*Amazons, Wives, Nuns, and Witches*

*Book Thirty-Two*
*Louann Atkins Temple Women & Culture Series*
*Books about women and families, and their changing role in society*

{ CAROLE A. MYSCOFSKI }

# Amazons, Wives, Nuns, and Witches

WOMEN AND THE CATHOLIC CHURCH
IN COLONIAL BRAZIL, 1500–1822

*University of Texas Press* ⌄ AUSTIN

The Louann Atkins Temple Women & Culture Series is supported by Allison, Doug, Taylor, and Andy Bacon; Margaret, Lawrence, Will, John, and Annie Temple; Larry Temple; the Temple-Inland Foundation; and the National Endowment for the Humanities.

First edition, 2013
First paperback edition, 2014

Requests for permission to reproduce material from this work should be sent to:
    Permissions
    University of Texas Press
    P.O. Box 7819
    Austin, TX 78713-7819
    http://utpress.utexas.edu/index.php/rp-form

♾ The paper used in this book meets the minimum requirements of ANSI/NISO Z39.48-1992 (R1997) (Permanence of Paper).

LIBRARY OF CONGRESS CATALOGING-IN-PUBLICATION DATA
Myscofski, Carole A., 1954–
    Amazons, wives, nuns, and witches : women and the Catholic church in colonial Brazil, 1500–1822 / by Carole A. Myscofski. — First edition.
        pages       cm. — (Louann Atkins Temple women & culture series ; Book thirty-two)
    Includes bibliographical references and index.
    ISBN 978-0-292-74853-8 (cl. : alk. paper)
    ISBN 978-1-4773-0219-4 (paperback)
1. Brazil—Church history—To 1822.   2. Women in the Catholic Church—Brazil.   3. Catholic women—Brazil.   4. Women and religion—Brazil.   5. Women—Religious life—Brazil.   I. Title.
    BX1466.3M97    2013
    282′.81082—dc23                                          2012050638

doi:10.7560/748538

*To Ted and Sonya*

# Contents

# Acknowledgments

M y work on the history of women's religious lives in colonial Brazil, first conceived as a series of independent research projects, has proceeded deliberately over a number of years, and the support of grants, foundations, colleagues, and friends has finally made this book possible. My preliminary studies on women and Roman Catholicism could not have been completed without the generous funding by the Fulbright Senior Scholar Research Award that I received from the Council for International Exchange of Scholars, American Republics Regional Research Program, for research in the libraries and archives in Brazil. Further support came from my Joyce Foundation leave, granted through Illinois Wesleyan University, for a semester's sabbatical to research concepts of gender and religious activities.

Illinois Wesleyan University has supported my work in several important ways. The Faculty Development Committee Academic and Scholarly Development Grants funded my travel to Brazilian archives and my research on concubines, religious women, and late colonial magic, the rather divergent topics that have been brought together here. FDC Senior Faculty Development Awards and course releases sustained my more recent studies on the images of Amazons and Luso-Brazilian concepts of honor, and the thoughtful advice of Associate Dean Irv Epstein encouraged me through the process of rewriting the manuscript. I remain grateful for the research funding that I received through the McFee Endowed Professorship of Religion for completing this project.

I wish to express my deep appreciation for the assistance from Brazilian librarians, archivists, and scholars whose guidance made my continuing research possible. At the Biblioteca Nacional, the library staff in the Seção de Manuscritos and in Obras Raras made my searches easier, and I thank them for facilitating my use of the card and digitized catalogs and the still-unwieldy texts. Eliane Perez, in particular, helped me manage the microfilm copies and machines. Historian Luciano Raposa de A. Figueiredo generously shared his own work, and counseled me on the hidden gems in the Archivo Nacional. And before the Arquivo da Cúria at the Catedral Metropolitana de São Sebastião in Rio de Janeiro had completed its revised cataloguing, archivists Paulo Lavandeira Fernandes and Aloysio de Oliveira Martins Filho lent me their invaluable assistance in locating individual texts and boxes of documents that had been transferred from convents in Rio de Janeiro.

I could not have overcome the challenges of this complex research without the help of many friends and colleagues along the way. Although I cannot name everyone who has assisted me with its many pieces, I would be remiss if I did not mention at least the most recent. Many thanks are due to the reviewers who offered sage advice for rewriting my manuscript and to University of Texas Press Editor Theresa May, who forwarded such encouraging notes, answered many and random questions, and arranged the final publication of this book. My colleagues at Illinois Wesleyan University have reviewed my work, encouraged my efforts, and responded generously to my requests for help. In particular, I would like to express my gratitude to Alison Sainsbury and April Schultz for their encouragement, and to Karen Schmidt for help with copies and permissions; in the Religion Department, I wish to thank Regina Linsalata for her help with editing and proofreading, and Tao Jin, Bob Erlewine, and my chair Kevin Sullivan for their unfailing support. My final thanks go to my husband, Ted McNair, who read nearly every draft, and to my daughter, Sonya Myscofski, whose sunny disposition cheered me even long-distance — thank you both for the gifts of love, time, and companionship on this journey.

*Amazons, Wives, Nuns, and Witches*

# Amazons and Others

On June 10, 1562, one of the first Portuguese missionaries in Brazil reported on the great successes of Padre Fabiano in conversions of indigenous women:

> He has also constructed another great house, . . . where live many girls of those Indians under his guidance and he teaches them to tailor, weave, and so on. Of these those already taught doctrine and instructed in good habits are married with young men.[1]

Padre Brás Lourenço, the putative author of the report, confidently declared that the young women had abandoned their former heathen customs so that they might serve the Jesuits, the Portuguese empire, and God. With their new womanly skills, they created modest clothing and thus might attend religious services and festivals—and provide merchandise for their future husbands and their Jesuit instructors. And with this short passage, echoed in letters from the Franciscans and Jesuits through the colonial era, women's roles in the colony were set: they were to be auditors of the patriarchal religious and political authorities, receptors of indoctrination in religious and social norms, and productive and reproductive laborers for the imperial government.

In this book, I focus on the lives of women connected with the Catholic Church in colonial Brazil, from 1500 to 1822, following their religious experiences in relation to prescribed women's roles and identity in the early modern period. Beginning with the perspectives of Jesuits and other missionaries toward the indigenous women at the opening of the colony, I explore the Catholic colonial views of the ideal woman, patterns in women's education, religious views on marriage and sexuality, the history of women's convents and retreat houses, and the development of magical practices among women in the colonial era. Each chapter depends on extensive research with primary manuscript and printed sources from Brazilian libraries and archives as well as secondary Brazilian historical works, and each is further informed by the most recent interpretive studies by Brazilian scholars on their own past.

My goal is to articulate women's place in the colonial society according to Jesuit missionaries, Roman Catholic Church officials, and Portuguese Inquisitors. Because of the Catholic Church's dominance in Brazil, any study of the colonial period is necessarily informed by its official statements, decrees, and reports. In those writings I find that women's daily lives and their opportunities for marriage, education, and religious practice were sharply circumscribed throughout this period. Those same documents also reveal the patterns of religious belief and practices that were especially cherished or independently developed by women for their own use, constituting a separate world for wives, mothers, concubines, nuns, and witches. There are, further, a few records which still retain the voices of women subject to the Church's power, responding to its power, and seeking their own place in the Catholic colony. With such a diverse set of resources, this book seeks to understand how Brazilian women lived their lives within the society created by the Portuguese imperial government and Luso-Catholic ecclesiastical institutions. With that as a first step, I intend to provide the foundation for women's own history, for the expression of how women experienced and understood their own lives within and against their political and religious constraints.

Since the history of colonial Brazil is relatively unfamiliar to North American readers, a brief overview will serve to introduce it here. In the late fifteenth century, the Portuguese began their successful exploration of the Atlantic with the establishment of outposts on the Azores, uninhabited islands, and coastal regions of Africa. Following the route to India initiated in the 1490s by Vasco da Gama, Pedro Álvares Cabral captained a fleet of thirteen ships southward from Portugal and, when prevailing winds and currents took them farther westward in the Atlantic, landed on an island off the Brazilian coast in 1500. There the Portuguese encountered indigenous Brazilians, claimed the land as the "Island of the True Cross," and sent news of their discovery to Lisbon while the fleet sailed on to India. In the following years, the Portuguese Crown funded expeditions to the coast of Brazil to exploit its natural resources for financial and political gain. By 1530, plans had shifted to the creation of a permanent colonial settlement, with the king's favored nobles and mercantile leaders receiving land grants to substantial sections of the coast and interior. The administrators of the hereditary "captaincies" financed fleets, recruited mostly male settlers, and established towns and plantations to cut wood and grow sugarcane, but little change came to Brazil beyond the introduction of slavery and sexual exploitation to the indigenous communities there.

In 1549, the Crown reasserted direct control over the new colony and sent a royal governor to Salvador, Bahia, along with bureaucrats, military officers, a few families, and six Jesuit missionaries. The first century of the Brazilian colony saw the haphazard growth of Portuguese control, but by the 1590s, the white population neared thirty thousand, centered in a few major towns and scattered across numerous sugar plantations. Portuguese elite immigrants dominated the colonial enterprise, holding political and economic power over lower-class immigrants and the subject communities of Indians, *mestiços*, and newly enslaved Africans. All required the oversight of an incipient juridical and economic system, an ecclesiastical organization of churches and parishes, and an extended visit of the Portuguese Inquisition to counter the heresies of Christians and hidden Jews in the new colony. The position and authority of women were quite meager: few European women voluntarily traveled to Brazil, but family life and urban markets flourished with the work of women of diverse origins.

In the late sixteenth and early seventeenth centuries, the political fortunes of Portugal and Brazil were shaken, but the colonial agricultural and mining industries developed independently and provided unforeseen wealth for the nobility and the *metropole*, the imperial center in Lisbon. The Portuguese throne, lacking an heir, was subsumed under Spanish control between 1580 and 1640, and the northeast cities of Brazil were attacked and even occupied by Dutch naval forces between 1624 and 1644. The colony expanded north and west, and the growing sugarcane industry and trade in African slaves were bolstered by the discoveries in Minas Gerais of gold in 1695 and diamonds in 1729. Communities there and in Mato Grosso and Goiás only later integrated mining with farming and ranching, but all saw their first bursts of growth during the gold rush. Cattle ranchers seized land far into the northeastern and southern interior regions where agricultural production was marginal, and raiders from São Paulo displaced or enslaved Indians in their quest for land, gold, and power.

In this colony, white patriarchal families retained financial and political precedence through their plantations and urban enterprises. Free and enslaved Indians and Africans, and the mixed-race descendants of Portuguese, indigenous, and African parents, occupied the lower ranks of the working classes and benefited the least from economic expansion. A few white women worked in towns or owned small farms, and free black and mulatto women created small enterprises or sold goods in the markets. Overall, women's lives depended on their male connections, but while wealthy white women "took a state" in arranged marriages or newly established convents, most women—of whatever ethnic origin—lived in consensual unions or concubinage. In urban and rural Brazil, women and men attended Roman Catholic services and joined confraternities or constituted their own informal and domestic religious practices at home or in celebratory festivals for Mary and the saints. The ecclesiastical institution expanded, with Jesuit oversight of schools, outposts, and indigenous conversions extending north and west into Maranhão and south into Rio Grande do Sul. New bishops in Bahia and Rio de Janeiro organized diocesan and parish congregations in those same regions.

Brazilian colonial society in the mid-1700s still clung to the Atlantic coast, with only a few inland towns inhabited or controlled by the Portuguese. Although Brazilian culture still retained the influences of the indigenous peoples, the communities themselves had been decimated, so that barely one-quarter of the original population remained at the end of the eighteenth century. As the mining boom ended, agricultural centers diversified—to coffee, tobacco, and rice—and provided a more stable economy for the colony as a whole. With its population over two million (as far as it can be determined) and its cities increased by resident whites and mulattoes as well as newly arrived African slaves, Brazil began political, economic, and religious reorganization, directed at some distance by the powerful Portuguese royal minister, the Marquis de Pombal. His efforts transformed the colony and eliminated one of its most influential religious and cultural institutions by expelling the Jesuit order. The educational and political system, however, still disenfranchised all but the scions of the aristocratic land-owning families.

While agricultural expansion increased wealth among the elite in the colony, the resultant inequities led to political unrest in the late 1780s and 1790s. Revolutionary groups in Minas Gerais and Bahia, inspired by events in the United States and France, attempted local uprisings for independence, but were violently repressed. The Brazilian territory expanded to its present borders by 1800, and the balance of power between the imperial government and its most important colony shifted at about the same time. The Portuguese court relocated to Brazil in 1806, retreating before Napoleon's army, and precipitated the most radical changes in the Brazilian cultural and political landscape. The king established the Brazilian National Library and its Bank, and permitted printing presses, new educational ad-

vances, and fuller representation of the Brazilian elite in imperial government. With new cultural awareness, women raised new challenges to the
limitations of their traditional roles and the insufficiency of their religious
and educational opportunities. The influence of the royal visit ended when
the court returned to Portugal in 1821, but the Crown Prince Pedro delayed
his departure and in 1822 proclaimed, "Fico!"—that he would "stay" in
Brazil—as the first emperor of the newly independent state.

## SEEKING THE HISTORY OF WOMEN

Women's religious lives were deeply woven into the cultural tapes-
try of colonial Brazil and critical to the maintenance of its society. But
their lives are now difficult to access. The primary texts that disclose their
struggles and accomplishments are kept only in the manuscript and rare
book collections of the national libraries and regional archives. When I first
ventured into these topics with the support of my 1990 Fulbright Foundation scholar's award to investigate "Women and Roman Catholicism in
Colonial Brazil," I had hoped to discover a lost treasury of letters or diaries
offering the richest details of women's traditions and transformations. But
without the personal documents that support histories of women's lives
in other colonial contexts, I instead labored to reconstruct the Brazilian
domestic religious scene using bits and fragments from collections of official documents penned for other purposes. Like other scholars, I worked
"against the grain" of the discourse of the imperial government and church
to bring women's contributions again into the light.

With the help of archivists in the *Manuscritos* section of the Biblioteca Nacional, the Arquivo Nacional, and the Arquivo da Sé in the Catedral de São Sebastião in Rio de Janeiro, I requested and read collections
of letters, provisions, notices, and local government orders sent from the
colonial capitals to the royal administrators in Lisbon. Occasionally, as was
the case with a box of "Juridical Documents Concerning Recolhimentos" in the Arquivo Nacional, my requests turned up manuscripts that had
disintegrated and were simply too fragile to read. Although relatively few
documents were composed by women before 1700, and those subsequent
to that date were sometimes countersigned by male family members or
officials to authenticate the intent of the authors, the available manuscripts
nonetheless revealed the extensive involvement of women in shaping colonial religion. Dona Ana de Sousa de Queiros, for example, offered funds for
the construction of "a seminary" in Salvador, Bahia, to educate the youth

"of both sexes" in 1798, specifying that Jesuit priests guide the curriculum there. Not all documents revealed favorable conditions, however, as several petitioners begged royal dispensation for renovations to their religious housing, or renewed support for their very survival. The mother superior of the convent of Santa Teresa in São Paulo requested that King D. João VI, for the "benefit of his subjects," suspend the tax payments due on their buildings in 1809 while she arranged for donations and the sale of property. In closing her petition, she assured the king that she and her sisters commended his "virtues" and would "increase their prayers for his prosperity."[2] These finds were enough for me to begin my researches.

The National Library also houses manuscript and print copies of regulations from the convents, informal religious houses, and religious schools for girls founded during the colonial era, all of which provided the foundation for my work on Chapters 2 and 4 of this book. Written by bishops, rectors, and local councilmen, these "Regimentos" and "Consultas" indicate the importance of constraints for colonial women — from the perspective of the men who sought to control them. In the Arquivo da Cúria Metropolitana, records from the Recolhimento de Nossa Senhora do Parto revealed the presence of independent women staying as paying guests, under the same rules of that religious house. Payments were accepted from the women themselves, and from husbands and fathers, to shelter and "sustain" wives, daughters, and their slave women for short stays or long residences: the "Book of Receipts" indicated payments by boarder Ignacia Batista to stay with her niece for 1786 and by Francisco Antunes de Andrade for his wife Maria Franca Capistrana for the years 1786 through 1794.[3]

In that same archive, I finally found a portion of the treasure that I had previously imagined, in a box of petitions collected in the Convent of Nossa Senhora da Conceição da Ajuda from girls and women aged eleven to twenty-five seeking to enter the religious life. The supplicants proclaimed their devotion to the Holy Mother Church and willingness to enter cloistered life, and they revealed their honorable lineage, recent donations, and other qualifications for religious life. Some of them wished to enter as pupils, some as novices, some as temporary residents under the convent's protection; still others petitioned to undertake life as a vowed religious sister, and all averred that they sought the convent "of their own free will." Each petition was signed — in some manner. Even Anna Acleta Felizarda de Menezes and her sister Josepha insisted, after describing their parents' donation of several houses, that they wished to enter "of their own free will and without any constraints," but still requested an extension for their younger sister, Isabel Maria da Conceição, who was only four years old.[4]

The most revealing and most difficult documentation, from the records of the Portuguese Inquisition, has become a central source for my investigations of the domestic lives of Roman Catholic women in Brazil. Since the publication of the edited collections of confessions and denunciations in 1925, scholars have explored the religious lives of outsiders such as heretics, women, and hidden Jews, to counter the dominant discourse of the imperial church. A manuscript copy that may have served as the preliminary version for the first publication of the denunciation records of the 1591 visit of the Portuguese Inquisition to Bahia, Brazil, kept in the Seção dos Manuscritos of the Biblioteca Nacional, informs the reader that it was "copiado do Codice no. 16 do Arquivo Nacional da Torre do Tombo" and indicates that only the repeated contextual reference—"in the houses of the Lord Visitor"—and vows of veracity to "the Holy Evangelists" were omitted from the published version. Although digital copies from the eighteenth-century visit of the Tribunal to Maranhão are now available online, access to the Portuguese archives for earlier visits is limited, so the print versions constitute the primary sources for details on magic, witches, and the daily lives of women who took refuge in that alternative spiritual world.

## THE HISTORY OF WOMEN IN COLONIAL BRAZIL

My path to this book has thus been neither direct nor uncomplicated, since the major primary sources that might support such study—women's own diaries, letters, or essays—are simply lacking for most of the colonial period. This difficulty has been reflected, until very recently, in the paucity of studies on women in the sixteenth through eighteenth centuries in the colonial cities and towns. Few Brazilian historians opened this subject before the twentieth century, and the books and articles they produced offer more insight into the modernist and progressivist perspectives of the late 1890s and early 1900s than into women's real lives and roles. Among these I would place—as an epitome but not the sole representative of the class—the book *Brasileiras célebres*, presented in 1862 by Joaquim Norberto de Sousa Silva to inspire imperial citizens to admire and emulate the virtuous women of the Brazilian past. Silva embroiders the rather sparse biographical sketches with laudatory comments, flowery descriptions, and a few bare statements of accomplishment, but the focal motifs of the tome emphasize the valor and devotion of Christian women to church, country, and family—in about that order. In such books one finds repeated archetypes, such as the noble/savage woman converted to Catholicism, the brave colonial matron defending her family from Dutch or other non-Portuguese invaders, the pious visionary petitioning for the opening of a new convent, and the stalwart abbess teaching the new generation of obedient daughters, but one gains little sense of what the women themselves might have thought or chosen.

Women's lives have rated only a few mentions in the histories of colonial Brazil, so that Brazilian authors through the middle of the twentieth century—from Sergio Buarque de Hollanda and Pedro Calmon to Caio Prado Júnior—offer few discerning points about women or family life in their sweeping accounts of the development of Brazil. And while Gilberto Freyre's social histories, such as *Casa-grande e senzala* (translated in 1946 as *The Masters and the Slaves*) recentered colonial studies on the intimate life within the plantation families, the impact of his work was not felt in women's studies until the 1980s. English-language studies by other well-known historians, such as E. Bradford Burns or Charles R. Boxer, typically displaced the lives of women in their focus on the plantation economy and the politics of patronage in Brazilian history through the eighteenth century. Boxer opened discussion of Latin American women within that framework, however, with the 1975 publication of *Mary and Misogyny: Women in Iberian Expansion Overseas, 1415–1815, Some Facts, Fancies, and Personalities*; while it remains a noteworthy book in the field, its research scope was severely limited.[5]

Studies of women's lives in colonial Latin America or of women and Christianity in the early modern period are few: most of them are anthologies with scattered subjects across the three colonial centuries. One exception is Asunción Lavrin's *Latin American Women: Historical Perspectives* with two important essays on colonial Brazilian women by A. J. R. Russell-Wood and Susan A. Soeiro, but other such collections rarely consider Brazil or the impact of religious institutions on indigenous, Portuguese immigrant, and African women there. Because of the specific history of Portugal and its unusual relationship with its American colony, studies centered on Spanish colonial history that simply add a paragraph or a footnote on Brazilian women cannot do justice to the developments unique to the colony in this time frame. The book that actually inspired my own work is Susan Migden Socolow's *The Women of Colonial Latin America*, which tucked brief mentions of Portuguese and Brazilian women into its accounts of the lives, marriages, and work of women from Iberia, indigenous women of the Americas, and enslaved women from Africa.[6]

Brazilian historical research since the 1980s has categorically redefined the contributions of women to colonial society, shifting the focus from political and institutional chronicles to personal and social experiences. The most valuable of the recent anthologies focused on women are *Família, mulher, sexualidade e Igreja na história do Brasil*, edited by Maria Luiza Marcílio, and *História das mulheres no Brasil*, edited by Mary del Priore, both of which include essays from contemporary Brazilian scholars on such diverse subjects as sexuality, magic, and motherhood. Priore's shorter *Mulheres no Brasil colonial* provides an overview of the issues and themes drawn primarily from her own work. New paths in colonial history have been blazed by Laura de Mello e Souza and Ronaldo Vainfas, whose studies of colonial demonology and sexuality redefined the colonial epoch, finally wresting its analysis from the institutional chroniclers. Recent social histories have been added with Alida C. Metcalf's studies on colonial family life, Anna Amélia Nascimento on the first colonial convent, Leila Algranti on late colonial convent life, Muriel Nazzari on women's dowries, and Kathleen Higgins on slavery in Minas Gerais, and I have attempted to follow their examples of careful primary research in my own work.[7]

### THE VIRTUE OF LIMITATIONS
### AND THE LIMITATIONS OF VIRTUE

In Brazil, from the era of Cabral's landing on the shore of the new colony in 1500 to that of the inauguration of the Republic in 1822, women encountered far more in the practices and teachings of the Roman Catholic Church than the path to salvation. Thoroughly invested in its secular role, the Church also demanded that women comply with the norms of the contemporary gender roles and social hierarchy as part of their spiritual submission to divine law. Native Brazilian women, immigrant Portuguese women, and mixed-race and African women thus faced diverse pressures to conform to dominant cultural expectations in dress, comportment, work, and worship. The civil laws and social norms were endorsed by the Catholic Church by means of religious teachings on the appropriate lives and activities for women, with promises of spiritual rewards for obedient Christian women and warnings of eternal damnation for the nonconformists. In the religious documents addressing women's appropriate roles, we can find two recurrent themes in the colonial era: limitations for women and the question of honor.

While Portuguese conquerors and missionaries envisioned their presence in the New World as the opportunity for civilization and conversion, indigenous women in the Brazilian colony learned a new set of restrictions for their lives. Over the subsequent centuries, the Roman Catholic Church helped inculcate norms for clothing, comportment, and activities that set limits on women's bodies, so that women themselves experienced colonization by the religious empire. Rules for dress and decorum were first set by Cabral's expeditionary force, so that women drawn to the Catholic services were the first to cover themselves in clothing suitable for the new roles they were to play: servants or workers in the new order. Once they were suitably dressed, indigenous women might then be consigned to the same domestic sphere that immigrant Portuguese and later mixed-race women inhabited, with limits to their mobility in the new plantations and villages. Whether working or worshipping, Christian women were taught the biblical lessons that left them few opportunities for life outside of a narrow set of expectations.

The Catholic Church itself offered only the saintly models, like the Virgin Mary, for women's proper roles in that institution. Women could not, of course, enter leadership roles in the Church nor learn very much about its core teachings beyond the barest minimum of indoctrination. For nearly two centuries after the beginning of the colony, women living in Brazil had little access to education or to any but subordinate roles in chapels or churches. Formal convents for women were not permitted until the late 1600s, so that even that opportunity for religious or personal development was absent. Enslaved and impoverished women probably understood little more than the basics of doctrine alongside the mandates of weekly attendance at Catholic Mass. Women of the leading families recited the requisite prayers and received the sacraments that led them closer to the front of the church, but well into the eighteenth century they still made few contributions to the emerging Brazilian Church. Barred from public activities and knowledge of the fundamentals of their religion, some women attempted to create their own spiritual havens at home or their own religious rituals, but informal or heterodox religiosity was quickly suppressed by the Church and the Portuguese Inquisition.

While elite women's activities were limited to home, and working-class or enslaved women were bound to servitude, colonial discourse nonetheless perpetuated the models of honor for society that had been most elaborated in medieval Europe.[8] For colonial Brazil, the definition of honor was provided in 1712 by Raphael Bluteau: "the respect and reverence with which we treat people on account of their nobility, dignity, virtue, or other excellence."[9] The social use of "honor" was claimed by the elite, that is, by the landowning nobility and the governing families of Brazil. As it had in Portugal, "honor" conferred privileges, favors, and other intangible benefits for that minority of colonial residents, and, not insignificantly, provided the means for distinguishing the leaders of society from their subordinates. Elite men claimed honor on the basis of such factors as public rank, family lineage, and personal conduct, but a woman's honor was determined by her adherence to the norms of gender role and religious morality prescribed by the Roman Catholic Church, and was most often linked to her personal sexual conduct.

Honor codes in medieval Portugal provided the foundation for conferring entitlements and status on members of the nobility and confirming the rights of rulers and landowners based on their public reputation for responsibility, probity, and virtue. For men, honor in the aristocratic ranks was supported by "cultural expectations" for appropriate masculine behavior, which might include competitive demonstrations of courage, wealth, and dominion over weaker men, lower classes, and women.[10] In contrast, women gained little honor by their public activities or public reputation. Women's honor, it has been argued, rested in a sense of "shame," in hiding their bodies and heads from public view and their behavior from public scrutiny. From the Portuguese perspective, a woman's failure to cover herself properly actually constituted a violation of honor and revealed her social and sexual vulnerability: shameless women were sexually immoral. Thus the failure of indigenous Brazilian women and enslaved African women to adopt European dress placed them into the category of the dishonored; dishonored women were "shameless," and their very nature as women and as moral beings was impugned.[11]

In Iberia and its colonies, honor was more than an aristocratic title or exhibition of virtue for men: it stemmed from family history and lineage as well, based on the inherent social status, religion, and race of the family as a whole. Families affiliated with the Iberian ruling classes and families of the owning and noble ranks, of governors and military leaders, gained and retained honor by demanding precedence in social gatherings and even in religious organizations and church processions. Men of such familial background accrued privileges in the establishment of commercial and land developments and in their access to government appointments. But the family honor rested not just on property holdings and political accomplishments, but also on an unquestioned lineage without impediments: honorable families possessed reputable ancestors who had been devout Catholics for generations and were recognizably white. Family honor rested on women's sexual honor as well, for the most assured continuance of that honor was through legitimate birth.[12]

Portuguese women shared in the family honor and were granted respect and privileged places in church and social gatherings insofar as their ancestral lineage was unmarred by connections with heretical religions or kinship with lower-status families. For women, too, legitimate birth continued ancestral honor, so that men and women alike were affected by the marriage status and chastity of their mothers. Women's honor also rested on the attainment of personal honor by their immediate male kin, that is, by their fathers and husbands, and a woman might enhance the standing of her natal kin through an advantageous marriage that linked them, through her, to a wealthier or more illustrious noble family. Conversely, women's personal behavior affected the family honor and their private transgressions and sexual incontinence brought dishonor to themselves and their male and female kin alike. While men rarely suffered from their sexual misalliances, the loss of virginity and the birth of children out of wedlock reduced women's honor drastically and might entail the loss of esteem for their lineage, male kin, and descendants.

Elite families in the Brazilian colony maintained their respected positions through personal accomplishments, and men of the elite, whether landowners or merchants, desired stability in social rank and sought inclusion in the town councils, the brotherhood of the Santa Casa de Misericórdia, and the Franciscan Third Order. An honorable daughter simply sought the best marriage match, to accumulate further prestige and money for her natal family and her progeny. For landowners or merchants in seventeenth-century Bahia or eighteenth-century São Paulo, family wealth and status—the ways in which they were treated, the prestige and deference they demanded, and the accommodations made for them—were thus bound to the honor of wives and daughters.[13] For women, honor and shame for the family were linked to the public perception of virtue, since the virginity of an unmarried woman and the chastity of a married or widowed wife created the reputation of appropriately controlled sexuality. Since women's behavior honored or shamed the family, and a daughter's honor determined the ranks into which she might marry, elite women were secluded by their families, but women in the lower classes were more "vulnerable to seduction or sexual attacks."[14]

In colonial Brazil, then, the system of honor was both robust and fragile, for family and male honor seemed to rest on ancestral, political, and religious expectations of prestige and virtue, yet still might be damaged by a single woman's sexual misdeeds. Women's relationships with the concepts of honor were paradoxical as well: a woman could not benefit directly from her honored status by securing a prized land concession or government appointment, nor could she contest with other women over issues of valor and worth. At the same time, however, women's obedient submission to contemporary norms for virtuous behavior played such a crucial role in the establishment and maintenance of honor for all of her family, that her daily activities might be monitored for compliance. Elite women and those who wished to achieve similar consideration seem to have been at once the least and the most powerful members of their families. Women outside of the upper strata, however, failed to receive honor from the governing and owning families, and indigenous Brazilian women and enslaved African women could not, almost by definition, be honorable. They were unprotected by their families, shameless by nature, and subjected to dishonorable treatment.

Honor for women was part of the same system of limitations in the colony and governed by the same religious expectations for feminine virtue expounded by the Roman Catholic Church. Bluteau in his 1712 dictionary had in fact elaborated the definition of honor to its full significance in relation to religious virtue: "True honor is, as Saint Thomas [Aquinas] defined it, *the reward given to any virtue*. That supports this definition, [that] without virtue, there is no true honor."[15] The foundation of a woman's virtue lay in her private and sanctioned comportment, and "included seclusion [and] anonymity." Expected to "live virtuously, calmly and in retirement, in her parents' home until a husband [came] to find her (or she was turned over to him)," an unmarried woman might demonstrate her worth through religious devotion, rigidly maintained decorum, and simple inaction.[16] A woman's public status, family prestige, and personal honor developed from her individual morality; far more important for her future than her heritage or male kin, her virtuous attitudes and behavior were determined by the gender-specific teachings that the Catholic Church provided. Within that feminine realm, chastity, fidelity, modesty, and obedience remained at the heart of women's honorable accomplishments. But virtue was irrevocably tied to the avoidance of sexual sins, and such sin might be quite broadly construed to include not just promiscuity or adultery but also personal autonomy, education, or any threats to the religious constancy of a devout woman. Thus women might also lose honor, damage the honor of their family, and bring dishonor to the men who controlled them—their fathers, husbands, sons, or masters—through their failures to maintain religious probity in all aspects of their lives.

The Catholic Church in colonial Brazil presented limitations and honor to women not only through its elaboration of the fundamental moral code for feminine virtue but also in its control over the two realms in which honorable women lived their virtue: marriage and conventual life. These realms will be discussed at length in Chapters 4 and 5. A woman first found sanctuary in her family home, but primary among her parents' duties was the settling of her fate into one of two "states" for her adult life. As a wife or vowed nun, a woman took another sheltered existence, but the portal to each of these, even when sought assiduously by wealthy families, was guarded by religious canon law. The Catholic Church had fiercely defended its sacrament of matrimony when challenged by Protestant reformers, and the doctrines of the Council of Trent (1545–1563) affirmed its importance second only to vowed chastity. The Church set new regulations at that point to bar clandestine and underage marriages, condemn fornication and abduction, and limit marriage by ordained priests to willing, unrelated partners whose intent had been well publicized. The ability of parish priests and bishops to adjudicate and dispense with certain restrictions, however, increased the authority of the Church over women, who might be married against their will and even to perpetrators of violence.

While the estate of matrimony was securely arranged, the convents of colonial Brazil were, as noted, late in establishment and limited in enrollment. Until the 1677 opening of the Convento de Santa Clara do Desterro in Salvador, girls of elite families might be sent to Portuguese convents with the blessing of their families and dowries appropriate to their status. With the family committed to their unified property inheritance, wealthy girls made the dangerous ocean passage to enter Catholic convents and undertake spiritual discipline supported by not only religious devotion but also sufficient funds for their life residency. A few women established independent and informal retirement houses in early colonial Brazil, but even those set strict demands on entrants, limiting access to only the young and unmarried from the wealthiest colonial families. The Catholic Church controlled religious residences, so that both informal and formal convents or retirement houses for women followed either the well-articulated rules of established orders, such as those of the Carmelite or Ursuline Sisters, or imitated them with their own local regulations. Women's virtues in convent life found expression in their daily devotional practices, in the clothing, movements, and ranks within the convent, in the hierarchy of officials governing the sisters, and in the very seclusion they inhabited. Considered a more worthy "state" than that of marriage, the cloistered life gave women a modicum of education and some autonomy in exchange for their lives as social beings and family members.

The stifling enclosure of women's lives, then, began with the limiting concepts of virtue and honor as part of the medieval aristocratic culture and the moral code of the Catholic Church. In colonial society, women's morality affected more than just their own fate and the prestige of their kin; the virtuous accomplishments of women also served the public good: "the honor of a woman was configured thus as personal good belonging to each woman, property of the family, . . . and also a public good, because it was at play in the preservation of good customs demanded by the moral code."[17] Women's lives in colonial Brazil may have been secondary to men's and their activities displaced from men's history, but they had no less of an impact on the shape of colonial history than the governors and colonels. Indeed, given the pivotal place of their behavior in the construction of the ideology of religious salvation and political honor in the colony, too little consideration has been given to them and to the efforts by the Roman Catholic Church to direct their destiny. This, then, is the subject of my study: the ways in which the Roman Catholic Church came to elaborate women's possible lives in colonial Brazil.

THE PLAN FOR THIS BOOK

The book is organized from the perspective of women, according to the roles and behaviors demanded of them, their attempts at fulfilling those roles, and their refusal to cooperate with the dominant religious discourse. Nonetheless central to this study are the concepts of gender, honor, and virtue, and the restrictions constructed by the Portuguese Roman Catholic Church and imperial government. To introduce those concepts, the first two chapters examine the expectations for women from the European male perspective, in continental and colonial literature. In Chapter 1, "Amazons and Cannibals: Imagining Brazilian Women," I have drawn together descriptions of early encounters between European conquerors and explorers and Brazilian Indian women recorded in letters, missionary reports, and imperial texts, to investigate the iconographical representations of the Native Americans at the beginning of the Brazilian colonial period (1500–1650). In the context of early modern European and Christian perceptions of barbarians and others, two images of indigenous women emerged, portraying them first as malleable and compliant creatures, then later as strange savages—the Amazons and cannibals of the title. These two images reflected not just the Iberian views of the indigenous Other, but also their responses to the alien lands they sought to inhabit and "tame."

Turning from indigenous women, Chapter 2, "The Body of Virtues: The Christian Ideal for Brazilian Women," takes a second look at expectations for women in Brazil through the lens of Luso-Brazilian Catholicism. This chapter reviews the concepts of womanly virtue, feminine honor, and the nature of the female body articulated first in ancient and medieval religious literature and echoed in early modern Portuguese hagiographies and colonial accounts of women's activities. The constraints on women's social, religious, and personal development left few opportunities for them to evade the imprint of the social body on their own lives.

In Chapter 3, "Reading, Writing, and Sewing: Education for Brazilian Women," I consider the efforts to educate women to meet the Portuguese and Brazilian ideals for the virtuous Christian woman, from European pedagogical directives to late colonial expectations for girls' training and women's occupations as adults. The concepts of family honor and privilege were conveyed directly and indirectly through colonial ideology and behaviors so that schooling took place in a variety of venues. Primary documents from the Inquisition and statutes from an eighteenth-century girls' school, however, indicate that little progress was made in women's literacy or education from the late Middle Ages in Portugal to the end of the Brazilian colonial era, and the limitations derived from the concepts of honor and virtue, still enacting the sacred norms, simply found new expressions.

Chapter 4, "Before the Church Doors: Women as Wives and Concubines," focuses on the discourse concerning wives, concubines, and marriage in colonial Brazil and the role expectations for women within the domestic sphere. While secular and religious authorities agreed that marriage was the consummate purpose for women's existence, conflicts arose in the discourse on gender difference, and the contesting powers in the colony—missionaries, church officials, local and overseas governors, and the colonial elite—entered a struggle for power that expressed itself in struggle for control of women. The study of these processes here entails considering the meaning of human relations in the colony and their historical context.

Chapter 5, "*Freiras* and *Recolhidas*: The Reclusive Life for Brazilian Women," undertakes a historical analysis of the lives of women in formal and informal cloisters. In cloistered communities in colonial Brazil, women found varied means for alternative personal and religious expression, so in this chapter I include an examination of the religious, social, and economic motives for entrants into convents and retirement houses, the religious behaviors expected of girls and women, and the uses of the cloister as prison and punishment for rebellious daughters and transgressive wives. With extensive use of records from Brazilian convents and other related primary documents from the national archives in Rio de Janeiro, this chapter provides a glimpse into women's accommodations to the rigid rules of cloistered life.

The final chapter of the book represents yet a different direction for understanding women in Brazil, moving from ideals, expectations, and rules to the rule-breakers and most marginal of women in the colony— women accused of witchcraft. Chapter 6, "Women and Magic: Religious Dissidents in Colonial Brazil," investigates women's uses of magic, following the trajectory of their alternative spiritual and magical practices from the first confrontations with the Portuguese Inquisition in the 1590s to the development of love magic, healing spells, and curses through the early 1800s. The evidence for women's continuing use of magic and healing comes from the records of the Portuguese Inquisition visits to Brazil in the late 1500s, early 1600s, and late 1700s, and from published accounts of trials and ecclesiastical regulations in several colonial provinces. While the earliest records of women's magical practices link them firmly to European folk practices, later accounts reveal the increasing uses of Brazilian Indian and African healing and divination rituals.

While most of my sources here are from representatives, of one sort or another, of the Roman Catholic Church, it is not my intent to suggest that the Catholic Church was merely a perpetrator of oppressions in this or other colonial settings. The colony in Brazil was not a religious enterprise, and its new dominators were not primarily engaged in the recovery of lost souls. Instead, the Portuguese royal authority administered all enterprises in its colonies, and inculcated conquerors and conquered alike more directly in their appropriate superiority and inferiority through law, constitutions, royal orders, and government mandates. The religious presence in Brazil, in the parish priests, resident and itinerant missionaries, appointed bishops, cardinals and nuncios, and visiting preachers, provided both the justification for the colonial enterprise in religious terms and its occasional critique. The Catholic Church had conceded spiritual authority to the Portuguese rulers in exchange for their guarantees that all conquered lands, from Iberia and Africa to Asia and finally the Americas, be occupied as Christian territories. Conversion to Christianity became the necessary adjunct to exploration and exploitation, and the Catholic Church used a small but influential network of workers to impose its theological worldview among the Brazilian indigenous residents and colonists. The power of their words should not be underestimated, then, for they had the ability to fabricate the very nature of the New World; the discourse they invented about Brazil shaped not just its institutional history, but also individual lives and personal relationships. Women's lives in the Brazilian colony were thus created and expressed in and around the religious teachings of their environment, in and around the Catholic Church.

# ONE

# Amazons and Cannibals

IMAGINING BRAZILIAN WOMEN

IN THE COLONIAL PERIOD

I n the first letter written from Brazil by a Jesuit missionary, the first published for eager readers awaiting news of the new colony in 1551, Padre Manuel da Nóbrega began thus:

The information that I can give you of these parts of Brazil, dearest fathers and brothers, is that this land has 1000 leagues of coast, all populated by people who go about naked, both women and men. . . .[1]

Here Nóbrega presented the primary information for his readers, that the land had some familiar characteristics (it was coastal, albeit excessively so) and one truly alien feature: the inhabitants were naked. His emphasis on the nudity of women was the first of many such powerful constructions entangling alien nature and alien women in the Brazilian colony.

The details from early colonial encounters between European conquerors and explorers and Brazilian Indian women were recorded in letters, missionary reports, and imperial texts, with a range of iconographical representations of the Native Americans created by the gaze of the startled male observer. Because the religious and military men charged with recording their triumphs did not expect to find the vast uncharted lands of the Americas or their unsettling residents, they struggled to find the images and metaphors to render alien places and beings comprehensible. They sharpened their understanding of the challenges in the new lands on the imaginary stone of European myths and legends and translated the nearly incomprehensible novelty of American otherness into the oft-told tales of alien creatures and lands from the European past. Gendered aspects of difference conveyed and constructed their sense of wonder and discomfort with the New World. In this first example from Nóbrega and more explicitly in other writings and visual depictions, the territory of the New World and the bodily nature of its people were inexorably linked. The alien landscape was repeatedly projected onto the bodies of its most alien residents, and Brazilian Indian women came to represent Portuguese and Spanish attitudes toward the new land and their troubled perceptions of its place in European consciousness.

Far from the European societies that had constructed the concepts of family and personal honor, Brazilian Indian women were offered little opportunity to understand the models for innocence, virtue, and shame to which they were to conform. Honorable women in Iberia drew upon their understanding of divine law and social norms for their willful actions of submission or rebellion, but women in Brazil were ignorant of Christianity and civilization and thus could not judge propriety unless direct instruction was given them. The European concept of honor was based on the knowledge of distinctions between good and evil, or virtue and error, and it was the task of missionaries and explorers to inculcate the knowledge that provided the basis for the "natural" life under such norms. The first experiences of colonization resulted in misunderstandings and confusion on all sides; for the Europeans, the behavior of indigenous women was so unlike the submissive decorum expected of Christian women that they might be considered to be innocent and childlike or irretrievably corrupt and depraved—and either designation served the purposes of the conquest.

Portuguese and Spanish accounts of the first encounters with Brazilian Indians, written from 1500 through the late 1580s, reflected incredulity at their discoveries, and other Europeans similarly faced confusion in their efforts to name, categorize, and comprehend the New World. Only rarely might these reports be considered reliable descriptions, or anything like a sort of early modern ethnography; rather, their authors evinced a drive to see and to discover—a paradoxical desire to encounter something quite different and then to convert it to the familiar.

Thus the Portuguese explorers and missionaries created a composite vision for the New World, portraying its land and inhabitants as starkly different while using familiar motifs to mark that difference. Their writings created two images of women, each expressing a different understanding of the colonial struggles. The earliest symbolic representations of Brazilian Indian women emphasized their innocence, compliance, and transparency. This set of descriptors drew a Golden Age ideal from the image of an uncorrupted Eve in an early Eden; Brazilian women as passive followers and willing converts resembled the conquerable virgin land. But when the Portuguese and Spanish found themselves entangled in fiercer battles over control of the land and its people, the descriptions of native Brazilian women changed and the discourse of innocence waned as the "major justification for the expurgation of diversity."[2] The second image of women emphasized their violent and perverse otherness within the unyielding wilderness, drawing on ancient motifs of the fierce Amazon and the savage cannibal. These dichotomous images, one of innocence and the other of violence, are often intertwined in the early colonial texts, but each set of symbols expressed a different set of challenges for the missionaries and explorers as they sought to impose imperial order during the colonial period. In this chapter I will explore these two paradigms, of docile and of fierce women, with special focus on the latter—the Amazons and cannibals. Here, the increasingly hostile portraits of women not only expressed the growing antipathy of the Portuguese and other Europeans toward the New World, but also justified the violence rendered to the land and its people—conquest and slavery were the results.

## THE EUROPEAN 'OTHER'

The representations of savages and barbarians in America, as has been suggested by recent historians,[3] emerged from a complex of traditional arguments in classical and Christian Europe depicting different types of human beings and a deep rift between the civilized world and the realms of wilderness. The trajectory of conceptualization about the nature of the human began in classical Greece, where the rational mind, carefully circumscribed by the social expectations for propertied Greek men, was the standard by which one might separate human from beast. The rational human was civilized, lived apart from the chaos of nature, and communicated with the clarity of the Attic Greek dialect. One may find, as Hayden White has argued, two complexes of beings outside the settled life of the Greek cities.[4] The first were lawless creatures who lived in the wildernesses of Europe or Asia and who stuttered and slurred in their guttural tongues; these non-Greek barbarians marked the limits of Greek understanding and threatened the dominant culture and polity. The second were the wild men and women, whose degenerate and outcast life in the nearer but wilder realms represented threats to individuals within civilization.[5] These creatures—the Other to the rational self—are found both in the ancient Greco-Roman mythology of fantastic beings of the forest or wilderness, such as satyrs and Dionysian maenads, and in the older Babylonian mythology of the wild man Enkidu.[6]

Early Christian writers utilized these asymmetrical dichotomies to distinguish those following the true Christian faith (in whichever preferred form) from the pagans, and the saved from the damned. Following Augustine of Hippo, most theologians were careful to add that even the most alien human beings were still endowed with a divinely constructed soul, such that all of humankind was susceptible of conversion. The image of the unconverted Other was split during the Middle Ages, however, to distinguish the barbarians whose souls were receptive to Christian doctrine from the soulless and inhuman savages. That dichotomy recalled earlier notions of aliens and resonated with European myths of the wild man—or wild men and women—who lived beyond civilization and its historical and psychological dominance. Like their Near Eastern and Greek predecessors, then, barbarians and savages both challenged civilized norms and renewed them with their (re)incorporation into the normative European community.

These images of otherness persisted into the early modern period and shaped the colonizers' views of and interactions with the native Brazilians. During the late Middle Ages and the Renaissance, novel concepts about racial and ethnic differences merged with prejudices about gender and national norms to confound attempts at recognizing the new peoples as similar to peoples of Europe. Thus the descriptions and characterizations of the native Brazilians in the New World began with the categories and mythologies of the Old World, formulated in advance of European explorations. The images presented by colonial reports also reveal another telling dichotomy: in the New World it was typically the missionaries who found "barbarians" to be brought to the light of civilization and the Christian doctrine, while conquerors and capitalists in search of slaves and profits found only "savages" to be enslaved or slaughtered.

The encounters with Brazilian Indian women drew on yet another discursive complex, this time from the entrenched misogyny of Western European cultures. Patriarchal cultures from antiquity through the Renaissance expected that women—of any nation—would fall short of male ideals in body and soul. Despite the expansive language of discovery to justify the conquest of new lands, women had few opportunities to contribute to the Iberian empire, its direction, or its governance in the sixteenth century. Repressive notions concerning the proper place of women interwove with the images of the wilderness and further distorted the descriptions of the New World from the earliest explorers and conquerors. The social conflicts of early modern Europe tended to heighten the dichotomous expectations, so that religious institutions there challenged the disparate forces of evil, and virtuous men denounced women as demons, witches, or sorceresses. Similarly, in the Brazilian colony, religious and secular leaders alike identified the shocking or anomalous behaviors of indigenous women as not just barbaric, but demonic.

## INNOCENT AND COMPLIANT: THE FIRST
## IMAGES OF BRAZILIAN WOMEN

As noted above, many of the earliest reports about Brazilian Indian women portrayed them as simple and vulnerable creatures. Barbaric customs aside, tribal women were extolled as healthy, vigorous, and sturdy workers who would be readily conquered by the superiority of Portuguese civilization. Once civilized and converted to the Christian faith, they might "evolve" into compliant catechumens and servants of the will of the empire. Missionaries, explorers, and artists alike suggested that the sincere efforts and material culture of the colonizers would be sufficient to begin the transformation of the barbarian women. Clothing would cover their shame while domestic artifacts would constrain the savage customs into which the degenerate community of native Brazilians had fallen. Further guidance in the norms of civilization, through instruction in the law, politics, and religion, would return the wild women to the proper path of human history and allow them to assume their rightful political and spiritual place—subordinate, servile, and saved—in the Portuguese Empire and imperial Roman Catholic Church.

The discourse in all of these reports portrayed the land and Indian women in tandem, with language that suggested their sensuality and availability. This by itself was not unusual, for surveys by European explorers in eastern North America similarly portrayed the "virgin land" as sexually available and desirable, free of constraints and rewarding to any man who approached it.[7] The malleability of the image of North American Indian women persisted into the nineteenth and twentieth centuries, particularly in the Southwest United States, where Navajo women similarly "presented a doubly powerful symbol of the unknown land, as they were twice removed from white man—the standard of true humanity—by race and by sex."[8] There, in the "lush wilderness," Anglo colonizers saw both the nobility and the savagery of the land embodied in the native "princess" who could be "safely admired" while she and the land surrendered to the "redeeming touch" of the civilizers.[9] The reports from Brazil that began with similar portrayals of open and accessible land and women, however, shifted quickly—perhaps after further observation or interactions—into astonishment and disgust at the more degenerate practices of the natives. Although many authors seemed to believe that even the more persistent vices of Brazilian Indian women would be eradicated by their integration into the colonial world, most authors also called for more heroic efforts from devoted missionaries. In all of these reports, then, we can perceive the reaction of the explorers, missionaries, and colonizers to their new milieu: it was at first an easy move, but the land was much more menacing than their early visions of compliant women allowed.

The expectation of compliance brought missionaries, along with Portuguese ship captains, merchants, and explorers, to regard indigenous women first, and slave and migrant women later, as mere instruments for the greater glory of the empire and church. The qualities and characteristics of women and their treatment by the Portuguese men depended on the perception of value and virtue, and the men seeking power and wealth employed their own codes of honor not only among themselves but also— at least in the preliminary encounters—with women under their authority. Indigenous women, however, fell fall short of the models for comportment: their immodest dress and bold behaviors left no doubt about their failures to conform, while their ignorance of status and imperial or religious ideology eliminated any justification for fair treatment. In response, religious and political leaders demanded rapid indoctrination so that the "innocent" women might grasp the Portuguese and Christian concepts of shame and guilt.

The first Portuguese report of Brazilian Indian women may be found in the letter of Pero Vaz de Caminha, who recorded the official discovery of Brazil by Pedro Álvares Cabral on April 21, 1500.[10] Caminha's letter, sent back to Portugal while Cabral's fleet continued on its planned journey around Cape Horn to India, described the wonderful new land and the brief interactions of the Portuguese with its inhabitants. As might be expected from the chronicler of a voyage of exploration, much of the report simply established the times of their travels and the resources of the new territories. Nonetheless, Caminha was aware of the proclaimed dual mission of the Portuguese conquest and conversion, and returned to the latter issue throughout his report. His account of the Brazilian natives repeated the expectations of the conquerors that conversion naturally followed conquest and was its imperial justification. In his summary of their first encounters with the inhabitants of the new land, Caminha wrote to his king:

The [Brazilian natives] appear to be so innocent that if we could understand one another, they would become Christians at once, because . . . they do not have any creed. . . . I have no doubt that they shall come into the fold of our Faith . . . [T]hey are good and simple folk, and anything may be impressed on them. And since God has brought us here, He must have some reason for all this. Consequently, since Your Highness' wishes are to extend as far as possible the holy catholic Faith, Your Highness ought to look after their salvation, and with the help of God it will take little labor to achieve it.[11]

Caminha included detailed descriptions, first of the Brazilindian men and their actions, and then, later, of the women. In both cases, he revealed the Portuguese fascination with the nudity of the Brazilian Indians and represented the alien, exposed, and innocent nature of the women in language consonant with the strangeness and vulnerability of the new lands themselves. Caminha offered only four descriptions of Brazilian Indian women, and in all of them he discussed their nude bodies and their visible (and available) genitals. In the first three, Caminha described their genitals—or "shameful parts," as the contemporary euphemism put it—directly, while in the fourth, his reference was more oblique. Such focus was not present in his wary descriptions of Indian men after their first meetings, in which he emphasized their skill at arms and defense of their territories. While Caminha connected the men and their accoutrements with the dangers of the new land, women represented its openness and vulnerability: they, like the land, were ready to be violated at the will of the conqueror.

After meeting Indian women on their fourth day near the coast, he first described their exposed bodies: "There among them walked three or four girls, quite young and docile, with very black hair that fell to their backs; and their shameful parts were so high and so tightly closed and so clean of hair that they were not ashamed when we looked closely at them."[12] In their next encounter, he briefly detailed the physical appearance of Brazilian Indian men and then, in greater detail, their female counterparts:

And one of those girls was totally painted from top to bottom, . . . and was so well formed and rounded, and her shameful part (of which she was not [ashamed]!) was so lovely that many women of our land, seeing such features, would be ashamed that they had none like hers.[13]

Caminha continued by recounting Cabral's activities on their island outpost, the first Catholic Mass said there on April 26, and the subsequent sermon by the priest on "the history of evangelization; and . . . our life and the discovery of this land, referring to the Cross." He claimed that the religious service evoked "great devotion" in the Portuguese congregants and great interest in the Indians watching from the near shore. When undertaking further exploration of the nearby river, they found more Indian men painted and armed with bows and arrows, and more women:

> Among them were also four or five young women, who were thus nude and did not look at all bad. . . . Another had her knees painted with curves, and also the tops of her feet; and her genitals were so naked and so innocently uncovered, that there was no shame at all in them. There was also another young woman, with a little boy or girl, held at her breast in a cloth (I know not of what material), such that only the little legs were visible. But on the legs of the mother, and on all the rest, there was no other cloth at all.[14]

In his closing pages, Caminha returned to his insistence on the docility of the Indians and the exploitability of the land; there, once again, the female body represented the land open to conquest. As illustration, Caminha described another Catholic service on the island that drew a few Indians to attend. The only woman present, however, disturbed the sacred ritual with her nudity; although the Portuguese attempted to cover her, she exposed herself—and probably her genitals again—when she sat down:

> Among those who came today I only saw one woman, a girl, who was present throughout the mass, and to whom they gave a sheet to cover herself, and put it around her. However, when she sat down, she forgot to rearrange the sheet to cover herself. Thus, Your Majesty, the innocence of this people is such that that of Adam was not greater—with respect to shame.[15]

As Caminha saw them, the young woman and her tribal compatriots lived thus in Edenic innocence, but were, like Adam, about to be subjugated to a greater will—to be covered by Portuguese rule as by Portuguese cloth and ultimately expelled from their isolated paradise.

In Caminha's report, the Indian women, like the land he encountered, exhibited pleasant but sometimes duplicitous characteristics. The available and desirable women he glimpsed seemed both innocent and dishonorable: they betrayed no awareness or understanding of the rules they violated in their dress and comportment, but their ignorance also left them vulnerable to temptation and susceptible to abuse by the Portuguese. Without the protections afforded by social connections or family status, their failure to comprehend their condition proved dangerous to themselves and their would-be conquerors. Other authors, particularly the later missionaries, argued that their ignorance and degradation would be transformed by their integration into the colonial world and their conversion to Catholicism. Those mid-sixteenth-century writers included Jesuit, Franciscan, and Dominican missionaries sent from Portugal, as well as French and Spanish prelates who accompanied their own national colonial excursions in Brazilian territories.

The Jesuit missionaries arrived in 1549 alongside the first imperial government imposed from Portugal, eager to begin their service to the Crown.[16] Padre Manuel da Nóbrega led his fellow Jesuits in the new colony and dispatched reports back to the *metropole*, providing ample records of their encounters with native Brazilian women. The Jesuits focused their missionary efforts on Brazilian Indian men and boys, judging that their evangelization would be most effective with the dominant members of the Indian families and villages. Still, their encounters with women and girls were duly noted in their letters, where they recapitulated the myth of the innocent and compliant native woman awaiting the command of her betters to ameliorate her lost and savage ways. The women and girls naturally sought conversion, the Jesuits recounted, and interrupted the catechesis of men or boys to learn about the true religion. A handful of devout women became prayer leaders and teachers of other Indians, supplementing the meager efforts of the Jesuits in the expanding colonial sphere. Here too the Jesuit accounts of women's presence among the catechumens and the converted embodied the attitudes they held toward not just the indigenous people but also the land itself, for as their successes among the Indians became less frequent, so too their harsh assessment of the land intruded into their writing.

The Jesuit paradigm of the ready and compliant convert developed alongside the related themes of heroism and triumph over the opposing cultures. In their first encounters with the native Brazilian women in 1549, the Jesuits were profoundly disturbed by women's nudity, which seemed to represent the danger of persistence in their pernicious customs. The reasoning of the Jesuits here drew on an ancient Christian tradition that, as a result of Adam's sin, all humans felt shame when naked. The native women apparently no longer experienced that "natural" shame after centuries of exclusion from the true religion, and their clothing, such as it was, served to decorate rather than conceal. While the Jesuits hoped to reinstate this most visible effect of Adam's sin, the nudity of the Brazilian Indian women proved to be the most trying native custom and the one most discussed by the Portuguese fathers. Padre Manuel da Nóbrega perceived their nudity to be an obstacle to conversion and wrote to his superior in Portugal in 1549 requesting "clothing, so that we might in the meantime cover the new converts, at least one dress for each woman, for the decency of Christian religion."[17] He went on to report that their nudity was especially distracting during religious services, but later in that same letter, he revealed that he had little concern for women once clothed and baptized, for they were merely to be the wives of the (more important) men that he taught regularly.

By 1556, Nóbrega's compatriot Padre Luís da Grã found fewer compliant converts and insisted instead that he and his compatriots faced dangers in the new lands, in traveling and meeting naked women:

> In visiting these villages, there is the difficulty that it is not good to travel alone, because on many occasions the roads are frequented by women, and it is necessary that we all go about in holy dread. . . . The bishop is disturbed that the Indians go about nude and has said that in this they sin against nature.[18]

Nine years after his first encounters, even Nóbrega altered his views of the innocent and compliant Indian women, and listed nudity as one of their graver sins. He then sought the intervention of the colonial government to establish the rule of law and the norms of civilization:

> The law, which they must give the [conquered Indians of the region], is to prohibit the eating of human flesh and undertaking war without the permission of the Governor; to make them take only one wife, dress themselves since they have enough cotton, . . . to draw them away from magic, to preserve justice among themselves and with the [Portuguese] Christians; to make them live quietly . . . with Fathers from the Company [of Jesus] to teach them doctrine.[19]

Once drawn from their sinful, unclothed lives, the native Brazilian women approached the ideal of compliance and innocence, and the Jesuits extolled the more tractable among them for their religious virtue. Nóbrega wrote of devout women who, under his tutelage and to his credit, had gone far beyond mere conversion:

These women, once deeply rooted in the love and knowledge of God, are to be sent to preach in the villages of their relatives and I am certain that in some of them I see the working of the highest virtue.[20]

Now as productive as the arable land, women from his missions could be the dutiful wives of converted Indian men or of Portuguese male colonists.

The younger Jesuit brother José de Anchieta, who rarely wrote about women, reported that Indian women seemed more eager for baptism and surpassed the men in their devotion to the new religious life:

We follow the same order [as reported earlier] in the doctrine for the Indians: every day they are called to the Church twice, with the sound of a bell, to which the women respond . . . and they not only learn prayers in their own language but also hear lectures and are instructed in the understanding of articles of faith. Some are so fervent that no day passes without their coming twice to the Church, without ceasing on account of the cold, which is very severe now; some have confessed and receive the sacrament of the Body of the Lord twice or three times a year.[21]

Like Nóbrega, however, he preferred their instrumental function in the colonial and religious work: "We have baptized all of the children and some girls, who, after they have grown, may marry the boys we are now teaching in the school." In the same letter, he recounted the tale of a young woman who, even when beaten, refused an arranged marriage with an un-baptized Indian man so that she might marry a Christian.[22]

Other Jesuits commended the women as they finally concealed their bodies and revealed their compliant nature. In 1551, Brother Pero Correia praised an early convert and exemplar:

And one Indian woman among these who have been taught doctrine arose one night to preach in the street of São Vicente, and with such fervor that [she put] the men and women in great confusion. And it is in this way that some of the women so taught are like mirrors [of good-ness] not only for their male and female relatives, but also for the many women of Portugal who are here.[23]

Luís da Grã admitted, in a letter to Loyola, that Indian women cared more about their spiritual condition than did the men, writing that "the women

are more clever in it and apply themselves much more toward the good."[24]
And Padre António Pires, yet another of the first Jesuits, collaborated with
an older convert in his work:

> After I say Mass for them, I teach them doctrine in the afternoon and
> sometimes preach to them. The interpreter is a married woman, one
> of the most honorable in the land, and one of the richest. And you,
> Brothers, should not be surprised to learn about these conditions, . . .
> With this woman I hear the confessions of some Christian Indian
> women, and I believe her to be a better confessor than I, since she is
> more virtuous. I commend her to our Lord.[25]

By the end of the first century, some of the Jesuit texts reflected the
heroic status they assumed as they confronted and overcame the challenges
of conquest and conversion. The new lives of Brazilian Indian women then
symbolized both the struggles in which the first Jesuits engaged and the
glory of their victories. Historian Padre Fernão Cardim borrowed those
themes following his tour with the Jesuit Visitor in the 1580s. As part of
his accounts of Jesuit lives and missions, Cardim included examples of the
exceptional religious state women might achieve under Jesuit guidance:

> The women for their devotion fast two or three days before [a holy mass
> or feast day], and all take communion devotedly, and some of them
> weep many tears: they confess in great detail and on the day of commu-
> nion return for reconciliation.[26]

Cardim also praised the once-naked women—not just for their religious
devotions, but for the fact that they remained clothed. In his description
of a 1583 procession of "new Christian men and women" in the colonial
town of Espirito Santo, he indicated the impressive changes and lingering
problems with this detail:

> And the Indian women when dressed are so modest, serene, sincere,
> and calm, that they appear to be statues leaning on their attendants;
> and at each step they lose their slippers, for they are not accustomed to
> them.[27]

The interpretation that the Jesuits created of their mission to the
colony, that is, that they had faced and heroically overcome the Ameri-

can challenge as they clothed the native Brazilian women and converted them to Christianity, resonated through the end of the 1600s. What started as a short list of challenges overcome by the Jesuits with divine assistance, gradually extended to a greater set of setbacks and obstacles, including the issues of recalcitrance and recidivism among their sought-after converts. These issues will be taken up again below, in the discussion of the resistance represented by cannibal and warrior women.

The image thus represented in the early Portuguese accounts — of the alien but compliant native woman — also emerged in non-Portuguese writing and art of the early modern era. Particularly important sources of this imagery were Jean de Léry, a Protestant missionary to Brazil in the 1550s, Claude d'Abbeville, a French Capuchin missionary to northern Brazil in 1612, and Albert Eckhout, a German painter working in the mid-1600s. In 1578, Léry published an account of his experiences as the Calvinist pastor for the first, short-lived French colonial outpost near present-day Rio de Janeiro.[28] Although the twenty-year lapse between his voyage and residence in Brazil and the publication of his reports certainly affected his interpretations of events, Léry supported the view that Indians lived in a savage paradise and that women were childlike and tractable. Tupinambá women, according to Léry, followed nature in their daily routines of social interactions and food collection and preparation. Léry praised their industriousness, submission to men, and natural breastfeeding and childcare habits. His perspective may be best seen in his descriptions of the Indian woman; these not only revealed his presuppositions about human nature, but also might be an early contribution to the physical anthropology that once linked physiognomy, racial stereotypes, and character.

Following his early encounters with the Tupinambá, Léry reported his astonishment that "both the men and the women were as utterly naked as when they came out of their mother's womb; however, to bedeck themselves, they were painted and blackened over the entire body."[29] This first mention in his *History* was followed by a more thorough discussion of their "natural qualities" and bodily appearance, emphasizing their lack of modesty. He assured the reader that the natives were not "monstrous," though they differed from Europeans in that they were "stronger, more robust, . . . more nimble" and of a slightly darker hue. He continued:

> Now this next thing is not less strange than difficult to believe for those who have not seen it: the men, women, and children do not hide any parts of their bodies; what is more, [they lack] any sign of bashfulness or

shame. . . . And yet, contrary to what some people think, and what others would have one believe, they are by no means covered with hair.[30]

Léry admitted that they did not fit his paradigm of alien savagery, for while they were complaisant and receptive, they were not hairy like the images of the European Wild Man.

When Léry described each sex, he noted some differences, for women were rarely covered with body paint, but instead wore some red string, a necklace or bracelet, and had long, unstyled hair. Returning to their immodest nudity, Léry repeated that

> among the things doubly strange and truly marvelous that I observed in these Brazilian women, there is this: although they do not paint their bodies, arms, thighs, and legs as often as the men do, and do not cover themselves with feathers or with anything else that grows in their land, still, although we tried several times to give them dresses and shifts . . . , it has never been in our power to make them wear clothes: to such a point were they resolved (and I think they have not changed their minds) not to allow anything at all on their bodies.[31]

The Tupinambá women had told Léry that their frequent bathing—several times each day in nearby rivers—made clothing troublesome, and he accepted their explanation as another practical choice made for their natural if limited condition. He ended his chapter on bodily characteristics with the personal note that the regular sight of naked women was no longer disturbing, and that their "crude nakedness [was] much less alluring than one might expect."[32] The lewd dress and cosmetics of Frenchwomen was, by contrast, much more provocative and shameful. The illusion of his enlightened perspective was shattered, however, in a later comment on his continuing efforts to clothe indigenous women:

> Even our women prisoners of war, whom we had bought and whom we held as slaves to work in our fort—even they, although we forced clothing on them, would secretly strip off the shifts and other rags, as soon as night had fallen, and would not be content unless, before going to bed, they could promenade naked all around our island. In short, if it had been up to these poor wretches, and if they had not been compelled by great strokes of the whip to dress themselves, they would choose to bear the heat and burning of the sun, even the continual skinning of their

arms and shoulders carrying earth and stones, rather than to endure wearing any clothes.[33]

With these last lines, as was the case with the Jesuit records, Léry's perception of native women as impressionable converts to Christian norms gave way to what may have been the more deeply held fears of the alien nature of the people and cultures that he had encountered.

Another French traveler in Brazil held similarly ambivalent views of the Brazilian Indian women he met further north. In 1614, Claude d'Abbeville published his accounts of the remarkably healthy and long-lived Tupinambá, including women in their eighties who purportedly bore and nursed their own children. He exaggerated the natural submissiveness of the Tupinambá women and thus challenged incipient French support for the education and autonomy of women.[34] But his characterization of the women as tractable, with a graceful willingness to accept the civilization and religion offered to them, faltered when he discussed the same custom that fascinated and baffled other European observers. He, like Léry, viewed their nudity as strange, for even the most barbarous of people wore some sort of clothing. Unlike Léry, however, d'Abbeville developed an exclusively negative assessment of this "unnatural" custom, and wondered how it might be that they, "sharing in the guilt of Adam and being heirs of his sin, have not also inherited the shame, consequence of the sin, as have all the nations of the world?"[35] He speculated that the Tupinambá ignorance of the Christian God had simply left them unable to understand divine justice or experience natural shame.

It was blindness to divine law, d'Abbeville concluded, rather than just the weight of the ancient custom among the women, for all humankind after Adam and Eve has felt shame like the first parents "when they opened their eyes, that is, when they were aware of sin and understood that they were dispossessed of the beautiful cloak of original justice. Shame arises, in effect, from consciousness of the malice of vice or of sin, and this results from the awareness of the law."[36] He noted that some might think it "a detestable thing to see this people nude, and dangerous to live among the Indian women, for the nudity of the women and girls would not cease to constitute an attraction, capable of casting those who contemplate them off the precipice of sin." Still, the nudity itself could pose no danger to him:

> In truth, that view is horrible, dishonest and brutal, since the danger is more apparent than real, and it is much less dangerous to see the naked-

ness of the Indian women than the attractive lewdness of the worldly women of France.[37]

The last source for the vivid imagery of compliant women in the Brazilian paradisiacal landscape comes from the paintings of Albert Eckhout, whose work in the early 1600s captured the persistent dichotomies of tamed and savage, docile and wild—in both women and the land. His work will be taken up at length at the end of the chapter.

The groundwork for the perception and treatment of women in Brazil during the colonial period had thus been laid by the first religious Europeans on its shores. Women's bodies were unrealistically portrayed—glorified, distorted, and refigured according to the transported imagery of the aliens, barbarians, savages, and "Wild Men" of European social mythology. In their letters and reports, the missionaries puzzled about the Brazilian Indian women: they were certainly not like the other aliens encountered in Africa or Asia, nor were they integrated into an identifiable civilization. European authors marked the differences from European women in terms of their virtue, docility, or simplicity. Those first reporters provided us with little by way of genuine ethnography of Tupí gender roles, but the primary interpretive discourse created in their accounts is remarkably consistent. First Caminha and then subsequent missionaries described the first ideal of innocence and compliance, naked and ready for conversion by the imperial and religious army. The Jesuit missionaries, inventing glorious histories of their own triumph over depravity and godlessness, used the images of the bodies of women as illustrations for their stories and shared with Caminha and later French missionaries a fascination with the naked and vulnerable Tupí women.

In the earliest reports about Brazilian Indian women, assertions about their innocence actually indicated the confusion of the observers: the women lived outside of the categories created for feminine value and virtue in Iberia. Although the women, like the land, seemed accessible and open, untouched by cultivation or corruption, they initially defied efforts by religious and civil authorities to regulate their lives and bodies. Their temporary status as innocents demanded civil protection and religious indoctrination, but only so that they might come to understand the full scope of divine law and human sinfulness. With the first moments of proselytization, their condition changed from innocent to shameless, and from invulnerable to dishonorable. As Brazilian Indian women proved increasingly resistant to conversion and conquest, however, the first paradigm that guided

European interaction with them gave way to a more sinister account. Innocence was lost, and remorseless condemnation followed.

RESISTANT AND VIOLENT: THE SECOND PARADIGM

The colony in Brazil was not, of course, a solely religious enterprise, nor were its new dominators primarily engaged in the recovery of lost souls; Brazil was to be both an extraction center — of raw materials such as gold — and agricultural venture for Portuguese investors. Indians were generally viewed as an available workforce, and, in response to the religious opposition to Indian enslavement, the Portuguese colonists developed elaborate systems for indentured servitude for Indians, based primarily upon two distinct rationales.[38] The first was that enemies in a just war might be enslaved, and so any Indians resisting conquest and conversion by Catholic Portugal could be captured and sold as slaves. The second rationale depended on the viewpoint that native Brazilians were in desperate need of the conversion and civilization offered by the Portuguese. Colonial enslavers therefore captured the Indians and then released them to the custody of individual Portuguese colonists as "wards" to be managed and educated. Most Portuguese, while making full use of the discourse of protection for their "wards," nonetheless treated them as slaves, counted their monetary value for tax credits, and passed them to their heirs as part of their personal property.

While the Portuguese extended their political and economic control, the discourse concerning women shifted, and a different image appeared more frequently in the letters and texts: the violent and perverse woman who fought back against colonial powers and their penetration of Brazil. This second set of images was dual, encompassing both the elusive Amazon warrior whose realms challenge male imperial hegemony and the rebellious cannibal whose appetite defies cultural norms. These two images came from the same complex of European ideology concerning barbarians and wild men from which the image of what would later be called the "noble savage" was drawn, and were, in a sense, its necessary complement. The portrait of the compliant body first encountered by Europeans was in fact sometimes accompanied by and nearly always followed by its inverse, articulating the resistance of the people and land. So while Caminha, in his first narrative from Brazil, stated repeatedly that the native Brazilians were innocent, ignorant, and tractable, he also conceded that the Portuguese felt uncomfortable with more than a few of them. The first Jesuits, otherwise stubbornly maintaining their views that the Brazilian Indian women were naturally devout, still worried about their perversions—including nudity. Both French missionaries Jean de Léry and Claude d'Abbeville tempered their admiration for the natural lifestyle of Indian women with concern over the tenacity of their ancient customs.

Through this new cluster of images one can see the changing perspective of the Europeans—colonists, exploiters, and missionaries—toward the land that they sought to possess. A wonderful place it had seemed at first to Caminha, not far from the Portuguese imperial metropolis, with a temperate climate and visible and exploitable resources on its shores. But its interior proved difficult to negotiate and conquer, its apparent availability repeatedly belied by the Brazilian Indians' aggressive defense of their lands and cultures as well as the truly alien nature of its forests and foods. Increasingly, missionary and colonial reports recorded clashes with armed combatants; complaints of impassable terrain, inclement weather, and insects; and struggles with famine and disease. By the 1560s, even the once-patient Jesuit José de Anchieta admitted that force would be necessary to maintain Christian devotion among the indigenous converts. While some of those reports dramatized the missionary struggles as part of the glorification of their successes, the emergent conflicts with the New World were real and indicated intolerable obstacles to the colonial enterprise. The New World was unnatural and dangerous, and its inhabitants were irredeemable savages among whose ranks must be counted Amazons and cannibals.

Amazon women were part of the mythology of the ancient world and reemerged in medieval and Renaissance folklore in Western Europe. For Homer, Hippocrates, and Herodotus, the Amazon was the Other at the borders of civilization—in Scythia, perhaps, or farther east—and within the borders as well; she was unlike the civilized male and a challenge to him because she was warlike, ungoverned, and female. For medieval Europeans, Amazons represented the wholly other—they were warriors possessed of corrupted femininity and disharmonious attributes. Part of the "wild space, which could enclose both women and quasi-bestial beings," "Amazons were clearly a paradoxical image of construed wildness."[39] The medieval West drew on ancient Christian images as well, portraying the wilderness as a place of negation, for withdrawal, penitence, and divine encounters. By the early modern period, however, ambivalence toward the wilderness was conspicuous: it was a place of depravity, a state to which wild beings retreated in their degeneration, but also the beginning of the "path to salvation and prophecy."[40] After 1500, in particular, the old European wild women represented not only the untamed inner self but also the peasant or primitive woman.

In the late Middle Ages, author Christine de Pizan offered an isolated alternative to the frightening alterity of Amazons when she extolled the virtues of Amazon life and Amazon queens in *The Book of the City of Ladies*. In that 1405 treatise, she laid "the foundation" for the City of Ladies with the help of Lady Reason and learned of the Amazons from Scythia who had lost all "male relatives" and chose to live without men in an independent state.[41] The bravest of Amazons "delight[ed] in the vocation of arms" and removed either left or right breast so that they were not hindered in carrying a shield or drawing a bow. Marpasia was their first queen, succeeded by the virgin Synoppe. Lady Reason recalled only a few of their "valiant ladies": "wise Thamiris" who beheaded Cyrus of Persia, Hippolyta who married the Greek Theseus, and Queen Penthesilea, who died fighting at Troy.[42] Still, their realm "lasted more than eight hundred years" until conquest by Alexander the Great, and, for Pizan, the descriptions of their valor, nobility, and prowess in war refuted more contemporary claims that women had only "weak bodies" and were thus "lesser" in virtue and "less praiseworthy."[43]

Inventive and popular travel accounts from that era provided even more details on Amazons to their readers. In the fourteenth-century narrative attributed to Sir John Mandeville, the traveler purportedly visited an island inhabited solely by women called "Amazonia" or "Feminye," and Marco Polo claimed that he found "the great riches of the women on the Female Island of the Arabian Sea."[44] Columbus, too, wrote of an island of women who "employ themselves in no labor suitable to their own sex, for they use bows and javelins . . . and for defensive armour have plates of brass, of which metal they posses great abundance." Those Amazons, he was told, took nearby male cannibals as "paramours" to father their children.[45] His *Journal* similarly placed an island of "women without men" near the fearsome Caribs, adding that they held "very much . . . gold or copper" in their possession.[46]

Indigenous American mythology may have contributed to the perpetuation of European myths of Amazons in the Amazon, with motifs of independent women or the separate creation of the two sexes. Women in the Tupian and Arawak communities in northeastern Brazil actually fought alongside male warriors and led separate women's sodalities—which may have confirmed European lore. Indeed, by the 1520s, more stories appeared in Europe to elaborate the ancient tales. Iberian romance literature

introduced brave and exotic warrior-women in a far-off Amazonian paradise in the New World who were challenged, conquered, and converted
to Christianity by male heroes.[47] Conquistador Hernán Cortés suggested
the name "California" for "the Amazon Queen Califia . . . of Montalvo's
romance" and for her eponymous island, and Queen Isabella herself endorsed the Amazon tales by offering a reward to the discoverer of their true
home in the New World.[48]

With this supportive background, it is not surprising that reports of the
discovery of Amazons in the New World emerged relatively early in the
colonial era alongside the misperceptions of indigenous women by European explorers and missionaries. The Jesuit missionaries themselves asserted that the Brazilian Indian women were at first pacific and compliant,
but nonetheless harbored suspicions that their unnatural wildness might
prove difficult to overcome. Indeed, more Jesuits reported their struggles
with converting women after the late 1500s, and fewer stopped to extol virtuous girls, dutiful wives, or enthusiastic prayer leaders. Thus Jesuit Simão
de Vasconcelos, in his 1663 *Chronicle of the Society of Jesus* in Brazil, emphasized the degenerate state in which his older compatriots had found the
indigenous women without indicating any natural mitigation. Instead, he
insisted that the land and its female inhabitants, fallen far from the human
and Christian standards, had required the nearly superhuman efforts of the
early Jesuit missionaries to effect a recovery. Calling them "wild, savage, . . .
and inhuman," Vasconcelos pointed to the women's nudity as the clearest
indication of degeneracy rather than innocence. They lived "without any
natural restraint," and "in them the light of reason was so dimmed" that
they were almost like wild beasts themselves.[49]

The ancient world may have given literary birth to the Amazon warrior, but the first account from the New World of Amazons and the eponymous river may be found in the *Relación* written by the Dominican brother
Gaspar de Carvajal who accompanied Captain Francisco de Orellana on
his first journey down the then-named Marañon River. Orellana had been
sent by Gonzalo Pizarro in 1541 to explore and raid the eastern Incan lands
for provisions, but he instead undertook an independent trip downriver,
traveling from Peru to the island of Cubagua, near present-day Venezuela.
Orellana failed to uncover the legendary wealth of the interior, but he
claimed to have encountered Amazons, the very "embodiment of a simultaneously rich and forbidding New World nature."[50] As part of his narrative of their survival in the dangerous worlds of the Maranhão, Carvajal reported that Orellana's ships encountered several great villages; most were

subject to a great inland prince, but in one impressive site—with a great temple honoring the sun—Carvajal learned that the inhabitants were "subjects and tributaries of the Amazons." They performed symbolic and ritual services for them, keeping and worshipping an "emblem of their mistress, who is the one who rules over all the land of the aforesaid women."[51]

In late June of 1541, the voyagers were attacked while traveling through and raiding several large riverside villages. After the Spanish had vanquished the fighters, Carvajal sought to learn why they had fought so well. Once again the report came that the villages were tributaries to the Amazon women. In that particular battle, the fighters had heard that the Spanish raiders were approaching, and they had gone to the Amazons for help. At their request,

> there came as many as ten or twelve of them, for we ourselves saw
> these women, who were there fighting in front of all the Indian men as
> women captains, and these later fought so courageously that the Indian
> men did not dare to turn their backs, and anyone who did turn his back
> they killed with clubs right there before us, and this is the reason why
> the Indians kept up their defense for so long.[52]

Carvajal continued with his own description of those putative Amazons:

> These women are very white and tall, and have hair very long and
> braided and wound about the head, and they are very robust and go
> about naked, (but) with their privy parts covered, with their bows and
> arrows in their hands, doing as much fighting as ten Indian men, and in-
> deed there was one woman among these who shot an arrow a span deep
> into one of the brigantines, and others less deep, so that our brigantines
> looked like porcupines.[53]

After another attack by well-trained fighters further downriver, Captain Orellana himself (who could not speak any Indian language) supposedly interrogated one of the captives, who admitted that he and his compatriots were also led and trained by Amazons. The captive revealed that the women warriors had "seventy villages" in the interior and dwelt in impressive stone houses. More details of their hidden lives then emerged when "the Captain asked if these women were married" and his captive "Indian said they were not."[54] As the interrogation continued, the ancient European motifs intertwined with the new story:

The Captain asked if these women bore children: the Indian answered that they did. The Captain asked him how, not being married and there being no man among them, they became pregnant: he said that these Indian women consorted with Indian men at times, and, when that desire came to them, they assembled a great horde of warriors and went off to make war on a very great overlord whose residence is not far from that . . . of these women, and by force they brought them to their own country and kept them with them for the time that suited their caprice, and after they found themselves pregnant they sent them back to their country without doing them any harm; and afterwards, when the time came for them to have children, if they gave birth to male children, they killed them and sent them to their fathers, and, if female children, they raised them with great solemnity and instructed them in the arts of war.[55]

Then the account reverted to details most likely gleaned from the lives and culture of Inca villages, with temples for worship of the sun, gold and silver vessels, and isolated communities of women. Carvajal subsequently returned to the equally fantastic—but invented—tale of Amazons, war, and danger for men who ventured into their land. The captive warned that men were usually banned from the land of the Amazons, but some were brought in to serve as consorts and warriors for the women. Again, he described the Amazons as being "of very great stature and white and numerous," but that while their land was rich in foods, it was cold and threatening to men, who might enter as boys but would leave as old men.[56]

The Jesuits, too, contributed to the lore about hidden communities of Amazon women. In 1553, Manuel da Nóbrega repeated another account of Amazons concocted by men returning from two years of gold prospecting in the Brazilian interior. Unlike the dangerous coastal Tupí, inland tribes supposedly resided in great cities and obeyed a great prince who assigned each day's work and distributed food to all. One of the vassal communities "that was nearest the Amazons fought with them" at the edge of the dangerous wilderness that still held the promise of material wealth for the Portuguese Empire and spiritual gains for the missionaries. Nóbrega provided further details of the New World Amazons who shared legendary traits with their Greek antecedents:

And these Amazons are such fierce warrior-women, that they war against the [local village], and take the most valiant men and conceive by them. And if they give birth to a son, they give him to his father or kill him, and if a daughter, they raise her. Because of their [warfare with] bows, they cut off their right breasts. And from among these Amazons came the news of gold.[57]

Here, as in Carvajal's writings, any authentic account of indigenous life has been lost under the myths first transmitted by the Greeks, and the travelers' failures to find gold and other riches have been reimagined as adventures uncovering the tantalizing opportunities for wealth and dangers just beyond the colonial borders.

Another contemporary chronicler of the colony, Gabriel Soares de Sousa, provided a further account of "Amazons." He wrote briefly of the many Tupí-Guaraní and Arawak tribes near the Portuguese coastal settlements, including the Ubirajaras near Bahia in northeastern Brazil. In Sousa's account of their "life and customs," he included detailed descriptions of their weaponry. Their longest spear, he noted, was useful for hunting as well as in their wars against Amoipiras who lived nearby, and in fighting against

> some women, who they say have only one nipple, and who fight with bows and arrows, and who govern and rule themselves without husbands, as was said of the Amazons.[58]

Sousa concluded, perhaps with some skepticism, that "of these we can discover no further information, neither of the lives nor of the customs of these women."[59]

The Jesuit historian Simão de Vasconcelos similarly included the Amazons in his 1563 account, *Curious and Useful News of Brazil.*[60] He reported all manner of unusual beings, such as extraordinarily short people and giants, and recounted the stories of "Almazonas" in northern Brazil in his conclusion:

> Finally that there was another nation of women monstrous in their way of life (these we now call Amazons, similar to those of antiquity, and from whom is taken the river's name) because they are warrior women, who live alone with themselves and do not traffic with men: they inhabit great villages in an interior province, cultivating the land, and sustaining themselves through their own work. They live between great mountains: they are women of known valor, who always live apart from ordinary contact with males; and even when by consent they come among them, [the men] come into their lands in certain times of the year, they

are received by armed women, holding bows and arrows, until they are certain that they come in peace, [as the men] first lay down their arms, [the women] take them into their canoes, and taking each one to a hammock, or bed, as it seems better to them, to take each to a house, and with her the guest is received, for a few days, which must be attended; after which, invariably they return, until the same time the following year, when they do the same. [The women] raise among themselves the females [born] of this meeting; the males they kill, or the more pious send them to their fathers, who then raise them.[61]

Amazons did not always present a challenge to the Jesuits, who typically allotted women—and the New World—only an instrumental role in indigenous or colonial life. For the Jesuits, women, like the land, served their higher purposes—the establishment of their new religious empire, with families of Brazilian Indians the new citizens and servants of God. So, just as the Jesuit José de Anchieta included female converts only so that males—Brazilian Indian or Portuguese colonists—might have properly Christian wives, so other missionaries mentioned Amazons rarely, and related only the contributions that Brazilian Indian women made to male lives, whether in the indigenous culture or as part of the colonial or evangelical conquest. One of the longer reports from early colonial Brazil was composed by Antonio Rodrigues, who wrote—at Manuel da Nóbrega's request—to the Portuguese Jesuit community of his travels in Brazil from the 1520s to the 1550s. Rodrigues mentions women only in terms of their service for colonists, or their economic contribution to an indigenous culture: colonists around the new town of Nossa Senhora da Assunção took the daughters of the local Carijós as wives, and the women among the Maias and Boroquis were remarkable spinners and weavers of cotton. He added briefly that some of his company had left to search for Amazons who were said to have gold and silver.[62]

Amazons thus corresponded with the reimagined dangers of the colonial territories beyond the coast and beyond even the nominal control of colonial authorities. Early colonial reports portrayed these "women without fear and without husbands"[63] as greater threats to the conquest of those lands than their male counterparts. While modern historians dismiss these reports as the enthusiastic imaginings of ignorant or impressionable men, contemporary Brazilian historians and anthropologists have taken a different strategy in their analysis. Most now agree that Carvajal was not hallucinating during his difficult journey or borrowing motifs of social inversions from the indigenous communities, nor did he simply embellish his *Relación* with a recognizable fable. Although the narrative cannot be historically or ethnologically accurate—there simply were no such white Amazons and Orellana spoke no indigenous language—Carvajal probably interlaced his captive's admissions with several stories about Inca villages, Virgins of the sun, indefatigable warriors, and warrior-women. Those embellishments both underscored the unworldly dangers that they faced and added an element of classical fantasy to his descriptions of daily fighting and river villages glimpsed in passing. They also suggested the fascinating contributions that his captain might make to the Spanish conquest. The Jesuit accounts may have had quite different literary or political impulses; they stemmed, at least in part, from the growing pagan resistance to civilization and conquest.

Brazilian historian Luiz Mott has suggested that the stories about Amazons in colonial sources conflated two different "equivocal ethnohistories"[64] of South American women. The first was that of Inca women living in conventual isolation and dedicated to the worship of the sun; their lives and customs probably inspired Carvajal's account, as noted above, as well as the other sixteenth- and seventeenth-century reports from Brazil of remote villages rich with golden implements. The second was that of coastal Tupí-Guaraní women, who not only fought alongside men but also occasionally lived independently of them, adopted masculine dress and roles, or cohabited with women. Indeed, accounts from the colonial period to the twentieth century have reported gender inversion and homosexual activity among Tupí women. The Jesuits themselves, in their praises of Brazilian Indian women who vowed to remain unmarried, may have unwittingly chronicled such women in their oblique fashion. A more direct account came from Pero Magalhães Gandavo, who in 1576 wrote of Indian women who determined to remain chaste:

> They abandoned all of the habits of women and imitated men and took on their tasks, as if they were not female. They cut their hair short like men, and went to war with bows and arrows, [and] to hunt, remaining only in the company of men. Each one had a woman who served her, and to whom they say she is married, and so they communicated and lived as husband and wife.[65]

The very presence of independent women would have been "the object of great curiosity"[66] for the neighboring communities as well as for later European men. Mott supports his contention with evidence for gender inversions among other Guaraní groups, a colonial dictionary of Tupí that includes the designation "çacoaimbaeguira" for a woman who has another "as a wife," the Jesuit confessional guide suggesting that friars question women about their sexual activities with other women, and the Inquisition accounts of homosexual acts among Brazilian Indian and mixed-race women.[67] For Mott, then, the myth of Amazons emerged from a tangled web of medieval European preconceptions about women, colonial confusion of stories about existent Indian women, and persistent ignorance — sometimes deliberately maintained — about the lives and powers of women in the New World. Through that web, we can glimpse the desire of those in authority to uphold social norms, even (or especially) at the cost of discovering the truth about the otherness thus reconstructed.

For the advancing Christian empires, Amazons were not the only women who embodied the obstacles within the Brazilian territories. In similar stories and parallel discourse, nearby Tupí or Tapuia tribal women presented more personal threats for the explorers and catechists. The Amazons, though frightening, were chiefly understood to reside far inland and away from the thriving coastal settlements, and descriptions of encounters with them receded quickly from the colonial reports. In their place stood women who posed a threat beyond death, a threat of loss, extinction, and desecration — for they were cannibals.

Although Pero de Caminha reported no clashes with cannibals in 1500, European explorers expected to encounter such alien creatures in American lands. Christopher Columbus established that expectation along with the central vocabulary of human consumption when he wrote in his *Diary* that Caribbean islanders had warned him that their neighbors were ferocious anthropophagi.[68] In recording his initial explorations of the Americas, he first rejected the attribution of anthropophagy to that nearby tribe, considering the practice too barbarous; he both accepted and named it, however, in creating the term "cannibal" for the dog-headed Caribs who ate other humans — a new term for a New World.[69] It was not a far step from that to the suggestion that those savage aliens would best be converted to the proper Christian life through capture and enslavement.[70]

Despite his failure to locate the perverse tribes that dined on their enemies, Columbus perpetuated his tales of cannibalism and corruption. He, like so many other travel-writers of his era, simply repeated the tales told by the ancient and medieval encyclopedists of wonderful and terrifying creatures found at the edges of human civilization. In the seventh century, Isidore of Seville had created a veritable catalog of "human monstrosities"[71] in the Indies, and the elusive author of the medieval travel writings of "Sir John Mandeville" repeated fantastic fictions of the various monsters of

Asia and beyond.[72] By 1511 in his first *Decades*, Peter Martyr d'Anghera had elaborated the cannibal reports from Columbus, rewriting the threats from fearsome Caribbean neighbors as a sort of cruel game of imprisonment:

> The natives of Hispaniola . . . complained that they were exposed to frequent attacks from the cannibals who . . . pursued them through the forests like hunters chasing wild beasts. The cannibals captured children, whom they castrated, just as we do chickens and pigs we wish to fatten for the table, and when they were grown and become fat they ate them. Older persons . . . were killed and cut into pieces for food; they also ate the intestines and the extremities, which they salted, just as we do hams. They did not eat women, as this would be considered a crime and an infamy.[73]

With so few restraints, the cannibal warriors destroyed neighboring villages and left them, according to Spanish reports, deserted huts with the remnants of their vile cannibal feasts.[74] Amerigo Vespucci confirmed the presence of cannibals "based on information gathered from the neighbours of these alleged anthropophagi,"[75] and confirmed the persistence of cannibalism among the tribes from not only the Caribbean but also Brazil.

Such influential reports perpetuated motifs from the European iconography of the other, in this case, of the "wild men" and "wild women" sketched in ancient and medieval lore. Details of the degenerate lives of those beyond the reach of civilization emphasized their nudity, hairy bodies, and exotic diet of wild and inedible foods, including raw meat and human flesh. Wild women violated the norms of Christian culture and their bestial appetites echoed the habits of demonic witches whose vices included lust, greed, and anger. These stereotypes were increasingly central to the European accounts of travels and encounters in Brazil, where defiant women symbolized the increasing hostilities among indigenous and immigrant peoples. To the imperial gaze, even customs once deemed harmless, such as communal housing and cooperative government, betokened the rebellious nature of Brazilian tribes. The nudity and hospitality of Brazilian women indicated the presence of evil, and, as the missionaries met further resistance to their catechisms, they also discovered that most vicious of customs among women—the uncontrolled appetites that culminated in cannibal rituals.

The images of cannibal women in the New World recalled more ancient myths as well: like the maenads of ancient Greece, they combined many of the signs of barbarity, including "lasciviousness, cannibalism, ingestion of raw meat, animal-like behavior, . . . and the clubs . . . used as weapons."[76] They continue the reversals of sex role that Amazons represented, for maenads and later anthropophagous women abandoned their domestic roles to live without men and hunt for food. The wild women of medieval European folklore challenged the norms of family life for they, like the fearful *lamia* spirits of ancient Greece and the witches of later Christian demonology, seduced and murdered husbands, tricked naive girls, and stole away unprotected children.[77]

In colonial Brazil, the most important and earliest source for the imagery of cannibal women came from a German soldier, Hans Staden, who recounted his captivity among the Tupí in his *Warhaftige Historia und Beschreibung*.[78] This *True History and Description* featured his misadventures begun in 1552 near present-day São Paulo where he was shipwrecked, abandoned, and finally taken as a hostage during battles between coastal tribes and the Portuguese colonists. His subsequent narrative detailed the cannibalistic customs of the Tupí who kept prisoners for later celebrations of victory, ritual sacrifice, and feasts. Captives like Staden might be kept, he explained, for up to a year and were even permitted to marry within the village, but they and their children were inevitably marked for death and desecration. Although many modern historians take Staden's account as an authentic report of his experiences, his emphasis on the central ritual role for women conflicts with other accounts of the Tupinambá—and is sometimes internally inconsistent.[79] It bears a strong resemblance, however, to the mythology of European witches' secret rituals, to an anonymous account written about Brazil in 1587, and to the burgeoning travel literature sensationalizing the savagery of Brazilindians.

Staden was, of course, the hero of his own travel tale. Seized near São Vicente and nearly freed during a skirmish with his captors' enemy Tupiniquin and allied Portuguese, Staden was spared a quick death because the "chief" wished to display him still alive to the women in the village so that they might have their customary "diversions" with him.[80] He was dragged, naked and wounded, to the Tupí village of Ubatuba and given over to the care of women there. Staden wrote that the women dragged him into the plaza by the ropes around his neck as they danced to the song dedicating their victims to be killed. Although he had been given as a captive to one of the leaders, Staden was nonetheless at the mercy of the women's blows and ministrations in preparation for death; he apparently expected to be "sacrificed" at that moment but misunderstood their plans.[81] The women mocked him, saying that he was "not yet" to be killed, and again danced and sang in a ceremony before the "hut where their idols, their maracás were." After shaving his eyebrows, two women dressed him with leg rattles and a feather crown, and demanded that he, too, keep time to their dance.[82]

The travel narrative portrayed Staden as a helpless victim, finally saved from the cannibal's blows by his own steadfast faith. In his early days of captivity, male captors had challenged Staden and demanded his death to avenge the murders committed by the Portuguese on the Tupí community. His protests of innocence were brushed aside, but his death was finally postponed following enemy raids and his intervention to cure the ailing chief.[83] The *True History* then recounted the events of his captivity and eventual escape, with intervening episodes of the Tupinambá men destroying nearby villages and consuming their enemies, but it only briefly mentions women's participation. The second section of his text, the "Brief Account" of "the Life and Customs" of the Tupinambá, provided fuller accounts of women's agricultural work, food and drink preparations, customary dress, and the care and raising of children. That section also featured the insistent reports that women took the dominant role in the cannibal rituals, overseeing the torture, ritual death, dismemberment, and eating of the captive enemy. According to Staden, Tupí women were first consulted for visions before a raid; subsequently they beat and decorated the victim, led him in a dance toward the central altar for sacrifice, and, after his ritual execution, butchered the corpse so that four women might take the four quarters in a procession around the village.[84] Women prepared the body portions for roasting, but only consumed entrails mixed with flesh from the head of the victim in a stew which was also offered to their children.[85] While Staden's narrative offered ample information on the bloodthirsty customs of village women, these latter images of the perverse and cannibal Tupí women came to dominate the visual representations of his tale and color the European understanding of indigenous Brazilian women as well.

The 1557 publication of the *True History*, in Marburg, Germany, was accompanied by vivid woodcuts, whose design Staden apparently directed. Each section describing the cannibal feasts featured images of the women's dancing and feasting. Male figures dominated only a few scenes of the captivity and killing, but women were present in each of those as well — placed close to the captive and to the center of the image. In fact, one of the most widely reproduced images portrayed a circle of women and children consuming the entrails, while another depicted a pair of women eating from a human skull. In later editions of Staden's narrative, the rather crude but evocative woodcuts were replaced with elaborate engravings created by Theodor de Bry, the author and illustrator of travel narratives encompassing North and South America. De Bry altered the images in two distinctive ways: first, he brought them into conformity with Renaissance ideals for art by creating vanishing points and introducing idealized human proportions and stances for the women and men.[86] Second, de Bry re-created the women's cannibal feast with significant additions to the women's figures: women seem to bite their arms and gesture wildly. His embellishment of the gestures and poses of the women—not part of any written accounts— also hinted at witchcraft, furtive sexuality, and the barbarous despair of the cannibal women even as they ate.[87] The images, thus embellished, both reflected and extended the condemnation now visited upon indigenous women and their traditional culture.

Accordingly, sixteenth-century Jesuits considered the very existence of cannibalism revelatory of the depth of degeneracy among the indigenous sinners, but they nevertheless held some hope for their final redemption. In 1549, Manuel da Nóbrega complained that although previous missionary orders had done little to counter barbarity, Jesuit missionaries found that some manageable villages already adhered to the "divine morals" of monogamous marriage, single-family residences with patriarchal ruling structures, regular farming practices, and generous exchange habits. The more treacherous groups were polygamous and lived in communal houses with a communal decision-making group; they were also predatory or warlike, hunted and gathered—and then only when needed—and ate human flesh. The Jesuits viewed cannibalism, like nudity and polygyny, as a token of the pagan nature of the Brazilian Indians, and marked true conversion to the new religion by the natives' abandonment of such practices.

In his early letters, Nóbrega remarked repeatedly on the horror of the ancient customs, and celebrated each case in which he found anthropophagy and other bestial vices abandoned. The Brazilian Indian women were of course notably present in the scenes of greatest cruelties and perversions. In August of 1549, he reported to his compatriots in Portugal that the vices of men among the coastal tribes were matched by women who participated actively in cannibalism, the "most abominable custom among those people." When prisoners of war were taken back to the villages, he explained, they were destined to be killed and eaten in subsequent festivals. Each male prisoner was apparently given a young woman as a wife, servant, and guard, but any children they might father met a similar fate. Although the original text was not clear, Nóbrega seemed to suggest that even the mothers shared in the feast: "if of them came some children, they will also eat them even if they are their [own] nephews and brothers, and at times their own mothers say that only the father has a part in them and not the mother."[88]

Nóbrega acknowledged that conversion in some villages was thwarted by women who still valued their barbarous feasts. In praising the work of Padre Navarro, Nóbrega revealed that violence against women was acceptable in this cause. While some former cannibals now "asked for his pardon, saying that they did not eat any dead [person], especially since the Padre was there," a nearby village proved more treacherous. There, among the

> Christian [Indians] whom we had baptized, the heathens one day ate a leg of an enemy that they had taken in war, but in secret and without a feast (as they were accustomed to do), so that we would not know of it; and when a Christian woman was found there, her husband beat her a good deal, and came to ask pardon of us, saying that he did not eat human flesh. Because of this we had all the Christians come together to exhort them to abandon all such bestial customs, and since that woman was ashamed to appear in our presence, this proved very edifying.[89]

In his 1551 letter to Coimbra, Jesuit Antonio Rodrigues developed criteria for distinguishing the tribes he had visited according to their culture and sustenance, emphasizing the native predilection for cannibalism. In his first travels, he and his companions enjoyed the company of "those heathens called the Timbos, who are many. They do not eat human flesh;" and their nearby compatriots, "the Mereatas, who brought to our ships fish cured in the sun, and much sustenance, for this is how they sustain themselves. They are a people who do not eat human flesh."[90] While the ethnically disparate Paris and Cameri, who were agriculturalists, hospitable, and "docile to receive the faith of Christ . . . did not eat human flesh," the Carijó tribal men were cruel and "ate human flesh."[91] Other Jesuit missionaries recorded that they followed the perspective Rodrigues had initiated and insisted that while the cruel warriors initiated war and practiced cannibalism for vengeance, women were the more violent and bloodthirsty participants. At the same time, missionaries and colonists encouraged intertribal warfare if not anthropophagy in order to suppress the indigenous population and sustain the justification for colonial domination, since any violent tribe might be massacred, and captives rescued from their cannibalistic enemies might be forced into slavery.

By 1573, Jesuit Simão de Vasconcelos admitted in his *Chronicle* that despite the many signs of divine grace in the land of Brazil, the people themselves remained "wild, savage, rustic, and inhuman."[92] For Vasconcelos, the savagery of the indigenous tribe emerged in their wars, for they fought for vengeance, brutally tormented their enemies, and ate their corpses. Women were by far the graver sinners in their lust for human flesh. He recalled that each "poor captive" designated for the cannibal ritual was met by a group of naked "old women who were fiercer than tigers and more loathsome than the Harpies, ordinarily aged in their role as in years, passing one hundred years old when chosen [for this role]." The women wore

> long necklaces of pointed teeth that they have taken from the bodies of the dead, which they had helped to eat in similar solemnities: and for their great amusement they go singing, and dancing to the sound of the pots which they carry in their hands to catch the blood and mix it with the entrails of the victim.[93]

For the Jesuit missionaries, women presented the greatest obstacles in converting these communities from their "natural" state with the civilizing forces of Christianity and patriarchal society. While the new customs— including monotheism, monogamy, and agriculture—attracted most men, a few women remained resolute in their savagery. The recurrent motif of the recalcitrant sinner thus appeared in this saga of incomplete conversion:

> One father of our Company related . . . that, penetrating the wilderness one time, coming to a certain village, he had found a very old Indian woman, at the end of her life; he catechized her at the point of death, teaching her about the faith, and thus completed his work. After tiring himself with things of such importance, and noting her frailty and lack of appetite, he asked her (speaking as they do in that land): My grandmother (and thus they call the old women), if I would give you now a little bit of sugar, or other taste for comfort from our part of the world, would you not eat it? The old woman, just catechized, responded: My grandson, I want nothing of this life, for everything now displeases me; only one this would now awaken my appetite: if I could just have a little hand of a Tapuia boy of a tender age, and suck on those bones, then I think I could take a little nourishment: for I (poor me!) have no one to go shoot one of those. It seems that this sufficiently explained the appetite of the people of Brazil for human flesh.[94]

For early Portuguese chroniclers, cannibalism marked the second Fall of human virtue, condemning the Brazilian tribes to barbarity long after Adam and Eve's first sin. Such diabolic acts deserved the fullest force of imperial and ecclesiastical repression, and so these claims about vicious heathens served the colonizing interests of both state and church. The con-

demnations of cannibal women went deeper than sixteenth-century political ideology, however, for they drew on the entrenched misogyny of European cultures. One can see those most clearly in the French missionary
reports of encounters with the Tupí women. Jean de Léry, noted above for
his matter-of-fact complaints about female nudity, underscored the violence and gluttony of cannibal women. In his account, as in Vasconcelos's
*Chronicle*, it was old women in particular who had "an amazing appetite
for human flesh," provoked men to bring them captives for sacrifice, and
licked their fingers as they ate.[95] Léry explained that while men and women
alike claimed their vengeance over enemies through the cannibal rituals,
only the old women—here much like European witches—found human
flesh "a delicacy."[96]

Brazilian historians Ronald Raminelli and Maria Cândida Ferreira de
Almeida have both remarked on the exaggerations in the written and visual
imagery that created and perpetuated the myth of cannibal women. Raminelli argues that the invention of cannibal women itself perverted the colonial accounts of indigenous Brazilian culture. Although Tupí men controlled village life and both created and demolished alliances with war, the
reports, maps, and illustrations found in the writings of Staden, Vespucci,
de Bry, and other European travelers increasingly "represent[ed] the feminine sex as the antagonist of the ritual and as the topos of cannibalism."[97]
The naked and contorted cannibal woman portrayed the vices of the indigenous cultures, and the motif of the old women who savored the cannibalistic feast not only perpetuated European fears of demonic witches
with unnatural appetites but also provided the justification for eradicating
Brazilian people and cultures. According to Almeida, cannibalism was the
primary "mark of barbarism" used to "define, qualify, name, and classify"
the otherwise unknown Brazilian people.[98] For the earliest discoverers and
explorers in Brazil, cannibalism thus represented the animalistic nature of
those alien tribes and characterized the most alien among them—cannibal
women.

The truly rare cases of ritual anthropophagy in Brazilian indigenous
cultures have multiple meanings and purposes, and the reports from colonial witnesses cannot all be trusted. Consequently, it may be impossible to
characterize its "real" function in those cultures and understand its value
to participants. As Claude Rawson has insisted, "cannibal accusations,
true or false, are usually expressions of xenophobia."[99] In these repeated
records of the "presence and enthusiastic participation of women in cannibal ritual,"[100] the colonial authors reveal their growing antagonism to
Brazil and its people. The idyllic Golden Age land dreamed of and briefly

glimpsed by the first European men had devolved to a hellish scene of rampant desires and appetites, and the innocent maidens who might be so easily civilized and converted had become fearsome Amazons and cannibals who clung to their depravities even as their villages were destroyed by the justified conquest of the imperial missionaries and slave traders. After only about ten years in Brazil, as can be seen in the accounts I cite, the records of the Jesuit missionaries began to enhance the heroic details of their efforts to save those devil-ridden savages, and they nearly abandoned the religious instruction of women to invest their energies in the conversion of young boys in new settlements. Supported by royal policies concerning just war and the enslavement of alleged cannibals, and by papal decrees designating "cannibalism, sodomy, and idolatry" as unnatural crimes, Portuguese colonial officials were encouraged to transform the indigenous peoples through the destruction of their sinful customs.[101] The imperial forces and ordinary colonists took the evidence of persistent savagery to vindicate their raids, massacres, and enslavement of the indigenous peoples—inducting them by whatever means possible into the civilizing powers of the Portuguese.

CONCLUSION

The paintings of Albert Eckhout provide us with the visual aids to understand the European colonial views of Brazilian women. Eckhout accompanied the new Dutch governor Johan Maurits de Nassau-Siegen on his inaugural trip to northeastern Brazil while the coastal cities were held by Holland between 1624 and 1641. While his work was based in his own experiences in 1640 or 1641, it was undoubtedly shaped by the factual accounts and fantastic travel narratives of the American land and its people that circulated in Europe in the sixteenth and early seventeenth centuries and by the classical norms for representation reaffirmed by the Renaissance. In three dramatic images, one can see the transformation of the wild woman—and wild land—into domesticity.

In the first painting, *Tarairiu Indian Woman*, a Tapuia woman serves as an "allegory of savagery and cannibalism."[102] She stands naked in a woods, with a characteristically Gê haircut, but with European facial features and bodily characteristics closer to the classical Greek than any native Brazilian. Her genitals are discreetly covered by branch bundles from the encircling locust bean tree, but her true savagery—her cannibal nature—is re-

vealed by the burden in the basket on her shoulders and in her hand: she
carries a severed human foot and hand, apparently her next meal. Around
her are the wilds of the land, and in the distance a group of Tapuia men
are armed for war. Eckhout offered her as the challenge of the land, the
savage and resistant body, corresponding to that set of characteristics outlined above.

In the second painting, a domesticated Tupí woman represents the
challenge of the land overcome, and indicates the Indians that Eckhout
imagined were in fact susceptible to conquest and civilization. In his painting of the *Tapuya or Tupí Woman and Child*, the figure stands passive and
expressionless. Bare-breasted, she is dressed in a long white skirt, probably
of native cotton, and her hair is long and bound by cords. With a child
on her hip, she mirrors the productivity and docility of the land, and she
carries cultivated foods and artifacts in her colonial-style basket. Next to
her is a banana tree—recently introduced to the colony—and behind her
are plantation buildings with the rows of its orchard tended by other Indians, probably enslaved. Within this transformed space, the Indian woman
has been domesticated, and the painting portrays the successful outcome
of her "pacification."[103]

In the third painting, *Mameluca*, Eckhout portrays the young daughter of a Portuguese man and Brazilindian woman, wearing a long white
loose gown, pearl jewelry, and a basketry headpiece adorned with small
flowers. In her right hand she lifts a basket of native flowers and herbs, and
her indolent stance gives her the appearance of a goddess of fertility and
vegetation—a young Demeter under a cashew tree. Her close surround-
ings include some native plants that gave nourishing fruits, but behind her
the lands have been cultivated, with fences and roads crisscrossing them.
In this symbolic image, the dichotomy of wild and civilized has been medi-
ated and not just displaced: she is the product of the two worlds in a single
person, thoroughly covered by the ancient image of tamed land.[104]

Eckhout's paintings—created nearly 150 years after the Portuguese
claiming of Brazil and nearly a century after the Jesuits began their mission
to re-create Brazil as a Christian outpost in the New World—preserve the
imagery of Brazilian women and the land as the Portuguese conquerors
and colonists might themselves have understood it. The otherness of that
place stands before them in these three women—once cannibalistic and
fearsome, then domesticated and cultivated, and finally replaced with an
entirely new being. The first ideas of the "compliant" and receptive savage
women may be seen through these, for the cannibal is quickly overcome

by the dominant culture. The final image, of the land and woman transformed, carries the vision of the imperial Portuguese civilization. Here, then, is how women must be.

The images discussed in this chapter, of compliant or savage women, were gradually eradicated during the first colonial epoch. As I have suggested here, the first encounters with Brazilian women were suffused with misunderstandings shaped by the European conceptions of the natural and wild world, and by extant dichotomous categories of tamed and wild, civilized and savage, saved and damned. The innocent women of the indigenous cultures fell outside of the imperial and religious codes of honor; without those rules impinging on their lives, they were—despite all claims of innocence—unprotected and vulnerable. When they resisted the imposition of the rules, they were subject to the harsh condemnations and oppressive conditions of the dominant religious and political culture: they were then deemed dishonorable or shameless. These two paradigms of Brazilian Indian women—the compliant women who awaited salvation and exploitation, and the resistant women who fought back against Portuguese colonial powers—were overthrown by the widely promulgated ideal of the good and virtuous Brazilian colonial girl and woman, with the appropriate characteristics, roles, and behaviors that merited honorable treatment in colonial society. In the following chapters I will focus on the expressive religious literature that defined the "ideal" for women in Brazil and mandated how women of Portuguese, African, Indian, and mixed heritage might best be educated, married, and cloistered to conform to Luso-Brazilian ideals of womanhood.

# TWO

# The Body of Virtues

## THE CHRISTIAN IDEAL
## FOR BRAZILIAN WOMEN

I n the early 1600s, the Jesuit Antônio Vieira preached to Catholics in Brazil that the failings of women began with their ancestral mother, Eve. After Eve's great sin, women had repeatedly abandoned the virtuous life that had been mandated for them, and exemplary women of Scripture were themselves trapped in perversion and ignorance. Vieira insisted that not all of the women named in Jesus's own genealogy were virtuous, for Tamar, Rahab, Bathsheba, and Ruth had failed to uphold the virtue of chastity. Magdalene, too, had been sexually "dishonest," bearing seven demons of unchastity before encountering Jesus's healing exorcism; the women of Brazil were scarcely less blameworthy. Still, he continued,

> why not introduce and discuss the examples or scandals of men, but only those of women? Because in women, just as this sin is more offensive, so is it more dangerous and pernicious. Consider the harms done in the world by the sin of dishonesty, and you will find that women were the origin and women the cause.[1]

Vieira in this sermon provided not just a commentary on women's nature and virtue but also a cornerstone for the ideal of the virtuous Christian woman in colonial Brazil, based in discourse begun in medieval and early modern Europe about feminine honor and its expression through women's virtues.

Male authors of the early modern era ascribed specific, gendered characteristics to the nature, attributes, virtues, and bodies of women. Drawing on ideas elaborated in the European Middle Ages, they warned of women's natural tendencies toward wildness and mayhem and recommended extensive social and personal restraint to reduce those tendencies. While the

first Portuguese reports from Brazil began with speculation that indigenous women might be naturally innocent and unaffected by the shame
of original sin, colonial attitudes quickly reverted to the longer-standing
understanding that all women were corruptible. The discourse went beyond abstractions to advocate control over women through religious and
civil laws, colonial regulations, and familial customs. When male writers
insisted that women be kept out of churches and other public places and
restricted to domestic service in their own or others' homes, women then
faced physical limitations to their daily movements and barriers to their
personal choices. By the end of the colonial era, Brazilian authors had furthered the restrictions so that upper-class women might seem to disappear
from the society at large and working women encountered more hazards
in their necessary defiance of such restraints.

The restrictive ideals constructed by early modern Portuguese and
Brazilian authors were neither new nor inconsequential, but rather constituted a complex set of constraints created for women within European
Christian society. There the centuries-old concepts of nature and sin in
what Mary Douglas termed the "social body" offered further restraints for
"the physical body" in the New World as well. Douglas contended that
the rules of the social body were impressed upon the physical body such
that the body "sustain[ed] a particular view of society" and expressed social
norms in "all the cultural categories in which it [was] perceived."[2] While
Douglas first identified bodily conformity as a "natural tendency" within
a comprehensive system, she further noted that "bodily control [was] an
expression of social control." Where strong social norms demanded for-
mality, one would find both the demand for "strong bodily control" and
increased pressure to reduce independent bodily expression altogether.
Social pressures, especially in formal and complex settings, mandated not
only extended distances between bodies but also the "pretense" that social
interactions "take place between disembodied spirits." Douglas concluded
her theoretical discussion of the "two bodies" by suggesting that enforcement of strong social norms would nearly eliminate bodily presence and
rigid social hierarchies would demand purity in social and ritual behaviors.[3]

While the images of Amazons and cannibals discussed in Chapter 1
reflected the alienation of the observers from the new Brazilian people and
lands, the later reactions to those images also reverberated with strong social
and religious norms, expressed in the expectations that girls and women
should tread a narrow path of virtuous behavior from birth through adulthood. A woman's virtue was a private attribute, unlike men's public claim to
privilege and prestige, and feminine honor began with an awareness of un-

avoidable shame for her very existence. Women were only honored if they first acknowledged that they were in fact not honorable, that their feminine nature was, as Vieira maintained, sinful and shameful. Vulnerable, foolish, even ignorant, a woman required the standards set by the church and wider society as guides for her amelioration; with men's protection under those standards, a woman might gain honor for her inviolability and submission to the virtuous ideal that the Iberian colony reproduced.

From the beginning of the colony, the Roman Catholic Church systematically developed plans for girls' and women's education in Catholic doctrine and Iberian culture. Under Jesuit guidance, indigenous and immigrant women were challenged to adhere to the religious teachings concerning feminine nature and virtue in order to gain (or regain) recognition as worthy beings in the religious and social spheres. Women's nature, as will be discussed further below, was perceived to be damaged and weak, and the attainment of virtue by women required dedication and devotion. In the religious sphere, honor was also "honesty," that is, sexual purity and modesty, so that an honorable woman was valued primarily for her virginity and chastity. While men's sexual conduct might bear public scrutiny, women's chastity was a private virtue and her honor depended on her obscurity: "if nothing was said about her, if no rumor circulated about her, then she was honorable. As the moralist wrote, *the best reputation is to have no reputation.*"[4]

In the Brazilian colony, women's bodies served as a peculiarly intense focal point for the imposition of social order by the dominant patriarchy. This had been so since the first ship's crews offered clothing to indigenous Brazilian women. Not merely an image of society, the female body was the image of the evils into which society might fall unless rigorous boundaries were enacted and "strong bodily control" exerted over it.[5] The development of feminine ideals and the creation of a "body of virtues" in colonial Brazil thus enabled religious and political writers to name the dangers they faced in the colony and inscribe indispensable limitations on women to avert the worst of them. Given the traditional imprimatur of the virtues thus advanced, most women had no choice but to accept them and embody them. Women's bodies and behavior, under scrutiny at the beginning of the colony, remained subject to restrictions as the colonists established plantations and chapels, towns and dioceses, and government and ecclesiastical institutions within this determinedly patriarchal society.

The elaboration of separate aspects of the idealized woman—virtues, character, and body—indicates the power of the dominant ideology over the individual in colonial Brazil, and may also reveal conflicts within the religious and social institutions as they confronted the colonial situation. The ways in which the female body was perceived, constructed by religious and social rules, reflected the cultural categories and boundaries deemed appropriate for all members as a *habitus*, the "durably installed generative principle of regulated improvisations." As Pierre Bourdieu has explained, such a habitus "produces practices which tend to reproduce the regularities immanent in the objective conditions of the production of their generative principle." Within the "commonsense world," women and men unconsciously produced and reproduced actions consonant with "the established order," so that their actions disclosed less of the intentionality of the agents and more of the "immanent law" of the *habitus*.[6]

While Iberian concepts of honor rested primarily with the elites, the virtues required by the Catholic Church pertained to women of any class or status. Elite women might achieve the pinnacles of the ideal, but even slave women — despite many contemporary prejudices — might sometimes be virtuous. Women of all ranks thus faced precise expectations for their religious activities and personal comportment. Variations for those expectations followed class and ethnic lines, so that white women of Portuguese descent met more rigid strictures in the ideal of the virtuous Christian woman, while mixed-race, native Brazilian, or enslaved or freed African women faced harsh demands for labor and submission. The religious and secular sources alike described the so-called feminine attributes, exhorted Christian virtues, and proposed suitable lives and behaviors for girls so that they might achieve the obedience and docility to enter their adult roles as wives and mothers. This chapter will consider the construction of the virtuous and honorable ideal in response to the threats posed by women's unruly nature.

## THE TRADITION OF FEMININE HONOR AND VIRTUE

The colonial notion of the virtuous Christian woman was not an autochthonous ideal grown in the hot tropical sun of Salvador. It had roots not just in Portugal but also farther afield, in ancient Greece and Israel. Greek authors rarely argued whether women might or might not be inferior, but instead they took women's inferiority as the beginning point for further argumentation. Aristotle, whose ideas permeated Christian moral thought through Augustine and Thomas Aquinas, assumed women to be deficient in their capacity for intellectual and moral excellence, but not without the subordinate virtues worthy of mothers and wives. Women, in his view, had the capacity to learn and to care for children, but their roles in nature were more material and passive, since they merely provided the substance for reproduction and the womb for nurturance of human life. Ruled in body and soul for their own good by men, women's purpose was limited to their service to men just as, to complete the dualistic patterns, slaves served masters and the body served the soul.[7] Women, then, should cultivate moral virtues of justice and temperance, but primarily in obedience to husbands and fathers; feminine virtues thus began in silence and were achieved in subordination.[8] While not every aspect of Aristotle's dubious assessment of women's value and nature entered the ancient Christian construct of feminine virtue and vice, his conclusions cast a long shadow on Christian literature.

The ideals for Christian women were also generated from ancient scriptural sources, notably the Genesis stories of creation and the collections of wisdom literature. The narrative of the creation of Eve from Adam and her subsequent flouting of divine command formed the foundation for doctrinal claims on women's nature, status, and proclivities. Created as a companion to Adam in the second creation story in Genesis, Eve ate "of the Tree of the Knowledge of Good and Evil" despite God's injunction against it, and in her disobedience reaped the blame for what Christians later called the "original sin." Cursed with pain in childbirth and expelled from the Garden of Eden with Adam, Eve was further punished as her husband was given "rule over" her.[9]

After Eve, few positive images of women are found in the Hebrew Bible, where the stories about strong and virtuous women such as Ruth, Naomi, Judith, Deborah, and Esther could not balance the weight of warnings about harlots and faithless wives. Women's sexuality and curiosity were corruptive, as the many stories and feminine images suggested, and unrestrained women were dangerous to the individual male and to the community. The wisdom texts collected the negative and positive stereotypes, with Proverbs 9:13 warning the "wise son" away "from the loose woman, from the adventuress" and encouraging him to choose instead the prudent housekeeper. A foolish woman was noisy, "wanton," and knew "no shame," but "a good wife . . . is far more precious than jewels." The virtuous woman in these texts was hard-working at home and in the fields, generous, financially astute, cautious in action, kind, and religiously devout. Her kindness was praised, but not her "deceitful" charm or her "vain" beauty.[10]

The sacred literature of the early Christian church scarcely advanced these notions, and the New Testament most often reworked the dichotomous portrayal of women inherited from the ancient world. More than one story from the life of Jesus offered an alternative role for women, with supporters of his movement such as Susana, avid learners such as Mary of Bethany, and witnesses or advocates such as the unnamed woman at the well and Mary Magdalene. Those were quickly replaced, however, by later apostolic interpretations that firmly replaced women in limited and oppressive roles and by institutional insistence on men's dominance.[11] The Pauline letters in particular articulated both the appreciation for the active leadership of women in the early Christian community and the need to restrain them at all costs. In the greetings or closings of his letters, Paul commended women who directed gatherings or taught, including the deacon Phoebe and noted workers Prisca, Mary, and Junias, among others. But the same author commanded that wives must "submit to" their husbands, that women cover their heads while praying or preaching, and that women simply "remain silent" because it was disgraceful for women to speak in church.[12] Finally, later epistles eliminated any doubt by asserting that women's virtues were submission, silence, and self-effacement. Women were returned to the ranks of sinners, but would yet be "saved through childbearing—if they continue in faith, love and holiness with propriety."[13]

Augustine of Hippo, the fourth-century convert and bishop, developed the ideal for women in his formulation of central Christian doctrines. True virtue—for men or women—derived from loving and seeking God, but all humanity deviated from the virtuous ideal in the quest for worldly pleasures. Women exhibited their innate inferiority through their physical differences from men, and their imperfections reflected their distance from the biblical "image of God." For Augustine, Eve's story explicated women's essential weaknesses, beginning with her subordination to Adam and vulnerability to temptation and sin. Sexuality, childbirth, sin, and death originated in Eve, and the resultant dishonor was borne by all humans after her. After her, and because of her, women were "intellectually, morally, and even physically inferior."[14]

Augustine was not the sole voice from early Christianity to offer this daunting argument against women's perfectibility and achievement of virtues beyond obedience and subordination, but his were the texts repeatedly cited to maintain women's subordination across centuries of social struggle and theological disputes. Thomas Aquinas furthered the construction of Christian virtues in the Middle Ages, with scholastic arguments that brought Aristotelian ideals within Christian teachings. For Aquinas, both men and women might cultivate earthly or natural virtues such as courage, justice, temperance, fortitude, and prudence, but women's weak intellectual and moral nature led them to inevitable failure in that task.

When questioning "whether woman should have been created" at all, he echoed Augustine's view that women were inferior to men and could not even "help" their male companions in the higher intellectual and spiritual pursuits. Since women only imperfectly reflected the image of God and were created secondarily to serve as the procreative partner for men, women might only achieve their divinely assigned earthly purpose through dutiful marriage and motherhood.[15]

After Aquinas, other writers on feminine virtue insisted that women's actions be controlled and their sphere of action circumscribed. Women's primary virtue was chastity, and protecting this virtue required more than virginity before marriage and strict fidelity during marriage; it signified the necessity of protection and confinement as part of the feminine ideal. Women were exhorted to cultivate modesty and restraint and avoid ostentation or profligacy, and their "intemperate and perverse loquacity" demanded that they be excluded from positions of authority in churches, legal courts, and schools.[16] Popular devotion enshrined the Virgin Mother of Jesus, but her virtues raised her above human accomplishment. In her place, Christian preachers offered women the model of Mary Magdalene as a reformed prostitute—invented from the accounts of several "Marys" and unnamed women in the New Testament—and emphasized feminine sin and penitence. Renouncing sexuality, liberty, and indeed volition, a devoutly religious woman could approach the virtues usually ascribed to men. Whether young or old, poor or rich, working or noble, medieval women were warned against independence and urged to find their lives within the family, as dutiful daughters, wives, or widows, or find their vocations within the church.[17]

For women who sought a virtuous ideal, author Christine de Pizan challenged the most pronounced misogyny of her day with *The Treasure of the City of Ladies or Book of the Three Virtues*, written in 1405 as "part etiquette book, part survival manual." Drawing her inspiration from "the three sisters" known as "Reason, Rectitude and Justice," Pizan advised that all "high-born ladies" must be inspired first by "the love of and the fear of Our Lord, for this is the cardinal principle of wisdom, from which all the other virtues spring."[18] Averting the "temptations" of arrogance, selfishness, pride, and related vices of "idleness" and "carnality," women might accept "the contemplative life" of religious recluses or the "active life" serving God through humility, patience, compassion, and generosity toward "the sick and the poor."[19] Sobriety, "moderation and modesty," and "chastity" in all personal relationships were the virtues that cultivated "Worldly Prudence"—the second-highest virtue—and preserved the lady's personal and family honor. Pizan counseled fidelity and prudence for all "ladies and maidens and ordinary women" who served at courts or had noble duties. Notably, even lower-ranking women might aspire to higher virtues through their household work, love and fidelity to husbands, honor to family, and maintenance of household order though knowledge and sensible management—from care of children to finances. Cleanliness, hard work, and attention to detail ennobled even housewives in Pizan's understanding of the virtuous Christian woman.[20]

Christine de Pizan and other late medieval writers expanded the ideal for Christian women, so that self-abnegation was no longer the full content of feminine virtue. Still, virtue and honor remained equally dependent on restrictions on women's activities, especially in their sexual conduct. For men, virtue—itself derived from the Latin term for men or manliness—drew on inner strength, and the masculine ideal of courage provided the public accomplishment of their natural roles. Women's virtue depended on a limited range of honorable behavior in the religious or domestic sphere. After 1450, women experienced a real diminution of their roles and opportunities, and the relegation of the woman's sphere to the decorative and the private all resulted from the reemphasis on classical ideas about men and women. Such restrictions on women increased during the sixteenth and seventeenth centuries.[21] These changes and retrenchments may be seen more starkly in the lives of women and the ideal set for them in medieval and early modern Portugal and its Brazilian colony.

IDEALS FOR WOMEN IN PORTUGUESE LITERATURE

Medieval Portugal cultivated the principles articulated by Augustine, Thomas Aquinas, and other Christian authorities, and so bound women with the same restrictive social and personal norms found elsewhere in Europe. Portuguese women of the highest social ranks experienced a few additional privileges and managed their own inheritance and dowries, while working women of the lower ranks breached custom out of necessity, but neither group escaped the rigorous standards for feminine honor set by their culture. Barred from most influential roles outside of the domestic sphere, Portuguese women in the Middle Ages and early modern era encountered mostly barriers and constraints in the feminine ideal constructed of chastity, silence, modesty, and piety.

By the time of the Portuguese voyages of discovery and the inauguration of the colonial era, humanist ideals had barely affected Portuguese concepts of womanly virtue, and few such ideas were transmitted to Brazil. Notably, no female authors, rulers, or patrons encouraged a shift in perspectives on gender roles in Portugal, and portrayals of women in Portuguese arts and letters were barely changed during the Renaissance. While Portuguese authors experimented with newer and more popular forms of literature, such as etiquette books, guides for the nobility, and collections of edifying stories, none attempted the satirical debates concerning women's roles that were popular in France and England. As a result, we find that the exemplary individuals in moral tales were pious and aristocratic men accompanied only occasionally by demure ladies and nuns. Since no printing press was permitted in Brazil until the eighteenth century, and then only briefly, the colonial elite in the new Brazilian cities of Bahia, Olinda, and Recife relied on publications from the imperial centers of Lisbon and Coimbra for guidance. From the sixteenth through the nineteenth centuries, secular publications from Portugal presented a virtuous Christian woman little changed from the Middle Ages, and the Portuguese religious writings recapitulated the discourse of restrictions for women predicated on ancient biblical teachings of sin and punishment.

The constraints for the sixteenth-century Portuguese woman emerged clearly in the tales transcribed by Gonçalo Fernandes Trancoso (1520?– 1596) in his *Contos de Exemplo e Proveito*. Trancoso, not unlike Giovanni Boccaccio over a century earlier, collected legends and proverbs representative of the national culture, but still emphasized a sharp distinction between the sexes. In his *contos*, domineering and arrogant men were the masters of honor and virtue, but independent women were met only with harsh punishments or condemned for a litany of "feminine" vices. His tale of "A Disobedient Daughter" offers a typical contrast between the "virtuous lady leading a good life" and her "lazy, gluttonous, envious, voluble" daughter. Seeking to settle her daughter into marriage, the elder woman instructed the girl to show herself to be "quiet and occupied in virtuous activity, as girls should always do, since restlessness and indolence in them commonly takes them to very dangerous thoughts, contrary to virtue, a good reputation, and a decent life." When the girl met her potential in-laws, however, they recognized her ineptness with a spindle, and her fiancé spurned her as an insupportable wife. In desperation, the disappointed matron poisoned her own daughter, and the editor added that daughters must attend to their family duties.[22]

Other *contos* repeated the same gruesome lessons for women, stipulating penalties for their persistent vices. In "The Honorable Woman Must Be Silent" ("A Mulher Honrada Deve Ser Calada"), Trancoso warned women that any conversation—especially witty banter—must be stifled for the womanly virtue of silence. Several short vignettes encompassed that particular moral, including the account of a young woman who fancied herself insulted by a passing man after she made fun of his nose. He countered her derision with this accusation: "You were not there when they gave out shame, or you would be silent!" When she complained to her husband of the affront, he chastised her for this disgrace and then beat her for her gossip and lies. Trancoso enjoined teachers to reward those girls who maintained silence and a downward-cast and modest gaze when walking abroad.[23]

A much longer tale, "The Envious Sisters," featured a young "virtuous and chaste" king who, indifferent to fortune, wed a woman endowed only with "virtuous habits, good blood and pleasing appearance." Respecting her beauty and modesty, he treated her with "honor" as if she were from a noble family. After her successful marriage, her jealous sisters, "taught by the Devil" himself, insisted that the queen had borne a series of venomous monsters. Cast out, the dishonored queen took refuge as a lowly servant in a convent for four years, until the deception was revealed and the lying sisters flung themselves into the sea. When finally discovered in her convent cell, the queen knelt to beg forgiveness of the king (although she had done nothing wrong) and to give thanks to God for his mercy, while the king simply reinstated her as consort. Trancoso's final comments disregarded the king's failings but underscored the punishments—deserved and not—for feminine vices.[24]

Two other tales affirmed the virtues of silence and self-abnegation for married women, even as their husbands abused them. "Grisela, The Obedient Wife" offered the lesson of a landowner's daughter whose noble husband mandated that she neither grieve nor contradict him. Agreeing to her fate, she swore her submission, vowing, "I must not do anything against your will, nor think it against your thinking, nor . . . contradict you in anything." Her husband then had their first two children kidnapped, blamed her "negligence" and her ignoble lineage for their losses, and threatened to repudiate her, while she only murmured that he was of course her "lord and husband" and "could do with her what he wished." Even when faced with her replacement—her own grown daughter in disguise—Grisela only expressed the wish that she might be a better wife to him. This tale of marital cruelty and deception concluded with the revelation that their two children had survived, and that Grisela had proved herself to be a truly obedient wife.[25] In "The Honest Maiden and the Righteous Duke," another woman faced with dishonor found neither dignity nor recompense. Finding an impoverished but beautiful maiden held by a cruel captor, the Duke forced the errant knight to marry the girl in order to regain his honor and a noble pardon. The man's brutality triumphed as he married his former captive, while the "honest maiden" was punished for her vulnerability. She was raised to "great honor and status," but never left her captivity at all.[26]

Taking a different approach to the virtuous ideal, Trancoso also created a "Moral ABC" in response to a lady's request for help in learning to read. He first admitted reluctance in this task, since she—at her advanced age and fixed role—should be content with illiteracy: "I rejoice that you wish to learn to read so as to pray from books, which is good; however, since you did not learn in childhood in the house of his lordship your father with your sisters, you must now be content with the beads [of the rosary], . . . since you do not read and you are married and already past the age of twenty."[27] If she were unsatisfied with that sage counsel, however, he offered an "Abecedário Moral" that she might memorize:

> The A [is] to say that you should be a friend of your house; B, well-loved in the neighborhood; C, charitable with the poor; D, devoted to the Virgin [Mary]; E, knowledgeable in your position; F, firm in faith; G, guardian of your property; H, humble before your husband; I, enemy of gossips; L, loyal; M, gentle; N, noble; O, honest; P, prudent; Q, docile; R, rule bound; S, sober; T, hard-working; V, virtuous; X, simple [or Christian]; and Z, zealous of your honor.

Trancoso's instructions echoed the rigid expectations for women: even if literate they must still remain enclosed at home, cautious, obedient, and self-effacing. Trancoso added, "When you made all this your own, as would be proper, you must believe that you know more letters than all of the philosophers," and repeated that a short list of regulations was an appropriate lesson for a feeble-minded woman.[28]

As Trancoso's "ABC" and collection of *contos* illustrates, a woman's chief virtue in the sixteenth century lay in her acceptance of her own limitations and her dedication to submissive obedience. In this literature, feminine honor began and ended in passivity, so a woman proved her value through restraint, self-denial, and self-effacement, and gained her meager successes through marriage and childbirth. Women's moral accomplishments might include chastity and modesty, but only men could award honor to her through their own honorable actions. A woman's efforts, then, were directed by and for men, with an eye to generating a usable necessity—children—for imperial or masculine glory. Supportive of the family honor above all, the ideal woman was rule-bound and humble before her husband, so that the world remained undisturbed by her or even unaware of her existence.

Portuguese marriage manuals of that era, circulated and reprinted later in Brazil, continued this theme, emphasizing that women should remain submissive, governed by religious instruction and their husbands' mandates. Even then, their speech in particular and actions in general were to be undertaken "with caution and moderation" so that they not "be unrestrained with strangers nor impertinent with their husbands." Above all, they could not correct their husbands' speech or ignorance on any subject, nor might they respond to arguments.[29] Secular sources rarely advised women on their moral values, however, leaving the inculcation of chastity and modesty to religious instruction. As will be explored further in the next chapter, even guides written for women offered little relief, since their authors viewed women's life as necessarily circumscribed. In his treatise on education for girls, for example, the Spanish scholar Juan Luís Vives concluded that a woman's world was narrow and her responsibility limited: "As for a woman, she hath no charge to see to, but her honesty and chastity. Wherefore when she is informed of that, she is sufficiently appointed."[30]

Few voices in early modern Portugal countered the prevailing wisdom that women should remain cloistered and constrained, and those observers were almost contradictory in their arguments. In 1572, Rui Gonçalves insisted on women's moral character and legal rights in his "Privileges and Prerogatives," dedicated to Catherine, queen of Austria and later regent of Portugal. As the first Portuguese author to have addressed "the issue of equality between the sexes," Gonçalves brought the European Renaissance perspectives of authors such as Christine de Pizan to the Portuguese world while at the same time creating the foundation for much later changes to women's lives in morality and education.[31] Gonçalves began his two-part treatise by contrasting the limited conditions in which women lived with their virtuous achievements and providing legendary and historical precedents to support his argument that women might actually excel men in some circumstances. Using examples from the Bible and ancient Greece and Rome, he argued that women did not lack such heroic virtues as "wisdom," "prudence in advice," "courage," "devotion" to God, and "mercy." That last "sublime" virtue, he reminded the Queen, was "very important and necessary to all persons, principally to Princes and nobility."[32]

The tone of his treatise changed to stronger apologetics, however, as he explained that—despite arguments to the contrary—women also excelled in the more social and personal virtues. Thus he noted that while women were sometimes considered avaricious, they still demonstrated great "generosity . . . as the Queen herself knows." Women were the equals of men in the "singular" virtues of chastity and conjugal love, and, as exemplified by the recently deceased Queen Mother herself, resisted the vice of "laziness" through their great industry at weaving, sewing, and other handiwork. Gonçalves concluded:

> And thus as the feminine sex was given these heroic and sublime virtues equally with the masculine sex one may count many other similar [virtues] which they hold; from these may be clearly understood that [the feminine sex] is as perfect as the masculine sex, and that man is not more perfect than woman, and it might even be said that in creation she was more excellent since she was formed by God from the rib of Adam while he lay sleeping in the terrestrial paradise. And the man was created from the dust of the earth outside of paradise in the field of Damasceno and afterwards placed in Paradise. Since woman was made of better material, and in a more noble place, because of this those who claim that the feminine sex is inferior and of worse condition have no cause.[33]

In the second part of his treatise, Gonçalves argued that women deserved legal rights in the Portuguese kingdom as, he asserted, his royal reader must already have known. Women were thus due just treatment at home from their fathers and husbands, and in the courts, especially when their persons and property were threatened. After providing an alphabetical list of "rights," Gonçalves insisted that dowries be granted to women during their marriage and remain intact without diminution afterward, to be used at their behest. Although Gonçalves defended women's dignity and autonomy in such cases, his concern was for the comfort and well-being of married, honorable, and "decent" women whose property was ordinarily controlled by men, and nowhere does he challenge the notion that women were "legally and morally bound to obey and serve their husbands."[34]

While Gonçalves might have provided the cornerstone for a new concept of the virtuous and honorable woman, influences from medieval Europe hampered Portuguese religious and secular writers for at least another century. Guide books, cultural commentaries, and pious biographies repeated the restrictive expectations for women, even within a historical or literary framework. Two such books were the *Jardim de Portugal*, the 1626 chronicle of exemplary Portuguese women by Friar Luís dos Anjos, and the *Adagios portuguêses reduzidos a lugares communs*, a compilation of medieval and early modern "adages" published by Antonio Delicado in 1651. Both works served parallel functions: they collected, in literary form, images illustrative of feminine virtue for the edification of the small group of literate nobles connected with the Iberian royal courts. The two authors inaugurated the genres of such compilations in Portuguese historical literature and, blocking humanistic or Reformation influences that might challenge Catholic traditions, established the constraints of Christian ideals even more firmly for their Portuguese readers.

Fashioned in the style of the sixteenth-century hagiographies published in Spain and Italy, the *Jardim de Portugal* or *Garden of Portugal* offered flowery portraits of historical women who might inspire others to excellence in virtue, beginning in the late days of the Roman Empire. The author narrowed the range of examples, however, to include only those women whose religious devotion best represented the monastic ideal, avoiding contemporary tales of heroic or literary figures. The women portrayed were chiefly pious noblewomen of the thirteenth through seventeenth centuries, from royal courts and royally endowed convents near Lisbon. The Crown Princess Dona Joana of Aveiro was one such example, for though born in 1452 to a royal role, she still dedicated herself to memorizing the Divine Office and "was much given to read[ing] devotional books" while still young. Even during her service as regent for her brother João II, she remained virtuous and devout until she could finally, in 1482, retreat to her houses near the Dominican convent in Aveiro.[35]

Author Luís dos Anjos considered the religious cloister the only suitable place for women, as he explained in his introduction to the short biography of Dona Joana, Marquesa de Elche:

> When one asks about a strong woman he does not intend [to consider] she who is good in whatever fashion, but [only] she who is adorned with all manner of virtues, since, as a certain doctor warned, for a man to be good ordinary goodness is enough, but woman is so weak that for her to be perfect nothing serves her but the greatest perfection.[36]

Female imperfections, then, so hampered women in ordinary life, that only the exceptional arduousness of an ascetic life might bring women close to men's ordinary goodness and the expectations of the Catholic Church for her. Dona Joana had married and raised her family, but only returned to virtue when she was widowed: she retired from the world and "thus, before dying she was dead to the world, practicing various penitences, giving herself to prayer, surrounded with the fear of God" until her last breath in 1588.[37]

Few women outside of the noble ranks matched that accomplishment, but Anjos included Adeodata de São Nicolau, a "poor orphan" taken in by the nuns of Vila Viçosa, raised "in the marvelous customs of penitence and prayer," and taught a livelihood with which she might support herself. Adeodata became "a friend of silence, of the hair shirt, of fasting, of prayer," and was accepted as a sister of the black veil—the lower ranks for nuns—by her confessor. Leadership in the secular or religious spheres was secondary to religious abasement, as in the life of Felipa do Espírito Santo of Lisbon, who was commended for her self-denial in her cell rather than for her advancements in the education of novices. Other noble women set the better examples in convents, becoming the "most perfect" of women, who never broke "the laws of goodness that God gave them, which was that they be sparing in their eating, moderate in their dress, docile in their behavior, honorable in their speaking, timorous in their conversing." As if to more deeply incise the feminine role, Anjos reserved his most effusive praise for women who endured self-inflicted penitences, those who fainted from hunger, preferred hair shirts as clothing, flagellated themselves willingly, knelt on stones to pray, and slept on the floor or a rough bed without comfort.[38]

A secular counterpoint to that hagiography, Antonio Delicado's *Adagios portugueses*, was designed to preserve the national character of the Portuguese vernacular and reflect the experiences of the Portuguese elite. Beginning with "Affeição" (Affection) and ending with "Ventura" (Luck), Delicado organized the proverbs in alphabetical order by theme—with an appendix on "adages of the months of the year."[39] Under separate titles, he listed over one hundred adages about women, with many repeating the hackneyed condemnations of dangerous, lustful, and voluble women: "A stubborn woman wants to be broken"; "A woman who loses her shame never recovers it"; "A woman and wine both take away a man's judgment"; or "A woman and a dog, both better when quiet."[40] His selections were rife with warnings about vain and irresponsible women: "If a woman is polished, her house is dirty and her doorway empty"; "The squire's wife [has] white bonnets and a black heart"; "A widow in the street is neither a widow nor married"; and "The [only] good and honorable woman is a widow in her grave."[41]

As in medieval religious literature and early modern etiquette guides, Portuguese women were advised by the adages to remain confined at home (or in figurative isolation) and quiet: "The man in the plaza, the woman at home"; "A married woman lives on a mountain"; and "A good woman is quiet when a man speaks." While women might contribute to children's lives, little benefit came of women's work or education: "From the sea comes salt, from a woman only evil"; and "A mule that sings and the woman who speaks Latin rarely come to much good."[42] A few adages praised beautiful faces and figures, stalwart if ugly servants, and—only dubiously— virtuous wives: "The wife of an old man shines like a mirror" and "A woman increases [in value] with a husband, like well-beaten gold." The powerful and conventional messages for women thus persisted through elite and folk literature, postulating unattainable ideals for women who, whether single or married, rich or poor, would always fail to achieve them. One last proverb from Delicado's collection seems to suggest that Portuguese women understood their cruel fate: "What is marriage, mother? Daughter, it is spinning, bearing children, and weeping."[43] With this collection of adages from medieval Portugal, colonists to Brazil had few expectations for creative, adventurous, or even independent women. Delicado's text and others like it from the same era sketched the limits of women's lives in the secular sphere, with little indication of contradiction from the religious.

### IDEALS FOR WOMEN IN COLONIAL BRAZIL

At the start of the colonial enterprise in Brazil, Portuguese explorers and missionaries drew their understanding of the ideal woman from the Christian and secular literature familiar to them. Though most had not read the most influential authors—or even the relevant scriptures— colonists and officials built their paradigm of the virtuous woman on the foundations of the medieval and early modern ideas found in writings by Rui Gonçalves, Luís dos Anjos, and Antonio Delicado. While the earliest reports from Brazil, as seen in the first chapter, portrayed the women of the New World as either wild or tamed, sinful or virtuous, those same writings presented the narrow expectations for feminine virtue. The rigid and often contradictory proclamations of women's meager rationality, excessive delicacy, inherent modesty, indulgent decadence, and tendencies toward both devotion and dissolution continued in Brazil. The bodies to be inscribed, however, resisted the imprint of the Catholic norms, fragmenting ideas about the feminine in two distinct ways. First, a heightened sense of the danger of feminine nature generated new warnings about sexuality and virginity, often connected with advice about clothing and marriage. Second, the universality of the ideal faltered, and, as the colonial period progressed, the finer virtues aligned with the Portuguese colonists while more of the vices were to be discovered among the rapacious Indian women, unrepentant African slaves, and treacherous *mestiças*.

The early colonial reports about native Brazilian women were at best ambivalent about their humanity and femininity. As noted in Chapter 1, Pero Vaz de Caminha revealed his own surprise that the graceful women seemed unaware of the European Christian principles for comportment and dress. His account of their first encounter was shockingly frank in its description of their nude forms and echoed contemporary European assumptions about women, women's bodies, and social control.[44] The freedom and sexuality embodied by shameless Brazilian Indian women violated the norms of Portuguese society, and missionaries and colonial officials struggled to establish European Christian order and propriety in Brazil. The effort to cover and control women began with the first encounter in 1500 and continued with the Portuguese Jesuit missionaries and later visitors in the 1550s.

Religious and cultural conversion of indigenous women challenged missionaries from the beginning of the appointed colonial government in 1549. The barriers of language and custom prohibited much meaningful interchange at first, but Jesuit letters, reports, and histories culled symbolic details from Brazilian Indian lives to portray the wretchedness of their circumstances and wickedness of their traditions. Women's behavior most often denoted transgression: women failed to cover their naked bodies, consumed human flesh with relish, changed sexual partners promiscuously, and cared little for their own children. As noted in Chapter 1, colonial authors emphasized women's perverse appetites as a mark of their difference, but even the missionaries, who intended to suppress women's desires, offered the same litany of feminine vices in their literature of encounter.

The missionaries sounded a note of triumph when they persuaded women to change their appearances, and by the early 1600s they had recorded a few successes in the imposition of virtue. In his report on the Mission to the Carajós, for example, Padre Jerónimo Rodrigues announced the impact of their efforts on women "old and young," remarking that "even though at times they go about nude, even in front of us, they do not come nude to church, not even a little four-year-old girl."[45] The Jesuit historian Vicente do Salvador explained their success with Indian women who, after relocating to mission villages under missionary instruction, had the opportunity not only to convert to Christianity and Portuguese customs but also to transmit the new ideas to their sisters and aunts along with the proper clothing and trade goods. Thus one Aymoré captive in the custody of Capitão-Mor Álvaro Rodriques da Cachoeira was instructed in "the mysteries of our holy Catholic faith," renamed Margarida, and sent to convert her family:

> After being well instructed and friendly to us, [the Captain] dressed her in her chemise or tunic of cotton cloth, which is the dress of our Indian women, gave her a hammock in which to sleep, mirrors, combs, knives, wine, and whatever more she could carry, and told her to undeceive her [people], as was done, showing them that it was wine that we drank, and not their blood, as they had worried, and the meat that we ate was of cattle and other animals and not human; and that we did not go about naked, nor sleep on the ground, as they did, but in hammocks.[46]

In these and other statements, the Jesuit missionaries confirmed that women's proper appearance symbolized the core feminine virtues of modesty and submission so that their catechesis could not disregard any aspect of the Christian ideal. Still, clothing and converting Indian women was but one step in the re-creation of that ideal in Brazil, for the Portuguese immigrants were also compelled to observe its dictates. The few Portuguese women present in the colony in the 1500s and early 1600s barely withstood the scrutiny of the patriarchy, and no breaches of honor might be accepted even under harsh colonial conditions. Women who worked in the fields, warded off attacks by hostile Indians, or managed large estates inherited from deceased husbands were praised with due caution as rare exceptions to Iberian expectations. When women assisted in the defense of the newly established village of Iguaraçu, historian Vicente do Salvador admired their fighting "spirit," but could not resist commenting that they also defied the stereotype of the garrulous female, adding "[it] was a very heroic deed for the women to have kept such silence." And after Dona Brites de Albuquerque, "the long-lived widow of Duarte Coelho [Pereira], the first donatory or lord-proprietor of the captaincy of Pernambuco," directed the captaincy during his absence, following his death in 1554, and during her son's subsequent absences, her extraordinary activities to secure the economic and political stability of the nascent state were briefly lauded and then forgotten.[47]

The Iberian "mentality" that had enjoined "the austerity of Portuguese women's lives" due to the stringent standards for feminine virtue was eagerly transmitted to colonial communities and provided the justifications for the "excessive zeal" employed in the "guarding" of elite women. This, too, was inscribed on women's bodies, as they were covered and controlled. Male colonists to Brazil in the sixteenth and seventeenth centuries argued that women must be "protected and secluded from the affairs of the world," so that they might reproduce the exemplary "life of an obedient daughter, submissive wife, and loving mother." Priests and officials alike enforced the "rigid double standard" that allowed men sexual access to any unprotected woman, whether European, Indian, or African, but condemned women for any minor transgression. Colonial religious and political leaders promoted the cult of Mary and other female saints as the appropriate base for women's identity while enjoining that impossible standard through ethical precepts, civil laws, and conservative attitudes.[48]

For the first colonial century and then in the remainder of the colonial period, women faced contradictory demands. On the one hand, as A. J. R. Russell-Wood put it, "Crown, Church, and colonist viewed womanhood as the repository of the virtues and moral qualities of the Portuguese people. On the other hand, she was hidebound by civil and canon laws, and the role prescribed for her both in continental Portugal and overseas was restricted to domestic and religious spheres." The divergent responsibilities and behaviors attributed to social classes and ethnic groups further complicated attitudes and the white man's expectations:

> The white woman, belonging to an elite, the future mother of his sons, must be kept secluded, having to be virtuous, honorable, and passive, since she was the one responsible for the transmission of the habits, patterns, and values of society. The black or *mulata* woman (whether free or enslaved) was the one who served to satiate his sexual desires and fantasies. Thus, a certain social promiscuity was already expected of the black or *mulata* woman, while the white woman of the elite must keep herself honorable.[49]

In the face of such demands, it may not be so surprising—as we may witness in the chapters following this—that while many women "accepted and adapted to the role demanded of them by society of that time," quite a few did not. Widows, wealthy married women, prostitutes, nuns, and witches might have responded to the incessant stipulations with disdain or even rebellion, but those who conformed to the "hidebound" role found comfort in their honorable status and praise for their acquiescence—at least at the opening of the colonial era.[50]

Religious justifications for restrictions on women echoed through the Brazilian churches in the seventeenth century. The popular preacher Antônio Vieira saw a direct connection between Eve's sins and the needful constraints on women's behavior in colonial Brazil. In his "Seventeenth Sermon on the Rosary," he insisted that women remain isolated from public view, even when they prayed: "Where should one perform the devotion of the Rosary? . . . To women . . . I say absolutely that each one must pray at home, and never outside of it." Vieira explained that the first woman, Eve, had not been created freely like Adam, but was instead "built like an edifice" from a single part, the rib, to remain by his side. Eve had, however, left Adam to venture outside the confines of Paradise where she had met evil and temptation: her sin of disobedience had been born of incessant wandering. In response, the "daughters of Eve" in colonial Brazil were to remain firmly fixed in one place and not counted "among the movables [like furniture]." The homebound woman might thus regain divine favor through her confinement.

Vieira was well aware that women might be compelled to leave their homes for work or for church obligations, but considered such trips a serious threat to personal honor and social stability, since "a woman who goes out to see women, also goes out to be seen by men. And . . . being seen endangers honor, endangers the person, endangers the family, and endangers the whole republic, and not just the one, but many [women]." No prior community guided by divine precept had permitted women to wander without incurring mortal and moral danger, and his own Bahia could not be the first to tolerate women's autonomy. To conclude, he cited the most ancient laws of the Old Testament, which required Temple visits of men but not women: "Thus it is, that God exempts women from this law of the Temple, releasing them from the obligation to go out but not [the obligation] to pray, valuing their seclusion more than their pilgrimages."[51]

The most dangerous of women's vices were those that kept them in the public eye and, in a later sermon preached within a convent, Vieira warned of women's natural inclination toward vanity. Since the time of Eve, he charged, women have been vain: "I say more: if the serpent had promised [Eve]: You will be like God; and the mirror had said to her: You will see your beauty in me; that Eve would have accepted the services and the offer of the mirror." Even the cloistered nuns and other religious women could not escape this failing: "The luxury and vanity of women has reached (I say) such excesses that even in the [Book of] Hours and the prayer books that they bring to church, among the pages are placed mirrors, . . . so that the fervent prayers do not reach God unaccompanied by those decorations." The cloistered sisters "idolize[d] themselves," replacing the inspirational "images of the Virgin Mary or Jesus Christ crucified" with their own like-nesses. He demanded their commitment to God, but despaired of their future, since their appetite for vanity was "inherited from the distant past, and . . . so natural and so appropriate to the feminine gender" even within the religious cloister. Their empty lives would be reflected in their refusal to "take down . . . the mirror."[52]

Male authors from eighteenth-century Brazil affirmed the necessity for submission and silence as well, so that the virtuous and ideal woman—whose characteristics might only be achieved by immigrant white women—would be not only chaste, honorable, and obedient but also absent from most of public life. As colonial governors struggled to impose the social norms of the stratified European community on the disrupted world of Brazilian Indians, enslaved blacks, and Portuguese colonists, they wrote about the need for control and restrictions—for women. While the colony faced upheavals from economic and political transformations, the virtu-ous Christian woman might engender the ideal social order that colonial leaders craved. Some of the later colonial writers ascribed the feminine virtues to women from birth, so that it was women's nature to be shamed, honest, hidden, and quiet, with her actions following her nature. Women who fell short in any way—especially women outside of the elite class of property owners—were "unnatural" women and deserved their destitute conditions and servile status. At the same time, most writers insisted that women must be taught to submit to men's rule in all things, as did Nuno Marques Pereira in 1711: "A woman is obligated to obey her husband ac-cording to Divine Law, and principally in those things which are directed to the served of God: and even in Civil Law is found written that a woman may not even cut her hair without permission, and the authority of her husband."[53]

Meritorious women faced limited choices on the path to virtue, for colonial writers—echoing Luís dos Anjos—lavished praise on those who suffered for their honor and preferred death to dishonor. Domingos do Loreto Couto provided another eighteenth-century colonial narrative for sanctity with a list of admirable women entitled "Pernambuco Illustrated by the Feminine Sex." Although that section is subtitled "News of Many Pernambuco Heroines Who Flourished in Virtue, Letters, and Arms," stories of virtue trumped all other notable accomplishments. Women—even with "the material of the body more solid" than that of men—had guarded their "honor, retirement, modesty, and restraint" in the regional struggles against the Dutch invaders. "Whether maidens, married women, or widows," they sought to resist the "depraved impulses of heretical immorality" and honor their homeland by "securing their own honor."[54] Some found their escape hampered by the very customs that kept them secluded, for the "grillwork" enclosing their windows and doors trapped them within their houses, on the brink of "losing their most precious jewel," their virginity, before divine intervention permitted their flight into the countryside. Still others died to preserve their chastity, which was threatened by the Dutch and the nearby "barbarous Tapuyas" among whom they sought refuge.[55]

Without stalwarts to defend them, women faced betrayal and "calumny" among the nobility and common folk alike, and Couto included tales of honorable women who survived years of degradation or imprisonment owing to "false testimonies" and tricks. Heartless men and faithless slaves conspired against them, but several heroic women overcame disease, abuse, and other dire "afflictions" while "divine Justice never failed them."[56] A few women left Pernambuco to embrace the sacrifices of the cloister. Notably, Mother Angela do Sacramento and Mother Margarida da Natividade served as inspired leaders in the Convento de Santa Clara in Coimbra and drew a small coterie of the young women from the upper ranks in Brazil to take conventual vows and "secure Jesus as their Spouse." "Heroic virtues" led other women to abandon the profane world and turn their village homes into cloisters as they, under the guidance of traveling friars, enacted the most violent penitence in their perpetual devotions. Here Couto, like others, reserved his most effusive praise for those who vanished within their own lives. The final romance of the feminine ideal was erasure from colonial society, as Couto put it: "To secure the purity of the body and of the soul, and to make them[selves] dwelling-places of God, many young Pernambuco women sighed for the retirement of the cloister and the quietude of the monastery, where, free of mundane insults, they might abandon themselves to holy meditation of the Divine attributes, and to the exercise of the Religious perfection."[57]

By the end of the colonial period, the tales of heroic women and exceptional recluses had faded, and, in the nineteenth century, travelers and historians alike turned prescription into history and the unusual into the commonplace. Ignoring the working lives of the majority of non-elite women and even the duties of wealthy women, they simply reported that a Brazilian woman's usual lot was to be secluded in her home, cherished by her family, and isolated from the mundane. Chief among the virtues of the ideal Brazilian woman, then, was a sort of invisibility: Portuguese authors had recommended confinement for women, colonial Brazilian authors demanded it, and historians—through the twentieth century—reported it as indisputable fact. One can see the shift from advice given in the 1700s to the descriptions of the 1800s, beginning with André João Antonil, who recommended that the male owners of sugar plantations construct "a separate house for guests . . . , for they can be better received [there] and with less disturbance of the family, and without affecting the seclusion in which one must guard wives and daughters and domestic serving girls, occupied in the work of dinner and supper." Antonil's advice was apparently well received, for a century later the invisibility of elite white women was a commonplace in the writings of European visitors to Brazil. L. F. de Tollenare thus reported: "When a sugar-mill owner visits another one, the ladies do not make their appearance. I spent two days in the house of one of them, . . . and I did not see his family either in the living room or at the dinner table. On a different occasion I arrived unexpectedly after supper at the house of another of them, . . . I noticed on the floor a piece of embroidery which seemed to have been tossed there suddenly. . . . The lady of the house prepared a choice meal, but I did not see her."[58]

The elite endorsement of seclusion had by then reached the lower strata as well, as Tollenare discovered in 1816–1818 when he visited the homes of small farmers and ambitious sharecroppers: "The *lavradores* are quite proud to receive on a basis of equality the foreigner who comes to visit them. . . . The women disappeared as in the homes of ladies, though I was always offered sweets." Visiting Brazil in the early 1800s, Mrs. Nathaniel Kindersley found no charm whatsoever in women's confinement but instead reported disdainfully of its effects on them: "After what I have said of the general character of the men of this place, you will not expect to hear much in praise of the women; brought up in indolence, and their minds uncultivated, their natural quickness shows itself in cunning. As their male relations do not place any confidence in their virtue, they in return use their utmost art to elude the vigilance with which they are observed; and to speak the most favourably, a spirit of intrigue reigns among them."[59]

According to Kindersley and other European visitors to Brazil, a woman's invisibility began early in her life, as soon as her presence and exposure rendered the family, its honor, and its property vulnerable. Rewriting the history of the colony, other chroniclers followed suit by praising the virtue successfully inculcated in Brazilian women of all races and tracing its practice from the sixteenth century. According to the revisionist historians of the 1800s, women's seclusion had begun in Brazilian Indian villages, where it had been instituted in obedience to God's law and to civilized order. In 1549, the Jesuit missionary Padre Nóbrega had in fact praised the acceptance of restrictions on women among his followers, claiming that the newly converted "heathens . . . already have had retirement houses for women as nuns."[60] But the Jesuits' calls for such institutions were rarely heeded, and colonial villagers who similarly sought informal or formal cloisters for girls and women met with obdurate resistance from the imperial Portuguese government and church authorities, as will be explored in Chapter 5. While girls in elite families had recourse to convents or even their own homes to hide from public view and await marriage with a suitable and propertied man, girls in the lower strata were made even more vulnerable by this unreachable ideal, for their visibility in public life meant availability to any predatory males.

The last element in the feminine ideal prescribed by Brazilian religious authorities and described in colonial records, then, was their absence. The innocent and uncovered woman and land had been covered and civilized into oblivion. And since only a few regions of the colonial land were tamed, so only a few elite women attained the ideal, that absence from self and society so lauded in advice books and histories. For them, the imprint of the full panoply of feminine virtues might finally transfigure their autonomy or identity and erase their very presence in Brazilian society. Marked to be saintly, modest, silent, and separate, elite white women carried the normative values of the colonial community even as they left its public sphere. Here, their double charge seems even more impossible, for how might they embody the virtues of the Christian ideal for the colony's residents and transmit its practice while vanishing from sight?

In the other households of colonial Brazil, women of color suffered under that ideal and were—like white women—castigated for their failure to achieve it. In their failures and in the persistent images of the subordination of indigenous, mixed-race, and African women, we find the recurring descriptions of a sort of primordial colonial chaos. As in Caminha's record of the first encounters, most histories disregarded Brazilian Indian women, who appeared only on the periphery, as slaves, servants, or concubines of the elite. Their status as women was further diminished by their benighted and alien culture. Their needs as women—in their own families or villages—were deliberately overlooked and their usefulness to colonial society underscored. Even Antônio Vieira, often named among the defenders of freedom for indigenous tribes, "could only manage to understand the [Native Brazilian] woman as maid, wet-nurse, servant or slave." At the end of his arguments for men's independence, Vieira conceded that some indigenous women could be pressed into service and then returned to their husbands or fathers for work at home.[61] The fundaments of the ideal of Christian virtue, so solidly grounded in centuries of European thought,

seemed shaken by the presence of others—and by the very bodies that refused to be confined by it.

### VIOLATIONS OF HONOR

"Honor," according to Raphael Bluteau's 1712 *Vocabulario portuguez*,
depended on another's view of virtuous behavior and acknowledgment of
"nobility, dignity, virtue, or other excellence." A woman's honor might be
perceived according to her "good repute . . . acquired with good actions."
For women, this definition of honor was linked to a narrowly feminine
virtue, a "feminine honor" called "*pudicîcia*" or pudic modesty: the "virtue
which teaches . . . the honesty in actions, & words, together with abstinence
from illicit desires."[62] Bluteau's remarks were refined in the 1789 *Diccionario da lingua portugueza* created by a "native of Rio de Janeiro," Antônio
de Morais Silva, who emphasized male honor "in virtue of an office" or
obligation. Still, "modesty, chastity and honesty" also constituted honorable behavior and a woman might be "honored" for her "virginal purity."[63]

If the ideal Christian women were to acquiesce to these definitional
constraints and contrive to be modest, chaste, and barely visible in the Brazilian colony, their efforts might encompass a whole life. Claims to honor
were, however, overbalanced by accusations of dishonor: women faced
charges of *desonestidade*, of immodesty and shamelessness at any failure
to maintain the public face of familial prestige and personal integrity. Brazilian colonial writers demanded that virtuous women demonstrate their
honor by withdrawing from public life and common society and repress-
ing desire, but that bodily disappearance might still raise problems in its
confinement. How might one admire the virtuous woman if she was not
meant to be seen? How might the elite families treat their daughters and
wives, so as to distinguish them from other ranks of Brazilian society, if only
one virtuous ideal were advocated? How could the priests and friars counsel women if they could not mention the vices which might lead women
astray? The identity of women still rested on their classification as "other,"
and their marked status was determined by men. Even their vices, then,
were different, and the borders of their bodily integrity were crucial to the
persistence of difference.

The primary marks of bodily difference for women were linked to sexuality, and, as seen in the European sources, virginity and chastity were
the primary achievements of virtuous women. Iberian authors in the early

modern period echoed the mandate that Christian women remain virginal before marriage and chaste afterward, and underscored their decrees with descriptions of the paragons of virtue from Iberian history. For the first missionaries in Brazil, virginity was valued above all else for women, and most Jesuits promulgated that value for all groups and classes. Padre José de Anchieta noted in 1554 with pride that a recent Indian male convert and his wife "have taken care to keep their daughters virgins" and expected their religious conformity to follow their bodily restrictions.[64] In later colonial documents, however, the Jesuit Jorge Benci abandoned the pretense that all women might achieve the vaunted ideal, scoffed at the expectation that Indian or African slave women would remain virgins, and even contended that slave women corrupted the morals of Brazilian society by prostitution.[65]

Although the failure to protect virginity was dangerous to the colony and adultery was just short of treason, other aspects of women's sexuality proved baffling. In an unexpected reversal of norms, penalties for sexual crimes were lessened for women, even when women were at fault. This apparent leniency reflected the ambiguous position of women's bodies and the recurring ecclesiastical debates over women's passivity in sexual relations. For example, the 1707 *Constituiçoens* established by the fifth archbishop of Bahia, D. Sebastião Monteiro da Vide, ordained that "women who one with another commit this sin" of sexual lasciviousness be punished with fines or three years' exile, while men faced "fines and exile, imprisonment and the galleys."[66] The archbishop mandated lighter penalties for crimes of incest because women were "weak" and unable to bear harsh punishment, and harsh judgments against men in crimes against a woman's "honesty and honor."[67] By some accounts, women were not considered capable of committing sodomy or bestiality, since these more serious sins were defined in religious literature as the active performance and completion of unnatural or illicit coitus. While the visiting Portuguese Inquisition in the 1590s heard denunciations of women's homosexuality and exacted punishment in Brazil, the 1613 *Regimento* instructed Inquisitors not to accept denunciations of passive sexual acts and thereby retreated from the controversial discussion.[68]

Colonial courts struggled to process claims for and against personal honor, especially in cases of rape and seduction. While elite families cooperated to extend male honor to cover and conceal the behaviors of women, women were obliged to conform to the more restrictive sexual norms as a matter of female honor. For single women in particular, honor "was indissolubly linked to the conservation of virginity," and their families were faced with undertaking legal procedures in cases of the "violation of honor and virginity."[69] While that legal recourse might restore some sense of family honor, the public admission of a woman's dishonor might never be recompensed. Girls who admitted to sexual relations outside of marriage—forced or not—lost personal honor, individual freedom, and family prestige. Suits brought against their rapists or seducers typically demanded paid restitution and subsequent marriage with the perpetrator—an outcome that might only be lauded in the pages of the *Contos* compiled by Gonçalo Fernandes Trancoso.

Women's clothing and ornamentation were also carefully monitored to assure not only that their shameful bodies were hidden but also that their frames and forms conformed to social expectations. Not unlike indigenous Brazilian women, black women inhabited a sexually charged, conflicted space: they were disparaged for their "loose" gait and *dishabille*, but their bodies were available for assessment and criticism nonetheless. Male authors, both Brazilian-born and visiting from Europe, commented on them as if they were mere portraits and property, as did Tollenare in the early 1800s:

> The black women generally have a flexible and elegant figure, the shoulders and arms very well formed. Many are seen who could qualify as pretty women if their necks were longer, giving more freedom to their heads. Their breasts are firm and fleshy, and they seem to understand their value, proving themselves very wise by concealing them. . . . It is unusual to see a black woman, even seventeen or eighteen years of age, whose neck has retained the shape which we prize so much . . . [When they walk about wearing only a thin cloth knotted above the breasts,] I must say that they are all attractive and very graceful. . . . Their legs are normal, but their feet are damaged by hard work and the lack of footwear.[70]

By contrast, wealthy young white women kept seclusion and wore complicated and more concealing attire, ornamented with "moderation and honor." Their older counterparts—those above the age of twenty-five— assumed less "elegant" clothing.[71]

By the end of the eighteenth century, more confusing guidelines were offered to distinguish white women by class and status:

> Women must also conform to the laws and regulate their clothing and ornamentation according to their [marital status], quality, condition and

principally according to the maxims and rules of modesty. For illustrious Ladies of distinction, more liberality is permitted in clothing, ornamentation and headwear, than to plebeian and inferior women: to virgins more than to married women, and to the latter much more than to
widows.[72]

Thus the colonial hierarchy of control began at home, among even the
most virtuous of women.

### CONCLUSION

The proliferation of rules and the precision of the directives concerning women's bodies and dress coincided with late eighteenth-century
efforts to centralize the colonial government under imperial control. The
stronger efforts to control the social body, as Mary Douglas suggested, led
to stronger efforts to control the individual, physical body—in this case,
to control women. Through the writings cited above and others from the
colony, Brazilian society concocted additional restraints for women, multiplying and intensifying the controls that women were to observe in daily
life. Their bodies, their behaviors, their clothes, their very thoughts were
under scrutiny by male authorities, who sought the smallest sign of non-
compliance. The seventeenth-century Jesuit preacher Antônio Vieira had
begun the chorus of calls for increased rules to bind women to home and
family, and to their status as legal and moral minors. Although his sermons inveighed against women's behavior, Vieira himself rarely addressed
women directly in any of his writings: he considered women too feeble-
minded to follow the rules on their own and "included [women] in his
list of 'imbeciles and curiosities.'" Instead, he wrote *about* women and
their failings, directed their priests, confessors, and male relatives to govern
them, and even blamed men for allowing them to sin.[73]

Later colonial writers completed the lessons that Vieira drafted, as
though stronger colonial norms might reaffirm not just their lofty position
in the social hierarchy but also the validity of their traditions. Those writers,
too, warned that women's minds and feelings were feeble and that heightened control over their bodies was the only recourse. Without the strict-
est sets of constraints, at least for white women, the virtue of the colony
might not be safe and the virtuous might not survive. Here, the gendered
construct—of a sinful and vulnerable woman—echoed again from early
Christianity and early colonial texts. But while the "role ascribed to the

female was marginal, isolating her from the main stream of development in the colony,"[74] those women who met or attempted the Christian ideal were held in high regard. Secluded and limited in behavior and dress, the white wife or daughter of a colonial official might be sexually chaste and protected from casual contacts, venerated as a suitable imitation of the feminine savior Mary. The path to such imitation was laid not only indirectly through advocacy in religious and secular tracts portraying the ideal for Christian women, but also through direct instruction of women for the virtuous life. The inculcation of the honorable ideal, then, came through the implicit norms carried across the Portuguese and Brazilian cultures and expressed in literature consumed primarily by fathers, husbands, and governors. More explicit education and indoctrination on feminine virtue and honor carried the same oppressive message directly to girls and women, as will be explored in the following chapter.

# THREE

# Reading, Writing, and Sewing

## EDUCATION FOR BRAZILIAN WOMEN

Writing in 1587, historian Gabriel Soares de Sousa noted with approval the transformations of indigenous cultures in northeastern Brazil through the praiseworthy efforts of Franciscan missionaries. The conversion of indigenous Tupinambá women to the religion and culture of Portugal was, however, still incomplete:

> The girls of these people who are raised and indoctrinated with Portuguese women, learn well the sewing and needlework, and do all the works with the needle that they teach them, for which they have much ability, and to make sweets, and they become remarkable cooks; but they are much desirous . . . of having love affairs with white men.[1]

Sousa, in this first comprehensive treatise on Brazil, thus offered a glimpse of the educational paradigm for women in the Brazilian colony: both indigenous and immigrant women were instructed by Christians in the comportment and domestic skills suitable for their gender. While their sewing and cooking had improved, according to Sousa, the religious formation of young Tupinambá women had not yet curbed their customary passions. In time and with additional instruction, they might still comply with the Christian ideals of chastity and submission for marriage to young male converts.

Sousa's *Treatise* is exemplary among sixteenth-century Portuguese and Brazilian texts in that he suggested the limits of contemporary educational efforts expended to bring women in the colonial society closer to the Christian virtuous ideal. As I explained in Chapter 2, male authors of the early modern era affirmed specific and gendered characteristics to the nature, attributes, virtues, and bodies of women. But the inculcation of the ideal

was not accomplished through religious exhortations or through any literary discussion among men as to its value and necessity. Along with texts
describing and justifying restrictive virtues for women came rules and regulations for the education of women. Production and reproduction of the
colonial norms required the strategic instruction and deliberate education of women in submission, from their youngest days as a child at home
through religious formation by missionaries and priests, and in religious
and secular schools.

The indoctrination of indigenous and immigrant women in the values
of Portuguese colonial society rested on the expectation of honor and virtue
in feminine life. For the most part, honor could not be taught—it was an
attribute recognized by others, expressed in personal conduct, family privilege, and social rank. Women could at best support and demonstrate their
personal honor through daily conduct, dress, and appearance; more often,
honor demanded their absence from dishonorable places and ignorance of
dishonorable people. Women might uphold family honor, but that was a
social attribute primarily linked with the occupation and behaviors of the
men of the household, and with the wealth, race, ethnicity, and lineage of
their ancestors. The privileges owed to an honorable family might not be
enhanced by a girl's education, but she could certainly demonstrate family
honor, mostly by the absence of evidence that might sully its reputation.
Social rank also conferred honor, whether recognized through imperial be-
stowal of land, noble titles, or simple acknowledgment in colonial society.
While women might not learn about or gain honor, the loss of honor was
still a singular problem, for sexual misbehavior—or any perceived diminution of reputation—might result in the forfeit of personal and family status.

Honorable women, then, might stand to lose honor, but seemingly
could not add to it. Honor was rarely a recognizable attribute outside of
the upper classes, but other women might have some measure of personal
honor because of personal virtue. For all women, then, religious virtue both
demonstrated and conferred personal honor, and the concepts and elements of virtue could be taught. Considered a natural part of the feminine
self, womanly virtue should have been understood naturally or discovered
within a girl's heart. Brazilian moralist Feliciano Joaquim de Souza Nunes
insisted in 1758 that a woman's "natural shame" taught her the ways of modesty and chastity, but that her virtuous reputation was "very delicate." One
word, he warned, destroys it, "one 'appearance' dulls its luster; one laugh . . .
defames it; one poorly articulated voice finally . . . annihilates it." Honor, he
explained, was falsely associated with wealth and family lineage; nobility
and honor were linked and only revealed in personal morality and public

actions. Nunes cited biblical examples for moral guidance and suggested that women carefully attend to the teachings of the Holy Mother Church, to develop the honorable demeanor that evinced the "four most precious jewels of *virtue, chastity, honor,* and *discretion.*"[2]

The delicacy of feminine honor thus dictated education for women so that, supported by social perceptions of privilege and rank, virtue was visible in virtuous women. Women fell short in so many aspects of their natural lives, lacking reason, discretion, and ambition, that even natural shame and religious inclinations could not guide their behaviors without some sort of formation and indoctrination. The first steps were, of course, undertaken by women themselves: mothers were the first teachers of natural morality and virtue to their children. But tutors, private schools, and dedicated religious women and men intervened to provide fundamental doctrinal teachings and advanced training in the suitable daily activities and personal habits for women of all ranks. The arguments supporting women's education ranged from later or humanistic reasoning that children, particularly sons, benefited from the advanced or scientific learning of mothers to calls for enhancement of feminine spiritual qualities through careful religious formation; most authors reminded the readers that education for women could only channel and control their abilities and introduce little or no change in their social status.

For the female self to understand and, more importantly, reproduce the constrained norms of ideal femininity, girls underwent training in the same religious practices, domestic skills, and academic subjects as their mothers. In that way, as Mary Douglas argued, the norms of the social body impressed its conventions on the physical body of the individual and provided not only a positive identity but also radical control over physical presence and development.[3] The ideal for virtuous women in Brazil entailed strong prohibitions and regulations for its enforcement, and the systems for training girls to meet the ideal provided the means by which it was inculcated—in reading, writing, praying, spinning, and sewing. Given the traditional imprimatur of the norms advanced, girls found their lives constructed through duties, customs, and even the style and colors of their clothing.

As a "medium of culture," the body functioned as its central text, as Susan Bordo has more recently argued. On its symbolic form, "the central rules, hierarchies, and even metaphysical commitments of a culture are inscribed," and the limitations of each culture produced on and for each body within that culture. At the same time, the bodies reproduced those rules and limits, often heedless of their origins and meanings, making them practical events and everyday exercises in conformity.[4] In the words of Pierre Bourdieu—especially appropriate for the Catholic society under study here—cultural values are embodied or "*made* body" through the "transubstantiation achieved by the hidden persuasion of an implicit pedagogy."[5] The appearance and actions of the body resonated with the values that inform the very organization of time and space within a culture, Bordo contended, so that "bodies are trained, shaped, and impressed with the stamp of prevailing social forms of selfhood, desire, masculinity, femininity." Female bodies have borne deeper inscriptions and limitations, the marks of intense control, of the "regulation [and] subjection" that was "habituated" in each woman's daily life.[6]

The norms of Luso-Brazilian culture were thus written, woven, and embroidered into the lives of the girls of colonial Brazil, and their everyday activities hemmed in by sameness and conformity. The medieval Roman Catholic Church laid the foundation for the implicit expectations for girls and women, but conflicts in the colony and the process of colonization itself created fissures within the homogeneity of culture transmitted from Portugal, and acquiring feminine roles necessitated repeated directives. The demand for conformity to a single, centralized set of norms faltered over the colonial era, so that the articulation of virtuous behavior under changing conditions could not be accomplished, as Bourdieu hypothesized, only within the "commonplace world," that is, within the daily interactions, structures of personal relations, and symbolic gestures that might have transmitted unspoken cultural principles.[7] The production of submission also demanded explicit guidelines for girls and women in religious, domestic, and civil knowledge, skills, and behaviors. Even the elite women made invisible by the Christian ideal were taught specific arts and behaviors to eliminate their tendencies toward the vice of "laziness" and occupy their hands and minds in appropriate activities while otherwise bound to seclusion at home. Girls outside of noble and elite families learned a limited set of occupations to serve their families and communities—and to support the inactivity of elite women. The efforts to force women to clothe themselves, act, work, speak, and think in accord with the Christian ideal for them continued, as colonial authors addressed and educated the "body of virtues" that women should inhabit.

## EDUCATIONAL MODELS IN MEDIEVAL
## EUROPE AND EARLY MODERN PORTUGAL

Women's nature, according to most ancient authorities, did not incline them toward creativity in the arts, sciences, or literature. Wealthy
women of ancient Greece and Rome had private opportunities for education, while women writers, artists, and scientists shared family values or
were singular models for women's accomplishments. The ancient Greek
philosopher Plato imagined an ideal society with roles for educated women
leaders who would not be barred simply because of their sex, but few other
male writers even suggested that women should be educated either for the
welfare of society or their own benefit.[8] The polarizing concepts of gender articulated by Aristotle allowed women little room for personal development or education. Women had only an "ineffective" intellect, he
insisted, and women's nature and virtues were otherwise characterized by
subservience and limitation.[9] Aristotle's precepts for women's subordinate
roles dominated gender concepts for centuries and were reiterated both in
the theological writings of Thomas Aquinas and in assigned readings for
the first European universities. As noted in the previous chapter, Greek
philosophical statements about women's inferior nature provided a parallel rationale to Christian paradigms about women's sins and failings, and
thus supplied part of the structure for the Christian ideal.

In medieval Europe, education in the feminine virtues that constituted that Christian ideal did not entail formal education or any training
outside the home. A girl's upbringing—even among the nobility—only
required her to learn household duties from her mother and female relatives under the guardianship and supervision of her father or male relatives.
Girls at home, then, engaged in the duties of what came later to be called
"home economics": she "had to be able to administer the family house and
property, solicitously multiplying, cautiously conserving, and prudently
distributing family goods."[10] Religious education meant "formation," that
is, sufficient instruction in basic prayers and irreducible articles of faith
so that a girl might recite an "Ave Maria" and "Pater Noster" and reply to
the catechetical questions posed before participation in sacraments such
as Penance and the Eucharist. In the household, a woman's father and
then her husband stood as the religious authority, as Paul had mandated
in First Corinthians, "to be her religious guide, an intermediary between
the assembly of the faithful and his wife." The "good wife" accepted her
husband's moral duty to guard, repress, control, correct, and silence her.[11]

Rote memorization and apprenticeship within the home served most women as their education, but a few in the middle and upper ranks of society also learned reading and simple arithmetic. During the Middle Ages, few church authorities recommended that women study complex subjects such as grammar or theology, but most admitted grudgingly that housewives needed to do basic sums to keep household accounts. Reading and writing skills were rarely approved since more harm might come from illicit texts and letters; books suitable for women and writing materials were scarce throughout the period. Hence girls rarely learned enough Latin to read ancient texts or even biblical passages — only available in Latin to prelates and their male pupils — or enough writing to do more than sign their initials. While noble families supported more learning among women, few owned enough books to educate them beyond a primary level. More often, their daughters entered convents — temporarily or permanently — where they might achieve a modicum of education in a properly safe environment. In several of the convents in Spain and in the royal convent in Lisbon, education for noble women expanded quite beyond medieval limits, so that abbesses and directors of novices became scholars and teachers in their own right.[12]

By the 1400s, when humanist ideas emerged in Italy and France and exceptional women like the author Christine de Pizan not only read but also wrote treatises on women's virtues, increased access to formal education benefited boys but not girls, and girls' studies were "limited and closely scrutinized." Lesson books for girls, still written by men for the most part, detailed the suitable subjects, topics, and texts in preparation for adulthood and, of course, marriage. Moral education still demanded model behavior, so the lesson books elaborated a woman's ideal comportment based on the virtues of modesty and obedience. Knowledge of sewing and other domestic handicrafts was valued alongside an understanding of cooking and property management. More women were granted the opportunity for literacy — and so they read a bit in books of religious devotion or translations of scripture but not as widely in the books their male counterparts read. The available libraries in a few noble homes added romances, adventure tales, epic poetry, and the collections of adages and moral tales — such as those of Trancoso or Delicado discussed in Chapter 2 — that represented the national ethos, but education for girls was still considered "impossible, futile, or unwise."[13]

Few women outside of the royal families in England, France, or Iberia required a humanist education in the 1500s or 1600s, and the small schools established in Europe for them taught "needlework, dancing, calligraphy, drawing and painting, moral instruction, domestic skills appropriate to their class."[14] Despite the exemplary and "accomplished" ladies found in laudatory lists written to inspire national pride and instruct students in the historical traditions, formal or classical education was not available to women; even so, "most schools for girls in early modern Europe taught little besides basic literacy and genteel accomplishments." Education for the middle and lower classes was rare and brief, even for boys, but in the early modern period in Europe—and in Brazil—women offered informal education in their homes to young neighbors and relations. For the most part, girls attended to learn reading, sums, and housekeeping skills to enhance their own marriage prospects; a few "enterprising lower-class girls" and their employers valued the additional education as well.[15]

In medieval Portugal, education meant the barest of accomplishments, even among the clergy and nobility. Children memorized their catechism and little else beyond the basics of Roman Catholic prayers and doctrines. Cultural instruction for women of the middle and upper classes was neglected for the most part, unless they might attend church sermons and lectures, observe church painting and sculpture, or listen to stories and proverb recitation by traveling bards. Formal education in Latin or letter-copying, considered a waste of time for women, was reserved for a few clerics and noblemen, but interest in literacy grew at the end of the Middle Ages, particularly when advances in writing and book-copying made Portuguese translations of classical Roman texts and "chivalric romances" like the tale of Amadís de Gaula more available. Most women received only training in "traditional household tasks, Christian dogma, and embroidery" at home, while a small group entered convents or private schools for education in religion and proper behavior.[16]

As the influence of new Renaissance values grew, instruction in Christian virtues, whether in a religious or domestic school, was deemed to benefit Iberian women in two ways: it directed their inclinations toward their own salvation and the service of their (future) husbands. The possibility for an exceptional education for girls emerged during the reign of Isabella of Aragon and Castile (1474–1504) when she extended her own education, begun in pious prayer and needlework, to include Latin, rhetoric, and writing. She collected books, founded two libraries, and encouraged the education of her own daughters Juana and Catalina (Catherine) of Aragon and other young women at her court. Notable educated women of that era included the Marchioness of Monteagudo, Maria Pacheco, and Beatriz Galindo, a tutor of Queen Isabella who was also professor in "Latin Classics at the University of Salamanca."[17] In her turn, Princess Catherine—later the first wife of England's Henry VIII—inspired Juan Luís Vives to compose his brief *Instruction of a Christian Woman*, "the leading theoretical manual on women's education of the sixteenth century."[18]

An influential adviser to noble families in western Europe, Vives tolerated little formal education for women and proposed that studies in modesty, chastity, obedience, and submission completed a woman's formation in the body of virtues. Indeed, his text offered only minimal directives for scholarship alongside a surfeit of instructions for feminine attire, posture, diet, and comportment. At the beginning of the *Instruction*, Vives admitted that women's education—and his advice to them—might be brief because "women yet may be informed with few words." Even a royal princess required little instruction, Vives warned, for "she hath no charge to see to, but her honesty and chastity. Wherefore when she is informed of that, she is sufficiently appointed."[19] When they were young, females must be sheltered from influences outside the home, and play and learn only among girls and women to encourage isolation from the "rude" wide world. Girls should only play with other girls and be watched over by women, to avoid the insidious influence of men's presence and flattery. Each girl must "not learn to delight among men" lest she overstep her virtues and bounds.

A girl's first schooling, according to Vives, might be in reading and writing, but must be accompanied by a thoroughgoing instruction in spinning "wool and flax," and then "cookery" to serve her family and guests and maintain household health. A girl's advanced education, dangerous if undertaken among men or under male tutelage, entailed the reading of books of "good manners" and excerpts from the scriptures, and the copying of hymns, biblical quotes, and "the sayings of philosophers." Girls learned best under the guidance of a "holy and well learned woman" who would avoid love poetry and romances of all sorts to teach her pupils "demureness and honesty."[20] Following her elders' examples in limited subjects, the future bride might "learn for herself alone and her young children," but rarely demonstrate her learning. Vives noted, "As for eloquence, I have no great care, nor a woman needeth it not, but she needeth goodness and wisdom. Nor is it a shame for a woman to hold her peace, but it is a shame for her and abominable, to lack discretion, and to live ill." Thus the most robust education for young women cultivated feminine frailty and submission, "because a woman is a frail thing, and of weak discretion, and . . . may lightly be deceived."[21]

In the latter chapters of his *Instruction*, Vives turned to "The Ordering of the Body in a Virgin," with painstaking directions for bodily conformity. Even a girl's food was restricted, with fasting preferred to the consumption of beer and spicy food that might endanger her chastity, for Vives warned, "how can a young woman that hath a body hot with [food] be sure of herself?" Her sleep must not be overlong on a too-soft bed, and her choice of clothing must be simple woolens and unadorned (and undyed) to indicate her "gravity, soberness, and chastity." Eschewing the vanities of perfumes or cosmetics, a girl should avoid mirrors, jewelry, and even shoes—so that she might be compelled to stay home. Vives suggested that girls were best adorned with a quiet "mind and conscience," and each was most suitable when she appeared "demure, humble, sober, shamefast, chaste, honest and virtuous."[22] Urging caution in any relationship with men, Vives was reluctant to countenance women's movement outside the home, since frivolous visits encouraged vices, and women were susceptible to the ruin of their reputations through gossip. If a woman were to go "abroad," she should prepare as if for mortal battle, travel with her own mother or "some [serious] woman that is a widow or wife, or some good maid of virtuous living," walk moderately, appear serious, ignore men's looks, not laugh, and neither give nor take anything from a man. Vives considered few trips to be warranted, "except it be to hear [Mass], and then well covered" under cloaks and veils.[23]

In this same period, educated women in Portugal actually received instruction in the classics and in Latin and other languages, although other demands were also made of them. Author D. Leonor de Noronha, notable for her 1552 translation of the *Enneades* by Italian humanist Marco Antonio Sabellico, reportedly read texts from "Cicero, Lucretius, Ovid, Virgil, Plato, Pliny or Horace" alongside her brothers.[24] Still, she would have been expected to observe rules of comportment and dress that diminished her potential for leadership and authority; among the most important was strict avoidance of the daily affairs of her noble male relatives. Contemporary moralist Francisco de Monzón failed to provide details for the education of noblewomen in his 1544 *Mirror of the Christian Princess*, but assumed that it left them fully prepared to read sacred scripture and demonstrate charity and devotion, while observing "seclusion and retirement" at home.[25]

The effects of guidelines such as those written by Vives and Monzón could be felt in sixteenth-century Portugal, where only a few women of the court had "literary pretensions" and "most of the elite ladies and all women of other social classes remained illiterate."[26] Outside of a few retirement houses and convents where girls might be sheltered, only the Convento de São Pedro de Alcântara, established in Lisbon in 1557, taught reading and counting to the *educandas* housed there. The Portuguese royal notice published in 1579, which required those who "teach girls to read, sew and embroider" to have municipal licenses, suggests that a few informal or home-based schools had begun by that date,[27] but most Portuguese instructors only reiterated the Roman Catholic ideals of obedience and modesty and taught women devotion and dependence on the Church for guidance. Secular Portuguese writers such as the seventeenth-century moralist Francisco Manuel de Melo, however, sounded a warning about diversions disguised as religious devotions and discouraged women's attendance at "extravagant devotions" that might distract them from domestic duties and personal restraints.[28]

In his *Letter of Guidance for Married Men*, Melo offered limited approval for women's religious activities but few options for women's education. On that subject, he first quoted Afonso de Portugal, bishop of Évora (and father of D. Francisco of Portugal, the first Count of Vimiosa): "The most learned woman should know nothing more than how to arrange a chest of white linen." Although he took issue with that extreme position, commenting that there must be many women "of great judgment," Melo insisted that education—even for elite women—threatened women's minds and safety. Women could not, after all, undertake traditionally masculine tasks or occupations, advise men on worldly matters, or lead independent lives. With limited understanding and limited opportunities, women did not—as some argued—need more education than men, and their studies led only to meaningless affectations:

> I assume that women know nothing of wars nor states, nor seek this. Some women annoy me by meddling in selections in government, judging games, taking challenges, initiating lawsuits. Others pride themselves on understanding verses, they gnash in different languages, deal with disputes of love and courtesy, memorize questions for discreet persons, remember difficult mottoes.[29]

Accepting the view that women's education was folly and that the affairs of state and other aspects of advanced learning should be left to men, Melo advised that women learn only what suited their station within the home. Women's education must prepare them for their home duties: "I said that it would be good to occupy the wife in domestic government; it is as good as it is necessary, not only so that she should be occupied, but so that the husband have less work. Such petty things should not encumber the thought of a man; and for that of women they are more appropriate. . . . The refrain is well said: 'For men the plaza, for women the home.'" Melo concluded with his advice for education: "The best book [for a woman] is the cushion and the embroidery frame; but not for this would I deny her the use of them. I do not praise those who always wish to read comedies, and know the romances of them by heart, and who recite them at length."[30]

In eighteenth-century Portugal, only a few religious schools educated a handful of elite and cloistered women, with most such convents and retirement houses providing shelter and religious activities but little schooling. The admonitions of Juan Luís Vives were echoed at the end of the century in the writings of Luís Antonio Verney, the humanist scholar who inspired and guided the reforms of Portuguese schools following the expulsion of the Jesuit order by the Marquis de Pombal. Despite the expansion of education for boys, girls remained excluded from most subjects and schools, for they needed only enough education to remain modest, manage a house, and instruct their young children. In the new colony, the boundaries of women's education were rebuilt, so that indoctrination in inferiority kept pace alongside the instruction in submission and religious virtues from the earliest moments of conquest and catechesis.

## IDEALS AND EDUCATION IN COLONIAL BRAZIL

The central ideas for girls' education, including the most radical limitations of it, were transmitted to Brazil at the opening of the colony. In fact, instruction of Brazilian Indian women in the doctrines of Roman Catholicism and Portuguese culture started during Cabral's visit in 1500 to the Brazilian coast when one Indian woman, appropriately covered, was purposefully brought to observe the Catholic Mass. The scribe Pero Vaz de Caminha—like many to follow in the early colonial period—expected that Brazilian women, owing to their ascribed feminine docility and subservient racial position, would be drawn to Christian teachings and susceptible to indoctrination in service to Portuguese colonists. The earliest missionaries in Brazil thus directed their efforts to retrieve women from their sins, bring them into the light of faith and service, and impose the divine plan for their lives. Teaching the naked and innocent captives entailed clothing and confining them according to the Portuguese Christian standards for feminine behavior, but rarely included liberative ideas or uplifting morals. In Brazil, the creation of the body of virtues and the protection of honor would be done through two means: first, nominal instruction in religious doctrines alongside training in domestic and social skills, and, later, introduction of a few academic subjects that might benefit familial and public institutions.

According to Brazilian traditions, the "first literate Brazilian woman" was Madalena Caramuru, daughter of an indigenous woman, either Moema or the more famous Catarina Paraguaçu, and an early Portuguese trader named Diogo Álvares Corrêa. Some nineteenth-century historians insisted that her father or her husband had taught her to read and write, and they regarded her as the paragon of women's achievements, claiming that she had written to the bishop of Salvador protesting the maltreatment of slave children in the region.[31] Despite this early exception, the education of women during most of the colonial era was limited to catechetics. The first Jesuit missionaries found women eager to accept a virtuous and spiritual conversion, as befitted their nature. While men represented an "obstacle" to religious formation since they could not be drawn from their customary vices, women embraced the new teaching, were "more clever in it," and applied themselves "much more toward the good."[32] And in 1556, José de Anchieta characterized Indian women as the more devoted supporters of the new village regimen, since they were more "fervent" in their acceptance of Catholic instruction.[33]

Once instructed, Indian women helped spread the new teachings to others, and converted and devout women were praised for their spiritual ascension. So Brother Pero Correia in 1551 praised indigenous women converts who modeled virtue not only for other villagers but also for Portuguese women.[34] Portuguese women occasionally labored alongside the immigrant missionaries, to extend the educational virtues that they themselves had assimilated. Padre António Pires recounted the devotion of one such, his interpreter Maria da Rosa, who later founded a retreat-house for women in Olinda. He insisted that she was among "the most honorable in the land," and even "more virtuous" than he was.[35]

In the sixteenth century, girls were rarely singled out for special attention by the Jesuits who dominated the educational institutions in the colony. When preaching among the Indians, they typically neglected girls, so much so that adults noticed the discrepancy and, in one case, called on Jesuit António Blásquez to write to the queen "to send them virtuous women to instruct their daughters [in the faith], since the Padres are instructing their sons."[36] Most often, Indian girls were trained by local colonists only in domestic tasks that fitted them for marriage and servitude. Jesuit Brás Lourenço reported thus of the construction of "another great house" where "a devout man and his wife" oversaw the domestication of young women for colonial service: the older woman had "many girls from among the Indians under her discipline and is teaching them to be seamstresses and to spin etc. These will be married to boys already taught doctrine and instructed in good customs."[37]

The Jesuit leader Manuel da Nóbrega included girls in his schemes for education, planning that they would "collaborate efficiently in the work of catechizing and converting the heathens and in the formation of authentically Christian families" among the indigenous peoples.[38] His ambition to create a network of retirement houses was thwarted, however, by his Portuguese patrons who could not imagine the utility of education for girls, particularly among Indians and the growing mixed-race population. Nóbrega's repeated letters to Portugal were unsuccessful, and he apparently never received the requisite royal license to open religious housing for women. He and his companions resorted to providing only nominal religious lessons to girls and women while focusing their educational efforts again on boys and men, ultimately creating a network of colonial schools and colleges limited to elite males.

For girls, the oral transmission of the Church's teachings and religious traditions sufficed to induct them into the service of the colonial empire. Some religious leaders, in fact, suggested that since religious truth had been revealed in oral form, missionary instruction should continue in that mode. The power of the Christian word, they claimed, was in its oral communication, and the direct encounter of the believer with the spoken lectures of priests or monks recapitulated the early Christian experience. Still, the traditional explanations that supported the understanding of scripture were in the written tomes of the Church and the cultural heritage of Portugal in its literature, so even the indigenous boys of Brazilian missions might be taught to read and thus brought more fully into "full adherence" to that culture and its hegemony.[39] Girls and women were closed out of the subtleties of the tradition and given only the roughest and most rudimentary fragments from which they might, if clever, fabricate a personal or domestic faith.

In the early colony, wealthy immigrant women from Portugal were the most likely to have educational opportunities beyond the minimal instruction in religion and service. Wives and daughters of the colonial nobility, business owners, and government officials had received some education in Portugal, and female relatives of the *donatórios*—owners and directors of the newly established hereditary captaincies—had been schooled privately or in convents before immigrating to their new positions of power. In fact, several women served as temporary governors or donatories during the early colonial era. Ana Pimental stepped into the role of acting governor for São Paulo in 1533–1534, and the Condessa de Vimieiro Mariana de Sousa Guerra succeeded her father as *donatária* in nearby São Vicente between 1621 and 1625. Brites de Albuquerque, the widow of Duarte Coelho Pereira, governed Pernambuco from 1544 to 1560, after her husband's death and during the absence of her son and heir Duarte Coelho de Albuquerque. And in Espírito Santo, Luísa Grinalda served as acting governor between 1589 and 1593, following the death of her husband, the *donatário* Vasco Fernandes Coutinho Filho. After her brief term as governor, however, she left for an extended convent retreat.[40]

These few women might serve, however, only as extraordinary cases. Colonial women were, for the most part, illiterate and rarely learned enough to sign their own names. The first documents of the visiting Portuguese Inquisition bear out this last point: while only a handful of men signed with just an 'X' or required the notary to sign on their behalf, most women did not sign at all. In the confession records of the first Visitation of the Portuguese Inquisition to Salvador, Bahia, between 1591 and 1592, twenty-six out of thirty-eight women could not sign their own names. These women were of all ages and ethnicities and occupied a variety of fields; among them were several well-to-do women who claimed the title "Dona" and two women who owned plantations. Only one is noted as having signed her name, but another twelve may have done so as well—the published accounts are silent on that point. In the confession records from Pernambuco of the same era, nine out of twelve women could not sign their own names. By contrast, only two out of the fifty male confessants could not sign their names in the published accounts from Pernambuco from 1594 to 1595.[41]

Barred from formal education, girls in the colony had other, less formal options for their inculcation in suitably feminine life: private and domestic schools in Brazil. One such school in Pernambuco came to light because its founder, Branca Dias, was denounced for Jewish practices: her former pupils explained their activities under her tutelage while denouncing her hidden religion to the Inquisitor in 1593 and 1594. According to their reports, Dias—who had since died—had escaped from Portugal after her imprisonment for Judaism there and followed her husband to his sugarcane plantation and nearby residence in Olinda, Pernambuco, in the 1550s.[42] In Olinda, Dias had schooled her own young daughters, Ines, Violante, and Guimar, her husband's illegitimate daughter Briolanja Fernandes, and a step-granddaughter named Isabel Frasoa at her home in the 1540s through the 1560s. Isabel de Lamas, daughter of mixed white and Indian parentage, and Joanna Fernandes, a girl of African parents (and probably slave to Dias), testified that other girls between the ages of nine and twelve had joined them in learning to sew, embroider, and work in the house and in the yard.[43]

The longest and most revealing denunciation came from Dias's own step-granddaughter, who explained that she spent three or four months in the house learning "to sew and do work" when she was twelve. Joined by her aunts, Felipa Paz, Andesa Jorge, and other girls, she observed Dias cooking, working cotton, and spinning coarse thread, while Joana Fernandes recalled her winding spindles of cotton thread into balls. On Saturdays, however, Dias and her sisters sent "the girls who studied" to the back yard to "work and rest" for a short time, while the household allegedly held Jewish services.[44] Felipa Paz had assisted one of the daughters—either Briolanja or Ines—in giving sewing instruction to Maria Camella, Ana Lins, and other girls. Ines may have helped with the basic literacy and arithmetic instructions, for she certainly possessed skills in "sewing, embroidering, making braids, and other things."[45] Ines was herself later denounced as having observed a Saturday "Sabbath" by resting and reading rather than working. Remarkably, none of the girls who were taught in Dias's home school came from elite families, and two of them continued in domestic service for some time afterward, their worth undoubtedly increased by their brief lessons. All of the young women later married white or part-white husbands, including a carpenter, a farmhand, a sugar-master, and the overseer of the plantation owned by Dias's husband. Only Isabel Frasoa, the step-granddaughter, might have married a man of property in nearby Varzea.[46]

In those same denunciation texts, recorders preserved accounts of the other "work" of young married women, who sewed, cooked, cleaned the beds, did laundry, and weeded the gardens—all part of the domestic life for women of most of the lower and middle classes in the colony.[47] None, however, learned more than housekeeping from the domestic schools in towns, since education in "math, reading, and Latin was an elite male prerogative for most of the Brazilian colonial period."[48] *Recolhimentos* or retirement-house schools were only gradually permitted in the late 1500s through the 1600s, following requests to the imperial Crown such as that of Nóbrega for "old and decent white women" to inaugurate and administer small residences for white daughters of Portuguese families in colonial towns. Even with permission to establish informal and formal religious housing for women in Brazil—examined in more depth in Chapter 4—barely one hundred girls might have been resident pupils in them by the end of the seventeenth century. Girls remained "completely excluded from any instruction" and hidden "in the recesses of the home" when the convent communities were finally allowed, for "the religious Orders for women that were established [in Brazil] dedicated themselves to a contemplative life, removing themselves from activities that might aim at the extending of intellectual cultivation of the feminine element."[49]

While immigrant women of the seventeenth century barely merited training, a few indigenous women welcomed the education that might still be had from catechists and missionaries. The more egalitarian gender roles among the communities along the Brazilian coast might have supported women's expectations for equal treatment by the missionaries, even though the gender equality simply permitted women to farm and fish alongside their husbands (and their husband's other wives).[50] Jesuits and Franciscans, at least in the last decades of the 1500s, praised Indian women who converted — perhaps because they had failed to convert the more resistant and bellicose men. Jesuit preacher Antônio Vieira, whose sermons lamented the susceptibility of (white) women to every innate evil, wrote occasionally about inspired and educated Brazilian Indian women. In 1654, for example, he reported that women led a village in prayer at night when the visiting missionaries were sure that the "village was silent with drink." The priests discovered that all were praying and talking about doctrine:

> Coming at last closer and noting what was being said in the first house, . . . [the fathers] found that what was being said throughout [the village] were prayers and declarations from the catechism, some of them [the residents] praying, others teaching, others learning, all stretched out in their hammocks. The sons corrected the parents, the wives admonished their husbands, since ordinarily the wives . . . are those who most quickly learn by heart.[51]

Two decades later, a young woman who "declared herself the daughter of the Indian Simoa" and the Portuguese colonist Eliador Eanes left a will naming her local vicar as the guardian of her only daughter, Maria. Claiming that her "freedom was under threat," Ana Bastarda—whose surname also identified her illegitimate status in the colony—implored him in the name of God to shelter her daughter in his house, "to teach and indoctrinate her in the love and service of God." Ana was an unmarried mother or, as she put it, a "poor, freed and liberated single woman," whose Indian heritage inscribed servitude on her own and her children's bodies, yet she understood that religious and domestic education provided protection for her young daughter.[52] At the same time, the lessons directed toward the virtuous and religious restraint of indigenous girls and women were sharply distinguished from the traditions that Portuguese women disdained. While

Ana's daughter might accept and even benefit from religious education, women of the elite classes eluded the options of religion and education. In that same era, Jesuit historian Fernão Cardim complained that the "great ladies" of the plantations of Pernambuco were unaccustomed to "frequent masses, preachings, confessions, etc.," and rarely attended them or benefited from them.[53]

The doors to literacy and formal education were thus closed to all but a few white women in colonial Brazil, women who, by most accounts, failed to appreciate the opportunity to submit to religious and patriarchal doctrines. Through most of the eighteenth century, girls learned only sewing and embroidery, even at the convent schools that began to open after the 1680s. Only a few Brazilian girls studied (and professed vows) at the convents in Portugal that were still open to them, such as Dona Maria Xavier, sent in 1740 to Santa Clara in Porto, and Dona Margarida de Campos, sent to São Bento in Évora, who were called "knowledgeable in letters" by their Brazilian peers. The first female Brazilian author, Teresa Margarida da Silva e Horta, was educated in Portugal, only shortly before the imperial order ended the practice of sending eligible girls back to the *metropole* and thus limiting the marriage opportunities of elite white men in the colony.[54] This superficial schooling for girls left deep impressions nonetheless, especially as boys' education advanced in the Jesuit institutions and—after the Jesuit withdrawal—in secular schools. Girls were more tightly bound by their ignorance of the wider culture and marked by the constraint to practice only the most trivial of manual arts.

Popular advice continued this sentiment, in books such as the 1728 *Narrative Compendium of the Pilgrim of America* by Nuno Marques Pereira. In that fictionalized account of a journey from Bahia to present-day Minas Gerais, Pereira interlaced descriptive episodes of travel with pointed, conservative advice for colonists. In one series of stories, he included somber warnings for the father of a young girl. Recalling one young woman who had learned to read and write just before running off with her tutor, Pereira cautioned that the father might do well to hire a "Master" to teach his sons, but "women are of a very different sex, and great prudence and virtue are required for their care." In place of the elderly gentleman who might teach boys, fathers must rely instead on "a prudent matron" for lessons in comportment and restraint, for the goals must be that the daughters be "less knowledgeable and more retiring."[55] Such reasoning—given to any who might ask—would safeguard not only the girl's but also the family's honor, providing few opportunities for rebellion or dissension and permitting her eventual assignment to a convent or marriage.

Fathers considering the necessity of a girl's education, then, considered her customary destiny and their family rank rather than her personal gifts or inclinations. Colonial noble families might send girls to convents in Portugal or to a newly opened girls' seminary in Brazil, but most others in the propertied classes took advice from Pereira and like authors in the colony and *metropole*. The basics of feminine education by tutors or in small private schools provided a girl enough instruction: she might learn

> to spin, to sew and to tailor, that she learn to write, but to write a letter, in order to record in a book that she made such and such provisions to live six months in their house; to record the time of service of the servants and dayworkers, or their salaries; in order to write in it the price of all comestibles, of all sort of cloth of linen, of clothes, of silk, of woolens, of furniture of the house; [and] the places where they are made or where they are sold most cheaply.[56]

Such instruction in arithmetic and writing permitted a young woman to manage expenditures in the extended household that included slaves and minor dependents; she might also calculate the benefits of domestic service provided by slaves or wages to be gained if they were sent out to sell sweets or to work for others. Still, many families simply refused to educate girls and young women because their travel either to Portugal or to the colonial cities put them at risk of physical and moral harms. Rather than damage family honor, girls stayed home—away from danger, intellectual development, and personal autonomy—and marked their time until they "took a state." The isolation of young women was excessive in the eyes of church officials, however, and even the archbishop of Bahia complained in 1751 that "the local girls could not be induced to attend the lessons given in the Ursuline Convent, owing to the opposition of their parents."[57]

By the end of the 1700s, however, girls' education was discussed more widely, and several important institutions were established in Brazil for the daughters of elite families. Educational reforms inspired by the powerful Portuguese minister Sebastião José de Carvalho e Melo, the Marquês de Pombal, created secular schools for boys in Portugal and Brazil, but girls' education still took place in convents or *recolhimentos* where nuns and lay sisters attended to their religious, moral, and domestic instruction. Under the guidance of devout women, girls could be educated not just for their own good, but more importantly for the good of their children and the future of society at large. Thus, the 1798 Statutes for the Recolhimento de Nossa Senhora da Glória in Pernambuco—discussed further in Chapter 4—proposed a "seminary . . . for the good education of daughters, of those daughters whom Providence has, from the cradle, destined to be Mothers, Teachers, Nuns, or Directors of the first steps of those [young women] who one day would shape the body of Human Society." Founder and local bishop José Joaquim da Cunha de Azeredo Coutinho insisted that young women required a moral foundation because they had "a house to govern, a husband to make happy, and children to educate in virtue" and could assist their more active and worldly husbands with social and moral improvement.[58]

Girls' paths to education, however, did not stray from the expectations of previous centuries. At the Recolhimento de Nossa Senhora da Glória, girls chose one of two directions for their instruction, one designed for future religious recluses and the other for those destined to be mothers. The domestic path taught girls reading, writing, math, sewing, and embroidery, all designed to support the married state in which they would educate young children and manage an extended household without lapsing into idleness. Coutinho added that girls, naturally of a more fragile and distractible disposition, should be entertained while learning, so that their lessons were to be arranged as games; even sewing and lace-making lessons might be accompanied by diverting and edifying tales. Instruction in religion centered on Catholic doctrines and included charitable works so that they might practice virtues and unlearn the "ordinary defects of their sex"—including both garrulousness and timidity.[59] Under Coutinho's more enlightened regime, a well-educated girl was still constrained in behavior while skilled in a few domestic tasks, rather than literate or knowledgeable about history, philosophy, or languages like her male counterparts.

As the Brazilian colonial era drew to a close, little changed for girls and young women seeking education of any sort. Impoverished girls and those of lower classes were occasionally admitted to training centers for household work, particularly in sewing and cooking, while the girls of white and elite families gained a limited literacy along with their advanced studies in embroidery. In the early 1800s in Rio de Janeiro, for example, a few schools advertised for pupils with promises that their instructors offered the best lessons in sewing, embroidery, reading, and writing, and even fewer suggested that they might teach arithmetic, languages, or music. Other advertisements individually mentioned education in "religion, morality, design, French grammar, English grammar, music playing, singing, household management, millinery, straw-hat making, stocking making, . . . hat cleaning, silk . . . washing, plain sewing, making of silk stockings, and good habits."[60] There are no mentions here of games or charitable deeds, but this

list of lessons presumed that girls needed little beyond a tightly circumscribed domestic sphere for their complete education. Indeed, at about
the same time in Portugal, a young nobleman wrote with pride of the accomplishments that his betrothed *lacked*: "My little lady is no rigorist of
manners: she does not know how to dance or play [an instrument]; . . .
she does not know how to visit in the parlor, nor to discourse about wars;
however, she knows how to satisfy me in all that pertains to the governance of the house, my and her arrangement, for this is her genius and her
upbringing."[61]

One last example will serve to conclude this discussion on girls' education for virtue, this from the founding Statutes of the Collegio de Educação de Meninas, to be dedicated to Nossa Senhora dos Humildes in Santo
Amaro, Bahia, in 1813. As the then-resident Portuguese Crown approved
more educational opportunities for girls in retirement houses or independent private academies, benevolent societies and town councils petitioned
for the creation of their own noteworthy institutions with a startling juxta-
position of high-minded sentiments and regressive rules for girls' dress and
comportment. Thus in 1813, the statutes for the small school for girls began
with the insistence that the impressionable minds of youth must be shaped
by diligent training, for "Women equally require Education: they make up
a part of the human society." As half of the human population, women,
too, must contribute to the family by assisting their husbands and, more
importantly, educating their own children "during the most tender years,
as their first Teachers."[62] The school was dedicated to that worthy task, and
honorable white women were to be engaged as the director, three teachers,
nurses, and doorkeeper to the school, all with suitable expertise and references for their demanding roles.

Warnings immediately followed in the statutes concerning the nature
and character of girls admitted there. In keeping with its ideological intent,
the Collegio would admit a small group of "poor Orphan Girls," each girl
with an affidavit from the Juiz de Orphãos guaranteeing both her status and
her virtue. The statutes specified their primary qualities: "First, that they
be white. Second, that they be truly poor and Orphans." The girls were to
be between six and ten years of age, with no contagious diseases or pox,
and "natives" of Santo Amaro or one of the nearby parishes.[63] After their
divergent training in skills and comportment, they might remain until age
fifteen. The orphan girls, sponsored by town grants and donations, would
be joined by "Wealthy girls" admitted as *porcionistas* or paying boarders.
Those girls—of the same race, age, and health—entered with permission
of the school's prelate and were expected to provide all necessities for them-

selves, including clothing, plus a monthly fee. Boarders might leave the grounds to visit home occasionally, but could only remain in the Collegio until turning thirteen.[64]

As the last group of students, the Collegio would admit "Girls who are not wealthy but are not poor, whose paying Parents wish to send them daily for lessons to this House, and finally all poor Girls, who wish to come to learn without payment in this College at determined times and hours." These pupils might come for schooling as long as they came well-dressed and "wearing shoes,"[65] and while their other virtues are not specified in the statutes, several other rules circumscribed their college-bound lives. First, no girls—neither residents nor day pupils—might dispense with the academic basics; as the statutes explained, "it will not be permitted that any Girl passes to the Class for Sewing, unless she first learns to read sufficiently." Second, the Collegio barred the doors to families seeking a residence for unwanted or even truant females with no intention of providing for their education. The statutes stated categorically:

> In this house is absolutely prohibited the depositing of Women, whether they are already married or to be wed; for it is not good that the innocent Education of Girls be offended by such examples.[66]

Early lessons from the Director of Girls entailed literacy, arithmetic, simple domestic skills, and religious doctrines, with moral lessons to be read aloud as they completed their daily tasks. Even young girls received instruction from the Second Teacher, in Portuguese grammar and orthography and "profane History." The Third Teacher taught all girls "to sew, embroider, make clothing, make flowers [and] decorations"; for girls older than ten, she added matters of household management and economy.[67] More than instruction was provided, of course, and the statutes elaborated the daily schedule and behaviors expected for all participants. After ten to twelve hours of sleep in the dormitory guarded by a teacher or nurse, girls woke at 5:30 a.m. for Catholic Mass, a bread-and-butter breakfast, and then classes until 11:00 a.m. After a midday meal with soup, meat, and dessert, girls resumed lessons until 5:00, with older girls completing their sewing or undertaking private lessons in French, music, or dance in the late afternoon. The girls finished the day with a light meal, then played or read until their evening prayers.[68]

The regimen was rigorous, and the statutes further insisted that few liberties be granted. Girls could only bathe weekly and use cold water to wash in the mornings. They were required to take their meals communally, so no special meals or exceptions might be granted to wealthier or more favored pupils. At the same time, their reading and leisure activities were limited, with the regulations repeating admonitions against "romance Novels" and other frivolous books. All girls were expected to appear with simple clothing and short hair, always wearing shoes and walking gracefully on their rounds, with a white dress with a blue ribbon belt reserved for Sundays and holy days. Only gentle punishments were allowed to miscreants, however, and the girls themselves were not to undertake any extraordinary religious penances or fasts, so that they might not be caught up in the peculiar defect of "fanaticism, . . . which falls easily on the feminine sex."[69]

Bound to their lessons and their lives, the girls of this and other schools continued to be measured against the Christian ideal for the virtuous woman. Even when the possibility of their education was inspired by notions of their social contribution, or by a glimmer of intellectual development, girls were bound—as much by the pale blue ribbon of their Sunday dresses as by the necessity of their moral and personal constraint. The details of the statutes from Nossa Senhora dos Humildes—Our Lady of the Humble—take very little from their late colonial era or the post-Enlightenment sense of individual freedom, for girls' education might only serve others—their families, their husbands, their sons, their state. Instructed in virtue and honor, they were thus instructed in submission through the daily and weekly diminution of their own lives and understanding of themselves. By the end of their stay at the Collegio, they embodied the principles deemed "natural" for women: their manner of walking as much as the content of their thoughts reflected the subordinate social category in which even the wealthiest girl must remain. Girls left the school at thirteen or fifteen, to await their next assignment in marriage or the convent, completing the peculiar "habituation" of one significant segment of society.

Girls and women of colonial Brazil probably experienced fewer changes in the moral ideal to which they were held than women elsewhere in Europe and the Americas, and they encountered fewer opportunities for education. The Luso-Brazilian cultural expectations for virtue, linked as they were to class privilege and concepts of honor, left little room for change. Even the Portuguese writers of the early 1800s introduced more freedoms for women than would be entertained in Brazil for decades. The habits of repression of liberty and governance that the imperial Crown maintained over the colonial lands lingered through the nineteenth century, then, and the subaltern classes bore the weight: slaves and mixed-race women met with few reprieves, married women of all classes gained few rights, and religious women found few opportunities for spiritual expression and leadership. The ideal of the Christian virtuous woman marked all women in the Brazilian colony and built a "commonsense world" in which daily violence against women inscribed their bodies and minds and ensnared them with demands of spiritual and intellectual abstinence.

Through the Brazilian colonial period, girls and women were subject to the visible bounds of behavior and space—they were limited to specified clothing, comportment, rooms, and buildings. Their explicit education in feminine action and roles enacted the implicit expectations of the Christian world around them, even as the colonial culture diverged wildly from the Portuese norms in politics and cultural and religious creativity. All of the Brazilian women, from the first industrious embroiderers under the critical gaze of Gabriel Soares de Sousa to the last fashioners of tea-cloths and flowers in the Collegio de Educação de Meninas, bore an ancient burden not unlike that represented by the national patron, Nossa Senhora da Conceição Aparecida, Our Lady of Aparecida. Long a medieval icon, Mary was transported to Brazil as a devotional focus for the early missions and especially for young Catholic women and converts. In the early 1700s, an elaborately carved wooden statue of Mary was recovered from a river near São Paulo, broken and damaged by years of exposure to the elements there. The body of the saint was found first, and its head lay not far away, the sections drifting apart as if under the very colonial norms for women that separated body and intellect, drowned under the same frigid constraints. The statue was reconstructed and claimed for the imperial cult, much like the women who devoted prayers to it, dressed in extravagant robes and enclosed in chapels—far from the intimate lives that might have flourished in freedom and autonomy.

# FOUR

# Before the Church Doors

## WOMEN AS WIVES AND CONCUBINES

In Bahia in 1591, Antonia de Bairos confessed to the visiting Tribunal of the Portuguese Inquisition that she had been living in a bigamous marriage for decades following her exile from Portugal for adultery. Anrique Barbas, her second husband, had arranged false witnesses, and they had wed "before the doors of the church" with the license of the episcopal official. She had fled from Barbas, however, because of the "wounds and blows" that he dealt her and her "bad life" with him. She had sought refuge in her village church. Although she herself was nearly seventy and all witnesses had died, Bairos still offered vivid testimony of her marriages and "begged pardon" of the Tribunal officers.[1] Three years later in Pernambuco, Breatriz Martins confessed that she had asserted to friends visiting in her yard that the married state, "made and ordained by God," was religiously superior to the orders of monks and nuns begun by mere humans. The wife of a carpenter, Martins explained that she had learned this heretical idea as a girl from a local teacher who had also instructed her in the womanly skills of cooking and washing. She was admonished by the Inquisitor Heitor Furtado de Mendoça that she should not discuss "what she did not understand" and sent to repeat her confession at the Jesuit monastery for her penance.[2]

The statements of these Portuguese immigrants indicate sharp contrasts in their experiences within marriage: while Bairos struggled with her husbands in conditions far from the idealized marriage of the era, Martins's satisfaction with the married state led her into sin. A close review of Portuguese and Brazilian writings about marriage in the early colonial era reveals similar discord and confusion about the nature and value of marriage for women. The Jesuit missionaries sent to Brazil, for example, extolled the virtues of marriage through sermons and lectures while neglecting the

marital status of their own slaves. The influential Jesuit author Manuel da
Nóbrega denounced the widespread practice of cohabitation and concubinage in a 1553 letter, while later sermonist Antônio Vieira recounted only
the virtues of the silent and isolated wife. These differences collectively suggest that this period in Brazilian history was not characterized by a single
vision of wedded bliss to which all aspired (though few achieved), and that
women's lives in marriage rarely conformed to a single religious norm.

With marriage, a bride might come close to achieving the elite and
Christian ideal discussed in Chapter 2: the honor of virtuous womanhood
that seemingly rested on her reputation for chastity and her removal from
the public sphere. Her other attributes and accomplishments mattered so
little in comparison that Feliciano Joaquim de Souza Nunes insisted honor
was the core value in a woman's "inestimable dowry," and without it, she
would "not be rich, noble, or beautiful."[3] Quoting Spanish Franciscan
Antonio de Guevara, he continued, "Honor is more valuable even when
life and property are lost; however, property and life have no value if [a
woman] loses honor."[4] From this perspective, those who lived with men
outside of the sanctified state violated the private yet public nature of the
virtuous ideal. The Catholic Church and the community identified extramarital sexual relations as sinful in part because they damaged public reputations—they were public sins. The attribution of virtue and honor, by contrast, depended on personal demeanor and private behaviors that remained
invisible to the public eye. An honorable matron was accordingly urged to
turn to religious ideals, to be "very devoted to our Virgin Lady, . . . to preserve chastity and free [her]self from dangers."[5]

This chapter focuses on the realm of marital relations in colonial Brazil, encompassing both the discourse on sexual relations, wives, concubines, and marriage that articulated the feminine behaviors deemed appropriate for women and the lived reality of women in reaction to religious
expectations.[6] While secular and religious authorities agreed that marriage
was, in the most general terms, the consummate purpose for women's existence, the emphases in their writings and the impact they sought on social
norms were not unified; when we include the most specific advice prof-
fered to women and men in the Brazilian colony on what were considered
to be the most pressing problems, surprising differences, even contradictions, appear. Inevitably, it seems, conflicts arose in the discourse on gender
difference, and the contesting powers in the colony—missionaries, church
officials, local and overseas governors, and the colonial elite—entered a
struggle for power that expressed itself in struggle for control of women.

Women's experiences in marriage also indicated deep rifts within the colony, especially between the Portuguese and landowning elite and the most marginalized of the Native Brazilian and African slave women. Few white women migrated to the early colonial cities and plantations, and even fewer spent their lives within the patriarchal extended family structure often taken as the domestic paradigm for colonial culture. For most women, married life was an unlikely situation, despite the contradictory efforts by the Roman Catholic Church and imperial Portuguese state to demand or inspire its institution throughout the social strata. The religious injunctions concerning marriage probably provided fewer opportunities for women and men in the colony to enter that sanctified state, and the efforts of the Church itself to both promote and prohibit matrimony may be seen in the historical records and discourse at the very same time.

## MARRIAGE IN MEDIEVAL AND
## EARLY MODERN PORTUGAL

Medieval Portuguese society emphasized—as did the rest of pre-Reformation Europe—the necessary unity of the Christian world under divine dominion, but perpetuated received notions that dichotomized good and evil, noble and peasant, and male and female. Ideas about restrictive gender roles and ideals for women, explored in Chapter 2, had found expression in ancient philosophical and religious texts that still circulated in late medieval Portugal. The Catholic Church honored the celibacy and chastity of the clergy first, but conceded the importance of fidelity and fertility in the continuance of lay society and asserted its control over the institutions surrounding marriage. Both women and men expected to marry at least once, and European society constructed individual identity, family ties, property rights, and concepts of honor on the marital bond. While traditional expectations and ecclesiastical precepts limited women's activities to the family household and women's sexuality to the marriage bed, marriage practices varied considerably by social class and wealth.

Medieval love poetry and romantic literature about courtship shaped few marital relationships for the Portuguese nobility, who accepted arranged marriages between suitable partners and for whom "free choice" marriages were protected by customary law.[7] Young women were pledged and given in marriage by their parents, and marriage ceremonies, contracts, and feasts celebrated by both families. In medieval Portugal, wealthy men paid a dowry to their wives upon marriage, and the sum appropriate to her status "signified the purchase of her body" from her family.[8] But many couples—even among the nobility—contracted marriages privately, avoiding dowries and duties. The Catholic Church inveighed against such "clandestine marriages" and demanded the appropriate fees for the lengthier process of betrothal followed by a "solemn wedding ceremony" held publicly in a church or "at its doors."[9]

Among the lower classes, simple oaths were exchanged either privately or publicly when women joined men in a new household, and the legitimacy of their children depended on the public recognition or church blessings of the marriage. Children born of adulterous relations, to single women, nuns, or the mistresses of married men or priests, might be granted legitimate status by the king, but complaints were raised in the fifteenth century about clerics "flaunting their concubines in public" and the numerous requests for "letters of legitimacy" for their children.[10] Any sexual relations outside of marriage were considered not only religious offenses, drawing penances and even excommunication for the most flagrant offenders, but also civil crimes, punishable by fines, flogging, exile, or prison. While cohabitation, concubinage, and prostitution were not unknown, women more often than men faced civil penalties and religious censure for sexual offenses. Men's involvement in extramarital affairs was tolerated at all levels of society and noblemen faced few penalties for it.

Duties for married women mirrored those mandated for all girls and women in Portuguese medieval society: devotion, fidelity, and obedience to men. The marital bond should generate a natural if restrained affection between the unequal partners rather than a sinful passion arising from carnal love. Any love must arise from or alongside the love for God and support each partner's religious growth, but a wife must also surrender her own autonomy in marriage and accept her husband's superior nature, reason, and estate. The very imperfection of women and their natural proclivities, Christian authors suggested, led them to commit themselves more passionately and completely to marriage while receiving less in return from their busy and dominant spouses. Accordingly, the sins that women might commit stemmed from their excesses of passions or failures to direct them toward their parents and spouses, but late medieval texts still debated whether women were by nature passionate or passive.

In the mid-1400s, D. Duarte of Portugal offered his royal guidance for marital love in O *Leal Conselheiro* (*The Loyal Counselor*), a "treatise" on ethics and behavior for his courtiers, dedicated to his wife D. Leonor.[11] Duarte developed his concept of "ideal love" in "four states of affection: well-wishing, desire of doing good, love, and friendship,"[12] and preferred rational friendship to the intensity of marital love. Constructing an unequal arrangement, Duarte insisted that women must love and fear their husbands just as humankind loved and feared God.

In the brief chapter "On the Manner which Should Be Kept so that Good Women Better Fear Their Husbands," Duarte directed men to comport themselves virtuously in order to elicit women's compliance. According to Duarte, "no better rule" brought submission and affection from wives than the "real and perfect fear of displeasure" in their husbands.[13] Women responded better to the dangers of loss of "some part of good will and sweet conversation" than to threats and wounds, he contended, and "good women" thus loved and feared their superior mates and "obeying them well, did as they commanded." When governed by a firm hand, women cultivated truly feminine virtues and developed their appropriate roles, but men who attempted to please those "good women" harmed themselves and inverted gender roles.[14]

Two centuries after Dom Duarte, Portuguese civil laws increasingly regularized marriage, while the Council of Trent promulgated its narrower perspective on marriage relations. Prohibitions against clandestine marriages, marriages between minors and cousins, and separation and remarriage challenged social customs in Portugal, but the council saved its strongest condemnations for the practice of concubinage. Unmarried and married men keeping concubines or mistresses were threatened with excommunication and punishments fitting "the character of the crime," while women were similarly to be "rigorously punished, according to the measure of their guilt" and expelled from "the city or diocese."[15] Under these strictures, women and men faced the new social disruption of colonial life in Brazil and turned to the religious and secular writing about gender roles and marriage for guidance.

## MARRIAGE IN EARLY COLONIAL BRAZIL: RELIGIOUS DISCOURSE AND EXCLUSIONS

As noted above, the expectations for women's lives in the Brazilian colony did not yield a unified discourse about marriage. The Portuguese empire favored a restricted but productive role for women in its colonization plan, especially for elite white women who maintained the property and power of the landowners. Secular writers then constructed the ideal of a submissive, isolated wife and mother according to medieval customs and early modern needs, though few might follow it.[16] Religious writers of the same era showed more diversity of opinion than might be expected, owing at least in part to the changes introduced by the Council of Trent and by the colonial conflicts themselves. Women, of both the common and elite ranks,[17] made the best of the limited choices, which more often entailed unsanctioned and consensual unions rather than the idealized sacramental marriage.

The path created for white women in colonial Brazil directed them toward marriage, deemed natural for all and essential for those of the noble, commercial, and governing families.[18] In Portuguese terms, women prepared to *"tomar estado"* (literally to "take a state"); while that phrase was also used to include entry into a convent, it signified that only in marriage was their existence settled. Virginity before marriage assured family honor through an untainted lineage, but any sexual activity before marriage, even if no child came from it, excluded an upper-class girl from the best marriage prospects. Public rumors about her were perhaps even worse than her actions; she was expected to be invisible to public scrutiny and kept under guarded seclusion. Preservation of her honor, that is, the reputation of her virginity, might be deemed a girl's only noteworthy accomplishment. A young woman might enhance her beauty, nobility, wealth, or youth, but equally important attributes such as shyness, modesty, and prudence only reinforced her self-effacement.

Parents in the governing families contracted a girl's marriage and dowry or marriage settlement, with fourteen an appropriately mature age for marriage. Roman Catholic Church Council decrees required public banns to preclude incest or bigamy and the bride's consent before marriage, but the rules had little effect. Once married, a woman contributed only within the domestic sphere, thus guaranteeing not only her own fidelity but also the family honor. Besides perpetuating the patriarchal lineage, a wealthy white woman managed the household stocks, meals, and clothing for her husband, servants, slaves, and later children—her own and those of the extended household. Cordial relations developed between a wife and husband and a few peers, but attachments outside the household, especially with religious women, were thought to endanger her loyalty. The virtuous wife was obedient to God and her husband, quiet, chaste, and frugal; without the strict guidance of a husband, she was more likely to be wild, garrulous, vain, and profligate. Religious devotions were deemed both enriching for married women and potentially dangerous if emotions were not appropriately restrained.

In her pursuit of religious devotion, a woman might encounter grave threats to her virtue, but she faced even worse dangers from extramarital affairs. Adultery "constituted a violation of the marital contract," a "'theft' of honor."[19] Law and tradition allowed her husband to kill her and her lover on suspicion of such betrayal. When faced with a husband's absence, a lone woman ideally opted to board for months or even years at a religious house to ensure her chastity. Her silent tolerance was presumed, however, for her husband's adultery and concubinage, and she might even be expected to raise his children from such relationships. In her natural destiny as a mother, then, the *dona da casa* ("lady of the house") bore strong sons and few daughters, instructed them and all household dependents in religious doctrine and practice, and exercised strict protection over the girls.

Given the dangers of the colonial life, early widowhood was not an unexpected outcome of a young woman's marriage to a husband ten or twenty years older. She inherited a portion of his estate—as she might also inherit from her parents—and could manage it and the estates of unmarried minors in nearly all legal details. Continuing her seclusion at home was proper, but remarriage was actually encouraged in the Brazilian colony when white women were considered a scarce commodity.

As the colonial enterprise progressed, the exhortations for marriage and progeny among white colonists increased, and writers echoed the truism that there were "too few" white women in the colony to sustain its governing population. Manuel da Nóbrega reported to his Portuguese superior that he had entreated the king himself to send "some women, who there had little chance for marriage" for the elite unmarried men of Brazil and added that these, "even if they had sinned," might redeem themselves and the lost souls of Brazil by their marriages.[20] He apparently intended that the primary candidates come from among the "orphans of the Queen," young women sheltered in a convent in Lisbon after the death of their fathers in service of the Crown. Their expectations for honorable marriages were limited, as Nóbrega knew, but Brazil offered new opportunities to fulfill their destinies. In the 1550s, some eighteen women disembarked in Bahia and found suitable spouses—some more than once—among the ranks of military and government officials of the colony.[21]

The prospect of such lives as these dominated women's expectations among the elite families, and even touched those of common or non-elite women so that all women felt honor bound. Brazilian historian Ronaldo Vainfas has recently argued for such a nuanced view of colonial society, rather than accept previous characterizations of colonial society as dominated either by harmonious if patriarchal family life or by "absolute unrestraint in sexual matters." He also rejected efforts to reinvent the colony as a paradise of "supposed 'sexual liberty'" without racial prejudice; those interpretations, he insisted, only serve to obscure the complex social struggles in the nascent colony.[22] Thus while contemporary secular and religious writing reproduced the elite women's ideal, as can be seen in the influential writings explored below, alternatives to that ideal were pervasive in the early colonial period and shaped the diverse social milieu of the late colonial centuries; those alternatives included common-law marriage and concubinage.

The ideal for Brazilian elite women was established through the writings of the sixteenth and seventeenth centuries. Secular authors—such as the influential Juan Luís Vives and Francisco Manuel de Melo—typically reduced the married woman to a single aspect of her life and role, such as chastity or obedience, without which a woman failed in her contributions to the human order or society. Religious writers such Martín de Azpilcueta Navarro and Antônio Vieira, contemporaries of the first pair, agreed that marriage was the proper place for women and sketched a suitably narrow role. They shared the restricted view of a wife's role, but bound women not to their earthly mates but to their Creator or church. Women's failure in her religious virtues led, of course, to deadly sins. Even these contrasting themes, further detailed below, left only the barest of lives for honorable women to inhabit.

The Spanish moralist and philosopher Juan Luís Vives wrote his influential treatise, "Instruction of a Christian Woman," for the daughters of the Spanish-born Queen Catherine of England.[23] The text, first published in Spanish in 1523, was rapidly translated and served as the central "theoretical manual on women's education of the sixteenth century . . . for the whole of Europe."[24] Vives set out his instructions according to a woman's life from infancy through maturity, noting to the reader that his advice for the education of women could be brief since so little was expected of them. Mindful of the demands that the government of a world state—or of a vast estate—might make on a noblewoman, Vives insisted that a woman's main "charge" was "her honesty and chastity."[25]

The development of virtue and honor should center a woman's life: her purity must be preserved in childhood, and, in preparation for marriage, she must learn silence, cookery, and moderation in appetite and appearance. Before marriage, a girl's virginity determined her sole worth: while "for men, many things are necessary," chastity was the essential virtue for women.[26] As a wife, she might please her husband through prudence, religious devotion, Bible reading, or domestic skills, but her "incomparable good" was chastity. Vives warned that a woman's virtue might be compromised by any number of disorderly acts—the use of too much makeup, the

reading of romances or love poetry, or the wearing of items of men's clothing, such as a plumed hat or dagger. His advice, clearly aimed at guiding the
political marriages of his patrons, might best compel a woman to inaction:
his instructions were rife with warnings and recommended an isolated,
limited existence for the few who might be esteemed as truly feminine.

Writing over a century later, Francisco Manuel de Melo published
*Carta de guia de casados* ("Guide for Married Men") with little to guide
men's behaviors and virtues, but extensive advice on the ideal wife. Melo
grappled with the humanist ideas on education for women yet still advised prospective grooms to treat women "like precious stones, whose
value increases or decreases according to the estimation that others make
of them."[27] Wise husbands must be solicitous of their wives—and their
own honor—and respect women of learning and judgment. But a learned
woman faced rigid restrictions at home so as not to infringe on her husband's natural rights: she must speak little, in a low voice, and dress som-
berly without makeup and ornament.[28]

While a husband must "be vigilant" to monitor even his wife's thoughts
lest she begin to "pride herself" on her domestic accomplishments and
begin to rule his life, a wife must refrain from offering her opinions to
him. Although Melo considered domestic concerns "petty" and beneath
men's concerns, men must still oversee and control women's behaviors
there.[29] A wife's connections outside the household should be few: her husband was to refrain from taking her to public entertainments, speaking of
her, or showing off her portrait, while she was to avoid female friendships
that might offer her any but the most limited glimpse of public life. Melo
deemed only a few religious activities appropriate for women, since women
could enact their submission to God with obedience to their husbands.
In a series of misogynist anecdotes, he derided extravagance of emotion
or devotion, reiterating hoary Portuguese axioms such as "Para homens a
praça, para mulheres a casa" ("For men the plaza, for women the home")
and "O melhor livro [para mulheres] he a almofada, e o bastidor" ("The
best book [for women] is the cushion and the embroidery frame"). To the
advice of D. Afonso de Portugal, bishop of Évora from 1485 to 1522, "A mulher que mais sabe, não passa de saber arrumar uma arca de roupa branca"
("The most learned woman should know nothing more than how to arrange a chest of white linen"), he added only that he was "certain that there
are women of great judgment" (although he names none), and that limited
reading and writing might be worthwhile for domestic efficiency.[30]

Religious writers of the period, including Navarro and Vieira, developed their discourse of gender roles from the same concerns as their secular

counterparts: to control women and limit their actions in a male-centered cosmos. The core of their arguments, however, invoked the sacral nature of the norms they wished to establish and the divinely ordained "natural" inferiority of women to men and men's rule. In the sixteenth century, religious advice and admonitions to women were irregularly linked with the new decrees of the Council of Trent, especially emphasizing the regularization of sacraments and marriage procedures.

Martín de Azpilcueta Navarro educated the first Jesuit missionaries to Brazil, including his nephew João Azpilcueta and the more renowned Manuel da Nóbrega.[31] Navarro's confession guide, *Manual de confessores y penitentes*, was among the first to promulgate the new doctrines of the Council of Trent for the Iberian churches.[32] While Navarro's aim was the maintenance of Christian virtue, he emphasized religious submission and chastity for married women in terms reminiscent of Juan Vives's *Instrucción*. His lists of sins corresponded to the biblical commandments and canonical laws but he offered a necessarily dichotomized view of women's nature. He followed Catholic teachings on the importance of free will, individual conscience, and personal autonomy, even for women, but acknowledged that they had less independence and discrimination in judgment because of their subordination to men.

The challenge for women emerged first in his section on the fourth commandment (to honor one's parents), which stressed filial obedience. A father might, Navarro insisted, sin mortally if he did not supervise a daughter's behavior with suitors or with her future spouse. Once she was established in her marriage—her proper place—her duties centered on her husband and he supervised her subsequent actions. Under the same commandment, a wife might sin grievously in her resistance to his supervision, when she "disobeys her husband notably," "does not want what he wants," "provokes him," or "despises to be subject to him."[33] Her husband assumed the power to guide her away from "her superfluous vanities and dishonest habits,"[34] but could not interfere with her religious devotions or other honorable activities. A husband could not force his wife into any sin or prevent her from complying with commandments or canonical law. While he could not beat her "excessively and cruelly," she might disobey him if "he wishes to be a vagabond" or abandons virtue himself.[35]

In the later chapters concerning the sixth commandment (against adultery), most warnings were directed to men, whose sins in act and thought threatened women. Women might sin through desire or persistence in a sinful relationship, but the author preserved traditional protections for women by condemning the tricks, lies, and force that men might use, even in marriage—including inordinate sexual demands.[36] The occasions for men to sin, however, ranged far beyond the marital relationship, while women's lives—at least in this document—have no other place. Navarro's confessional opened no doors for a woman's creative life, and even the range of her vices was narrowed in his text.

Antônio Vieira, called "the greatest Portuguese and Brazilian preacher of the seventeenth century,"[37] presented his views on marriage in letters, chronicles, and reports, and in sermons preached in the royal chapel in Lisbon and the bishopric cathedral in Bahia. As in Navarro's *Manual*, Vieira's varied writings revealed his struggles to maintain the Catholic—nearly humanistic—doctrine of individual autonomy while still insisting on masculine dominance over women. Vieira's statements exhorted all Christians to the free-willed acceptance of divine command, but still denounced women's independence as unnatural. As an active missionary in Brazil, he called for the conversion of individual Brazilian Indian women—so they might then surrender their autonomy to the imperial civilization and religion he introduced there.

Vieira's letters from the Amazon region exemplified his persistent efforts to introduce Iberian status and gender norms among the indigenous converts. He applauded the success of Indian women—strictly segregated from male converts—in learning Catholic doctrine or attending religious service, but offered limited opportunities for further involvement for women. He denounced the practice of separating Brazilindian wives from their families to serve colonists in domestic slavery, but promulgated a list of rules for Jesuits for the same end in his report as Visitor to Maranhão (1658–1661). Arguing against the expansion of Brazilindian slavery in that short treatise, he nonetheless endorsed domestic service and slavery for Indian women, in tasks as wet-nurse, table-server, or maid for "some poor [white] woman" who had no other help. He stipulated that these "exceptional cases" were only appropriate for older "unattached" women, and that harvest work could be undertaken by some women "with their husbands"; otherwise, he warned, their salvation might be compromised.[38] In a later letter, he boasted of the cloth made for his male students—by twenty-four Brazilindian women employed exclusively in spinning and weaving.[39]

His classically baroque sermons, especially the series on the Rosary, recommended personal piety for women, but he still castigated them as foolish, vulgar, and prone to evil. As noted in Chapter 2, Vieira argued that a woman's virtue was bound to her submission to marriage and to a husband's authority, and her vices were revealed in her defiance of marital norms. In the "Sermão Sétimo do Rosário," for example, he denied any virtue for the women listed in Jesus's genealogy (in Matt. 1) and contended that they were notable only for their sexual infidelity. The sin of infidelity was characteristic of women, and in women it was "more offensive [and] more dangerous and pernicious." Since chastity before marriage and fidelity in marriage comprised women's virtue, infidelity "encompassed all sins" they might commit.[40]

In the "Sermão Décimo Sétimo do Rosário," Vieira returned to the theme of the proper seclusion of all women within the home, insisting that they "must pray at home, and never outside of it."[41] In his later "Sermão Vigésimo Segundo do Rosário," however, Vieira reproached the elite women who preferred Latin offices and private religious services to the vernacular rosary and church services attended by "common women":

> Of old the greatest splendor in the churches . . . were the Portuguese ladies, when they came to worship God with their faces covered. They used to confess in the church, take communion in the church and hear the mass and sermon in the church. But what was once only permitted for extreme infirmity today is conceded for extreme vanity: the confessor must go to their houses [to] hear confessions there, say mass there, give communion there.[42]

With these specific and seemingly contradictory admonitions—stay home and pray but leave home to pray—Vieira expounded the central principle for women's religious lives: submission to patriarchal command. He returned to the repeated theme of obedience to his own religious authority and to the dominance of their husbands. This is presented clearly even in the two contradictory passages above: obedience, whether to father, husband, God the Father, or the Catholic padre, was the sole virtue to which women might aspire.

Vieira's discourse on women matched that in Navarro's *Manual*: both religious writers argued about virtue while creating the means to control women. For them as well as for Melo, the honorable woman was obedient and isolated within her marriage and household. Her activities, thoughts, and sense of herself found their essential beginnings in marriage; otherwise, she defied her divine creator and her human master. Still, these authors differed on the origin of feminine disharmony, that is, on why women were so dangerous and disruptive. Vieira ascribed to women's nature an inherited tendency to chaos and sin, as descendants of the sinful Eve. In this, he made their sin almost inevitable, their guilt undeniable, and the need for religious control imperative. Navarro, by contrast, considered men and women equally vulnerable to sin but still identified women's failure to maintain marital submission primary among their misdeeds. The discourse created by Melo differed in the significance that economic power, rather than religious constancy, played: vigilance was necessary to keep the domestic sphere separate from the public sphere and under its dominion. Honorable women might assume additional duties in the household, as long as they did not stray from their seclusion. Vives, with his emphasis on chastity, added yet another note of conflict to the discourses. He tied control over women's sexuality to women's submission to religious authority, with a political purpose: the fidelity expected of elite women not only upheld family honor but also guaranteed the patriarchal lineage. With these four writers having bound elite women by their nature to one virtue, one sphere, and one function, subsequent writers penned only a few creative embellishments. The realities of the colony itself created manifest obstacles to a single code for honorable women.

In the early Brazilian colony, missionary reports, Inquisition records, contemporary histories, and government documents constructed not one but two gender roles for women: the ideals usually proclaimed for all women were in fact directed to elite European-descended women, while Brazilian Indian, African, mixed-race, and poorer Portuguese women found a different set of standards shaping their lives. The differences arose from the economic conditions of the colony and the growing concern, especially between 1550 and 1650, that the social norms of Portugal had not been fostered in Brazil. As Brazil grew prosperous from its sugarcane industry and hence drew increasing attention from imperial ministers, the need for a regulated society was articulated as a need for white women bound within the institution of marriage.[43] Despite the insistent demands, however, few families achieved the ideal of the multigenerational patriarchal family and few women negotiated the narrow path to live as its *dona da casa*.

Brazilindian, African, and mixed-race women or Portuguese women of the lower classes in Brazil found no secular or religious guidebooks to offer advice on their marriages and few preachers to exhort their virtuous submission to their husbands. The ideals for elite white women certainly extended to them, but girls outside of the elite group prepared themselves more for a working life than for a good match. White women of the lower strata and mixed-race women were encouraged to preserve their virginity before marriage but converted Brazilindian women struggled to comply with the religious expectations of early missionaries: the Jesuit José de Anchieta reported with pride in 1554 that one recent Indian convert and his (unnamed) wife "have taken care to keep their daughters virgins."[44] Virginity was not, however, expected of most Brazilindian or African women; slave women were usually perceived as licentious and corrupting, and, when unsupervised or freed, liable to become prostitutes. Colonial men of all classes took advantage of that fiction, and documentary records indicate that Indian and African slave women bore the "natural" children of their married and single male masters. Men confessed to the visiting Inquisition their heretical claims that having sexual relations with unmarried women was no sin, even suggesting—as did Dominguos Pirez in 1618—that it was "no sin for a man to sleep carnally with a black woman if he paid her."[45]

Missionaries separated Brazilindian girls from boys for doctrinal instruction and deprived the girls of the additional education in reading and writing provided to their male counterparts; plans were made but never realized for "virtuous women" to teach girls to sew and spin, so that they might marry converted youths.[46] Among the lower classes and mixed-race families, girls learned to spin, sew, cook, and complete other household production tasks. Such were the skills taught by Branca Dias in Pernambuco in the 1550s. As noted in Chapter 3, she trained girls between the ages of five and fifteen to wash, starch and iron linen, cook, and spin cotton in her own home. The results of her efforts were mixed, for some of her young female students married well among the lower working class, but the women who identified themselves as daughters of immigrant Portuguese men and their Brazilian slaves left their marital status unclear.[47]

Following the Council of Trent, marriage under a priest's blessing was preferred for aspirants to higher position in society, but this was rarer among the lower classes. Women who had some white parentage, especially those whose parents had married, expected formal marriage "before the church doors" with artisans, merchants, sailors, and small landholders. Cultural expectations and church regulations made matrimony for slave women, whether native or African, an elusive goal. Native Brazilindian women were condemned by the missionaries for their "loose morals" but barred from marriage before their conversion to Christianity, while early colonists routinely disregarded the "natural" or consensual marriages of native Brazilians when separating families in order to enslave the adults. African women, who made up less than 40 percent of the slave population, had few opportunities to marry. Slave owners preferred to prevent permanent relationships, especially those blessed by the Church, so that they might sell individual slaves without legal or ecclesiastical reprisals. The colonial government also limited the possibility of marriage for Brazilian Indian women and African women when officials introduced laws stipulating that free men took on the bondage of their wives. The Catholic Church itself made marriage more difficult for impoverished and marginalized women by requiring the publication of banns in the couple's hometowns—a nearly insuperable obstacle for African slaves—and fees for the ceremony.[48]

Still, marriages among slaves and between slave and free blacks provided a fundamental family relationship, especially in rural areas where African and Brazilian-born slaves lived together on larger farms. Alida C. Metcalf discovered that in eighteenth-century Parnaíba, "slaves married without restrictions in the parish churches" and, perhaps uniquely in the New World, they "actually had a marriage rate comparable to that of free persons" in the mid-1700s.[49] In that district, slaves most often married others from the same estate, but some also married free blacks, slaves living nearby, and even Brazilian Indians. Still, since most Brazilian slave owners had fewer than twenty slaves and lived in urban areas, slave women had relatively little opportunity to find and wed a suitable spouse. Instead, they headed small slave households with no support from the white men who typically fathered their children.

Rather than marriage, mixed-race women and native Brazilian women faced long- or short-term consensual unions, such as concubinage or cohabitation with single men (including priests), and clandestine or coercive sexual relationships with married men, as will be explored further below. The sexual exploitation of native Brazilian and slave women was encouraged in several ways by the colonial system; in some parishes, marriage could only be contracted by those women who were baptized and active in the Church, and who had passed a lengthy quiz on Christian doctrine. The resident priests apparently did not discourage concubinage or cohabitation, and the Constitutions of the Archbishop of Bahia of 1707 "closed its eyes" to the sexual relations between landowners and slave women. Jesuit missionaries valued compliance with Catholic doctrine above conformity in relationships for the converted Brazilindians.[50]

While elite families and those aspiring to such status provided dowries, lower-ranking and poor families had little property to grant to their daughters before marriage. The Brotherhood of the Misericórdia in Bahia, however, set aside a small fund for the daughters of freed black women and "unknown" fathers.[51] Few women from families of artisans and small-farm owners might remain cloistered within the home after marriage; since their labor was necessary for family survival, they could not avoid acquaintance with other women and men. Many poorer women—especially in temporary or consensual unions—instead prepared for independent existence as innkeepers, bakers, or "shopkeepers, vendors, peddlers, . . . seamstresses or

laundresses."[52] Since the norms of the Brazilian slave society tied the upbringing of children to their mothers, unmarried or abandoned women
might also expect to be single parents and heads of households; in São
Paulo in the 1789 census, 46 percent of the households were headed by
women.[53] Colonial residents were suspicious of such households, however,
and the Inquisition in Pernambuco accepted charges of witchcraft against
a "woman who has no husband" or of homosexual sins against "a *solteira*
[single woman] with children."[54]

   Married women—rich or poor—might dedicate themselves to appropriate religious devotions and church activities, and find some solace there
from their subjugation. Small sodalities and prayer groups grew around
devout white women, and women of African descent found themselves
welcome in the prestigious lay religious brotherhoods such as Our Lady
of the Rosary in Salvador and Our Lady of Mercies in Minas Gerais. The
Brazilian brotherhood of the Rosary, established for the religious and social
benefit of Afro-Brazilians, admitted all blacks "regardless of social position and sex, both free and slave." Single as well as married women might
be members, and several leadership positions were reserved for married
women. In addition, "female members of the brotherhood played a vital
and essential role in providing social services for brothers and their families
stricken by sickness or poverty."[55]

   For women of the lower classes as for those in the families of plantation owners or colonial governors, the emphasis on the Christian ideal in
literature, sermons, and (one suspects) colonial conversations served to
maintain the illusion of a unified society. At the same time, the restrictions
placed on marriage for poorer, biracial, and enslaved women reserved feminine honor for the elites. The reserve of unmarried and sexually available
women was thus assured for the colonizing enterprise that the political and
religious authorities planned. The increasing efforts to manipulate the roles
for women of the lower strata and restrict them within the virtuous ideal
indicated the growing power that the nonwhite, non-elite Brazilians were
gaining in the colonial society.


CONCUBINES AND COMMON-LAW WIVES


   From the earliest colonial period, missionaries and government officials reported that there were "too few" white women in the Brazilian
colony to provide suitable wives for the predominantly male immigrant
population. The migration of Portuguese men, rather than families, to Bra-

zil and the sexualized image of Brazilian Indian and African women, explored in Chapter 1, increased the likelihood of relations considered illegal or immoral, including bigamy, consensual marriages, and concubinage.[56] As elsewhere in Portuguese imperial colonies, indigenous and enslaved women were exploited as part of the conquest, and impoverished women and those of mixed racial heritage entered casual and even abusive relationships with single and married men in military or government positions or in incipient farming and mining enterprises. The eventual establishment of the colonial order did not introduce legal and stable bonds between partners in illicit relationships or foster the honor of single or married women. Unequal gender roles and marriage expectations set in Portuguese and canon law reduced women's options for matrimony, and colonial institutions reproduced the very conditions that perpetuated such inequalities.

Portuguese law through the sixteenth century acknowledged two types of marriage: marriage "at the doors of the church," and "presumptive marriage," which was often called "*por palavras de presente*" based on the vows spoken by both spouses before witnesses as the intended beginning of their marriage.[57] Couples who had promised to marry might begin to cohabit months or years before the marriage, and this arrangement, though condemned by the Church, was tolerated outside of the highest levels of society as long as the sacrament of matrimony eventually blessed the couple and their children. Even after the 1500s, cohabitation might not be challenged if no public scandal arose, and local civil authorities might not prosecute couples who lived "as if married" without causing public discord. At the same time, the laws concerning concubinage seemingly ignored brief affairs, or even longer-term relationships, if partners did not cohabit—even when priests or married men were involved. Portuguese civil law extended to its colony, and even more informal arrangements may have been tolerated by residents there. Following the Council of Trent, however, religious authorities challenged the popular acceptance of informal and so-called clandestine marriages and affirmed that any sexual activity outside of a sanctified marriage was sinful. Religious laws defined any kind of adultery as concubinage, since any relations between single or married men and unmarried women—whether brief or of long standing—contravened the commandments.[58]

Concubinage was prohibited by the first religious laws written for the Brazilian colony, beginning with a sharp distinction between occasional adultery and the more vilified practice of cohabitation. According to the *Constituiçoens Primeyras* promulgated by Archbishop D. Sebastião Monteiro da Vide in 1707, concubinage consisted in "an illicit relationship of a man with a woman continued for a considerable time."[59] Couples could be denounced by neighbors or authorities, and "those who are guilty . . . of living in concubinage with infamy, scandal, and perseverance in the sin" received first "admonitions and penances," then criminal penalties. If one partner was already married or if the crime continued, the fines increased substantially, and the couple faced "prison, exile, or excommunication."[60] Most women found cohabiting in an unrelated man's house or in a priest's residence were considered concubines, though the definition failed to address the vulnerability of servants and enslaved women. Surprisingly, Vide expressed concern for women's safety, even suggesting covert accusations of concubinage to prevent violent reprisals from fathers or husbands.

The warnings against informal marriage, cohabitation, and concubinage were barely heard by a populace that seemingly avoided the formalities of matrimony. Some working-class and poorer Portuguese men apparently did not hesitate to purchase or live with an Indian or African woman—freed or not—as sexual partner and housekeeper. Similarly, landowners, farmers, and civil officials, even when married with white women, exploited the sexual availability of their female slaves and servants. In most cases, marriage with nonwhite women was out of the question; for poorer men, the fees charged by the priests were prohibitive, and for richer men, marriage was unnecessary or impossible because of wives living in Portugal or the negative effect of a mixed marriage on their own or their sons' social position. Little is recorded of women's reactions to these relationships; the records more often repeat the convenient image of the sensuous woman of color—native, slave, or mixed-race—to excuse their male partners and assign sinful blame to the "concubine."[61]

Such was the response to the mistresses of parish priests in Brazil, as witnessed in the 1707 *Constituiçoens*. Archbishop Vide warned that clerics were to "flee from the company, sight, and activities of women, from which may come ruinous suspicion, thus because they should not give occasion to the devil, but should always guard against falling in to them." He mandated that priests avoid the company of women in convents or in private homes, hire only women over the age of fifty, and dismiss "any female server from whom may come any suspicion or danger, even if she is his own slave." Guilty clerics escaped public disgrace and received only a secret admonishment and fine for their first crime; after that, they might lose part or all of their goods and benefices. Women found guilty of concubinage with the priests, however, fared much worse: "The woman, who has been convinced to go into a sinful state with a clergyman, always will have a greater penalty than she who is in this way with a lay person."[62]

Following the 1707 *Constituiçoens*, denunciations of concubinage swamped some of the local religious courts. As Brazilian scholar Fernando Torres-Londoño discovered, as many as 80 percent of the statements during ecclesiastical visits in Mato Grosso in the late 1700s concerned concubinage, and between 60 and 85 percent of the accusations in Ilhéus and Minas Gerais in the late colonial period featured such crimes.[63] Kathleen Higgins uncovered figures that revealed that colonial Sabará exceeded those figures: over 93.2 percent of denunciants called before the Visitor in 1734 answered for the crime of concubinage. In Sabará, barely 5 percent of the men were married, and only 15 percent were married when the Visitor returned three years later, indicating that "concubinage was thus largely an alternative for marriage."[64] While colonial residents still denounced their neighbors' sins of fornication, adultery, and prostitution during pastoral visits, the "public scandal" of concubinage drew most of the charges. Other scholars have suggested that even birth records in colonial Brazil indicate widespread concubinage in regions where 25 to 65 percent of all live births were registered as "illegitimate."[65] The shifting population of the frontier effaced the records of illicit relations, but in the early 1800s in São Paulo, as many as 80 percent of the accusations made to the ecclesiastical courts named partners in concubinage.[66]

Concubinage touched all levels of society, but across the colony it was mostly unmarried, impoverished, and enslaved women who entered illicit liaisons with older, wealthier men of higher social status. Most women in consensual relations or concubinage were single, but in Mato Grosso and São Paulo, a few justified their concubinage by failures in their marriage: they had been abandoned by their husbands, either temporarily or permanently, or they had decided to separate from their husbands.[67] Their relationships involved priests, single men, or married men, none of whom might choose to marry the African, Indian, or mixed-race women who shared their households. In Minas Gerais, fewer marriages were contracted between unequal partners during the early 1700s, in part owing to the transient, mixed population of the colonial towns. But poverty alone did not determine marital relations: richer men in particular avoided marriage since widows and their children legally inherited family property. White, upper-class men partnered with mixed-race or black women and even recognized their "natural" children as heirs, but failed to extend their wealth and status to mistresses and concubines. Priests, too, kept servants or slaves in concubinage and were thus less likely to denounce the sexual sins of their neighbors.[68]

Concubinage constituted a sort of parallel to legitimate marriage in some regions and some levels of society in colonial Brazil. As Torres-Londoño has argued, this "other family" might have even been "commonplace, accepted by many social strata, tolerated by others and known by the better part of the population, including civil and religious authorities."[69] In the mid-seventeenth century, neither the Church nor the state had the power to identify and eliminate the illicit relationships in the "fluid" society of the frontier or in the upheaval of the mining districts. The Catholic Church had fewer priests and bishops to enforce its will in the colony, so it relied on sporadic ecclesiastical visits and the spiritual penalties and rewards that drove neighborhood spies to denounce those who lived "as if married" and the men who kept an unmarried woman either at home — "*de portas adentro*" — or in an independent household. Where fewer priests officiated, unmarried couples might cohabit for years, even decades, before the declaration came that they were causing a "public scandal," a key notion used by the Church to restrict otherwise private behaviors by identifying them as a threat to the community.[70]

## SLAVERY AND CONCUBINAGE

The development of slavery in Brazil seemed inexorably linked to the sexual abuse of native Brazilian and African women. Such women and their daughters were enslaved and dominated by the male colonizers, and their bodies violated for the benefit of the expansion of the empire. Patterns of inequality interlaced the illicit relations but dominance was always held by the men, such that white men of the elite classes of government officials and landowning families kept native Brazilian, African, or mixed-race slave women as concubines, lower-class white men kept mixed-race, freed, or enslaved concubines, and mixed-race men and freed or slave men had slaves as concubines.[71] Even as they blocked marriages among slaves and between slaves and masters, neither religious nor civil authorities succeeded in restricting the masters' exploitation. Religious condemnations of concubinage resounded from the first through the last colonial century — to little avail, it might seem, given that the priests themselves used their female slaves as concubines.

Jesuit missionaries in the 1540s and 1550s wrote disparagingly of the intemperate and temporary liaisons they found among native Brazilians, but found little virtue in the relationships that they subsequently fostered in the colony. Manuel da Nóbrega first condemned the "great sin" of male immigrants: "almost all of the men cohabit with their [Indian slave women] as concubines, and they ask from other Indian men their free women" to take as wives. When he challenged the practice, Nóbrega reported, "all excuse themselves to me [saying] they have no [white] women to marry."[72] The priests of the colonial cities did the "work of the devil," he complained, for telling the men "that it is licit for them to live in sin with their [Indian slave women], since they are captives"—and for their own sexual misconduct with slave women.[73]

His companion Irmão Pero Correia similarly recounted the entrenched vices among the residents of São Vicente:

> It has been a long-standing custom in this land that married [white] men who have twenty and more women slaves and Indian women take them all as wives, and there were and are husbands with *mamelucas*, who are the daughters of Christian [white] men and Indian women. And they have set that custom at home, such that their very wives with whom they were received at the door of the church bring them their concubines to their beds, and if the women refuse, they beat them severely. And not long ago I remember asking a *mameluca* whose Indian slave women she was taking along with her; and she responded that they were the wives of her husband, whom she always took with her and over whom she watched like an abbess with her nuns.[74]

After only three years of religious endeavor, however, Correia triumphantly announced that women in his church no longer tolerated such treatments or the threats that accompanied them.

Rather than separate the women from their partners, Nóbrega, Corriea, and other Jesuits first demanded that couples found in concubinage marry, but met with resistance from white men who refused to marry their slaves. Because of the widespread "misinformation" that marriage to a free man conferred freedom on an Indian slave woman, colonists fought church efforts to sanctify their illicit relationships, seeing a loss of profitability in the change in status. Nóbrega wrote to his superiors in Portugal asking that they contact the king on his behalf to "mandate that the masters be disabused of this, that married slave women do not become free" when they marry. Nóbrega assured them that since slavery was such "a profitable thing for these parts," the white masters of the colony would not marry unless they kept their wives in bondage.[75] In similar cases, José de Anchieta preferred that male colonists abandon their partners:

Much fruit has been gained, for some contract marriages with their slave concubines; and others are beginning to live on the path to salvation, separating themselves from them. In this shines above others the virtue of a great and noble gentleman who has joined the right path to salvation, repudiating the concubine with whom he had lived for a long time and with whom he had children.[76]

With no protection from the church or from civil law, Indian servants and slave women continued to be the victims of sexual dominance wielded by more powerful men, including priests. As part of her 1591 confession to the visiting Tribunal of the Portuguese Inquisition in Salvador, Bahia, for example, Isabel Marquez identified herself as the daughter of Canon Diogo Marques and "Isabel, an Indian woman of this land." More explicit evidence is provided in a later statement by the Canon Jacome de Queiros in which he confessed that he had raped two minor girls. Under the influence of alcohol, as he put it, he had assaulted a young *mameluca* slave girl who sold fish in the afternoons, and later he raped his own slave Esperança whom he subsequently sold.[77] In those same records, seventeen of the confessants identified themselves as "*mamelucos*" or "*mamelucas*," that is, as the sons or daughters of white men and Indian women. Five men explained that they were the sons of a white man and his Brazilian Indian slave, while six confessants specified that their white fathers had been married to their Indian mothers.[78] In Pernambuco in the 1590s, Salvador de Albuquerque confessed to the visiting Inquisitor that he had attempted to persuade "various Indian women" to have sexual relations with him by claiming that there was no mortal sin in consensual sex outside of marriage. He added that most seemed to understand that it was indeed sinful excepting "two women, Antônia and Filipa, Brazilian slaves of his brother Joao de Albuquerque, who it seemed to him, being more simple, could have believed it not to be a sin as he told them." He admitted that he knew the act to be mortal sin, and that he had only said this to the women "to ingratiate himself." His efforts were foiled by at least one woman, for he also admitted that he had propositioned "Pelônia Ramalho, a single woman of the world," who had only mocked him for his efforts.[79]

As Visitor to Maranhão in the early 1600s, Antônio Vieira recognized that matrimony brought little remedy to the "common" problem of concubinage for the native Brazilian women. In his experience, few masters or free white men would marry their Indian concubines or permit them to marry other slaves. As for marriage between free Indian men and enslaved Indian women, he admitted that "under the name of matrimony these marriages come to be a sort of captivity," since husbands were forced to serve their wives' masters; to avoid these "grave problems," he admonished missionaries that they carefully instruct the men so they would not be tricked.[80] In the seventeenth century, however, increasing numbers of African slave women in Brazil were similarly trapped into sexual relations with their white masters. In the Inquisition records of 1618, for example, three men of Bahia who identified themselves as "mulattos" were born of white fathers and—in their words—"captive women." João Fernandes, a "free mulato," was the son of Portuguese Anrique Fernandes and the "single black captive woman" Catherina da Costa. Joseph Fernandes was a "mulato" slave, son of Martim Fernandes and his master's slave Anna. Bento, the "captive of Pero Garçia," was the son of an unnamed *mameluco* and his master's slave Francisca.[81]

Even the exacting lists of sins in the *Constituiçoens* of the Archbishop of Bahia failed to include the sexual exploitation by slave masters of female slaves, although it condemned cohabitation among whites and among slaves. Vide warned that concubinage among slaves required "prompt remedy, though it is usual and almost common [custom] among all to leave them in the state of condemnation, which they, owing to their coarseness and misery, do not heed." Masters could not impose penalties themselves, but were to admonish their slaves, and arrange for them to "leave their illicit affair, and ruinous state, or by means of marriage, (which conforms better to the Law of God and their masters may not impede them in it, without a very grave burden on their souls,) or for another that might be convenient." The religious authorities, however, could imprison or exile slaves who persisted in such sins without considering the losses that their masters might incur.[82] In that same canon, in Book 1, Title 71, "On the Marriage of Slaves," Vide mandated that "according to Divine and human law, male and female slaves may marry with other captive, or free, persons and their masters may not impede the marriage" by threats of removal or sale. The same penalties befell slaves and masters alike when such marriages were thwarted, especially when slaves lived in immoral conditions.[83]

At nearly the same time, Jesuit moralist Jorge Benci in his *Economia cristã dos senhores no governo dos escravos* (*Christian Economy for Masters in the Governance of Slaves*) argued that slaves who "lapsed" after marriage were no more "brutish" than their errant masters, and that matrimony and the other sacraments should not be withheld from the enslaved: "Have them marry, when they wish; that in this way you will satisfy your obligation. And if after being bound by Holy matrimony, they are corrupted; call them . . . to give an account to God of their sins." Once married, slaves must not be further impeded by masters "separating the husband from the wife and leaving one in the house, and ordering the sale or residence of the other in parts so remote that they cannot have a conjugal life."[84] This would have been equivalent to divorce, a concession rarely granted by the Church. He went further than Archbishop Vide, astutely criticizing the masters for their sinful example: "How can one persuade them to live a restrained and chaste life, seeing that the master keeps a concubine in his own house, and however much that same master may teach them that God wants them to remain chaste?" Even worse, he concluded, was the man who abused his own slave:

> Is it not a scandal, and the most abominable in the eyes of God, for the master to establish a relationship with his slave woman? And is it not even worse and more abominable, to oblige her by force to consent to sin with her master, and punish her when it is repugnant to her and she wishes to end this offense to God? No Catholic would deny this. And should the master expect to be saved who does this? . . . What we must say that besides eternal punishment, with which they merit to be punished in the next life those masters who so violate and oblige their slaves to sin, even in this they merit the temporal death imposed by common law and the particular law of Portugal on all those who violently or in another manner force and oblige women to sin of whatever quality they are, even those who are vulgarly called worldly women?[85]

Despite the efforts made by slave owners and Catholic priests to block their legitimate marriages, slaves lived together as couples and, rarely, as family units. In some situations, as reported by the Jesuit André João Antonil in 1711, plantation owners simply mandated the arrangements: "Some masters . . . not only ignore their cohabitation, but start it, saying: You, so-and-so, in your time you marry so-and-so; and from then on they allow them to live as if they were received as husband and wife."[86] During the 1700s, however, lopsided sex ratios, especially among African-born slaves, made family constitution difficult: in the sugar plantation regions the ratio of men to women reached 2 to 1 while some areas in Minas Gerais found ratios of 9 to 1.[87] When marriage was possible, slaves from Africa at first tended to marry other Africans, particularly within their own ethnic groups, while Brazilian-born slaves married among themselves or with mixed-race slaves. By the end of the century, marriages crossed ethnic lines but few slaves married or managed to develop stable relationships. Where slave families formed, they were headed by single mothers who bore the children of their African or mixed-race companions or their white masters. While the "high mortality rate of slaves in all age groups broke up families" and left mothers bereft, the potential benefits of a possible marriage, including legitimacy and inheritance, led slave women to endure or even encourage relationships with the higher-status white men.[88]

## COMMON-LAW WIVES AND PROSTITUTES

Given the dominance of male immigrants and slave owners and the rigidity of religious edicts, it is not surprising that one finds little evidence of cohabitation among equals in colonial Brazil. The proofs and ceremonies demanded by the Council of Trent, the scarcity of the clergy in frontier regions, and even the great distances within the colony led women to create long-term relationships without the benefit of ecclesiastical sanctions. Cohabitation was "a commonplace relationship and, as such, accepted" among a wide range of women despite the efforts by the Catholic Church to define all extramarital sexual activity as "sinful" and maintain the paradoxical demands that all illicit sexual activity end without "altering the prerequisites for marriage."[89] The impoverished and marginalized sectors of the population—designated the *desclassificados* or "declassified" by Brazilian historians in the 1990s—had little means to marry and establish families, so single and widowed women established independent households and provided a stable home for their children, children's partners, grandchildren, and other relations.[90]

The working poor resorted to marriage sanctioned by the Catholic Church when needed or possible, but consensual unions were relations of expedience at every level of society. While younger or poorer women might live with a lover because of affection or need, older women found fewer reasons to sanctify the relationship through the sacrament of matrimony. Women of the elite families could cohabit with their partners when marriage was promised or postponed, but faced the loss of their financial independence at the doors of the church. Widows might even avoid marriage when the law mandated that they forfeit control of their inherited property to a new husband; some wealthy women instead simply invited a prospective mate for lengthy "visits," without much harm to their honor or reputation. When marriage was impracticable, free women typically cohabited with free men, but, as noted previously, many temporary and even consensual relationships involved women with socially superior men, leaving slave, freed, and mixed-race women more vulnerable to violence and abandonment. Some elite men, with spouses in Portugal or little to lose in status or honor, even found consensual relations preferable to the legal entanglements of matrimony. And white women, even of an elevated social status, might enter longer-term consensual unions with members of clergy who, despite the rules of celibacy, subsequently petitioned the Portuguese Crown to legitimate their "sacrilegious children" and claimed their own "human weakness" and folly to excuse the years of lapses.[91]

Prostitution in colonial Brazil was condemned by religious and civil authorities as the erosion of the moral order, and brothels denounced as the refuges of dissolute women and decadent courtesans, but the stark reality for prostitutes was harsh indeed. With only the most meager means for survival, poor and marginalized women, especially in the mining regions of colonial Minas Gerais, turned to prostitution to support themselves and their families. Brazilian scholar Luciano Figueiredo discovered that despite the idealized "chastity of women of the privileged social class," or perhaps because of it, mixed-race women, freed black women, and poor Portuguese women established brothels in the cities, towns, and villages of the colony, where they might live, work, and raise their children.[92] With few prospects for marriage for most of the dispossessed population, "prostitution represented . . . an accessible alternative in which free mulatas and black women, and more rarely white women, might guarantee the means for their own immediate survival and that of their dependents."[93]

For too many, concubinage came to be associated with the practice of prostitution, so that the illicit relations of women who could not marry lapsed into their exploitation by other men. Witness the church court case against Joana da Costa in Vila do Príncipe in 1756: an unmarried woman, freed and of mixed-racial parentage, she had lived for years with one man, but it was "'public knowledge and notorious' that she also went with other men."[94] Prostitution grew alongside the other small business enterprises conducted by women and continued in the women-centered households they maintained, though some were pushed into prostitution by parents, step-parents, and even their own legitimate husbands. There, according to Portuguese civil law and the *Constituiçoens Primeyras*, was the beginning of criminal behavior, for though prostitution itself was not a crime, forcible sexual relations, establishment of a brothel, and profiting from prostitution were all illegal.[95]

Accusations of prostitution followed independent women, especially when they were associated with other censured behavior, such as theft, fraud, or witchcraft. Women banished from Portugal for witchcraft might find themselves repeatedly accused of that crime after they had resettled in Brazil — and of prostitution as well. In 1610, Maria Barbosa was denounced by "numerous witnesses" for her multiple offenses as "a troublesome citizen and poor Christian." Exiled from Évora as a witch and brothel-keeper, she was accused of beguiling residents of Rio de Janeiro while she dishonored her husband as "mistress to many men." She was even accused of inducing a young Isabel Roiz to join her household and accompany her to liaisons with wealthy men.[96]

Slavery also fostered prostitution, since slave owners forced their female slaves to accept sexual relations with the family's guests or kin, provide sex for pay for unrelated males, or even take to the streets to solicit customers. Assenting to contemporary preconceptions, slave owners attributed lasciviousness and lax morals to slave women of African descent, and thereby excused their own complicity in this exploitative work. In colonial Minas Gerais, the church records of 1753 provide two examples of this sort: Manuel da Silva was accused of forcing his female slaves to work longer hours for the expected wages of sin and bragging of his growing wealth, and Maria Franca rebuffed criticisms of the prostitution of her slaves by arguing that she lived well by their earnings and simply met the demands of local men. Procuring prostitutes or renting space for their activities was also lucrative for slave owners, who might even lease the slave quarters as a brothel.[97]

By the early 1700s, Portuguese and Brazilian authors warned of the mistreatment of female slaves and the dangers that their imperiled morals presented to other women. Writing in 1704, Nuno Marques Pereira chastised the plantation owners for their own covert immorality and then advised against allowing the "virtuous daughter" to associate with a "dishonest slave woman": "And what more (I might ask) would a public prostitute have than a dishonest slave woman? . . . . I have seen little girls of nine and ten years of age already lost: and when they do not soon sin, yet they are going to learn" to commit such outrages.[98] Jorge Benci tallied multiple offenses committed by careless or wicked masters who took little notice of the practices of prostitution among their own slave women. He proclaimed his astonishment over masters who cared little for the scandals created by slaves who came and went freely from their houses "at whatever hour of the day, whether night or day, knowing that that will result in many offenses to God," or who reproached their slaves who seemed less industrious but who preserved their little virtue thereby.[99]

Benci reproached those who created the most oppressive conditions by demanding payments from their own slaves, "distributing among them the sustenance of the house, and charging to each her portion! To one the flour or bread for the table, to another the meat or the fish for the plate; another must pay the rents." Benci asked them:

> Where must your slaves search, to satisfy these payments? Perhaps they have some income, from which they might take that which you order and impose upon them to pay? Certainly not. Then where will they turn, if not to sin and the shameful use of their bodies? And supporting yourselves with this filthy lucre and with these sins; what are you but a living and active sinner [yourselves]?

Even this was not the final outrage, Benci wrote, for "the scandals of the slave masters of Brazil do not stop there; for they are not content to induce, counsel, consent, and even order their slaves to sin, they go much further, obliging them with punishment or threats that they offend God, and fail to keep his precepts."[100]

With less concern for slave owners' culpability, André João Antonil offered the briefest of references to prostitution in his account of management of sugarcane plantations. Though he deemed *mulato* slaves more tractable than any others, he warned that their intemperate emotions might lead them to rebellion or worse: "To free unquiet *mulatas* is manifest perdition, for the money that they give to free themselves rarely comes from sources other than their own bodies, through repeated sins; and, once freed, they continue to be the ruin of many."[101]

MARRIAGE AND RELIGIOUS DISCOURSE IN THE
EIGHTEENTH AND NINETEENTH CENTURIES

After the first colonial century, little beyond confirmation of gender stereotypes may be found in religious and historical literature. Portuguese or Brazilian chroniclers such as Ambrósio Fernandes Brandão (writing in 1618) and Domingos do Loreto Couto (in 1757) typically reported little of Portuguese women's lives in the colony and their few statements were more likely to be generalizations about elite women rather than critical historical information. Thus, Brandão retold a Jesuit story about the employment of a "very virtuous" married woman in the catechizing of Brazil-indian women, while Couto provided lists of women accounted virtuous for their gentle demeanor, chastity, and religious devotion.[102] Even Luís Vilhena, who offered insightful details of life in the colonial capital in 1802, repeated the standard condemnations of white women for their luxury and of black women for their seduction of young white men.[103]

Two important sources for the later era, André João Antonil in 1710 and Nuno Marques Pereira in 1725, continued the religious tradition articulated a century earlier by Navarro and Vieira and provided just a few details of quotidian life alongside their reiterations of the ideal for chaste girls who might become obedient and faithful married women. Antonil, as noted above, stressed the duties of the plantation owners to govern their slaves and women, and to ensure the limits of each in a defined role. Patriarchs had few reciprocal duties beyond providing dowries for their daughters and restrictions for their wives. Wives, by contrast, might corrupt or bankrupt the prudent managers of their estates by usurping the governance of a plantation or sending funds to quiet the pleadings of a spendthrift son. Children would find the "best education" in their own parents' behavior and the "most secure rest" in the estate proper to each; for a daughter, then, the secluded existence of a virtuous wife was both her model and her due. Social propriety and Christian virtue still demanded the separation of the sexes, and Antonil insisted that male guests be housed apart from the family and servants, even in isolated plantations. Their presence would then prove no "obstacle for the family" and not "disturb the seclusion in which must be kept the wives and daughters and house servant girls occupied in the preparation of lunch and supper."[104]

In his fictionalized account of a "Pilgrim" traveling through the middle regions of the Brazilian colony, Pereira pulled back the curtains on turbulent family life in colonial Brazil while his protagonist provided trenchant advice to plantation owners on their wives and daughters. As reported in Chapter 3, Pereira determined that the foundation for such advice was "Divine precept" which, like "Civil Law," required obedience from women: "a woman may not even cut the hair of her head without the license and authority of her husband."[105] Marriage, he reminded a concerned father, was instituted by God for Adam and Eve and saved the souls of all who enter its sacramental state:

> God with his presence authorized the first state of marriage in the world: to show us the great excellences and perfections that are contained in it, and the obligations, that married persons have, to live according to divine precepts, uniting them both in one sole will, establish-

ing it in many diverse and copious virtues, showing themselves grateful to one Lord, who so honors them with his presence, and so sustains them and favors them with his providence and will.[106]

Obedience and duty rather than passion or pleasure drew the faithful to marriage, but agreement in wealth, status, and "inclinations" allowed the growth of appropriate affection.[107]

In the tales that Pereira recounted, women were responsible for their own and for men's failings and were advised to accept the most restricted existence for the development of virtue. Since husbands "jealous of their honor" suspected adultery when they glimpsed "the least reduction" in their wives' proper seclusion at home, wives must redouble their efforts to protect themselves against their imagined flaws and actual proclivities. Adulterous women brought miserable deaths to their lovers and their husbands through their deceptions, while the "precepts of God" freed women and men for contented lives.[108] Concubinage and other illicit relations with slave women led only to sin and death, for murder and even suicide might result from the evil conflicts with their masters and with women themselves. Pereira warned that the married couple and their children suffered from the scandal, but the slave women themselves only gained in "daring" from their apparently elevated state. A man tempted by concubinage might turn from sin to marriage with a poor but honorable woman, Pereira contended, and cling to her as to "a plank in a shipwreck."[109]

Pereira's counsel to women reiterated that of previous authors, and he barely balanced his presumption of feminine iniquity with exhortations of integrity. A virtuous matron should, in his view, flee all occasion of sin, give no cause for mistrust, and, finally, prefer to "lose her life, [rather] than violate the virtue of chastity, that she so loved." Lest she fall at the "pawning of her honor," the married woman should accept no gifts, live strictly within her own means, and dress modestly. She might indulge in no friendships with other women and no casual conversations with men other than her own husband, and only respect the clergy from "some distance," for while they were "supposed to be comparable to Angels, it has happened many times, [that] from the path of virtue they entered the street of evil."[110] In personal relations, Pereira warned,

> married women must be strong, discreet, and prudent: in their homes, prudent; outside of them, modest; and on all occasions, exemplary; and more prizing of suffering than of irritations, because for the most part all the disorders, that happen between married couples, are due to the

lack of [tolerance for] suffering and impertinent jealousies, because from words they go to disputes, from disputes to shouts, from shouts to threats, from threats to blows, and from blows to deaths.[111]

His last words underscored the physical dangers that followed the violations of divine law and personal codes of honor. Virtuous women could not "speak ill of their husbands in the presence of others," for fear of offending God and inciting their husbands' righteous vengeance. In this regard, women could not be like a "rock" struggling to overcome the "sea" that is her husband, for he would wear her down to a pebble. Instead, she should be "navigable" even in the tempestuous storms so that the sea might bring her "through a safe journey to the port of salvation." Pereira completed his advice to docile matrons with two anecdotes, "one lamentable and the other humorous." In the first case, a long-suffering husband confronted his noisy and jealous wife, and "since the wife did not wish to accommodate him, the man took up a cutlass and with blows and stabs killed her." In the second case, the humor all but eluded the narrator, for he described the failures of a weak wife to accede to her husband's demands. When she threatened to drown herself in a nearby lake, she was astounded that no one came to prevent her, for the rest of the household dutifully followed his absolute commands. She "returned to the house, and from that time on lived much in accord with her husband."[112] Such quiet devotion was preferable to immoderate love in Pereira's view. He concluded that "women should occupy themselves in good practices and not be jealous. Be very devoted to our Virgin Lady, for this is the best means, that a creature might find, to preserve chastity and free oneself from dangers."[113]

The criticism of married women in the late colonial discourse from Portuguese and Brazilian writers was duplicated by the first foreigners to travel widely in Brazil after 1750. Little encouragement was offered by the French and British authors in their accounts of the dissipation of the Brazilian elite. Their disdain for the lives and attitudes of colonial women was reflected by the few facts and fewer compliments in reports that criticized customs as decadence, hinted at indecency, and anticipated little intelligence or sense from women living in Brazil. One such account was written by Mrs. Nathaniel E. Kindersley, an English traveler on her way to Calcutta, who visited Salvador, Bahia, in 1764, but had little opportunity to meet and talk with Brazilian matrons during her short stay there. Her letters indicate not only her persistent curiosity about "nunneries" and the domestic arrangements of those "Portuguese ladies" kept from her, but also a readiness to censure them.[114]

Based on the reports gleaned from other residents, Kindersley concluded that while women in Brazil were "brought up in indolence, and their minds uncultivated, their natural quickness shews itself in cunning." Mistrust and prejudice led only to further evils, she insisted, and women's defects resulted from the failings of Portuguese men and the perversions of colonial society: "As their male relations do not place any confidence in their virtue, they in return use their utmost art to elude the vigilance with which they are observed; and to speak the most favorably, a spirit of intrigue reigns amongst them. Were I to tell you what the darkness of the evening conceals . . . , it would look like a libel on their sex."[115] After the insinuations that their sexual lives were immoral, Kindersley provided ambivalent descriptions that similarly hinted at corruption in the female sex. She admired the "delicate features" of younger women, but added that their sallow complexions were "disagreeable" and they "look old very early in life." And while she acknowledged that their attire was "calculated for a hot climate," she nonetheless criticized the layers of clothing "without any stays" and "massive" quantity of gold jewelry assembled for formal attire.[116]

After the turn of the century, travelers' accounts added little to these judgments beyond surprise when their own experiences called them into question. John Mawe was astonished to meet several married women during his mineralogical expeditions to the state of Rio de Janeiro in 1809, but mocked those who avoided him: "The few females we occasionally saw at any former place generally secluded themselves" and even "ran away" from him "as if they had been accustomed to be frightened at the name of an Englishman." During his visit to the home of Captain Rodrigo da Lima, he discussed clothing fashions and cooking with the wife and daughter of his host and commended their conversation as "gay and enlivening." Disappointed that the "lady of the house" apparently took little interest in "housewifery," he offended her by praising her supervision of "domestic work," but concluded that the evening with them was passed "agreeably."[117]

The British traveler John Luccock, who spent the years from 1808 to 1818 in Brazil, offered the same critical particulars as did other reporters: Brazilian women were poorly educated, ill-mannered, oddly dressed, and indolent. He considered their behaviors with him "sly and coquettish" and contrasted the pleasing attributes of girls with the unfortunate flaws of matrons a few years older: a woman was "corpulent" at twenty, and "at twenty-five, or thirty at the most, she becomes a perfectly wrinkled old woman."[118] He explained that women's failings might be attributed to their seclusion and repression, but nonetheless blamed them for surrendering their lives to the dominant customs. Ladies of the leading families only ventured out-of-doors to attend religious services and then swathed themselves in heavy cloaks for privacy; at home, they remained seated while attendants brought them food or drink as required. Their few accomplishments were spinning, lace-making, and occasionally directing the cooking of desserts. Luccock, who found little to admire in Brazilian society, concluded that a woman's "constitution [was] enfeebled and ruined by inactivity" and her intelligence checked by patriarchs who treated girls and women alike as "dolls, or spoiled children."[119]

Two quite different accounts emerged from the voyages of Captain Louis de Freycinet, the first from author Jacques Arago and the second from Rose de Freycinet herself, but both found fault with the morality of married women in the colony. Arago had little good to say of the residents of Rio de Janeiro from his brief layover there in 1817, but found women over-dressed with so little style that they reminded him "of those old-fashioned dolls" found in English millinery shops. Their choices failed to hide their "sallow complexions," which he observed during a "procession" of ladies in the street. On the streets and in church, he complained, the women of elite families seldom wore "hats or bonnets" and seemed irreverent at religious services, where they avoided the few seats available so that they might instead display their best attire. After castigating the ladies for their vanity, Arago derided the "public prostitutes" of Rio de Janeiro for their boldness and, oddly, their rebuffs of potential customers. He claimed that they were "disgustingly ugly," but added that, like "honest women whose husbands are absent," they hid themselves deep within heavy velvet cloaks.[120]

Rose de Freycinet accompanied her husband on his travels and, like Arago, encountered a few respectable ladies in Rio de Janeiro. She was, however, slightly more generous in her assessment. She frankly acknowledged that she "did not have an opportunity to meet any Portuguese women" during her visits to various homes there, but had observed them in the religious "spectacles" she attended. Given that "they are allowed to leave their homes only to go to church," she found little fault beyond their primary shortcoming: "Their main concern is to be attractive rather than to pray to God." She noted the "beauties" in attendance and the popularity of the nighttime festivals, but, without further acquaintance, could only add a single anecdote, concerning the refusal of a washing bowl, to bolster the prejudice that the elite women of Brazil were self-centered and "generally lacking in personal hygiene."[121]

From these later sources come uneven accounts of women's behavior in marriage, and silence concerning concubinage and common-law spouses. Portuguese and Brazilian chroniclers offered specific advice for the patriarchal ideal that instituted control over daughters and wives; still, they extended their criticisms from women to the failings of the patriarchs themselves. Here, the first widely published writings by foreign travelers revealed much more about the expectations and prejudices of the authors than about their Brazilian subjects. In the local and European sources alike, elite white women were still expected to restrict their lives to their do- mestic confines. Poorer women repeatedly fell short of the ideal when they attempted to provide subsistence for their families, and African women, whether slave or freed, furnished characteristics for the very opposite of the ideal in their behaviors and traits.

CONCLUSION

The religious discourse articulated for the Brazilian colony attempted the creation of a single ideal for women, with the expectation that a good Christian woman perpetuated her own and her family's honor by remain- ing virginal before marriage, marrying a suitable spouse in her youth, and effacing her social presence though her preoccupations in the domes- tic sphere. The attempt failed to shape lives much beyond those of a few governing families in the colonial elite, for women outside of that lofty circle simply could not presume to attain that ideal. Indeed, the further marginalized their origins, the further removed were women from such expectations: poor, mixed-race, and enslaved women could not remain virgins, marry, or withdraw from the public sphere. The slave culture of colonial Brazil made nearly every aspect of the married ideal unobtainable for women outside of the elite families, yet still condemned these women for their deficiencies.

The common theme of the writings during the first two colonial cen- turies was that the ideal for women compelled them to marry, so that what might have been a call for a return to morality or a restatement of medieval values instead became insistence on marriage, articulated by those most observant of what they felt to be the dangers in the social reorganization of the colony. Vives, Melo, Navarro, and Vieira all warned that each woman — even the Queen of England — must exercise personal restraint, guard against incursions from without, and maintain constant watch against trai- torous thoughts. Control over social chaos, then, could be gained through laws, or at least endless rules, that codified the religious norms for women in exacting detail and created the safeguards that might carry the dominant classes through the turbulent era. By the end of the colonial period, chroniclers detailed the wrenching effects of the disintegration of such norms, so that Benci, Antonil, and Pereira rehearsed the failures of the ideal married woman in misalliances, adultery, concubinage, prostitution, and death. Efforts to attain and preserve women's honor barely achieved that goal, and foreign visitors ridiculed both those who managed it and those who did not.

From the 1500s through the early 1800s, the representatives of the Catholic Church itself delivered mixed messages to Brazilian residents. While Portuguese common law permitted fewer formalities in the establishment of marriage-centered households, Church officials under the edicts of the Council of Trent instituted the most restrictive conditions for sacramental marriage—and then regularly waived them for some petitioners who could not post banns in their previous residences, find sufficient witnesses for their single status, or locate a priest to sanctify a relationship. Other petitioners were granted stipulated exceptions to marry a near relative, legitimize their "natural" children, or contract marriage before the legal age. At the same time, the Church escalated its penalties for sexual sins with the earliest church rules, the 1707 *Constituiçoens Primeyras* of Archbishop Vide, which condemned concubinage and adultery and endorsed the imprisonment of women denounced as prostitutes and concubines. The results were even deeper divisions in colonial society and corruption within its institutions: plantation owners and government officials could buy their way out of religious or civil judgments while forcing women, both elite and otherwise, to pay for their sins.

In *Casa grande e senzala* [*The Masters and the Slaves*], Brazilian sociologist Gilberto Freyre portrayed the results of the matrimonial expectations for plantation-owning families and the white urban elite as detrimental at every level of society. The daughters and wives of the governing classes lived stiflingly confined lives, isolated in their homes as if in a cloister or harem, bound to preserve their family and personal honor through chaste maidenhood, early marriage, debilitating pregnancies and childbirth, lost health, and early death. Native Brazilian women and African slave women embodied natural but depraved sensuality in this scenario, for while some nursed and raised the offspring of their masters, others were sexually exploited as the mistresses for the youth and *senhores* of the same family. But in Freyre's account, neither the sensuous *mulata* nor the sexually exploitative "white lad of the slave-owning class" were blamed for their corrupt morality. Rather than place responsibility for the fragmentation of social and familial bonds on the lapsed priests or abusive male colonists, Freyre faulted the "Brazilian patriarchal system," citing the "enormous capacity of that system for morally degrading masters and slaves alike."[122]

A sharper criticism of the "system," however, must begin with the exploitation of women from the earliest moments of colonization and cannot excuse those who benefited from it. Marriage was reserved for the elite, the property owners and the governing families, and restricted to them by elaborate laws and customs so that "only the dominant classes considered Catholic marriage a social requirement."[123] By the end of the colonial era, matrimony seemed to be a marker of social superiority, but unmarried couples continued informal relations, and concubinage in itself entailed neither immorality nor promiscuity. Throughout this era, the virtues demanded of married women, especially fidelity, were not demanded of married men but could be discovered among those with no legal bonds whatsoever. Married women might still be admired, but not to the extent that historians have proposed, and marriage "was not the bond that held together the family," as can be seen in records such as the 1804 census in Vila Rica, Minas Gerais. There, as Donald Ramos concluded, the numerical dominance of women-headed households suggested "the need to reevaluate the role and status of women in traditional Brazilian society."[124] There, while some women barely survived under the burdens of the married ideal, many lived successfully at the edges of the ideal, and many more thrived just beyond its reach.

AUTHOR'S NOTE: The preliminary interpretations in this chapter were first published, in a significantly different form, in "Bounded Identities: Women and Religion in Colonial Brazil, 1550–1750," *Religion* 28 (1998): 329–337.

# FIVE

# Freiras *and* Recolhidas

## THE RECLUSIVE LIFE

## FOR BRAZILIAN WOMEN

I n Rio de Janeiro in 1756, Thiodara Francisca Evangelista formally petitioned the Convent of Nossa Senhora da Conceição da Ajuda to admit her daughter, Thereza Rosa, as a pupil "until she reaches the age to decide whether to profess as a nun." To support her case, Dona Thiodara explained that the girl's father had died in the Lisbon earthquake while attempting to secure her a place in a convent there, and her aunt was already a professed nun in the convent. At the same time, she offered a twelve-year-old companion, an impoverished "Mariana" who could "serve while in the company of the said nun."[1] With this request, seven-year-old Thereza Rosa might anticipate an honorable future outside of marriage but still within the bounds of social expectations for elite white women. Dona Thiodara's letter reveals that the social and economic circumstances of a family, rather than the religious proclivities of the entrant, might lead women to the religious houses of colonial Brazil.

Women's motives for entering the convents and *recolhimentos* of colonial Brazil and the rationales for founding those cloistered houses are complex and interwoven, and most historians opt for one of two paradigms in their overall analyses, stressing either the social or the religious dimensions of conventual life. Social historians have emphasized the political and economic concerns that drove the leading families in Brazil to petition for the creation of religious houses. Women who entered, either willingly or compelled by family interests, must then have accepted the practical necessity of their celibate and cloistered life and reaped the additional benefits of independence and education. Religious or ecclesiastical historians, whose views dominated Brazilian history through the mid-twentieth century, have underscored the virtues of the religious life and its less tangible

rewards for the saintly women who pursued it. In my own research, I have
found each perspective to be incomplete, and together the two may mask
the complexity of women's lives and choices in the colony. For this chapter,
then, I will hold in abeyance the interpretations centered on the institutions of colonial Brazil and consider instead what I deem central to understanding the reclusive life: the motives expressed by women themselves.
More than a few documents remain from the colonial era that contain
statements from women who sought to be or were recluses, sisters, and professed nuns. In those petitions, letters, and reports, they demanded entry
into the sacred enclosures so that they might pursue the devotional life
*and* — in nearly the same texts — escape the burdens of the secular world.
I will begin this chapter with women's motives for the religious life, and
then turn, in subsequent sections, first to the founding of *recolhimentos*
in colonial Brazil and the rules established for their residents, and then to
the founding of convents and the rules for professed nuns. This chapter
includes a full, if brief, history of the primary cloisters of the colony, but
viewed from the perspective of the women who sought to enter, reform,
and leave them.

Most girls and women in colonial Brazil, like seven-year-old Thereza
Rosa and her mother, expected to live in perpetual relationships controlled
by men — with their fathers as they grew up, with their legal or common-law
husbands as adults, and with their sons as they aged. Enslaved women also
found their fate determined by male, not female, owners and managers. In
the upper classes, daughters, sisters, and wives of property owners, colonial
government officials, military officers, and skilled workers might also spend
a significant portion of their lives behind the walls of temporary or permanent cloisters, as residents of a retirement house (*recolhimento*) or convent.
Even there, their relationships were primarily governed by the men who
established the residences, allocated funds to support them, and decided
which girls and women might reside there. The rationale for women's religious enclosure, as for their education, was that they thus served their male
relatives and their Father God and Jesus.

As noted in previous chapters, the colonial Brazilian discourse concerning the proper lives for women centered on the ideal role as Christian wife and mother. If that ideal was not yet achieved or was somehow
disallowed, women might also accept another honorable estate, living in
seclusion apart from marriage and families. The primary institution for this
was the cloistered convent, the *convento* or *mosteiro* for cloistered nuns,
which devout women of the elite social classes might enter for life. *Recolhimentos*, or retirement houses, were less formal structures created for

either the proper seclusion and education of girls in preparation for their own later marriages or vows as nuns, or the informal religious life of a few older women, especially widows, who might spend their last years in seclusion and prayer. In practice, however, many convents often included girls as students, married women in residence, and a few older women, while *recolhimentos* were often begun where convents were not yet allowed by government and ecclesiastical license.

For the first two centuries of the Brazilian colony, only one formal convent for women was permitted by the imperial Portuguese government and approved by papal decree. The restrictions in Brazil did not extend to other Portuguese colonies, and Spanish colonies had no such limits. By the time of Brazil's first convent—Santa Clara do Desterro in Salvador, Bahia, in 1677—twenty-eight formal convents had been founded in Mexico, and a total of more than seventy formal convents had been created in the Spanish colonies. In other Portuguese territories, royal decrees had sanctioned thirteen convents in the islands of the Azores, with another four on the island of Madeira by the year 1690.[2] The religious circumstances of Brazil were not significantly different, but its social and economic situation clearly prohibited cloistering for more than a few white elite women.

In the sixteenth century, despite the hopes of would-be founders, the Brazilian colony lacked both the workers and the wealth needed to construct the buildings and endow and maintain the comfortable lives for the residents of cloisters. The colony barely produced enough to sustain its own immigrant population after paying fees and taxes owed to the Portuguese Crown, and through the middle of the seventeenth century the imperial government insisted that the establishment of a large and predominantly white Portuguese population was essential to the success of the colony. Only the growth of the sugar industry through the 1600s and the emergence of mineral extraction—especially gold—in the 1700s brought sufficient capital and population to permit the seclusion of elite women in religious houses.

It is nevertheless surprising that Portugal's indisputably Roman Catholic culture failed to establish religious centers for women in the new colony. While men's devotion had varied outlets, the colonial norms limited women's spirituality beyond church attendance to a few private devotions. Women still sought new modes of spiritual expression, either at home or in small informal or larger formal communities, and attempted not just to join but also to inaugurate religious groups. I will explore the motives that women and their families offered for entering *recolhimentos* and convents in Brazil. I will then consider *recolhimentos* and convents separately, examining the reasons given for their establishment, the lives that women led within their walls, and the responses of women to their cloistered existence.

## MOTIVES FOR ENTERING THE RELIGIOUS LIFE

Women of the elite white families in colonial Brazil were bound by social and familial expectations to lives as wives and mothers, or as nuns in a cloistered setting. Their own choices thus limited, a few nevertheless asserted their own understanding of them and made entry into a convent or *recolhimento* part of their own life path, without reducing it to mere compulsion or reluctant obedience. In her impressive study of the convent of Desterro in Bahia, Anna Nascimento offers an effective analytical model by situating that convent within the lives of the women who inhabited and governed it.[3] Insisting that the key to understanding the motivation for residence there lay in the status of women in colonial Brazil, she outlined the options for the independent life that elite white women might find at Desterro. Education, devotion, refuge, shelter, safety—these were the terms that defined many women's new lives within those walls. While few black or Indian women or women of mixed ethnic ancestry had that life available to them, elite and wealthy white women—and a few orphans, widows, and abandoned wives—actively sought the suitable alternatives that *recolhimentos* and convents offered. Bearing in mind the challenge of this task—given the widely divergent lives led by residents of *recolhimentos* and convents and the changes in social, economic, and political conditions between 1500 and 1821—I will follow Nascimento's lead and attempt to preserve the complexity of real women's lives from the few documents that reveal their motivations and responses.

### Religious Motives

For women, the motives for entering the religious cloister emerged from the teachings of the Catholic Church concerning the self and salvation in a dangerous world. Nuno Marques Pereira, in his compendium on colonial Brazil, found only three suitable life choices, three "states in which humankind may remain in the grace of God: Matrimony, Religious orders, and Celibacy."[4] Unable to remain independent and celibate, women among the elite classes were to be "given" by their fathers to the more appropriate states of matrimony or the religious life; in either "state" they maintained personal and family honor. But a woman avoided "fire of sensuality" only in "the religious life, where she might learn to control and sublimate the desires of her own body, or discipline them through the sexual norms imposed by the sacrament of matrimony."[5] Seeking control, discipline, devotion, and seclusion, Brazilian women turned to the exclusionary roles of religious activities in the convent. My discussion of women's motives here will begin with the religious expectations for women and the devotional intent that they themselves claimed, continue with consideration of social and familial expectations, and conclude with the enforcement of cloister without women's consent.

As the dominant cultural institution of the Portuguese empire, the Roman Catholic Church provided comprehensive social and gender role expectations for Brazilian women. As noted in previous chapters, Church officials both dismissed women as powerless in the temporal or spiritual spheres and disparaged them as the wellsprings of evil and the originators of sin in this world. As might be seen in late medieval portrayals of the Virgin Mary, however, feminine nature readily accepted revelatory guidance and was capable of deep religious passion and self-sacrifice. Thus it would seem that women were best suited for a life of religious devotion and most in need of the religious merit that such a life secured.

In the sixteenth century, Portugal still favored cloisters for religious women, using as models the Virgin Mary, her mother Anne, Augustine's mother Monica, and other virgins and martyrs prominent in Iberian popular Catholicism. Missionaries in Brazil inculcated Catholic virtues through the veneration of Mary and of feminine figures such as Santa Ursula and the Eleven Thousand Virgins, whose relics were taken to sanctify the colony in the 1550s.[6] Devotion to virginal and reclusive saints and the ascendancy of the cloistered Order of Saint Clare testify to the power of the self-effacing and monastic ideal for feminine devotions. It is hardly surprising, then, that the women aspiring to the religious life assented to such ideals and offered primarily religious motives.

Women's desire for religious expression and seclusion is revealed in only a few documents preserving women's own voices concerning the religious life to be found in *recolhimentos* and convents. One of the last came from Clara da Paixão de Jesus, who petitioned the Portuguese king in 1817 to grant her royal sanction for a residential "House of Prayer" in the bishopric of Mariana in Minas Gerais. There "women, dedicated to the Service of Our Lady of Piety, might live cloistered, sustaining themselves by the work of their own hands." Inspired by the "Holy life" of a local woman who experienced visions of Christ crucified every Friday, they had been "gathering to create an exemplary and edifying life" of "pure devotion" under the

guidance of the priest tending a small chapel. Despite impious persecutions, they "have not ceased to live with the same regularity of purity of
habits; practicing every day the exercises of Piety, proof of the truth of their
vocations." Clara herself vowed "by the soul of the [late] Queen . . . and
her precious relics," that the women who sought this religious life would
"not cease praying to God for the health, and the spiritual and corporeal
life of Your Majesty and of all the Royal Family, [and] for the conservation,
growth, and prosperity of the Kingdom."[7]

Although ultimately unsuccessful, Clara was not alone in requesting
royal sanction for the creation of a contemplative religious community. In
1757, Dona Maria de Albuquerque, then age seventy, had sought to establish a retirement house for herself and her five sisters, "all older than 60."
Her petition was approved, but in that same year, Dona Sebastiana Pereira
da Conceição, already living "in seclusion with a sister and two nieces," was
refused. She had proposed, with "many promises of donations," to create
a *recolhimento* for girls "dedicated to prayers, above all praying to God for
the temporal and spiritual life of the King Dom José."[8] In 1809, Manoela
de Santa Clara and Rita de Santa Ignêz had petitioned the king, stating
that they, "inflamed with the ardent desire to serve God, [had] retired
from the tumult of the secular world" and aspired to join "others of their
same sex who might wish to follow the path of virtue" in a new *recolhimento* supported by their independent income. Their advocates, including
Bishop Mateus de Abreu Pereira of São Paulo, attested to the adequacy of
their virtue and fortune, adding that a refuge for orphaned and devout girls
would serve the region well.[9]

In the eighteenth century, Jacinta de São José and Rosa Egipcíaca
were inspired by their own visions to found new religious houses. Part of
the history of "obstinate women" in Brazil,[10] these two could not have been
more different in social background—the former was a white woman of
wealthy noble background, the latter an abused African who endured the
worst conditions of Portuguese slavery—but they both overcame daunting challenges in pursuit of religious validation. Jacinta de São José, born
Maria Jacinta Aires, struggled from 1744 until her death in 1768 to establish a convent in Rio de Janeiro, confronting direct opposition from Bishop
Antônio do Desterro there. Unable to travel to Portugal to enter convent
life, Jacinta began reclusive life in a run-down farmhouse where she experienced "ecstasies, visions, [and] illnesses," suffering on behalf of sinful souls.
She gathered other devout women to practices of devotion and austerities
under the Carmelite rule, guided in her personal quest by visions of Jesus,
John of the Cross, and Teresa of Ávila. Thwarted by contradictory direc-

tives from the governor and different ecclesiastical officials, Jacinta never saw her dream realized: she died in her Recolhimento de Santa Teresa in 1768, while the remaining devoted recluses finally inaugurated the Convent of Santa Teresa in 1781.[11]

Rosa, by contrast, was taken as a slave from Africa at age six and, after living in Rio de Janeiro until age fourteen, worked as a prostitute in Minas Gerais from 1733 until 1748. Experiencing fainting spells and bouts of illness attributed to demonic possession, Rosa turned to religious devotion, distributed her ill-gotten gains among the poor, and was freed from slavery by her confessor. Her visions of a "beautiful young man" dressed in blue drew her back to Rio in 1751, where further visions of the Virgin Mary directed her to found the Recolhimento de Nossa Senhora do Parto as a shelter for indigent women and reformed prostitutes.[12] In 1757, Madre Rosa Maria Egipcíaca da Vera Cruz, as she was then known, entered seclusion with twenty-two women, twelve of them white, seven African-Brazilian, and three of mixed ancestry; only one, beside herself, had any sinful past to repent—most were young unmarried women seeking religious and social shelter. Five years later, her visions and increasingly outrageous prophecies took her before the Tribunal of the Portuguese Inquisition in Lisbon, where her eventual fate is unknown.[13]

Many of the existing convents and *recolhimentos* of the colonial period claim an inspiring woman or group of women as the first director or sisters, even where the ecclesiastical histories attribute the honor of establishment to religious men or government officials. In most cases, men composed the initiating letters requesting convents and *recolhimentos*, and only men in the Catholic Church and Portuguese government could grant the licenses required to create a sanctioned house for sisters, nuns, and recluses. Women were not left without options, however, and if the ecclesiastical and royal officials denied permission, informal houses "where women could lead a life of piety, cloistered in a simple house under the direction of some *beata* and her confessors"[14] were nonetheless organized.

Colonial convents and *recolhimentos* welcomed young women with explicitly pious intentions, especially in the late eighteenth century. Statements from young women seeking to enter the Convent of Nossa Senhora da Conceição da Ajuda in Rio de Janeiro offer us a glimpse of the discourse typically adopted. Luiza Michaella de Vasconcelos, for example, expressed her "great desires" to "employ herself in the service of God" when requesting admittance to the school in 1751. In 1754, Joanna Maria da Conceiçam asked "of her own free will, and without constraint by any person" to begin her novitiate in the convent, sure that "in the Religious Life she may better secure her salvation." A year later, she began her life as a professed nun with the name Joanna Bernardina. And in 1758, Anna Corrêa de Souza averred that "because of a special vocation and superior impulse," she "greatly desires to live and profess [vows in] the religious life" and would take the name of Anna Maria de Jesus in sign of her devotion. Even the younger girls expressed their eagerness for the cloistered life under religious guidance: Clara Jacinta de Santa Rosa, a "minor eleven years old" in 1756, declared her wish to "live free of the dangers of the Secular world" in the convent until she was old enough to become a novice and nun of Ajuda.[15]

Once within convents like Ajuda, young entrants found a demanding monastic life, directed toward the "path of perfection" for nuns.[16] Brazilian novices and nuns participated first in dramatic rituals of renunciation of their secular lives, then commenced the spiritual exercises of daily Mass, chanted prayers, solitary meditation, and readings from scriptures at mealtimes. Most convents also staged novenas, vigils, and other popular religious practices for their residents, in addition to processions and saints' day celebrations that their families might attend. Private devotions included meditations on the lives and experiences of Mary and Jesus that might culminate in emotional outbursts of penitence for Jesus's suffering and death. Novices, *recolhidas*, and nuns created small religious shrines in their cells for personal veneration, and the chapel housed devotional images given as part of the required dowry for entrance. Self-mortification, fasts, and devotion to the Eucharist were also recommended for the "individual experience—of seeing, consuming, and encountering God."[17]

After the novitiate, women became "brides of Christ," with a special naming ceremony on the day of the solemn profession of their vows of poverty, chastity, and obedience, and a change to more somber—usually black—clothing. While professed nuns held higher status in Brazilian convents, they faced more stringent demands for religious dedication and self-denial. Guidebooks for the nuns recommended strict attention to their vows, scrutiny of their daily lives, and additional penitential practices to enhance "the interior life and the love of God" as they journeyed on the "path of perfection."[18] Nuns of the "white veil"—usually poorer women of more questionable background—held lower ranks in the convent and served the more elite wearers of the "black veil," but some might be regarded as their spiritual betters. Such was Maria de Cristo, whose name in the Book of Entries for the Convent of Santa Teresa in Rio de Janeiro included an appended comment that she was "very humble and obedient and very devoted to Our Lady."[19] *Recolhidas* and sisters in the colonial *recolhimentos* enjoyed even less social prestige, but distinguished themselves religiously nonetheless. In the Recolhimento da Luz, for example, four sisters entered as "religious recluses," served variously as mistress of novices, doorkeeper, and director, and all—living past the age of seventy-five—were regarded as "full of virtues, favored by extraordinary grace."[20]

The religious ardor that drew women to the reclusive life was tempered by the regulations of the Carmelite and Conceptionist orders in the earliest convents in Rio de Janeiro and São Paulo. Founded or reformed by Iberian women during the time of the overseas expansion of the Spanish and Portuguese empires, those communities transmitted the early modern ambivalence toward women in religious life alongside the necessary means for their spiritual improvement. Their cloisters for women thus reflected both the "Iberian views of the proper roles of women and the devotional life of Iberian religious groups to Mary, through the Immaculate Conception or Mount Carmel."[21] For devout women seeking the religious life, then, *recolhimentos* and convents offered special opportunities for an expressive spiritual life closer to God and a greater assurance of salvation. That is not to say, however, that religious devotion was the sole motive for refuge in the colonial religious institutions.

### Social Motives

While women clearly articulated religious motives in their petitions for a new religious house or entry into an existing community, familial and social motives appear regularly as well. Girls seeking an education and protection from early or risky marriages might petition for a place as a pupil or *educanda* at a recolhimento or convent and remain resident there until the opportunity for a proper marriage or a place as a professed nun opened. Orphaned girls as young as five or six—as was seen in the case of Thereza Rosa—might enter a convent to live with an older aunt or cousin, and students as young as six enrolled in convent schools. In at least two colonial convents, over 20 percent of the entrants were younger than fifteen at the time of entry, and many, finding their religious vocations there, stayed to enter the novitiate.[22] This was the case for Barbara Francisca Xavier, a novice who petitioned to profess formal vows at the Convent of Ajuda in 1796. She testified in her sworn statement that she had "entered this Convent at age five or six, and . . . stayed in it until the Novitiate which was very much by her own free will."[23] Three sisters sought a similar situation in 1756, petitioning for "the grace to be admitted to enter, . . . taking the habit and fulfilling [all] obligations as Pupils until they achieve the age for the novi-tiate." The youngest of the three, Isabel, had her entrance deferred since she was only four years old.[24]

Temporary residence in a religious house was appropriate not just for young girls but also for any woman without suitable male protection. Widows entered as lay sisters, and wealthy young women of the elite classes took refuge in the convents and *recolhimentos* to preserve their status, honor, and family prestige while their fathers or husbands traveled. By agreement with the governing board, they paid an entrance fee and stipend for their weekly or monthly support, but some remained long after their original reason vanished. Ana de Santo Agostinho, for example, entered the Rio convent of Santa Teresa with her widowed mother but stayed on when her mother resumed public life; Ana first directed the convent choir and then held nearly every office in the convent after taking final vows in 1781.[25] A few women found themselves with no other choices and turned to the religious life as the only alternative when marriage failed. So Messias de Arruda and Anna de Arruda requested permission to create the Recolhimento of Divine Providence in a small town outside of São Paulo in 1819, following the model of such houses in the nearby city. Devoted to the life of Jesus, they envisioned a house for thirty-three maidens, but added that in their village "the feminine sex exceeds by two times in number the masculine sex."[26]

Lay women who resided in convents or *recolhimentos* might do so for one year—or a dozen. In the Convent of Nossa Senhora do Parto, fifteen different women rented individual cells between 1786 and 1797 in exchange for yearly payments. The records of "Receipts and Expenditures" for 1786, for example, list four girls as boarders or "*porcionistas*," six married women, three "daughters," and two female slaves.[27] During that decade, most of the lay residents were married women whose husbands paid yearly rent and support expenses directly to the convent. Jozé Francisco de Miranda, for example, paid yearly fees for his wife Caetana Maria de Jesus, who was accompanied by her daughter and one female slave during her nine-year residence there. Only three women had sufficient funds to pay for their own stays: Tereza Maria de Jesus enrolled as a "voluntary and unmarried *porcionista*" for 1793, Dona Catarina de Azevedo Coutinho supplied her own rent and sustenance fees during 1795 and 1796,[28] and in 1796, D. Eugenia Angelica de Santa Anna leased a room for her two daughters while she traveled to São Paulo "to see her husband."[29]

## Mixed Motives

Many women undoubtedly chose the cloistered life for more than one reason, weighing financial and personal considerations in their decision. Entrance into the leading convents of colonial Brazil conferred a privileged status on a woman and her family, allowing her to "take a state" (*tomar estado*) with the entrance fees and yearly support calculated at a much lower cost than a marriage dowry. The family property, in which daughters had an equal share with sons, remained intact—for neither nuns nor the convents could inherit by law—while social prestige and personal honor increased. Since only elite white women were accepted as professed nuns, it has even been suggested that some entered the convent to suppress any questions about legitimacy and ethnic origins. Thus entrance into the cloisters affected more than the woman herself—it proved a family's devotion, honor, status in the community, and purity of blood.

As may be suggested by the large number of younger girls entering convents and *recolhimentos*, not all entrants stepped willingly into the cloisters; the records of departures reveal the limited options that Brazilian women faced. Temporary residents who found shelter and protection as lay sisters in religious houses departed freely after brief stays, but *recolhidas*, novices, and nuns needed permission from the male directors or regional bishops for even brief leaves from their cloisters. Most departures were by younger women, but some records suggest that even long-term residents left when possible. Some, cloistered by male relatives or at a relatively young age, departed when they found the means or the opportunity. For example, three of the four daughters of Manuel Gomes da Costa in the Recolhimento of Santa Teresa in Rio de Janeiro left before taking solemn vows, despite their lengthy residence there in the mid-1700s. Maria da Assunção was granted leave for health reasons after her sixteen-year stay, but her sisters Escolástica da Assunção and Ana Maria de São José left without permission after more than sixteen years, forfeiting their large dowries and any possibility of return.[30] Another long-term resident, Ana de São Francisco, left the *recolhimento* after thirty-two years, avoiding the formal profession of vows and leaving her own substantial dowry there just as the Santa Theresa was transformed into a cloistered convent. Vitória Rodrigues da Fonseca, the wife of José Ferreira da Costa, brother of the founder, left the Recolhimento das Macaúbas immediately after his death, abandoning "the cloister with the permission of the bishop who granted her half of the inheritance, to which she had claims." Her daughter Catarina Maria do

Coração de Jesus followed Costa's instructions to remain there, supported by the remainder of his donation in her religious life.[31]

While a few married women probably took refuge from their husbands in convents or *recolhimentos*, many more women were forced into cloisters by angry or abusive husbands, disappointed relatives, or disapproving officials. So José Gomez Pereira in the late 1700s petitioned that his wife Mariana Maria de Jesus, already resident in the lay *recolhimento* of the Santa Casa da Misericórdia, be moved to the more restrictive convent of Our Lady of Lapa in Bahia. He insisted that her "illicit and abusive" friendship with another man had not ended during her stay at Misericórdia because she had more liberty there, and that he would pay all costs incurred for the move.[32] The convent of Nossa Senhora da Ajuda in Rio de Janeiro also received similar petitions from husbands claiming deceit: Paulo Fernandes was denied entry for his wife in 1816, but Mariana Inácia de Sousa and Ana Teotínia Leal, both cloistered by their husbands under accusations of adultery, remained in the convent despite their pleas to leave.[33] Maria da Piedade e Castro first entered the Santa Casa da Misericórdia after she herself admitted "her indecency" in an adulterous relationship. She later begged the local police commissioner for permission to leave, insisting that she had only confessed to escape her husband's violent threats and could now return to her father's house. Despite the evidence of abuse, sufficient to initiate a divorce plea, her request was denied.[34]

A more dramatic case is that of Dona Luíza de Nascimento e Oliveira, whose stay at the Convento da Lapa began in 1789. Her husband Manuel Joze Froes, a local merchant, proclaimed her "dishonesty and infidelity [contrary to] what she owed him as a wife"[35] and accused her of a secret relationship with a military officer. Luíza petitioned to Lisbon for release from her near-imprisonment in 1794, beginning over ten years of charges and countercharges. For her part, Luíza asserted that she was only cloistered because of her husband's "tyranny" and that her long stay and his failure to pay for proper food and care had resulted in illnesses such as "repeated fluxes, debility [and] stomach pain." Other residents and officials of the convent offered supporting statements, with the abbess suggesting that her proposal to take shelter with her sister proved that she had no ulterior motives for departure. Three nuns signed an affidavit for Luíza, swearing that she was exemplary in modesty and obedience but that her husband, by contrast, had disrupted the community with his frequent visits pretending reconciliation. While a doctor concurred that she had indeed suffered physically, the vicar insisted that her pains and claims of diminished funds were both false, but she did seem to be honest and decent in comportment.

Her husband then protested that his contributions to Luiza's support were substantial, secured the sympathies of the Lisbon officials and the Bahian bishop, and managed to have her placed under lock and key for a short time — before the abbess herself contravened the religious mandate and released her. By 1802, it seemed that the case might be settled: the Convent Regente mandated her release with the archbishop's permission and an order from Lisbon in 1803 approved her departure; records from 1807, however, place her within the walls of the convent, still cloistered after more than twenty years.[36]

For elite white women, a cloistered convent served as refuge or prison, then, depending on marital circumstances, but other women with fewer choices might also be sequestered in religious or lay retirement houses. Two *recolhimentos* in Bahia accepted women who transgressed the social and sexual norms of the community: the Recolhimento of Senhor Bom Jesus dos Perdões sheltered "devout ladies who wished to lead a penitent life" beginning in 1723, and after 1761 the Recolhimento of São Raimundo accepted women accused of adultery or other sexual sins, so that they might repent and "lament their errors" under religious guidance.[37] The Recolhimento of Santa Casa da Misericórdia served as a shelter of last resort for some, as was probably the case for an unnamed woman found "crazy and furious, contending and accosting one and other" in Maragogipe in 1798. After she interrupted the "divine offices" sung in church, a local official had her "taken" but, because she was "dark-skinned," he could not place her in a well-regarded convent or retirement house. Instead, he requested that she be "retired in the Santa Casa de Misericórdia so that she be kept with those of her quality."[38]

As noted above, servants and slaves were also present in the convents and *recolhimentos*, but rarely by their own choice. Religious and lay houses alike allowed for a small number of slaves and servants for the service of the community as a whole, for all sorts of manual labor, and to farm or manage other properties that made up their patrimonies. Some slaves also worked outside the convents, giving their wages or other earnings to the convents. Cloister rules permitted one or two personal servants or slaves, provided that the nun or sister pay for any additional boarding costs, including food and clothing. In Bahia, the statutes governing the Convento do Desterro allowed servants "as necessary," and at some points there were more servants and slaves than professed nuns in the cloister. With similarly large numbers of slaves at the Convento da Ajuda, novices and nuns were regularly reprimanded by vicars and the bishop for the numbers of slaves found within the cloister. Even at the less prestigious *recolhimento* in Macaúbas, thirty-seven women petitioned in the late 1700s to enter the religious life accompanied by one or more slaves, with eight of those requesting three slaves to serve them not only within the convent grounds but also as messengers and workers outside of the cloister. In some cases, however, private servants were prohibited by the religious statutes but still admitted when entrants requested them. So, for example, in 1743, Norberta Rosa do Paraíso petitioned that three slaves be allowed to enter with her as part of her entry donation. And in 1767, Maria do Nascimento petitioned for a single slave to enter with her and was granted her request.[39]

While a number of women chose to enter a convent or *recolhimento*, women's choices for a life in the Brazilian colony were severely restricted by their ethnicity, status, wealth, family, and communities. Further restrictions began with the established gender roles for women of the different social ranks and continued with the individual expectations and experiences of the women themselves. With so few records of women's own perspectives on their religious lives surviving from the sixteenth and seventeenth centuries, the handful of documents that remain offer us a valuable glimpse of their opportunities despite seemingly insurmountable odds; at the same time, we cannot forget the majority of women whose lives were hemmed in by servitude, slavery, and violence and who might have welcomed a respite behind cloister walls. In recalling the women who inhabited the cloisters, we must bear in mind, then, the very few opportunities for women's freedom during this time, and take seriously the religious motives alongside the very real and compelling social, economic, and political pressures that led to the gates of convents and *recolhimentos*.

### RECOLHIMENTOS: INFORMAL SECLUSION IN BRAZIL

The first choice for Brazilian women seeking a dedicated religious life was the *recolhimento*, a less formal but still regulated and cloistered house for the sheltering and retirement of the unmarried and the unmarriageable. In late medieval and early modern Portugal, *recolhimentos* were acceptable communal residences "where women of different status [took] refuge . . . under rules of cloister and obedience to the Director." In imperial Lisbon, the recognized *recolhimentos* were primarily lay houses that encouraged religious devotion in seclusion, while institutions with lesser status housed orphaned girls or "fallen women," with few expectations for religious rigor.[40] The establishment of *recolhimentos* in Brazil is linked not just to the imperial and ecclesiastical history of Portugal, but also to the religious blueprint created for the spiritual conquest of the New World and its piecemeal realization.

The institutional and ecclesiastical histories of the *recolhimentos* in Brazil, ranging from the more historical approaches of José Wanderley do Pinho to pious accounts such as that of Antonio Alves Ferreira dos Santos,[41] may lead the incautious to imagine an orderly system in which individual religious centers for women emerged regularly and according to international plan. That contemporary scholars such as Riolando Azzi and Maria Valéria V. Rezende could produce a credible chronicle of women's religious lives in the colony[42] is a testament to their labors in research and analysis and belies the real disorganization of the Catholic Church and the contradictions of faith during the colonial period. Their work, alongside such contemporary histories as *Desagravos do Brasil e glórias de Pernambuco* by Domingos do Loreto Couto, allows us to understand the context for the first *recolhimentos* as well as the reasons for their institution in the colony.

From the beginning of intense colonization in 1549, the Jesuits dominated the Catholic Church in Brazil, attempting to convert Brazilian Indians and later African slaves while maintaining some semblance of orthodoxy among the nominally Catholic immigrants from Portugal. That the latter task was as difficult as the former is revealed not just by the ensuing visits by the Portuguese Inquisition in the 1590s and 1610s, but also by the paucity of records of guiding directives from either the imperial government or, indeed, from the papal see itself. With the impetus of the Council of Trent and the ensuing Catholic Reformation, the coordination of the far-flung religion was slowly taking shape in Europe, but the systematic elimination of challenges to church authority and doctrine would not reach Brazil until much later.[43] As had been the case during other times of change and social stress, however, the first demands for allegiance and submission fell on women; in this light, we can see the creation of and support for *recolhimentos* as an extension of control not just of one sex but of Catholic Church members generally.

During the late Middle Ages in Western Europe, more women of diverse social ranks had participated in the spiritual life of the Catholic Church; in particular, there was a "marked increase in the number of women who consecrated their lives to God"[44] in a wide range of religious communities. Following the Tridentine decrees, however, women's path to religious perfection was restricted to formal cloisters. In Brazil, where few convents were available during the colonial period, a multitude of private and unsanctioned retreat houses were initiated by and for women seeking a devoted and secluded life.

## The Beginnings

The term *recolhimento* designated "diverse types of institutions for women," and the same retirement house might in reality "serve more than one purpose."[45] Azzi and Rezende identify four different types of *recolhimentos*: boardinghouses to seclude and educate girls until marriage, shelters for "fallen women," cloisters for "women seeking a more pious life in prayer and penitence," and *recolhimentos* "of women destined for a monastic life," "organized in a conventual model" with the hope that it later be approved for a religious order.[46] The earliest *recolhimentos* in Brazil were not, however, for fallen women or would-be nuns, but were organized among indigenous converts to Catholicism. In 1551, Jesuit missionary Manuel da Nóbrega reported to his colleagues in Coimbra that indigenous women converted by "two Castilian friars" in southern Brazil had "received the doctrine so well" that the friars had already established "cloistered houses for women as nuns."[47] Concerning his own efforts in northeastern Brazil, Nóbrega worried that the mostly male Portuguese colonists would not find suitable wives from among the indigenous Brazilian women without his intervention. As he converted unmarried women to Catholicism, then, he convinced them to remain near the Portuguese colony in a house "in which they may retire and from it marry working men little by little." The Jesuit shelter for women proved so successful that Nóbrega recruited some of the women as catechists for other potential converts from their home villages,[48] and subsequently boasted to Portuguese King João III:

> We have ordered built a house for the retirement of all girls and women of the heathens of this land who have for many years lived among Christians, and are Christians and have children from white men; and those very men who had them ordered this house, because there they would be taught doctrine and governed by some old women among them, and from then on most will marry and a few will remain with fewer occasions for sin; and this would be the best way that we can see for them not to return to [their] heathen [ways].[49]

Following this precedent, local religious and government officials requested that the Portuguese king under the right of royal patronage grant license to create *recolhimentos* in the growing towns of the Brazilian colony.

As in Nóbrega's letter, the reasons for the establishment of colonial *recolhimentos* were clearly stated, but social, political, and economic reasoning dominated the later discourse, both in the letters from colonial officials and in the royal responses. Many *recolhimentos* sheltered women whose honor was in peril or already damaged, but the reasons most often invoked were the preservation of family status and the conservation of the family's fortune. The new elite of Brazil wished to avoid the division of property among their heirs and preferred the lower entrance fees for the informal religious houses to the greater expenses of travel to Portuguese convents or of marriage dowries. The earliest requests for cloisters were rejected by the imperial government, on the grounds that the colony's success depended on an expanding population rather than communities of celibate women. In the late seventeenth century, with the larger coastal populations losing men to the interior for more lucrative farming and mining, royal concessions were finally granted to house unmarried women.

One of the first petitions to create a *recolhimento* in Rio de Janeiro advanced a religious justification while still reflecting the economic and social concerns of the colonial elite. The officers of the Town Council or Câmara wrote that recent financial "calamities" challenging the stability of many elite families left them unable to provide a dowry for more than one daughter; the rest of their daughters faced "either their own degeneration [by] marrying officials or men of lesser quality, or the risks of damaging their honor."[50] Another petition from the council in 1694 requested a shelter that might protect the honor of "no more than 30 orphan girls" who, fatherless and without sufficient dowries, might be cloistered in "this very pious creation." The petition, while appealing to the "singular piety" and Christian virtue of the king, also stipulated that only "white souls" would be admitted, and only maidens "not less than twelve or older than forty, which is the age at which honor is less endangered."[51] Of the four religious shelters permitted in the sixteenth and seventeenth centuries, three—in Salvador, Rio de Janeiro, and São Paulo—were quickly transformed into convents under Portuguese religious orders. With the fourth, in Pernambuco, the history of Brazilian *recolhimentos* commences.

## Histories of Brazilian Recolhimentos

The captaincy of Pernambuco welcomed the first *recolhimento* for women of Portuguese descent, the Recolhimento de Nossa Senhora da Conceição in Olinda, whose origins date to the 1580s. Maria da Rosa, the widow of wealthy landowner Pedro Leitão, abandoned secular life to live in "a sort of convent" for girls and women of religious inclination.[52] Licensed in 1595, the *recolhimento* added a chapel and school for girls while drawing other wealthy unmarried women—and their legacies—to its shelter. Briefly abandoned during the mid-1600s, the *recolhimento* was restored in 1722 with the royal order that only honorable women live as *recolhidas* in the cloister. The formal statutes established in 1741 by Bishop Luis de Santa Thereza for behavior and worship were rigorous and demanding. Permitted only close family visitors, the cloistered sisters dressed in a full Franciscan habit except while sleeping and performed religious prayers and rituals for three hours daily, with strict silence kept for another nine hours.[53]

In the late 1770s, residents in Pernambuco realized the establishment of another *recolhimento*, that of Nossa Senhora da Glória in Boa Vista. Although its director, Ana Maria de Jesus, had hoped for a convent, the bishop thwarted her plan, and in 1798 his successor presented an elaborate organizational structure and daily schedule—detailed below—to educate poor girls under the direction of honorable *recolhidas*, asserting his to be the best means to inculcate essential social virtues. In the village of Iguaraçu, the controversial Jesuit Gabriel Malagrida assumed direction of a group of devout women that had been meeting daily to pray with local Franciscan fathers. With them he created the Recolhimento do Sagrado Coração de Jesus, receiving the royal license in 1754 with local support but opposition from other religious orders over alms distribution. Malagrida went on to found numerous recognized and informal houses for the education of girls and the sheltering of disreputable women until his conflicts with the Marquis de Pombal and the Portuguese Inquisition led to his death in 1761.[54]

In Bahia, as in the neighboring captaincy of Pernambuco, a great number of *recolhimentos* were created in the eighteenth century, with the first few established in the city of Salvador for so-called fallen women. The recolhimento of Senhor Bom Jesus dos Perdões thus opened "to shelter a limited number of devout women who wished to lead a penitent life" and in 1723 enacted statutes for admittance, daily behavior, and preferred religious practices.[55] By 1759 its thirty-five *recolhidas* were admired as "great examples of virtue," but lived "in the hope that they might become professed nuns."[56] The Recolhimento de São Raimundo was begun in the 1750s "to harbor twelve women who, repentant, went to seek that asylum where they might lament their errors,"[57] and formalized its statutes in 1761. Around the same time, the Recolhimento do Vale das Lágrimas functioned as a private retreat for devout women, with austere rules and plans to educate a small number of local girls. When the legitimacy of the *recolhimento* was challenged by the bishop, founder Isabel Maria, daughter of João da Silva Guimarães, replied "that she had never petitioned for a license to live piously in her own house with her female relatives and friends, because she had not believed it to be necessary."[58]

Other Bahian *recolhimentos* such as that of Santissimo Nome do Jesus existed briefly in the 1700s, while the last established in the colonial period was probably that founded by Padre Ignácio dos Santos e Araujo in Santo Amaro da Purificação. Destined to be a school for "poor and Orphan girls, rich Girls as Boarders, [and] Girls, who are not wealthy but not poor, whose paying Parents wish to send them for daily lessons," the Recolhimento de Nossa Senhora dos Humildes received formal statutes in 1813.[59] Its rationale emphasized that "women need education" equally with men, since

> they form part of the human society; they have a house to govern, a husband to make happy, Sons to raise and educate in virtue [in their] most tender years, as the first Teachers that Nature provides us; and finally they are partners and co-helpers of their husbands in the economic management and domestic government of a Family.[60]

The *recolhimento* was not, however, to become a depository for repentant or discordant women—married or not—so that the innocent girls studying there would not be distracted by scandal.

Unlike Pernambuco and Bahia, the southern captaincy of Rio de Janeiro saw few requests for *recolhimentos* during the colonial period, and even fewer records remain concerning the reasons for their establishment, their names, and their founders. The first royal permit was finally granted for a shelter in the small village of Rio in 1695, but languished until its reissue in 1732. A new order then directed that the unused permit be transferred to the institution proposed by Martin Correa Vasqueanes.[61] By the end of the era, two of the more noteworthy *recolhimentos* had become convents (discussed below), and the presence of the Portuguese royal court and new city status as the capital of Brazil deferred the inauguration of any less prestigious religious institutions.

In the captaincy of São Paulo, however, two important religious houses drew women for centuries. The Recolhimento de Santa Teresa was initiated in 1685 by the visiting bishop of Rio de Janeiro as a retreat for "pious women."[62] The first *recolhidas* were three girls, the daughters of Manuel Vieira Barros, who entered with elaborate ceremonies, taking the simple habit of the order of Santa Teresa—the Discalced Carmelites—but no formal vows. Funding was provided by wealthy men such as Lourenço Castanho, who befriended the bishop and intended for his own granddaughters to take up residence there. By 1715, however, that retreat was in disrepute and officials in São Paulo petitioned the king for yet another refuge for women, claiming that the city itself had fallen into decadence. Narrowly avoiding demolition because of persistent scandals, the community was reorganized in 1744 as a school for girls, who learned reading, writing, mathematics, and domestic skills alongside their daily prayers in Latin, and by 1798, the *regente* reported that her thirty-one *recolhidas* and three pupils were thriving.[63] In 1809, her successor Maria Angelica do Espirito Santo painted a more dismal picture of the *recolhimento*, and her petition to the Portuguese Prince João VI for tax exemptions asked that he "deign to look with compassion on her and her Recolhida sisters who live in misery and poverty."[64] With few wealthy patrons and shortfalls in payments from renters, she had been forced to sell community property to feed and clothe her charges. Her brief letter was accompanied by a supportive document from members of the City Council attesting to the "real poverty" of the religious women who had merited only "the greatest esteem and public approbation" of the residents of São Paulo. Leaving past scandals aside, the councilors reported that the "sweet scent" of "their irreproachable behavior and the exercise of virtues . . . flows through this city to the great edification of all resident in it."[65]

The founder of the nearby Recolhimento da Luz da Divina Providência, Helena Maria do Espírito Santo, first found shelter in the Recolhimento de Santa Teresa. Admitted there because of her visionary experiences, she was only permitted entrance as a lay attendant due to her lower social status. Further visions inspired her in 1774 to found her own more inclusive religious community, with the support of her confessor and the provincial governor, under the Portuguese-reformed regulations of the Order of the Immaculate Conception; her piety and humility, not to say poverty, drew twenty-three *recolhidas* and fifteen slaves to her house in São Paulo by 1798.[66] In other, smaller towns in the captaincy, devout women made private vows to remain cloistered alone or in small groups in their own homes. In Sorocaba, one such *beata* or "holy woman" was Maria Pais de Jesus and in Itú, Margarida de Jesus and the "great Third-Order penitent" Margarida de Cortona were honored for their pious and sheltered existence.[67]

Other captaincies held fewer opportunities for informal cloister. Among "innumerable *recolhimentos* in Minas Gerais," the best-known institution was the Recolhimento das Macaúbas, founded by Felix da Costa in 1716 for his own nieces and the young women of the few other elite white families there.[68] Dedicated to Nossa Senhora da Conceição, the religious house eventually sheltered not just *educandas*, girls undertaking a modicum of education before marriage, but also widows seeking religious seclusion, and married women living apart from their absent or abusive husbands. In 1727, the visiting bishop from Rio de Janeiro found women in daily prayer living according to conventual rules, and he not only approved the community's continuance but also formalized its statutes, undertook new construction for better housing, and spared them from fees for their confessors. His successor, the first bishop of Mariana D. Manuel da Cruz, sponsored three girls whose father's death left them without yearly support. While records indicate that several girls of mixed ancestry resided there — probably in an effort to benefit from the status of the *recolhimento* — most of the residents were white girls of Portuguese descent supported by the burgeoning riches from their families' gold and diamond mines.[69]

Nearly every region of the Brazilian colony welcomed the establishment of *recolhimentos*, especially during the seventeenth and eighteenth centuries. Among them, especially outside of trade and commercial centers, were small, isolated *recolhimentos* associated with individual pious founders or well-regarded holy women. In São Luis Maranhão, for example, the itinerant Jesuit Malagrida opened one of his many *recolhimentos* in 1752, drawing local Ursuline sisters to oversee and educate the thirteen girls chosen for admittance. And a short-lived *recolhimento* was begun by the *beata* Joana de Gusmão in Santa Catarina, near her shrine to the Child Jesus. She directed the house beginning in 1762, but left only two *recolhidas* there after her death in 1780.[70]

In the larger colonial cities, women in need of shelter — before, during, or after marriage — also turned to lay *recolhimentos* such as the Santa Casa de Misericórdia, whose buildings housed a number of social support systems. In Salvador, Bahia, a new retirement house was built with support from the bequests of João de Mattos de Auguiar and opened in 1716 for "young girls of middle class families who were of marriageable age and whose honour was endangered by the loss of one or both parents."[71] When a girl met the conditions set by the charter, notably that she be white and impoverished but of unquestioned virtue, she resided in the house for up to four years until her marriage and not only received a basic education but also a suitable dowry. Soon after its establishment, and with the urging of the king, married women and widows were also permitted to reside in the *recolhimento*, paying for their own room and board. Beginning with only three *encostadas* or recluses in 1716, the *recolhimento* housed thirty-three young women in 1755; for most of the eighteenth century, however, fewer than ten older women boarded there.[72]

*Life in the* Recolhimentos: *Seclusion and Restrictions*

Each *recolhimento* founded in Brazil, whether religious or lay, began with specific expectations for the comportment of its residents and a daily schedule of activities; the strict regulations were derived not only from the rules of an existing religious order for women, such as the Franciscans or Carmelites, but also from specific statutes created for the house by the founder or another local political or religious authority. Many statutes were determined by the mandates of the Council of Trent, whose new sacramental emphasis strengthened the cloister and severely restricted secular activities for religious women.

Most regulations for *recolhimentos* centered on disciplinary control of the residents, imposed by the directors but gradually internalized and assumed by the women themselves. Since most of the Brazilian *recolhimentos* were founded with plans for later conversion to convents, the lay sisters, *educandas*, and *recolhidas* followed conventual rules that centered on cultivating "the three great virtues: obedience, poverty, and chastity."[73] Obedience in the *recolhimentos* entailed submission to God's will and to every ecclesiastical representative deemed to exercise proper authority over the sheltered women; thus every order from their own *regente*, as well as from confessors, priests, bishops, and the king himself, was to be summarily obeyed. This virtue proved to be the most difficult to cultivate, and all breaches of the rules, from the failure to keep silence to the flouting of visitation rules, were considered resistance to the first virtue of obedience, and offenders faced censure, fines, and expulsion.

The virtue of poverty was paramount as each *recolhimento* began as an independent, fully funded institution dependent first on direct donations and later on the rent or interest paid on their communally held donated properties. Poverty in their accommodations was equally important, so that any social distinctions among the residents might be diminished and all might seek to cultivate this apostolic virtue through simplicity in food, household goods, furniture, and attire. The particulars of their apparel typically garnered lengthy descriptions in the founding statutes, and most sisters wore clothing inspired by convent habits, with simple blue or white cloth in a plain style for dress, mantle, and head covering. Each *recolhida* had only a single room or "cell," with sparse furnishings and small images of Jesus or the saints for private devotions. Common areas included a private salon, dining room, and chapel, along with servants' quarters and a parlor to meet guests, all plainly representing the humility and poverty essential to the religious life there.

Chastity entailed not just virginity and sexual continence but also numerous restrictions on interpersonal relationships. Women were to spend their time silent and alone, separate from male and female friends and most family members. Modesty of dress and behavior reinforced the isolation of the individuals, as did restrictions for the public rooms in each house. Submission of the will to the rules enforced by the *regente* was also part of chastity, and in that we might see — as Foucault has suggested — the transformation of sexuality into discourse or its conversion into silence.[74]

The expectations for women in Brazilian *recolhimentos* may best be seen in the statutes written in 1798 for the Recolhimento de Nossa Senhora da Glória in Pernambuco. When its unnamed founder petitioned for its conversion to a convent, she received a sternly worded refusal from the Portuguese imperial government, criticizing her efforts to mimic the religious houses of Rio de Janeiro and Bahia "where women bury themselves alive."[75] The officials advised that she turn instead to the betterment of the population of Pernambuco by establishing "the method to Raise, Educate, and Teach the Residents, and raising them from infancy in the purity of habits, and securing good Teachers, to Instruct [them] in the work of Sewing, making Lace, Embroidery, and other similar Occupations."[76] After such an education, all "idleness, indolence, and laziness" would vanish from their lives as the young women left for marriage and introduced improved personal and social qualities to their new families.[77] Indeed, when Bishop José Joaquim da Cunha de Azeredo Coutinho published the reformed rules for the *recolhimento* in 1798, he prefaced the specifics of daily life and behavior with a similar rationale for the education of young women. Struggling as they were against the "crimes and disorders that disrupt Societies and the Church" and the "passions of corrupted nature," educated wives and mothers served the common good through the private cultivation of virtues in their husbands and sons.[78] Peace, a pleasant home, success in marriage, and, ultimately, the future prosperity of human society thus depended on girls' proper education. The remainder of his short book provided the guidelines that might achieve that admirable end.

Although the *recolhimento* was instituted as a seminary for elite girls, Coutinho was most concerned with the regulations for the small cadre of teachers who would guide his pupils. Official roles were fixed for a group of twelve virtuous women, with nine appointed in different tasks as "Superior, or *Regente* of the House," "Vice-regent of the Choir," "Procurator," "Sacristan," "Doorkeeper," Keeper of the Turn-box," "Nurse," "Keeper of the Dispensary," "Keeper of the Refectory," and three "Mistresses of the Pupils."[79] Each woman admitted to these honorable positions might be from an impoverished family, but was to be white, a longtime resident in the colony of Pernambuco, from a legitimate marriage, and of good reputation. Teaching candidates between the ages of sixteen and thirty had to prove they could "read, write, and count" and, during a trial period of fifteen days, demonstrate to the founder and the Board of Trustees other personal qualities that they might teach their charges.[80] While their duties were focused on "the business of the instruction of youth," the personal lives of the teaching *recolhidas* were sharply restricted: they dressed in plain clothes without decoration, lived in small cells with simple furniture, and cultivated the virtues of charity, humility, and modesty, "the distinctive trait of the feminine sex."[81] Rising to pray at 5:00 a.m. each day, the directors and teachers of the *recolhimento* then prepared themselves for the day, joined their sisters to pray the Divine Office in Latin at 8:00 a.m., and performed assigned duties until the midday meal. Vespers, or afternoon prayers, began at 2:00 p.m. and work resumed afterward. After their 7:00 p.m. dinner was a half-hour conversation "directed by the *Regente*"; all retired to their rooms at 10:00 p.m., and at 10:15 all lights were extinguished.[82]

The statutes created by Bishop Coutinho specified that the pupils admitted to the care of the virtuous women at the Recolhimento da Glória were to be white, orphans or fatherless daughters of legitimate marriages, and at least seven years of age with no lingering illnesses. Their admittance to the seminary was but the first step of their life paths, and, although they were "obliged to bring their [own] bed, clothing, and furniture such as their poverty allows," the charity of the institution supported them entirely: "from that point on [they] would be sustained, and clothed at the cost of the *Recolhimento*, until the age of sixteen, if they had not up to that point married [or joined a convent], or [accepted] another honest means of life, in which their honor and status would be secure."[83] Their future lives determined which of two curricular models the girls might follow: those destined for the convent learned "the mortification of their own will," Latin, and music, while those planning for marriage and motherhood cultivated domestic virtues and skills.[84] The latter included reading, writing, math, sewing, and embroidery, with special instruction in the proper means for governing her little "Republic" of servants and slaves through "justice and economy in expenditures."[85] Coutinho advised that the girls' studies be designed as games, so that they might learn more easily, but insisted that their caretakers give attention to their "tender" nature and cultivate obedience and other virtues, by beginning studies in Catholic doctrine.[86] While the girls learned their catechism, they were also taught to "use reason to know

God" and to practice good works that might prevent the "ordinary defects of their sex" such as timidity, fear, gossip, and indolence.[87]
The proposed statutes for another college for girls, the Recolhimento de Nossa Senhora dos Humildes in Bahia, offer further details on expectations for the orphaned and impoverished girls admitted there.[88] Admitted only with permission from the local judge and prelate, the girls dressed in plain white clothes, kept their hair cut short, and learned to walk gracefully and modestly. Their teaching mistresses were assigned specific subjects, with the first responsible for moral lessons on virtues, the second for methodical teaching of reading, Portuguese "Grammar and Orthography," and history, and the third for instruction on how "to sew, embroider, make clothing, [and] make flowers and decorations."[89] The girls boarded in the *recolhimento*. They had few visitors or opportunities to visit home, and their recreation hours and activities were limited: they might play and read, but no "love novels" were allowed.[90] Fanatical religious practices were also banned, and the girls were permitted no extra fasts and only weekly baths.[91]
The *educandas, recolhidas*, and *regentes* of the colonial *recolhimentos* met the varied and stringent demands of such statutes, enacting near-perfect imitation of the religious life provided by convents. Whether drawn to the devotional life or placed there for a brief education or perpetual confinement, girls and women in the *recolhimentos* dwelt in the shadow of the more prestigious and powerful convents of Bahia, Rio de Janeiro, and São Paulo, with only the modest accomplishment of persistent virtue to bring their communities public recognition or esteem.

CONVENTS: FORMAL CLOISTERS IN BRAZIL

The founding of convents for women in Brazil was delayed at the behest of the imperial government for the first 177 years of the colony. Far fewer women lived in cloisters in Brazil than elsewhere in the Hispanic American colonies, even by the end of the colonial period. In Portugal as in other European countries, convents functioned not just as cultural and educational refuges for religious women but also as depositories for unmarried daughters, adulterous wives, and unattached widows. In Brazil, convents were undesirable to the Portuguese state because they isolated the elite white women deemed essential for the stability and expansion of the colonial enterprise. In 1603, for example, the Portuguese king rebuffed colonial requests for convents, concluding: "It is therefore not regarded as convenient to erect in those regions convents of nuns—since they [the lands] are so vast that in order to populate them many more inhabitants are necessary than are there at present."[92] In response, the colonial elite sent young women to Portuguese convents throughout the colonial period, along with substantial funds to support them, even flouting the 1732 imperial decree forbidding the transport of unmarried women without royal permission.

From the Brazilian colonial perspective, two primary reasons drove the unceasing requests for the establishment of convents. The first was religious: girls, families, priests, bishops, even city councils argued that women be accorded the opportunity to live in devout service to God and the Church. Even that reason, however, might prove inadequate if imperial officials concluded that women's submission to God conflicted with their duties as wives and mothers in submission to social progress. The second reason for convents, then, offered social benefits: convents could serve as temporary or permanent housing for women who could not marry. Citing economic stress, political exigencies, and social pressures, colonial leaders petitioned the Portuguese crown for license to create convents and thus an honorable status for unmarried women, while preventing the loss of population and money to Portugal. In Salvador, Bahia, especially after 1650, few elite families had sufficient wealth to endow more than one daughter for marriage or to allow the division of the family estate among additional heirs, and the women themselves had fewer eligible suitors. Thus, as Susan Soeiro has convincingly argued, convents "performed a valuable service for the colonial elite by cloistering its undowered daughters" while also isolating in subservient positions the "unprotected, violated, unchaste, and rebellious women" that might otherwise disrupt colonial society.[93]

While the town council of Salvador sent a series of letters to Portugal citing the dangers to its economy and its young women, officials in Rio de Janeiro joined with Bishop D. Francisco de São Jeronimo in a petition seeking relief from "the very universal sorrow in the honors for their families" and requesting a convent "where their relatives and sisters might take refuge."[94] The Overseas Council agreed that transportation for so many women to Portugal was both dangerous and inconvenient and, in 1703, recommended that the king concede the license as requested—and so he did, fifty years later. Women seeking a place in a Brazilian convent, however, could anticipate only profound isolation and separation from normative domestic roles. For a few elite women, the colonial convents offered asylum from socially marginal roles, and—perhaps only once entered there— the attainment of a secure, independent, and vibrantly creative life within religion. Eduardo Hoornaert has argued that Brazilian women chose the cloister as an "exit" to a new and different life:

> Only religion was unencumbered of duties for the Brazilian woman of the Portuguese period. She took advantage of this possibility to the maximum extent so as to keep alive the flame of faith, of hope and of love. . . . It is clear that, [by joining a convent], many women became religious for less than religious reasons, and transformed the convent into a place where there might be more possibilities for personal initiative, independence and social achievement than in the conjugal life. In a society centered on men and governed by men, religion constituted a respectable alternative for the woman, in the sense of liberating her from the male control that in reality was the control of the system, since the woman already served to bear and raise children for the system.[95]

## *Histories of Brazilian Convents*

The first colonial convent, Santa Clara do Desterro, was established in Salvador, Bahia, in 1677. Over sixty years later, three more Bahian convents received royal permits in the seventeenth century under the auspices of the Ursuline or Franciscan orders: Nossa Senhora da Conceição da Lapa in 1733, Nossa Senhora das Mercês in 1735, and Nossa Senhora da Soledade e Coração de Jesus, first as a *recolhimento* in 1741, then as a convent in 1751.[96] The residents of Rio de Janeiro, whose petitions to the Portuguese Crown began in the early 1600s and were renewed in the 1670s, received royal permission for two convents in the colonial period, the Convento de Nossa Senhora da Ajuda in 1750 and Convento de Santa Teresa in 1751. The city of São Paulo received no such permission before 1821, despite the clamor to transform its Recolhimento de Santa Teresa into a cloistered convent. The nearby Paulista city of Sorocaba sought to create a convent near the family shrine protected by two devout sisters, Manoela de Santa Clara and Rita de Santa Ignêz; while its petition finally received royal assent in 1811, the convent itself was never established.[97] The creation and institution of each of these few colonial convents, detailed below, followed remarkably different paths, with spiritual inspiration from visionary women and missionaries or political calculations from wealthy men on the town councils.

## Convents in Bahia

The Convento de Santa Clara do Desterro received its royal permit only when the colonial population and local economy had grown sufficiently for the Crown to ease some restrictions on women's lives. Among the families who had grown wealthy from the sugarcane plantations of the northeast, fewer than 20 percent of eligible women married in the seventeenth century, and many white girls — even from the merchant and artisan classes — were sent to Portugal to assume the honorable status of nuns.[98] Requests for a convent had begun in the early 1600s and grand buildings were designed to house the large numbers expected to reside there. When royal permission was finally granted in 1665 and the first four nuns of the order of Saint Clare arrived in Salvador in 1677, the stage was set for the most elite religious center of the Brazilian colony. Petitions for the convent had originated among the men of the Câmara and it benefited their daughters first, with the statutes allowing only fifty professed nuns "of the black veil." These ranks were quickly filled by women who were able to draw on family wealth for the "substantial dowry" and the "costly and extravagant life-style" created at Desterro.[99] Another twenty-five places were reserved for novices and sisters "of the white veil," an "inferior rank" held only by those awaiting an opening in the upper echelon or ineligible — due to lower social and economic status or personal humility — for such promotion.[100] A petition for augmentation of the fifty places at that first convent was denied in 1697,[101] and after 1760, places in the convent became more difficult to obtain, in part due to the king's insistence that all nuns obtain royal approval of their religious vocation. Wealthy parents then donated not only large dowries for girls seeking either the white or black veil, but also funds for buildings, furniture, and chapel decorations at Desterro.

From the beginning, the convent also accepted young girls as *educandas*, though later amendments to the statutes forbade nuns to invite young relatives to live with them as full-time wards. *Educandas* who entered at the age of five or six might remain at Desterro their entire lives; if no place among the nuns opened for them, they might join the devout widows and independently wealthy women residing as *recolhidas* there, with less prestige but fewer restrictions placed on their behaviors and activities. In any case, the nuns, *educandas*, and *recolhidas* all met the same basic requirements: they were white or nearly so, from old Christian families (rather than recently converted Jews), and able to pay the entry fees and yearly maintenance costs. Each nun and *recolhida* also entered with at least one personal servant or slave, and the community sponsored numerous "servas da casa," who were orphans or poor but pious young women seeking shelter and a life of religious devotion. By 1755, the religious population of nuns, pupils, and recluses exceeded one hundred, with an equal or greater number of servants.[102] In the biography of Archbishop D. José Fialho from the 1740s, his secretary marveled at the splendor of the religious institution at Desterro and the virtuous examples of its residents, but noted that Fialho had expelled more than ninety women who resided there comfortably but without religious vocation.[103]

Three other convents were established in Salvador in the middle of the eighteenth century, two of them in the 1730s. The Convent of Nossa Senhora da Conceição da Lapa had its origins in the 1733 petition from João de Miranda Ribeiro and Manuel Antunes Lima, who declared that the Convent of Desterro was not sufficient for the religious women of Bahia. They received royal permission for a new convent for twenty nuns that same year—on October 25, 1733—with specific stipulations concerning the building and its residents.[104] The *provisão* from Dom João V insisted that the petitioners assume fiscal responsibility for the small convent:

> I the King make known to those to whom my Provision goes, that having respect for João de Miranda Ribeiro, . . . that he will build at his expense, and create to the ultimate perfection a Chapel [dedicated to Our] Lady, as he intends, with Manoel Antunnes Lima and other men . . . who have daughters, to make in that Temple at their own expense a Convent for Franciscan Nuns, . . . which will include twenty Sisters, more or less, with a limited number of communal servants.[105]

Ecclesiastical consent for construction of the convent followed in 1734, but when Archbishop Dom José Fialho arrived in Brazil in 1739, he found the building still incomplete and unoccupied. His successor D. José Botelho de Matos wrote the statutes for a Franciscan Conceptionist community, so designated "in virtue of their consecration to honor the mystery of the Immaculate Conception" of Mary.[106] In 1744, a small number of nuns from the Convento do Desterro moved to Lapa, joined by five daughters of the founder João de Miranda Ribeiro and girls from other wealthy Bahian families, and in 1747 the Ursuline order assumed direction of the convent.[107] By 1756, however, the residents of the cloister and the city felt that the number of places for nuns was too small. Two founding members, Maria Caetana da Assumpção and Josefa Clara de Jezus, wrote to King D. José, arguing that twenty women could not fulfill all of the duties of the community, especially since the climate, food, dependence on slaves, and other social norms of Brazil inclined "persons of the feminine sex" to limited vigor or outright laziness. With thirteen more places, they continued, the "perennial praise of God" would be restored.[108] Permission was granted for the additional spaces, and the imperial government subsequently mandated that additional funds be raised to restore the finances of the expanded convent and that each entrant to the convent provide fully for her own personal expenses.[109]

The third convent founded in Salvador, the Convento de Nossa Senhora das Mercês, was inspired by Dona Ursula Luiza de Monserrate. Having inherited the "fabulous fortune" of her father Pedro Barbosa Leal, she petitioned the Crown for permission for a new cloister, where she avoided the "many wolves" who sought to marry her.[110] With government authorization received on January 23, 1735, to construct a convent for fifty nuns, she first established a temporary community, and then, as abbess, led four pupils and a small number of novices and nuns to the finished convent on September 23, 1745. Of those, two of the young *educandas* were sisters, as were four of the nuns. The eldest novice entering—a wealthy woman who had already funded an independent hospital "in her own home"—was fifty-two.[111]

The retirement house that would become the Convento de Nossa Senhora da Soledade e Coração de Jesus was begun in 1739 by the Jesuit father Gabriel Malagrida as part of his network of establishments for poor and pious women in the northeast. The local Confraternity of Our Lady collected alms for Malagrida, and in 1739 fifteen "decent maidens" entered the newly constructed cloister.[112] Soledade first received royal approval as a *recolhimento* in 1740, with papal approval for up to forty recluses at that site following in 1741, and Ursuline sisters managed the convent following its conversion in 1751.[113] While the convents of Desterro, Lapa, and Mercês welcomed the wealthiest and most influential women of the colonial capital, Soledade at first housed the more impoverished and pious nuns. Still, its abbess, Beatriz Maria de Jesus, received her income from a large slaveholding plantation, another nun had a similar property for her personal fortune, and five later residents came from a sugarcane estate. At the time of its conversion to conventual status, in fact, a few of the original recluses lacked sufficient funds for the larger yearly allowance and could not take their places as professed nuns.[114]

### Convents in Rio de Janeiro and São Paulo

In Rio de Janeiro, the drive to establish distinguished religious refuges for nuns was led by two quite different women, Dona Cecilia Barbalho, a widow who became the first abbess of the Convento de Nossa Senhora da Conceição da Ajuda, and Madre Jacinta de São Jose, a lifelong recluse who died before the conversion of her *recolhimento* into the Convento de Santa Teresa. The first house, Ajuda, also began as a small *recolhimento* guided by the Franciscan Provincial official Cristóvão da Madre de Deus Luz. Having escorted nieces to Portugal to enter convents there, he was inspired in 1674 to create a religious center in Rio and collaborated with his brother, another church official, and Dona Cecilia to found a convent there. For her part, Dona Cecilia began a private *recolhimento* for herself and her three daughters, and, with the Franciscans' support, gained the approval of the Câmara of Rio de Janeiro for her project. They sent their petition to Lisbon in 1678, praising the pious mother who spared her children the dangerous sea voyage, and instead "resolved to create a Recolhimento near the Church of Nossa Senhora da Ajuda in that city, and in it took shelter on the past date of 26 June with her three daughters" and other women who were all nobles and persons of quality.[115] Since the women were already following the rules of a cloistered convent and such an institution had not yet been created in their city, the Câmara requested royal approval; the Overseas Council in Lisbon consented in 1687 but other royal officials only granted permission for a *recolhimento*. With the installation of an influential bishop in Rio de Janeiro and its emergence as an important colonial town, residents again sought royal license for the convent and succeeded in 1705. Papal approval and the final *alvará* from Lisbon were delayed until 1749, but in 1750, five nuns traveled from the Convento do Desterro in Bahia to begin the new religious community.[116]

The second convent in Rio, Santa Teresa, also met with repeated delays, not because of imperial dissent but because of conflicts between its would-be founder and the city's bishop. Born in Rio in 1715 to wealthy and aristocratic parents, Jacinta de São Jose chose the religious cloister after her visions of Teresa of Ávila revealed her life's vocation. Prevented by injury from traveling to Lisbon, she and her sisters moved instead to a small farm on the outskirts of town in 1743 or 1744, where "they lived by prayers and fasts, privately planning the construction of the future convent."[117] Over the next decade, other women joined the two in their observance of the Carmelite rule — inspired again by Teresa of Ávila — and the governor of the captaincy first provided funds for their new chapel and monthly sustenance and then helped them move into the city to establish a *recolhimento* in 1749. Bishop D. Antônio Desterro received license to construct a new convent in 1750 but denied it to Jacinta's community in 1753, claiming that the royal and papal approval had specified a Franciscan order.

The determined woman, now the Regente Madre Jacinta de Jesus, went to Lisbon that same year to plead directly for royal permission to realize her dream of a cloistered convent; the recluses remaining in Rio refused to admit any visitors — including the bishop himself — while her pleas went unheard. Madre Jacinta died in 1768 while further disputes hindered the inauguration of the convent, but in 1780 the Convento de Santa Teresa was established under the Carmelite rule and Jacinta commemorated as its visionary founder.[118]

As noted above, the captaincy of São Paulo inaugurated no convents during the colonial period despite the efforts of local families and ecclesiastical and governmental officials. Instead, *recolhimentos* flourished in São Paulo and surrounding towns in the later colonial years and maintained conventual standards without the requisite royal permission. The cloister at Santa Teresa managed to achieve the levels of exclusivity and prestige of the Bahian and Cariocan convents when Bishop D. Bernardo Rodrigues Nogueira, perhaps frustrated at delays in the Crown's response, rededicated it as a convent in 1746 and rewrote its statutes to follow Carmelite rules. New donations and entrants from the wealthiest families invigorated the would-be convent and set new challenges for other religious institutions there. At the end of the eighteenth century, the Recolhimento de Nossa Senhora da Luz followed suit by establishing rigorous guidelines for religious behavior, but only the Convento de Santa Clara in nearby Sorocaba obtained the royal *alvará* for its residents to take formal vows as members of a religious order. The founders there received permission directly from the Prince Regent D. João in Lisbon, and Frei Antônio de Santana Galvão allowed the residents to take vows and initiate the stricter rules of conventual life. Still, ongoing conflicts with the governors of the captaincy kept the *recolhimento* as a school well into the nineteenth century.[119]

*Life under the Rule in Brazilian Convents*

Life within a cloistered convent was an isolated and restricted existence under the Franciscan or Carmelite rules preferred in Brazil. Entrants were tested as novices, usually for one year, before being accepted as candidates for the formal profession of vows; women who took that final step foreswore personal comfort and social pleasures for hours of prayer and service. Still, as can be deduced from the different reasons given for the establishment of convents in Brazil and the different impulses that drew women to them, the lives of women in the convents varied widely. I will begin here by relating the expectations placed on the professed nuns according to their orders' rules and conclude by exploring the evidence for resistance to those strictures expressed in letters, wills, and personal accounts of life within the cloisters.

With the stringent expectations of the Tridentine Catholic Church, novices and nuns faced community discipline and prescribed activities designed to remove them from the secular world and attitudes and re-form their bodies and souls to the dictates of saintly life. The ideals that permeated women's lives in Brazilian *recolhimentos*, described above, were exceeded in the strict demands within the formal convents. For the professed nuns, the discipline was accepted permanently and the formal vows of obedience, chastity, and poverty were unbreakable bonds that held them in the cloisters during their lifetimes and on the path to divine perfection afterward. The emphasis on the "path to perfection" made obedience the first and most important of the vows, signifying the renunciation of personal autonomy and the full subordination of the self to the will of God under the direction of the ecclesiastical authorities. After that, the demands of poverty, by relinquishing comfortable clothes, furnishings, and foods, or of chastity, by severing friendships and familial relations, were ancillary duties performed naturally as each woman completed her virtuous steps on her own path. Women renounced homes, children, and the small corner of the public sphere to which they might have had access in the secular realm, so as to assume an elevated position in the religious realm. Their vows still conformed to the feminine gender rules, however, as nuns surrendered control of their independence, wealth, and sexuality to masculine authorities and won only the privilege of deferred rewards.[120]

For Brazilian convents, each entrant was committed not only to uphold the community regulations but also to make full and irrevocable donations upon her profession of vows and every year afterward. Most colonial convents thus grew wealthier with patrimonies established through gifts of houses, ranches, farmlands, and income from crops and rents. The first convent in Salvador, Santa Clara do Desterro, required significant dowries of its entrants along with yearly allowances, and provided loans from its accumulated properties. As Susan Soeiro notes in her studies of its role in the colonial economy of the Brazilian northeast, Desterro maintained "intimate ties" to the most powerful families and served the region as a "banker, landlord, and slave-master."[121] Other religious houses did not require entrance fees, but acquired houses and land from nuns who sustained themselves with rental income and then left the property to the convents upon death. At the same time, loan failures, family disputes, and poor planning left the convents vulnerable, and resounding complaints of shortages in food and personal comforts were heard by the end of the eighteenth century.

The writings of Bishop D. Antonio do Desterro for the Convento de Nossa Senhora da Conceição da Ajuda permit us a glimpse of the idealized expectations for professed nuns as well as the difficulties they experienced with them. The "Rule" for the nuns began with a florid description of the religious devotion that might bring a woman,

> inspired and called by our Lord, wishing to leave the vanity of this world and take up the habit of this Holy Convent, and join herself to Jesus Christ our Redeemer, honoring the Immaculate Conception of His Blessed Mother, to make a vow to life always in obedience, without property, in chastity, and in perpetual cloister.[122]

Since entrance to the convent was a "singular offer" created by Jesus through "his glorious Mother," not every woman might be admissible. The candidates were to be "full Christians, not suspect of any error," older than twelve, and capable of accepting the "harshness and difficulties that they will encounter" on their chosen path.[123] After a year under the scrutiny of the prelate, *regente*, and community of nuns, each woman repeated this oath:

> I, X, for the love and service of Our Lord and the Immaculate Conception of his Glorious Mother make this vow and promise to God and to the Glorious Father Saint Francis, and to all the saints and to you Mother to live my whole life in obedience, without property, in chastity, and in perpetual cloister, under the Rule that His Eminence Pope Julius II conceded to Our Order and confirmed.

Completing the ritual, the abbess responded: "if you keep these [vows], I promise you eternal life."[124]

The first section of this extended text, enacted in 1750, outlined the ecclesiastical guidelines for clothing, property, and behavior, each explicitly linked with the formal vows. Thus, the vow of poverty required each nun to dress plainly and donate her property to the community, including all income needed for her own expenses. The vow of obedience enforced attendance at all religious activities, and the vow of chastity bound each woman to "perpetual incarceration within the cloister," covered in dark robes, and sleeping in a small and separate cell.[125]

The "Constitution and Laws" for the convent, enacted one year later in 1751, affirmed the Rule and established the governance of the nuns and terms for the admission and training of novices and nuns.[126] Here the primary concerns were for the perfection of the self, based in deprivations and submission. First, only those who were white, "of clean blood, honest and retiring" and who truly "aspire to religious perfection" might be considered for admission. Of those, the preferred candidates were "intelligent," "accommodating," and between the ages of fifteen and forty; older women adept at reading Latin and singing might still be admissible by the prelate.[127] The number of professed nuns was limited to eighty, and each entered with a substantial dowry, yearly income, and one or more virtuous servants according to her needs.

The women at Ajuda under the formal vows began their restricted lives with the perpetual cloister, examination of conscience, and the mandated spiritual exercises. The rule called all novices and nuns to church for hours each day, beginning in the morning with the Divine Office, choir singing, and Mass. The schedule included one hour of "Mental Prayer" daily, but here the author warns of religious extremism. Meditative prayer was spiritually vital, but because it was "also Most subject to tricks and illusions, principally in Women," Bishop Desterro demanded that "all Nuns according to the Merits of Holy Obedience" report any "revelations, visions, ecstasies and trances" experienced. The prelate or religious leader would faithfully guide them to "disillusionment," that is, to the realization of their mistakes, thus avoiding "the great harms that may come to Nuns in Prayer."[128]

The remaining activities of the novices and nuns were defined negatively in the text: special meals, games, and recreation were forbidden, as were most conversations, glances, and personal contacts among the women themselves. Each nun lived "chaste, and pure in the composition of her external actions, in the modesty of her eyes, and in the decency of her words, but [also] in the mortification of the appetites" so that her full being was "restrained with Reason."[129] Personal love and friendship only entered the cloister in distant charitable acts, replaced by love for God. At the same time, the creation and composition of each nun's habit demanded extraordinary scruple to express the simplicity and poverty of her vows. In particular, no fancy sewing, "curiosities," or flower-making might be completed unless the decorations were to grace the common areas or the chapel altars.[130]

A significant portion of the "Constitutions" directed the care for the sick and rituals for the dead, and the document concluded with the duties of the distinctive offices of the convent. Thus, the abbess maintained the "honesty" of the cloister, the vicar was the "mistress of ceremonies," and the most intelligent among the "discreet counselors" kept the convent account books.[131] The door-keeper controlled visitors and the nurse cared for all minor ailments, while the mistress of novices guided the souls of the youngest women to docility, restricting their daily acts and prohibiting the practices of "mental prayer" and "speculative mysticism" among these most vulnerable residents.[132] The text warned, finally, of the dire threats that emerged among sinful women in the convent, discriminating among light, medium, and grave faults. Here, the gravest sins were incorrigibility, "sins of indecency," physical assault of other residents, and abuse of office among the convent leaders.[133]

The expectations for the perfected religious life at Ajuda were apparently not met by its first residents, for Bishop Desterro wrote to the nuns just ten years later to condemn the many abuses he found there. With his own holy mandates and mercy upon the "miserable creatures blinded by their internal passions," he warned that the accumulation of so many errors at the convent attracted the "Infernal Enemy" and his army of demons to ruin their souls. Much as the small glance from Eve or the "small fault" of David had led to dismal evils, the small crimes of the residents would lead to the loss of their sanctity so that they would be "useless for the religious life."[134] The details of the letter indicate that the elite women drawn to the convent were loathe to abandon their secular lives, for their crimes included the spending of money for the lace and fine fabrics in veiling and time in unfettered conversations through the exterior windows. To stifle sinful impulses, the bishop ordained that the mistress of novices inculcate self-mortification among the young women and that all nuns and novices gather for a common meal at which the Rule, the Constitutions, and his warnings would be read aloud at regular intervals. His final act established a weekly ritual of public admission of sins, so that each erring sister might beg mercy from the community for her failings.[135]

## Conflicts and Resistance

The "abuses" revealed in Bishop Desterro's letter were not unique to the Convent of Ajuda, nor to Rio de Janeiro in the eighteenth century. From the first, Brazilian convents and *recolhimentos* faced unavoidable conflicts between the ideals of the perfected life and the reality of women

who variously sought social, economic, and religious refuge in their cloisters. The religious life demanded no less than self-annihilation in submission to God, and the nuns, novices, and sisters could not but fall short of
that highest goal. Indeed, since convents and *recolhimentos* offered a safe
haven for women with no alternative (and no vocation) and many were
forcibly confined in them, it is not surprising that colonial records include
repeatedly reformed statutes and visitors' reports of violations of vows and
cloister.

In the eighteenth century, more *recolhimentos* and convents were
begun without prior imperial or ecclesiastical approval, and their varied
functions and governance structures resulted in not just confusion but
also the regular abrogation of conventual rules. While the earliest petitions for cloisters included some mention of religious functions, later *recolhimentos* and convents underscored social and political needs, and
their residents perceived them as alternative housing rather than as sacred
grounds. Decisions concerning their building, statutes, and religious requirements were typically made by political and religious leaders who envisioned their daughters or nieces bound to quiet seclusion, but daily life was
overseen by the resident *regente* or prioress and a small set of powerful and
astute women whose lives were increasingly removed from colonial norms.
With little religious supervision, the recluses—by choice or by necessity—
abandoned religious practices or replaced them with lessons in music, art,
and sewing, while the few literate residents read aloud from the lives of the
saints or other devotional texts.[136]

Most complaints about convent life centered on the presence of outsiders within the cloister and failures to maintain the communal life.
Women who entered the convents without religious vocations re-created
their secular social worlds inside those walls, and the strict boundaries of the
cloisters became permeable. At the Convent of Santa Clara do Desterro in
Salvador, pious residents clashed openly with recluses who maintained external businesses and welcomed visitors into their well-appointed cells for
repeated or lengthy stays.[137] At the Recolhimento da Luz da Divina Providência, Bishop Mateus de Abreu Pereira warned that without barred doors
and windows, "laxity, discredit and perdition" entered to tempt the residents: "In truth it is lamentable that so many young women well-behaved
in their parents' houses, without the liberty to socialize even with their own
brothers, once in the cloisters are free to meet with the whole world!"[138] His
1788 statutes mandated modesty and decency in the few permissible meetings, and other religious houses followed with new emphases on silence,
eliminating visiting rights and live-in servants. Pereira added communal

gatherings for meals and devotions, maintaining that perfection might be realized even among the "fragile sex" through poverty and common property,[139] but other religious houses dropped the mandatory meals and meetings that created financial burdens on the convent patrimony.

Internal conflicts were not the only reason for abandoning shared meals and communal festivals in Brazilian convents and *recolhimentos*. Most religious houses faced financial problems by the end of the colonial period, as donations dried up, debtors defaulted on the desirable low-interest loans, and the financial support for residents reverted to individual means. The waning of religious vocations also meant that fewer women were willing to submit their personal fortunes to the oversight of the abbess or the external control of men from rival leading families. Women within the cloisters recognized the power they might gain from establishing an independent household there, beyond the reach of their families and the limits of secular laws. In the wealthier establishments, each resident might surround herself with younger family members, servants, and slaves, creating a small family with a private income from property, the sale of embroideries, baked goods, or candies, and even the hiring out of slaves for wages.[140] Funeral inventories from Santa Clara do Desterro reveal that many nuns owned not just religious objects and books, but also "objects of silver, gold, furniture, jewelry and fine china" with which to entertain friends or guests; barred from marriage or a larger inheritance from their families, nuns received these goods as a sort of recompense for their restricted lives in the cloister. Poorer women in the same convents or in small *recolhimentos* "practiced fasts, vigils, used sackcloth and mortifications, [and] followed the dictates of charity and poverty."[141] The residents of the lesser institutions with "nothing or almost nothing" lived on alms and wrote endless letters petitioning religious and political leaders for funds to offset their expenses, having sold their patrimony and lost all but a few elderly recluses.[142]

Bound to the cloister for life, some Brazilian women resisted conformity and flouted the statutes and religious expectations of the convents. They refused to attend daily prayers, learn the required songs, or adopt appropriately modest attire. They spoke to family members and friends through the barred doors and high windows, exchanged gifts through the turn-boxes, and accommodated friends and relatives in their cells overnight.[143] Before their final vows, a few nuns and *recolhidas* abandoned the cloisters briefly and returned, repeating such excursions until forced by the external administrators to choose between the convents and their family homes. Others took refuge in artistic expression in the convent choir or orchestra, directed religious pageants and processions celebrating local saints, or introduced traditional or popular devotions without church approval.[144] With new lives created within the convents and *recolhimentos*, even those with no religious vocations might find some solace and some individual autonomy—contrary to the best intentions of the founders and their ephemeral ideal of the submissive Bride of Christ.

CONCLUSION

The convents and *recolhimentos* of colonial Brazil drew numerous women within their gates and have left modern interpreters with a set of paradoxes. The question that ends this chapter is simply this: did convents and *recolhimentos* benefit women? Did their positive aspects—shelter, education, and power—outweigh the restrictions and burdens?

While women outside the white and elite classes had few opportunities to voluntarily enter the formal or informal cloisters, the religious houses nonetheless represented unique opportunities for colonial women. For hundreds of women, they were the only place of refuge from a stifling, narrow life of restrictions and drudgery under the patriarchal demands of fathers, brothers, and husbands. As the doors of the cloisters opened, so did women's lives, with education for young girls in convent schools, temporary residence for married women while husbands traveled, protection for abused women, and housing for the abandoned and widowed. In the demands for shelter from visionary women and orphaned girls one can glimpse—albeit only rarely and briefly—the possibilities that the colonial convents offered to them and other women. A few women from beyond the sheltered courtyards and closed cells visited their relatives and friends, cooked and sewed for residents, or sold lace and candies to them, and both visitors and residents benefited from the interchange. And women whose paths in religious expression were otherwise barricaded found opportunities for spiritual growth in the convents, where they might be both quiet in prayerful meditation and exuberant in independent leadership.

At the same time, the convents and *recolhimentos* were not successful in nurturing expanded freedoms for women in colonial Brazil. Too many women were forced to enter these shelters by their families, and there found a life that must have seemed like a pale imitation of the home life they had left. Still limited in nearly every dimension of their lives, with their clothing, living spaces, relationships, roles, and behaviors constrained, women in the cloisters may have found the isolation only exacerbated their sense of restriction. They were there "entombed," to paraphrase the infamous colonial declaration. Women outside of the white elite families, of mixed ethnicities, impoverished, or enslaved, had no choices at all regarding cloistered life: they entered or were barred from entry as others dictated, and no recovered documents reveal their responses to their losses.

These studies and reflections on the contributions of convents and *recolhimentos* to the Brazilian colony have led to some unexpected conclusions. The introduction of cloisters, intended to marginalize excess women and restrict their presence in the larger society, eventually resulted in the ceding of a place where women might develop more fully in religious, personal, and social dimensions—but only after considerable delay. By the end of the eighteenth century, a changed discourse had emerged in founding documents that emphasized the importance of women's education—then for the greater social good—and argued that women deserved fairer treatment and greater opportunities for personal and social development. Confirmation of this trend may be seen in the increasingly younger ages of entrants to convents in the last fifty years of the colonial period: most entrants to convents in Rio and São Paulo were younger than thirty, and as many as one-third were younger than fifteen.[145] Only a few notes remain from this later era concerning women's eagerness to establish new convents or *recolhimentos* or to enter the existing cloisters, however, to balance the considerable evidence that the establishment of educational institutions in Brazil lagged far behind European counterparts. While powerful and wealthy young women were briefly educated within the cloisters before marriage or before their permanent vows, literacy for women in Brazil remained marginal through the end of the nineteenth century, and the convents themselves declined precipitously over that same century. The positive contributions of the colonial cloisters might finally be seen in the twenty-first century, in the delayed women's movement and in the women's colleges which today occupy a few of the original convent buildings.

# SIX

# Women and Magic

## RELIGIOUS DISSIDENTS

## IN COLONIAL BRAZIL

O n August 20, 1591, in Salvador, Bahia, Brazil, Paula de Siqueira confessed that she had learned a small repertoire of prayers and rituals for obtaining and securing the love of her husband. Among them was a spell using the Latin words of consecration from the Catholic Mass that, when whispered to her sleeping spouse, would cause him to "put all of his affection on her."[1] Two years later, in the agricultural center of Pernambuco, Isabel Antunes denounced her neighbor Ana Jacome, who was said "by the good and bad of this land" to be a witch. Jacome had taught her the trick of placing an inverted stool and trivet near her door to prevent the entry of witches to her house but had also — Antunes claimed — bewitched and killed Antunes's newborn daughter.[2]

Nearly two hundred years later, in the province of Grão-Pará in 1763, Constança Maciel denounced Luduvina Ferreira, a white woman known in the town for her magical healing. Ferreira attributed mysterious ailments to *feitiçaria* (or sorcery), and used cigar smoke, a *maracá*, and a water-filled gourd to empower her cures. During one ritual healing, family members heard thumps and shouts coming from the darkened sickroom, after which Ferreira reported that spirits had uncovered the magical objects or *feitiços* that had brought the illness. Maciel reported that Ferreira had done such "deviltry" on three occasions and was teaching her own daughter to continue her work.[3]

These examples provide a glimpse into the world of women's magical practices during the colonial period from the late 1500s to the late 1700s. The confession by Siqueira and denunciations of Jacome and Ferreira only begin to indicate the diversity of women's alternative religious activities in Brazil, the subject of this chapter. Their magic, sorcery, and witchcraft was gathered from a range of changing European traditions, including personal and private rituals, objects, and words developed outside of the realms of ordinary religious and political power or bypassing ordinary means of communication and expression. Most magic, from the time of its Western origins in ancient Greece and Judaea, sought alterations in the material world for the benefit of its practitioners, although that scarcely distinguished it from the religious rituals of the Imperial Roman Empire or Christianity. Magic did not always address the highest divinities, but still implicated supernatural powers, often displacing a strongly theocentric religious tradition. Instead, women in colonial Brazil, as elsewhere, attempted to exploit the inherent but hidden properties in the natural world, primal relationships among persons and objects, or inclinations of the entities and powers beyond human understanding.

The traditions of magic, in Brazil as elsewhere, were open to manipulation by women of all social classes, but few openly admitted to their use. While participation in a restricted set of religious activities might have enhanced a woman's perceived status—or at least have caused no diminution—magic and sorcery brought intimations of danger and harm, especially to a woman's honor. Accordingly in his 1728 *Vocabulario*, Raphael Bluteau noted that women might magically enhance their own beauty or delve into others' secrets, but that "even today" most of women's magic was demonic deception.[4] Women's faults were exaggerated, and as Diogo de Paiva de Andrada warned in *Casamento perfeito*, vanity, gossip, curiosity, and even idleness led to their downfall: "idleness is a door wide open for disordered thoughts; and since our nature always inclines itself to the worst, and the devil has more entry where there are few cautions, . . . idleness gives them occasion to be tempted." Strict obedience to marital life and observance of Christian virtues might be women's only refuge, for without such controls, even a small fault could damage their honor.[5]

The examples of Siqueira, Jacome, and Ferreira illustrate two distinctive trends during the colonial period, beginning with the diversification of women's magical practices and ending with increased condemnation of their aberrations. Colonial records suggest that women's magical arts first expanded from their early focus on interpersonal relationships to encompass community concerns, changing from love magic (for example) to curing illnesses and removing curses. At the same time, women increasingly adapted indigenous Brazilian and African religious elements, changing the traditional structure and practices of magic in the colony. The diversification of purpose and practice was not, however, the only change that one might observe. The second trend, casting an ominous shadow over the religious lives of the colonists, was the increased demonization of magic and witchcraft due to the changing perspective of the Roman Catholic Church. Whereas in the 1590s, the Inquisition records contain many reports of the suspicious behaviors of colonists of Jewish descent alongside the few confessions and denunciations of superstitious magic, the documents of the 1700s bear long descriptions of divinations and healing ceremonies clearly attributed to unnatural and hence demonic powers.

Through the Inquisition reports and other contemporary texts, we can see these patterns unfolding. This chapter is centered on the effort to separate and trace these two developments, the increasing diversity in women's magic and the demonization of that magic and sorcery from the ecclesiastical perspective. The results were, of course, a shocking clash of ideas at the heart of what it meant to be religious in the early modern colony. I will address this in three sections. In the first I will introduce the history of the Portuguese Inquisition and magic and briefly summarize the issues of approaches to the study of magic, and in the second and third I will turn to the characteristics of magical practices during the early colonial period from the 1590s to the 1620s, and during the later colonial period of the mid- to late 1700s. In my conclusion, I will bring the separate issues together again to relocate the issue of magic and interpretive perspectives in women's lives.

## MAGIC, WITCHCRAFT, AND SORCERY

The conflict between magic and religion in Brazil reveals a landscape of shifting boundaries of belief and rival claims of power. At issue for Church officials and the men and women who confessed their own sins and denounced the sins of others was not just what was done but also why. Central to the study of magic, then, is the consideration of how any act came to be identified as "magic" rather than "religion." As I have drawn from a variety of sources, the center of my studies will still concern what constituted magic, witchcraft, and sorcery according to the perspectives of the Catholic officials, and what sense the practitioners and participants themselves made of these practices. The focus on women does not remove methodological considerations from this particular topic. Before I continue, then, I would like to comment on the usefulness of ritual theory, anthropological methodology, and definitions of magic and religion emergent from studies other than the present case.[6]

The scholars of the nineteenth century who inaugurated the field of comparative studies in religion drew sharp boundaries between "religious" rituals on the one hand, and "superstition" or "magic" on the other. Following the theories of Edward B. Tylor,[7] James George Frazer famously defined religious prayers as heartfelt pleas for divine intervention and magical spells as formulaic rituals compelling hidden spirits to act. Frazer proposed that magic was like primitive science—both were based in misunderstood resemblances and ineffective attempts to control the environment—and that magical acts were either sympathetic analogies or imitative gestures.[8] The origins of such dichotomies may be found in the ancient Israelite condemnations of the "false religion" of magicians and idolaters, but the more likely influence is, as Stanley Tambiah has convincingly argued,[9] the Reformation authors seeking to challenge the apostolic descent and power of Roman Catholic rituals. From those beginnings, Émile Durkheim transported the discussion of magic and religion to the realm of social analysis by insisting that magic was personal and pragmatic: with no "*Church of magic*," practitioners drew on fragments of rituals and symbols to relieve their own disease and misfortune.[10]

Following his extensive studies in the Trobriand Islands, anthropologist Bronislaw Malinowski argued that magic emerged as an irrational set of procedures designed to extend the limits of primitive science, create a (false) sense of security in a frightening world, and support the development of the more intellectually and emotionally satisfying beliefs and rituals of religion.[11] British anthropologist E. E. Evans-Pritchard contended that the specificities of individual cases—including his own work among the Azande—rule out the possibility of any universal theories of magic or sorcery.[12] In his African examples, witchcraft appeared as innate transformative power and sorcery as the deliberate acquisition of spells for evil and harm to others, providing an Azande explanatory system for disease and death as well as the means for negotiation of enmity and harm.[13]

Social historians of European magic have generally relied on Frazer's original dichotomy alongside Durkheim's distinctions to interpret magic, witchcraft, and sorcery, and explain their relationship to institutional Christianity. Arguing that magical practices continued alongside Christian sacraments and devotions, Valerie I. J. Flint marked the minimal distinction between magic as coercive and religion as propitiatory interactions with supernal powers.[14] Richard Kieckhefer, however, adhered more closely to European Christian perspectives, which distinguished between the "different types of causal principles."[15] Keith Thomas has insisted that sorcery utilized material manipulations while witchcraft relied on invisible powers, but conceded that the two were intertwined during the decline of magic in England.[16] Brian Levack followed Evans-Pritchard in his explanation that even in early modern Europe, witches were "regarded as individuals who possess some sort of extraordinary or mysterious power" and contrasted witches' manipulations with the priest's powers of religious supplication of "superior beings."[17] But these scholars rarely consider Iberian magic, whose history and form reveal quite divergent trends.

In his studies of Spanish witchcraft, Julio Caro Baroja mapped the shifting patterns of credulity and skepticism in Christian views of magic, noting that authorities in sixteenth-century Iberia typically followed Thomas Aquinas's admonitions to view witchcraft and sorcery as devilish illusions, while elsewhere in Europe trances, dreams, and magic were deemed part of devil worship.[18] Similarly, José Pedro Paiva found that few Portuguese in the 1600s consistently distinguished between the witch or *bruxa* who had a pact with the devil and the sorceress or *feiticeira* who learned magical lore and rites. The Catholic clergy, lay people, civil authorities, and magical practitioners, Paiva explained, were concerned less with "the processes used by the agents of magic, but more in the concrete results of their actions."[19] Finally, Brazilian scholar Laura de Mello e Souza followed past practice in calling the conjuring of demons and creation of pacts sorcery, apart from the ordinary and syncretic practices of magic or witchcraft. At the same time, she emphasized the specificity of the early modern mentality that accepted the "tension between the rational and the marvelous, between lay and religious thought, between the power of God and that of the Devil" in a world "where the religious plane occupied a place of prominence, revealing itself present in the most diverse sectors of daily life."[20]

For this chapter, I follow the examples set by Baroja and Paiva, to allow—as best as can be managed across the gulf of language and time—the definitions and categories to emerge from the early modern Luso-Brazilian world. As I present the textual accounts of magic, sorcery, charms, curses, and cures created by women, most attention will be paid to their own dynamic understanding of these acts especially as they utilized terms and labels available to them. Here, I concur with Malcolm Gaskill's concern for understanding witchcraft in its context, accounting for "first, competition for power and resources; secondly deviance, criminality, and the resolution of disputes; and, finally, the mentality shaped by belief within a universe governed by supernatural forces."[21] Women's concerns, including their conflicts over property and propriety and their often desperate efforts to survive under unbearable conditions, were enacted in their practices of magic and their accusations of others' sorcery. By "taking discourses of witchcraft on their own terms, however much those terms might conceal as well as reveal meanings,"[22] I hope to offer some new insights into women's spiritual imagination during the colonial period and into their religious experiences and the ways they made sense of them in Brazil.

## Magic in Medieval and Early Modern Europe

Medieval and early modern European magic depended on a complex world of "mysterious forces and invisible beings of awesome power"[23] compelled by the will of the witch, healer, and necromancer. The religious power wielded by the priest was not separate from that of the sorceress, for each relied on unseen forces, efficacious rituals, and traditional knowledge. The Christian church, however, reserved to itself the right to appeal to divine and angelic forces and condemned those outside of its hierarchy who dared manipulate the supernatural. By the early modern period, however, a sharper difference could be seen between the learned scientists and conjurors who developed occult systems of astrology and alchemy, and popular witches and women healers whose domain encompassed fertility rituals, magical cures, divination, and weather predictions.

Magical traditions in the Middle Ages perpetuated a complex of beliefs and practices, some from the ancient religions of the Near East, some from autochthonous European religions.[24] Specific material elements, such as colored gemstones for protection, and techniques, such as the creation of personal effigies for harm, have long histories in the Western world, and participants from nearly every class of society have relied on herbal cures, protective amulets, divination practices, and the use of occult symbols, drawings, and incantations. Beginning in late antiquity, Christian authorities confronted "a wide array of beliefs and practices, ranging from astrology and alchemy, charms and amulets, to sorcery and necromancy, trickery and entertainment, as practiced by both clergy and laity, by those of high and low social status, educated and uneducated, and found in diverse sources and contexts, including scientific and medical treatises, liturgical and other religious documents, and literary texts."[25] Christian leaders condemned practices that undermined the exclusivity of priestly privilege, but magic and religion were notoriously difficult to distinguish, and some local traditions thoroughly integrated the Christian elements.[26]

Faced with the endless tasks of survival, European peasants relied on rites for planting and harvesting and for protection and fertility, with private and community-wide celebrations following an annual calendar. Natural calamities, such as storms and earthquakes, were addressed by local witches or magicians on behalf of the community, especially when the work of priests fell short. Blessings of the Church were supplemented by amulets, prayers, and potions to bring about love, marriage, and conception, and midwives and women healers relied on folk traditions and accumulated experience to protect mothers and their children through dangerous passages.[27] At the same time, sorcerers or sorceresses could not only curse enemies and damage personal or community prosperity, but also uncover the origins of such curses. Divination and astrology were also part of the local repertoire in medieval magic, and the powers of the dead were raised by necromancers who manipulated spirits for success in love and business.

Much of the commonly known beneficent magic was part of oral culture in medieval European villages, where wise men and women taught their remedies, spells, and blessings, while the literate tradition of occult sciences drew the learned of the church, including monks and priests who transmitted ancient herbal and medical texts.[28] In the late Middle Ages and early modern period, however, the attitudes of the elite shifted so that "the Devil was presumed to be behind every non-approved religious activity, sowing among the faithful doubt in the veracity of the [Christian] ritual or outright desecration of the same."[29] Challenges to the spread and consolidation of Christian authority were considered not just dissidence but heresy, and heretics—witches, diviners, and healers—were Satan-worshippers, relying on Satan's power to thwart the Church.[30] By the mid-1500s, popular magic and witchcraft had become the target of Inquisitors and diocesan courts in Spain, Italy, and France, and the witch hunts began.

The religious atmosphere of Europe in the sixteenth century was marked by conflict between reformers and the established Church that played out—no less symbolically—between lay leaders and the clergy, and diabolical forces and divine power. Villagers and elite alike perceived an increased threat from witches and instigated more widespread persecution of marginalized individuals, especially women. Northern European regions guided by the Reformation turned to secular courts for redress against the burgeoning threat of the witches' subculture; southern Catholic countries petitioned the popes for ecclesiastical courts and Inquisitions to examine their cases of heresy and apostasy. In Italy, France, Spain, and Portugal, however, the potential for destabilization caused by Lutherans, Muslims, and Jews was at first far more menacing than the challenges that witches might present. Still, the arguments for prosecuting witches and witchcraft were felt in Catholic countries as well. By the mid-1600s, the accumulated propaganda of the *Malleus Maleficarum* (*Hammer of Witches*) by Inquisitors Heinrich Kramer and Jacob Sprenger and the *Démonomanie des sorciers* by Jean Bodin was sufficient to convince the elite Roman Catholic clerics that magical practitioners were linked in a devilish conspiracy to suborn the Church and the papacy.[31] The resultant "institutionalized repression" of witches and sorcerers created the dark mythology of the witches' Sabbath, coalescing fragmented or local beliefs in magical transformative powers with animalistic and orgiastic images of nocturnal rituals with the devil himself.[32]

In western Europe, especially after the 1300s, it appears that women more often than men were accused of witchcraft, sorcery, and demonic practices. Even in the face of contrary evidence, the demonologists of the late Middle Ages assumed that all or nearly all those involved in witchcraft were women, with the authors of *Malleus Malleficarum* and *Démonomanie des sorciers* insisting that women were inherently prone to such evil and outnumbered male practitioners fifty to one.[33] Recent studies have revealed that women accounted for only 10–20 percent of the accused in northern Europe and 50–70 percent of the accused in Germany and France, but in localized cases in England, North America, and central Europe, women constituted 80–95 percent of those accused or brought to trial during the worst witch hunts, leading some scholars to conclude that witchcraft was increasingly identified with women as a "feminine crime."[34] The misogyny expressed in such persecutions of women may have emerged more readily during times of socioreligious and political turmoil, but the elite and the local perspectives differed on women's propensity to demonic influences.

In European villages, women were accused of malevolent magic when their behaviors threatened—or appeared to threaten—their neighbors' well-being or their communities' sense of feminine propriety. Older and poorer women repeatedly faced persecution as carriers of illness or bad luck, and women healers and midwives were suspected of causing or exacerbating disease, especially during local famines and epidemics. Local opinion may have tied disasters to the workings of witchcraft, so that villagers suspected marginalized individuals of demonic influence. Under patriarchal structures that mandated the submission of women to religious and social norms, women were not only the more likely victims of witchcraft accusations, but were also more likely to accuse other women or make claims about magical powers. By these means, they might challenge or resist the pressures from dominant males, or seek to gain a modicum of power for themselves in a relatively powerless situation.[35]

For the European elite who composed the demonological literature and created the witch hunts, medieval Christianity had shaped the predominantly negative concepts of women and feminine nature. Theologians named Eve as the first woman to surrender to the devil's suasions, and all women after her were deemed more susceptible to immoral acts and carnal desires. Considered intellectually and morally deficient, women were associated with "powerlessness and passivity" but still held accountable for their sinful choices.[36] Women's social position in Europe was similarly ambiguous. Women played crucial roles during the most uncertain moments of human life—whether caring for children, the ill, or the elderly, preparing meals for the family, or in funeral preparations. At the same time, most women were themselves socially vulnerable, so that with their limited power in the family or in political, juridical, or economic arenas, and their limited recourse to judicial courts or for family support, they were more often targeted during the witch-crazes and may have turned to magic "as an instrument of protection and revenge."[37] As will be explored below, women in Portugal and Brazil were no less vulnerable, and in both regions were most often accused of magic, witchcraft, and sorcery.

## Magic in Portugal

While some European countries developed elaborate definitions of and legal defenses against magic and its practitioners, and a few were ravaged by the so-called witch hunts of the fifteenth and sixteenth centuries, Portugal was singularly unaffected by the severe repressions witnessed elsewhere, and Portuguese women were spared the worst of the attacks. Nonetheless, Portuguese civil and religious law specifically prohibited magical practices, and royal, ecclesiastical, and Inquisitorial courts all claimed jurisdiction to prosecute crimes so defined.[38] Civil decrees against magical practices dated from the fourteenth century, and included the 1385 royal edict against magical "binding," demonic prayers, and divination. The Ordenações Manuelinas promulgated in 1512 defined "witchcraft" generally as a crime, extended royal law over a wider range of illicit practices, and permitted capital punishments in extreme cases. At the same time, ecclesiastical decrees, beginning with the Synod of Braga of 1281, granted the regional bishops power over witchcraft, magical rituals, and divination, and Portuguese bishops encouraged local diocesan priests to extirpate heretical beliefs, rituals of divination, diagnosis, and healing, and abuse of sacred objects for demonic purposes.[39] Episcopal punishments were limited to monetary fines, religious penances, appearances in autos-da-fé to repudiate the forbidden acts, and, for reiteration of the same crimes, exile and excommunication.

Portugal was not alone in its diversification of juridical authority in opposition to magic and witchcraft. Across Europe, at least until the 1550s, most charges of witchcraft or sorcery were individual offenses brought to local village courts or ecclesiastical tribunals by those claiming physical injury or property damage by curses or ill will. Political elites accepted the possible threat, if not the spiritual reality, of magical practices, while ecclesiastical authorities in Italy and Spain soon adopted the new theological discourse concerning magic that emerged from the Council of Trent. That "ecumenical" council, called by Pope Paul III (and his two successors) in response to the growing unity of the Protestant Reformation, enacted a new institutionalization of Catholic theology and ritual behavior. Among its far-reaching results was a new perception of the salvific importance of the sacrament of penance and the creation of several important penitential manuals that included lengthy descriptions of the crimes of magic and witchcraft.

In response to the teachings of the Tridentine Council, new confession manuals were written to guide clergy concerning individual virtues and vices and to inculcate sacramental behaviors. One of the most important for the Iberian churches was the *Manual de confessores y penitentes*, published by Martín de Azpilcueta Navarro in 1556 and in Spain in 1570; in that formidable text, Navarro detailed the sinful magical practices that were to be confessed before the priest and God.[40] Navarro noted that all "false religion" and superstitions constituted sins against the first commandment to worship only one God, and he vilified excessive piety alongside misdirected worship. He first condemned the invocation of demons, whether done "expressly" through spells, conjurings—even in one's own heart—and prayers, or tacitly through the attempted manipulation of the hidden "virtues" of natural objects and sacred words or in the occult sciences of necromancy and treasure hunting.[41]

Navarro continued with a demonic litany of sorts, listing mortal sins connected with all manner of magical arts. Even without the aid of demons, sinners might still err if they created curses and enchantments or the means to undo them, consulted fortune-tellers, created potions or powders using sacred elements of the Church such as holy water, treated holy statues and amulets like charms, or trusted the hidden meanings of dreams. Most of the lists castigated "anyone who" might indulge in superstitious practices, but Navarro stipulated that gypsies, superstitious healers, and diviners also "sinned mortally" if their consultations replaced true religious rites. In particular, *santiguadoras* and *ensalmadoras*—women who cured using liturgical prayers, the sign of the cross, and psalms—should be "forbidden this occupation because many times vain and superstitious things [were] mixed in" with their devotions. Even if the women were "virtuous, discreet, and commonly known for living a good life," their practices must end, since "simple folk" could not discern the licit from the illicit in prayers. The mere belief in sorceresses and their powers also constituted mortal sin, although the acknowledgment of the powers of the devil to mislead the gullible did not.[42]

When Navarro instructed sinners to abjure all superstitions associated with witches and witchcraft, he assigned their penitence to the confessional, but not to the Inquisitorial Tribunal since that institution was tied to political rather than religious concerns. The Portuguese Inquisition had been reestablished in the mid-1500s to address the problems raised not by witches or heretics but by the recently converted Jews, known as *novos christãos*, taking refuge from repressive measures introduced by monarchs Isabel and Ferdinand of the neighboring Spanish kingdoms. Requested of the papal authority in 1515, 1525, and 1531, the Inquisitorial Tribunal was begun in 1539 by Portuguese Cardinal D. Henrique, appointed Inquisitor General by his brother King D. João III and conceded by Pope Paul III in 1547. The Inquisition adapted the fourteenth-century Inquisitors' Manual created by Nicolás Eymerich as well as the sixteenth-century confession manual of Navarro, and under its own aegis added magic to its list of banned practices. The Inquisition *Regimentos* listed magic and magical practices as criminal practices with its first two edicts, in 1570 and 1613.

The most powerful and extensive of its regulations, the *Regimentos* of 1640, dominated Inquisitorial practice for 130 years and established the harshest judgments against magic and its practitioners. Under its rule, Inquisitors condemned "witchcrafts, sorceries, and divinations" as demonic and heretical, and included capital punishment—carried out under the civil justice system—as appropriate for the most dangerous criminals. Exile, physical and religious penances, and penitential sentences were also exacted, but more merciful judgments might be levied for those who willingly confessed their crimes before their neighbors denounced them and religious leaders arrested or investigated them. Paiva estimates that as many as 60 percent of the Portuguese seized by the Inquisition for magic and witchcraft were tortured during their imprisonment.[43] The last *Regimento* promulgated by the Inquisition in 1774 radically transformed the religious assessment of witchcraft, magic, and superstition. Ending the demonization of heretical practices and beliefs that had begun in the late Middle Ages, the Inquisition redefined magical practitioners as ignorant "imposters" and their rituals as illusions. Inquisitors were instructed to deal carefully with these dangerous but foolish men and women, and lead them back to the true religion and away from their "superstitious" ideas.

In Portugal, beginning in the Middle Ages and extending well into the early modern period, cunning men and women had used practical or "traditional magic" for healing, protection, and influence over people and the future. Relying on plant and herbal medicines, arcane symbolism, inherited knowledge, but few books, those *curandeiros* and *feiticeiras* rarely asserted their own or other supernatural powers and so were not always considered dangerous to the political and ecclesiastical elite.[44] Their specialties might be suggested by the terms assigned in Inquisition reports, for they were variously identified as "curers," "healers," "potion-makers," "witches," and "sorcerers," but their activities overlapped. Denouncers and Inquisitors focused more on their activities and goals than on their titles and means of accomplishing magic.[45] In the cases recorded in seventeenth- and eighteenth-century Coimbra, most accusations of witchcraft or sorcery targeted women—up to 67 percent of those named to the Inquisition—and most of the evil practices were attributed to women. The majority of women accused were either unmarried or widowed, and the few detailed accounts suggest that they were poor or considered indigent and unlettered.[46]

While elites and commoners resorted to healers and diviners of both sexes, women specialized in personal magic, "in the area of feelings and will," which included love magic, arranging or improving marriages, reconciling estranged friends and lovers, and divining the location of missing persons and objects. The assistance rendered might be removal of curses or the casting of spells, the use of "devotions, conjuration, *cartas de tocar* (magical touch-letters), *fervedouros* (brews), invocations of demons by circles or *signa Salomonis* drawn on the ground, formulas for charms, *lançamentos de sortes* (casting of lots), and communication with souls."[47] Divination in particular seemed tied to women, and they offered information about the whereabouts of long-lost relatives or missing goods. *Feiticeiras* or sorceresses, who had learned their craft from local elders, listened to spirits, prayed over "a napkin, cheese, bread, and a knife," or read the pattern of an egg yolk and white to obtain hidden knowledge about missing husbands. Witches or *bruxas* were considered to have some inborn power to help or harm; with that power, they might construct or destroy an effigy or *feitiço*, or dispel persistent bad luck or bad health—known as *quebranto*—due to the evil eye. Such powers were closer to demonic forces, even when the *bruxas* claimed that they wielded a "divine gift," and they were more likely to draw the attention of the Inquisitorial and ecclesiastical courts.[48]

While the Portuguese Inquisition, especially following the 1640 *Regimentos*, considered magical practitioners to be heretics and prosecuted any who stole sacred objects or "expressly invoked diabolical spirits,"[49] no witch hunt resulted from its attention. Little of the "European witch myth" emerged in the statements to the Inquisitorial Tribunal or in cases transferred to the civil courts: there were no references to night flights or the so-called witches' Sabbath. With their attention focused on hidden Jews, Portuguese political or religious officials did not consider illicit magical practices an "important crime": few cases were tried and even fewer resulted in convictions.[50] Rather than merge the divergent practitioners into an apostate underclass, the church and state treated the *feiticeiras, bruxas,* and healers as aberrant individuals and assigned the abjurers to religious penances and subsequent public spectacles, imprisonment, and exile. In the early eighteenth century, European diabolism waned and Inquisitors expressed outright skepticism toward magical practitioners; one of their pamphlets even ridiculed the claims of village healers, proclaiming that "God no longer provided mere mortals with healing powers."[51] By 1774, the Portuguese Inquisition and royal courts considered magical practices to be nothing more than trickery and superstition and only persecuted those who persisted in defrauding their neighbors through their fantastic deceptions.[52]

## Magic in Brazil

As Portuguese explorers, missionaries, and colonists opened the Brazilian territory, magical practices and practitioners accompanied them. By some definitions, magic had preceded the European presence in the New World: native Brazilians certainly practiced no religion recognizable to Europeans, and hence were either innocent of all religious sentiment or guilty of devil worship. From the perspective of some early missionaries, then, indigenous shamans and their rituals were no more than magicians and their magic *mutatis mutandi.* The expectation of magic—like the expectation of Amazons and cannibals—had its roots in the ideology and experience of religious life in Portugal. In this section I will focus on women's magic in the colonial period: what magical practices women created or continued and why women might have utilized magic for their new lives in the New World. Of special interest is the change in content and purpose for magical practice and practitioners across the era from the late sixteenth century to the late eighteenth century, as far as we can determine from the limited records and limited cases.

The accounts in the Portuguese Inquisition documents provide glimpses into the nature of magic and its use in Brazilian colonial society. Women's statements before the Inquisitorial representatives painted sketches of their religious and personal lives in the colony, shaped by needs and desires for comfort and company. The statements are rich in some details—providing the words for magical spells or the ingredients in a potion for love—but rarely offer us insights into women's motives for their acts of magic, denunciation, and confession. Here I will examine women's magical lives through the lens of their own and others' descriptions of magical practices and beliefs, beginning with an overview of the sources and context of colonial society and a brief discussion of what constituted "magic" in colonial texts. The clustering of historical records allows for investigation of two different time periods, and so the first focus will fall on women's magical practices during the early colonial period, including Inquisition records from 1591 to 1618, followed by a shift to the end of the colonial period, with the Visitation of the Inquisition from 1763–1766.

Women's lives in the Brazilian colony are known to us not from their own writing, but from the gaze and writings of men. As was true concerning the concepts of feminine virtue enacted for women's education, sexuality, and spiritual development, the limits of women's rights and liberties to practice magical arts were set by fathers, husbands, sons, confessors, and critics, who inscribed the details of their lives, ideal and real. Women's magical arts fell far outside of the ideal, so the ecclesiastical and juridical powers of colonial Brazil recorded the official efforts to extirpate magic and, with it, a burgeoning set of alternative religious practices. For this reason, the primary source for the study of women's magic is the documents of the Portuguese Inquisition, where church officials from the *metropole* confronted dissident ideas and behaviors in the colony.

The Roman Catholic Church did not establish a permanent commission for the Inquisition in Brazil, but instead appointed Portuguese officials for three major Visitations—in 1591–1595, 1618–1620, and 1763–1766—to coordinate ecclesiastical institutions there and enforce adherence to the mandates issued by the Council of Trent.[53] Since the Portuguese Inquisition had not been established in response to a significant heretical sect or suspicions of demonic sorcery, the Visitor General, his secretary, and the accompanying officials and guards took more general concerns about religious lapses to the Brazilian colony. There, the Visitor heard confessions and denunciations from elites, familiars, commoners, padres, and even African slaves concerning neglect of religious duties, breaches of faith, sexual sins, and—occasionally—magical practices. The Inquisitorial vigilance was supplemented by the oversight of Jesuit and Dominican missionaries, by episcopal Visitors appointed for occasional regional inquests, and by regular ecclesiastical courts from which local bishops sent a few grievous sinners and recidivists to Lisbon for religious or civil trials.[54]

The first *Visitação* of the Portuguese Inquisition in the 1590s was headed by Dom Heitor Furtado de Mendoça and convened in two locations, Salvador, Bahia, the colonial capital, and Olinda, Pernambuco, the agricultural center of the colony, with brief subsequent stays in two other towns near Olinda. From 1580 to 1640, Portugal was under Spanish dominion, and Spanish concern for political and religious hegemony directed the Inquisition to all regions under its control. Such imperial attention linked Spanish political and ecclesiastical officials with the Inquisition in Iberia, and in the New World the Visitors of the Inquisition focused their attention on exiled criminals, elusive suspects from other Portuguese colonies in the Atlantic sphere, and Jews seeking refuge from Spanish and Portuguese persecution. According to the documents proclaiming their establishment, the first Visit of the Inquisition intended to uncover the presence of "hidden Jews" in the colony, along with miscreants guilty of a longer list of sins.[55]

The second Visit of the Inquisition directed by Inquisitor D. Marcos Teixeira took church representatives to Salvador, Bahia, in 1618–1620. Texeira apparently followed no new directives, but continued the search for Jewish residents and refugees, especially from the Protestant countries whose increasing trade with the colonial cities unsettled Spanish plans. More frequent contact with the British and Dutch forces and the threat of invasion probably inspired the Spanish and Portuguese officials to secure the political and social allegiance of residents in the colonial capitals through what was, in effect, the religious branch of Iberian imperial power.[56] The recorded documents for the third Visitation of the Inquisition in 1763–1769 to Pará under Inquisitor D. Giraldo de Abranches were only recovered in 1963 and published in 1978. Historical reports suggest that the battles against heresy, Jewish influences, and the lax authority of the local bishop and Jesuit community repeatedly roiled the newly important Amazonian town. At the same time, Portuguese interests in maintaining religious and political conformity in that economically important region, dictated by the Portuguese Minister Marquis de Pombal, might have been inspiration enough for the last inquisitional visit.[57]

While the primary motive for the Inquisition's visit in the late sixteenth and early seventeenth centuries was the discovery and eradication of hidden Judaism, that was not the only sin the Inquisitors sought to eliminate. For the visits in the 1590s, Bishop Dom Diogo da Sylva issued a "Monitorio do Inquisidor Geral," that is, a notice to all residents that they must inform the Inquisitorial officials concerning any crimes against God and the Catholic Church. That *Monitorio* warned against those "who did not fear our Lord God, nor the grave dangers to their souls" with their "crimes of heresy, and apostasy against our said Holy Catholic Faith," and ordered reports from any persons who had "known, seen or heard of those who are heretics." The edict then specified heretical and apostate acts in six different categories: (1) following "Lutheran errors"; (2) observing Jewish religious or domestic customs, including special practices on Friday or Saturday, fasts or food avoidances, celebration of Passover, Jewish prayers and blessings, and avoidance of Catholic sacraments; (3) prayers or customs related to "the sect of Muhammad"; (4) bigamy or the denial of any of the "Articles of the Holy Catholic Faith," such as the efficacy of sacraments; (5) magical practices; and (6) possession of a Bible in the vernacular.[58]

In this edict, magical practices were distinguished from the religious, and in fact fell first at the top of the lists of sins—literally so, since these acts were considered heretical offenses against the First Commandment. In the *Regimentos* for the Portuguese Inquisition, confession manuals dispatched to the new colony, and proclamations of each new visit, officials condemned the practitioners of any banned ritual or occult science as heretics, for they defied the commandment that worship and obedience was uniquely due to the one Christian God, and there were to be no "other gods." This had been established in the most widely known manual for the Inquisitors concerning the nature of sin, the *Manual for Inquisitors* of Nicolau Eymerich, first printed in 1503.[59] That text, along with others such as Navarro's *Manual for Confessors*, explicitly condemned heretical magic, which consisted in sorceries using sacred materials and adoration or invocation of the devil. No alternative practices or spiritual powers might be considered in the face of Christian demands for allegiance, and magical practices were thus considered superstitious, heretical, or idolatrous.[60]

Confessors and Inquisitors also required confessions and denunciations of any "magical and demonic practices," presented in most edicts in general terms. In the first *Mönitorio* for Brazil, the Inquisitors demanded reports on anyone who had made "certain invocations of the devils, going about with female witches at night in the company of demons, like malevolent sorcerers [or] malevolent sorceresses" with prayers to "Belzebut, and to Satan, and to Barrabas, renouncing our holy Catholic Faith, offering to the devil a soul, or some parts, or part of their body and believing in him, and adoring him, and calling to him to tell them things that are to happen, knowledge about which belongs only to God all powerful." The text adds

that anyone having "books or scriptures, in order to do . . . the said inventions of the devils, or [has] some other books or book" specifically banned
by the "Holy Mother Church" must also come forward for confession or
be denounced.[61] Thus, for each visit of the Portuguese Inquisition to Brazil, practitioners of magic, witchcraft, divination, and sorcery were called
to confession before its tribunal, and those who had witnessed, had known
by secondhand accounts, or had even heard rumors of such beliefs and
practices were called to denounce them to the Inquisitors and officials.
For most sessions recorded by these early visits, men's and women's confessions before the Inquisition revealed an interesting pattern of difference by
gender: while men's sins indicated their regular and persistent failures to
achieve the minimum of the Roman Catholic code of religious behavior,
women's confessions revealed excesses in religious behavior, including the
additions of folk practices from Europe of Jewish or non-Christian origin.[62]
Further differences are revealed when the focus shifts to magic.

For my studies of the Inquisition texts, I have used Roman Catholic
precedent to distinguish magic and sorcery from other unusual religious
acts on the basis of three criteria: first, use of Portuguese terms for magic,
witchcraft, witch, or sorcery by the Visitor, confessant, or denouncer;
second, descriptions of European practices commonly deemed "magic"
there; and third, any accounts of demonic or unnatural powers.[63] Most
of the statements about magic identified the practitioner or practice with
one or more of the specific Portuguese terms, using *feiticeira* or *feiticeiro*,
*feitiçaria, feitiço, encantimento, bruxa* or *bruxo*, and *embruxado*.[64] The etymology of each term may shed some light on the Portuguese and Brazilian perspectives on magic and its uses. The first set of terms derived from
*feitiço*, itself the Portuguese word for an object that is "crafted" or "made"
by human artifice, apart from a naturally occurring phenomenon. Such
terms were not employed to identify magical crafts in ancient Greece or
Rome, but similar constructs are used in other Romance languages and
may indicate Christian efforts to distinguish the limits of human creativity
and culture from divine creation and associate the *feiticeira* or sorceress
with demonic powers. The term *encantimento*, or *encantada*, was derived
from "call" or "chant," but was used almost exclusively to indicate magical enchantments. The words *bruxa* and *bruxo*, here translated as female
and male witch, have no Latin derivation but were used in other Iberian
languages and dialects, including Castilian and Galician. The etymology
for these terms is not yet determined, and while they seldom appeared in
the early colonial records, their use increased through the later period. In
these Inquisitorial records, then, the identification of magical practices as

*feitiçaria* and practitioners as *bruxas* signaled their departure from ortho-
dox religion, but that connotation was not consistently accepted, as will be
discussed further below.

## Women and Magic in the Early Colonial Period

Between 1591 and 1620, over 750 confessants and denouncers came
before the visiting Portuguese Inquisitors in Pernambuco and Bahia to confess and denounce their own and their neighbors' sins; in the published
records are forty-two statements detailing women's use of magical powers,
powders, and enchantments.[65] As they explained the forms that magic took
among the colonists, many also justified their use: women practiced magic
because it worked and because it was both familiar and common. In all
of these cases, the Roman Catholic Church remained resolute: magical
practices of any sort were prohibited and penances must be assigned to
their practitioners. Wary of aggrandizing these practices, the Portuguese Inquisition tended to reduce them to foolishness, superstition, and ignorant
breaches of basic Catholic Church teachings, even while their threat might
be characterized as demonic or heretical. The visiting Inquisitor during the
first sessions of confessions, Heitor Furtado de Mendoça, conformed to the
canonical understanding that magical practices were merely "inventions"
and admonished Guiomar d'Oliveira "that she not believe in these magic-
spells and things, for they were all superstitious abuses with which the devil
fooled weak people."[66]

The witchcraft and magical practices attributed to women during the
first two Visitations of the Inquisition were recognizably European magical practices, preserving the use of centuries-old phrases, ritual objects,
and gestures. While many different actions were described and attributed
to witches and female healers, all may be grouped into five categories according to the central goal of the act; these are, listed in order of numbers
of occurrences: magic to harm an enemy or control events with marvelous
powers; to gain or secure love; to discover the unknown; to cause transformations; and to cure common or mysterious ailments. There are, in addition, claims and accusations of witchcraft with few details that are therefore
harder to classify, as will be discussed below.

Most of the *feiticeiras* during this first era confessed to or were denounced for their powers to control the world around them, principally
by inflicting harm on perceived enemies or by claiming supernal powers.
Between 1591 and 1620, eighteen women were denounced for the magical harms they wrought, and three more confessed that they had made

claims to such powers.[67] Women's statements in the 1590s revealed their use of magical inscriptions, charms, and potions familiar from medieval sources, but few indicated any connection to occult or demonic powers. Paula de Siqueira, a forty-year-old Portuguese woman married to an accountant, was first among these; she confessed to a variety of magical and sexual sins—and was later denounced for them as well. She admitted that she had been given a powerful *carta de tocar* or "touch-letter," a magical token with writing on one side; she had, however, neither read nor used it, but had burned it instead. On that same day, Catharina Froiz confessed that she had "some charms" made up to kill her detested son-in-law who mistreated her newlywed daughter but that she threw out the materials despite her daughter's own pleas. And Guiomar d'Oliveira followed an elaborate recipe with ground nuts mixed into chicken soup to give to a landlord "so that he would not press her and her husband so much about the rents." She explained that an old friend named Antonia Fernandez had also promised her a magical glass bottle that, when filled with onion and vinegar, would reveal "whatever one wanted to know" so that she might increase her power. When questioned, d'Oliveira conceded that "the said *feitiços*" were created of diabolic magic but that she "expressly did not speak nor call on the devils" and had not consented to their use nor understood all that they entailed.[68]

Most of the denunciations from Bahia and Pernambuco during the 1590s claimed that witches and sorceresses had used curses, magical books, or their own personal powers, sometimes through the manipulation of personal objects, to control, harm, or even kill.[69] For such causes was Joana Ribeiro denounced for taking a newborn's caul or afterbirth, performing secret rituals on it with salt from a church, and causing the child to "sicken and turn black" over its first month of life. The young mother confirmed that Ribeiro had "bewitched the said child" and that he "wasted away" and died.[70] So too was Ana Jacome, mentioned at the start of this chapter, denounced for causing the death of the daughter born to Isabel Antunes just six days previously. After offering Antunes some advice on keeping witches away from her vulnerable child—by piling a broom atop an overturned trivet and stool—Jacome suddenly "approached the side of her bed," cursed her child, and spit at her and her servant. Antunes fell ill with "a fever and chills" while her "unbaptized child who before this had been well and taken the breast well began to cry loudly." The "bewitched" child developed black spots at the corners of its mouth and on its belly, and died a day later after a hasty baptism. Antunes added that Jacome had a twisted eye and was "generally said" to be a witch. The young Jesuit Baltezar de Miranda similarly recalled the death of his younger brother from the curse of a witch whose name he had forgotten, recounting a strange tale of a black cat appearing to jump over and put out a candle, and then to bewitch the hapless six-day-old infant—who later died shriveled and with a "thin beard." Witches endangered adults as well, writing spells that caused an accuser to "spit blood from his mouth" and threatening town officials with unspecified harms.[71]

Repeated tales about marvelous powers to harm or intimidate focused on two women—Breatiz Corea and Maria Gonçalves Cajada. Corea, twice denounced for her magical creations or *feitiços*, allegedly kept a jar with a cobra that caused ships to go off course or come to port—an important power when overseas exile transported more than one accused witch to the colony.[72] Gonçalves Cajada, famously known as *"Arde-lhe-o-rabo"* (Her-tail-burns-her), drew denunciations of diabolical acts like a magical lightning rod. Claiming to have ecclesiastical powers "like a bishop with his miter," Gonçalves Cajada could also redirect the passage of ships, hide fugitives by her magical powers, or compel victims to act as she wished by means of a magical table. More than one denounced her claims that she spoke and slept with the devil himself, and a young widow from Bahia reported that Gonçalves Cajada called devils to work for her to avoid their harassment. In fact, she had seen a deep wound in the foot of the "vagabond" *feiticeira* where devils came to feed unless sent to cause mischief elsewhere. And while Gonçalves Cajada might visit the bottom of the ocean to learn more spells, she also called demonic powers from inside an inscribed "sign of Solomon" while holding a bit of consecrated oil "in her mouth."[73]

While recurrent magical threats menaced the lives of Brazilian colonists, women's powers to influence love and marriage balanced on the edge of threat and promise, as can be seen in the twelve Inquisition statements in this second category. Love magic offered women an intimate opportunity to direct their own lives, often by ameliorating their own marriages. For this end, a popular formula from Portugal utilized the words of consecration as noted in the chapter introduction: a woman whispered the phrase *hoc est enim corpus meum* ("this is my body") into the mouth of her lover while he was asleep or engaged in sexual acts in order to bind his love.[74] Paula de Siqueira learned several more remedies from other women who recited complicated ritual blessings to her. Her friend Maria Villela confided that she had "used many things so that her husband would love her" and had "first called upon God about this, [but] after she saw that God did not want to improve her husband she called on the devils" and their magic instead. Siqueira and Villela together concocted a potion using wine and a bit of powdered altar stone; in other accounts, wives added to their husbands' meals combinations of special herbs, ground bones, transformed and ground hazelnuts, or even his own semen.[75] Villela herself—the text notes—was called before the Inquisition; she "was reprimanded and sent to confession and warned not to use these superstitions again."[76]

Women also professed magical powers to initiate or secure relationships, conferred by consecrated materials like baptismal oil or other unspecified charms or powders during rituals that typically included chanted words naming the intended and the intention.[77] So, a woman with the colorful nickname "Vinegar Piss"—claiming no fear of the Holy Inquisition—had promised Maria da Costa that she could "make her something" to promote a longed-for marriage, and the "well-known" witch called "Nobrega" was denounced for her vague claims of love-inducing spells. Lianor Martins was similarly named in 1593 for having knowledge of a root shaped like a woman, a "card of Saint Arasmo," a wolf's claw, and seeds collected on the eve of the feast of São João, all of which she used to "make men love women or women love men as she wished."[78]

After magical threats and love magic, Brazilian colonists might also consult several "well-known" witches for divination seeking to learn future events or the whereabouts of a missing person or thief. Most divination—the third category of confessions and denunciations to the Inquisition—simply relied on women's innate gifts or familiar European magical techniques. Thus was Brisida Lopes denounced twice for predicting an unexpected voyage to Portugal, and five other women were censured for their magical knowledge of love and crime. In Pernambuco, for example, Domingas Brandoa dressed a broom in skirts, leaned it against the wall, and "began to speak calling on Barrabás and other names" to advise Maria Escobar about her marriage prospects. Escobar denounced the seer and repented of her dabbling in magic, admitting that "the aforesaid seemed wrong" to her—and she "saw no results." Felicia Tourinha, in prison for witchcraft, apparently continued her practices there, for she was denounced for her ritual involving a boot suspended from the points of scissors and a call to "the devil with the disheveled hair, devil with the big ears, shaggy devil" to reveal the road taken by a missing man. The boot then rotated in a half-turn when the right path was named, and the denunciant—who blessed herself with fear—confirmed later that the divination was accurate.[79]

As some sought to learn a future husband's name or the route of a disappearance, others sought to recover stolen goods and discover the villain using the European book-and-key ritual. In 1618, Maria de Penhosa admitted to helping a neighbor to divine the identity of a thief. She explained that she took "a Book of the Hours of Our Lady, and put in the middle of the pages a key." She then closed the book, keeping her hand on the key. With an eight-year-old boy as an assistant, she proclaimed: "I conjure you in the name of God and the Virgin Mary by virtue of these Hours that you tell me who took such a thing." She then named the suspects and "the said Book gave a turn when she the confessant named the person who committed the theft." She recalled having learned the technique from the wife of a carpenter and a Frenchwoman who had since moved to Peru.[80]

Alongside the tales of divinations, these early colonial records include five odd denunciations of magical transformations—the fourth category of women's magical practices. In these cases, witches might appear in non-human form to intimidate opponents, impress potential clients, or simply evade detection. The first report was in Bahia in 1591, as Dona Lucia de Mello offered details of an encounter that still distressed her after forty years. Knowing her to be timid, one of her boarders had warned that she planned to scare her, and not long after, a large butterfly "with huge eyes" circled around her candle late one night and frightened her and her sister from their sewing. Days later, when the boarder asked if she had seen anything unusual, Dona Lucia described the strange butterfly, and the unnamed woman promptly claimed that she had taken that form to frighten her. Dona Lucia added that while "it seemed to her that she said that as a joke," the woman had in fact been accused of sorcery—so Dona Lucia hid her children away so they could not be bewitched. Just one day later, on August 17, 1591, Padre Baltezar de Miranda suggested that the "large cat" that "jumped over and put out the candle" in his family home had been the witch, strangely transformed, who bewitched and killed his newborn brother.[81]

Later that same year, three Portuguese-born women of high status, Maria da Costa, Custodia de Faria, and Isabel de Sandales, all offered a long list of suspected witches and then denounced one or more local sorceresses who had been seen out walking "in the form of ducks." Costa reported that it was "publicly known" that the woman called "Twisted-Mouth" had been spied in that shape only twelve days before her testimony, while Faria repeated a secondhand account from Breatiz de Sampaio that Violante Ferreira, Dona Mecia Pireira, and Paula de Siqueira had been seen in their transformed state. Sandales, who repeated other stories from Sampaio, claimed that her source was the more reputable sister of the local curate and, later, the curate himself. Nearly ten years earlier, they had told her "that a person walking from the city toward Villa Velha at night . . . had found two honorable women of that city in the form of ducks, and one of them was Dona Mecia." She added that only a few days later, that same Dona Mecia had passed beneath the window of the curate's house, and he quipped, "There goes Lady Duckling."[82]

Transformed or not, Brazilian women were rarely associated with the healing arts, unlike men of the same era in Bahia or Pernambuco or women of previous centuries in Europe. Only three cases of women using magic to heal ailments appear in the denunciation records of Bahia and identify activities that come closer to harmful magic and the creation of powerful potions and spells than to traditional herbal remedies. In two cases based on hearsay, witches only known by nicknames are denounced: the first report was that "the woman from Minas" was known to cure "by the devil's art with herbs," and the second that a tall Portuguese woman called "Borges" had attempted to free a man from a binding spell by pricking his legs to draw blood to feed to demons. Maria Gonçalves Cajada, who had been denounced for curses and love magic, was similarly accused of having secret powders wrapped in bits of paper "so that she might cure," though the ailment to be healed was not specified.[83]

In addition to the five categories of magical practices detailed in the confessions and denunciations, many statements included the simple assertions that one or another woman was "commonly known" to be a *bruxa* or *feiticeira* along with her other magical crimes. Gonçalves Cajada was thus identified in five different denunciation statements as a *feiticeira* according to "*publica fama*" or "common knowledge." Isabel Monteiro Sardinha, for example, testified that "they said" Gonçalves Cajada had been "married in Portugal, exiled from Pernambuco to Bahia as a *feiticeira* and placed at the door of the church with a [conical witch's] cap." Margarida Carneira also reported that "public knowledge" had revealed Gonçalves Cajada to be "a vagabond woman who . . . called to the devil and slept and dealt with him." Similarly, Tareja Roiz, a widowed gypsy who insisted that she herself had come willingly to the colony, reported that Gonçalves Cajada had been "exiled to Bahia as a *feiticeira*" and that "it is public knowledge" that she "speaks with demons."[84] Breatiz Corea, Caterina Roiz, and the witch known as "Twisted-Mouth" were all denounced for the "public report" of their witchcraft, and two unnamed women were similarly accused.[85]

The statements found in the Inquisition records of the 1590s through the 1620s reveal that the Portuguese women colonists faced a dauntingly complex situation and relied on unorthodox means—including magic— to respond to the challenges they met. From the details of the confessions and denunciations, one may glimpse those new lives and the interplay of old and new demands in them as the colonists reflected on the place and meaning of the magical and spiritual practices prevalent amongst them. Their motives for magic and their appearance before the inquisitional board are not immediately apparent, although some of the personal details mandated by the officials may reveal inclinations and intentions. Many confessants and denouncers must have been inspired by a pious duty to the Holy Mother Church and a dread of the Inquisition, or at least the sincere aim of conformity to the demands of the ecclesiastical or civil law. Confessions given during the grace period included petitions for mercy, and so might have been motivated by genuine remorse and the hope of escaping the more serious penalties of the *auto-da-fé*, imprisonment, whippings, exile, and execution. Since the Inquisition relied on secret testimony, more than a few who confessed might have spoken out in fear that they might be denounced by their neighbors and friends, as indeed happened in a handful of cases. Paula de Siqueira, for example, confessed her magical crimes on August 20, 1591, only a week before her friend Custodia de Faria denounced her for witchcraft. And on August 22 of that same year, Margarida Carneira reported the public reputation of the absent Maria Gonçalves Cajada as a witch only ten days after Gaspar de Gois denounced her and three days after his father-in-law Diogo Martin Cão accused her of using love magic on them both.[86]

While the Brazilian confessants and denunciants had reason to fear the Inquisition's power to arrest and punish malefactors, most were not compelled to appear. There is little clear evidence that the visiting Inquisitors forced either confessions or denunciations, especially in the earliest reports, and many statements specified that the individuals came "without being called." Women colonists had no additional compulsion to confess or denounce magic, and they were not, as a group, socially marginal or economically vulnerable. Women came to confess their magical practices in roughly equal numbers to men—four women and five men—and their social standings were remarkably similar. Further, the women who confessed to magical practices were all of Portuguese descent, married, between the ages of thirty-seven and fifty, and relatively prosperous: Catharina Froiz was married to a city bailiff and Guiomar d'Oliveira to a shoemaker. None, however, could sign her own name or read, with the possible exception of Maria de Penhosa, who owned the Book of Hours of Our Lady used in divination.[87] The women denunciants came from a wider swath of colonial society and included married women and widows—though only one unmarried maiden—between the ages of eighteen and fifty-five. Most had emigrated from Portugal, with only one from Galicia, one from Africa, and four specifying a colonial birth; of the immigrants, two noted that they had been exiled from Portugal by the Inquisition there—one in connection with a murder and the other after false accusations of homosexuality. Few women mentioned an occupation, excepting Caterina Rois (married to a brick mason), who was a weaver of cloth, and two women with long-absent husbands (Maria de Escobar was a baker, and Caterina Vasquez "kept a store to sell food and other merchandise.")[88] While most denunciations identified women from the same social ranks, several—especially those of witches with disparaging nicknames—noted that the woman was "a vagabond" or "without a husband."

While age, social rank, or occupation might not distinguish these forty-two statements concerning the magical arts from the others recorded by the visiting Portuguese Inquisition between 1591 and 1620, analysis by gender reveals several patterns. First, most of the confessions and denunciations regarding magic were presented by women, with twenty-six of the total statements coming from women. Four of those were confessions, with admissions to a range of magical beliefs and practices, each of which *also* identified at least one other woman involved in the described activities, as a teacher, witness, or client. The remaining twenty-two were denunciations by women from Bahia and Pernambuco in the 1590s, typically accusing only one or two women for their magical practices. Second, most of the statements—thirty-two of the forty-two—denounced women, focusing partly or entirely on women's magic. This second pattern may not be surprising, since the paradigms linking women and witchcraft were predominant in Europe as elsewhere in the Americas.

More important than these two patterns, however, are the links among women: women named other women almost exclusively in their denunciations and confessions. While men denounced both men and women for magical crimes, all but one woman named only women as witches and sorceresses in the denunciation statements. The exceptional statement was given in Pernambuco in 1591 by Maria d'Oliveira, who denounced a list of individuals for crimes of blasphemy, heresy, and magic—all based on hearsay and "public knowledge." She added that it had been told to her husband some "four or five years ago" that Mateus, a captive from Guiné or African slave, had performed "diabolical sorceries" to ascertain knowledge about "things done." Mateus had, she recounted, "caused a white pan to move about in such a way" that no one could discern who pushed or pulled it and "that this was by the devil's art."[89] The denunciation of an African slave for African-derived magic—an accusation against another individual marginalized by the colonial power structures—may not in fact be so different. But while other women similarly recall magical practices of the near or distant past, and many rely on hearsay as their source for magical events, all but d'Oliveira named women—their friends, family, acquaintances, even strangers—as the practitioners of magic in Brazil. In this early colonial scene, then, the presence of women dominated: witches and sorceresses shaped and perpetuated magic, women observed and used magic, and women decried it before the ecclesiastical and colonial officials.

The importance of magic in the colonial period, particularly in the two colonial centers of Bahia and Pernambuco, is attested in these accounts of potions, spells, threats, and supernatural occurrences. Many confessants and denunciants who detailed the magical practices and practitioners spoke of them as powerful and efficacious, even appropriate for their ends. Some used the common European discourse for religious folk traditions, calling them "devotions" or "remedies" and their accompanying spells "prayers." A remarkable number of records indicate that the observers—whether willing pupils of elder witches or scandalized witnesses of the occult arts—believed that magic worked. Many women who denounced the malevolent powers of witches, evidenced in their curses, threats, or transformations, did so because of the apparently only-too-real results: Isabel Antunes's newborn child had indeed died after the witch's curse, according to her account in Pernambuco, and Isabel Antoniane insisted that the reputed witch Maria Gonçalves Cajada had truly disappeared from her locked house.[90]

A surprising number of denunciations and confessions of divination and love magic similarly affirmed the efficacy of the magical practices to the Inquisitors, even in the face of questioning. The accuracy of divination was scarcely doubted by the denouncers, who revealed the names of practitioners *because* of their powers. Futures were accurately foretold and lost objects recovered, according to the various accounts. Even reluctant participants were convinced: Francisca Fernandes da Silva claimed that she had at first doubted the words of the reputed witch Brisida Lopes, but acknowledged that the predicted voyage to Portugal had later taken place. In her denunciation of Felicia Tourinha (coincidentally the daughter of a cleric), Domingas Jorge similarly insisted that she disapproved of divination by scissors and boot and had reprimanded the practitioner, but added that Tourinha had identified the thief correctly.[91] And a few of the confessants even bragged about the success of love magic, as did Paula de Siqueira, who reported that Breatiz de Sampaio had taught her a spell of love magic that had made her previous two husbands "so obedient" that she could order them to kiss her feet. Guiomar d'Oliveira claimed that her husband was much "improved" after her use of magical powders and, when questioned further by the Visitor Heitor Furtado de Mendoça, she replied that "she found by experience that the said [spells] had worked."[92] Useful and dependable, the practices of divination and love magic thrived under the harsh conditions of colonial life, for they offered participants knowledge of the future, comfort against the unknown, and control over their turbulent relationships.

Many statements, however, not only cohered carefully with the Inquisition's perspectives on magic but also concluded that the magical practices reported were wrong or at least ineffective. Women who witnessed attempts at magic often dismissed them, as did Francisca da Silva, who denounced an acquaintance for divination and, after some prodding by the visiting officials, insisted that she could only "unburden her conscience" since "she did not believe in it." Similarly, Magdalena de Calvos ended her denunciation of a friend for love magic by adding that she had not wished to participate and knew that her friend had tricked others. When questioned about the reports of witches transformed into ducks, Custodia de Faria responded that "it seemed to her that Breatiz de Sampaio is a liar and there was nothing in that" story.[93] Others seemed torn between affirmation and rejection. Thus, Catharina Froiz confessed to learning love magic, but added that such *feitiçaria* "did not have any effect" and she "did not want" to use it. And finally, Paula de Siqueira ended her lengthy confession about her use of love magic by saying that she had not in fact tried to bind her husband's love with a touch-card or magical chant, and had seen no "improvement" in him after she had stirred powdered altar stone into his wine.[94]

Two preliminary conclusions may be drawn here, both emphasizing the familiarity and traditional nature of magical practices during the early colonial period. The first conclusion addresses the fact that most accounts of magic, witchcraft, or sorcery—whether done for good or ill—detailed efforts by individuals to influence the world close around them, painting a small world for these alternative spiritual acts and beliefs. The accounts mentioned neighbors, relatives, friends, acquaintances, and nearby townspeople as those who taught the spell or ritual, or who sought to learn its power. Even confessions or denunciations of events far in the past related connections among the women: they not only named the magical practitioners, but knew their birthplace, age, and marital status. In particular, claims of magical power to help or harm were reported by near neighbors and acquaintances, and denunciants knew by name or at least sobriquet those whom they claimed had bewitched or killed their loved ones. Love magic, too, was a localized, even private practice primarily done by a few women to ameliorate their own marriages. Finally, even the denunciations of frightening or demonic changes described women down the street or on the next block, seen near the denunciants' own homes.

The issue of proximity suggests two quite different perceptions of magical practices—either that early Brazilian colonists saw demonic forces around every corner and submitted to intimidation from the Inquisitors, or that magic and witchcraft were simply common among the popular religious practices. Some scholars would support the first view and have suggested that fear of the Portuguese Inquisition drove women to implicate family and friends in criminal practices. Thus its European history was just the beginning of the repressive efforts of the Church and state to dominate the lower classes, women, and colonists. The Inquisitors in Portugal certainly used secrecy, permitted hearsay evidence, cultivated local *familiares* as spies, and created "chains of accusations, impregnated by a pervasive, omnipresent dread" in their efforts to dominate peasants and workers and eradicate any element of the popular tradition that contradicted Roman Catholic orthodoxy.[95] In Brazil, the Holy Office attempted to control the colonial capitals, but the infrequency of the visitations in this early period and the failure to re-create the requisite network of officials allowed the colony and its residents the opportunity to continue popular religious and magical practices for centuries.

The full statements of confessions and denunciations, however, lend more support to the second point: those appearing before the Tribunal of the Inquisition did not explain magic, witchcraft, or sorcery within a realm of frightful and uncontrollable experiences in a New World rife with hidden and dangerous powers. Rather, many accounts registered an unexpected complacency about and even acceptance of the magical or miraculous powers, indicating the possible permeability of magical and religious worlds in that era. Maria de Penhosa—a respectable though illiterate fifty-year-old woman—provides a final example on this point. After confessing to book-and-key divination, she insisted that she no longer performed such rituals and had no pact with the devil to aid her noble clients. The Inquisitor pressed her further, asking "whether it seemed to her that [her ritual] was done by the work of the Devil or by Divine miracle, and if she knew that the Holy Mother Church forbade such fortunes for being acts that the Devil might help?" Penhosa replied that the unmasking of the thief might be "a work of God and not of the Devil," and that she herself supposed that it was "a little thing and not forbidden."[96]

At the same time—and this is the second conclusion that I draw—the beliefs and practices were not only close but in fact quite familiar, continuing centuries-old traditions of European and Christian magic. Nearly all of the forms and elements in the early colonial statements of witchcraft, magic, and sorcery may be found in earlier and contemporary accounts from Italy, England, Spain, and Portugal. Love magic, divination rituals, spells to direct the will of others, even the curses and bewitchings were common practices in late medieval and early modern Europe, and had not changed significantly in their transport across the Atlantic.[97] Even more importantly, Christian phrases, symbols, and materials were used for magical cures and spells, so women attributed failures of life and love to forces that might be addressed with well-known Latin phrases or remixed rituals; God, the saints, angels, and devils were within the reach of the faithful, and might improve spouses and circumstances. The world of the witches was—for magical practitioners at least—not alien from the world of *Nossa Santa Madre Igreja*.

The Inquisitors and representatives of the Church neither sanctioned women's creativity in this alternative tradition of rituals and prayers nor relinquished their own power over the sphere of the supernatural. The Church leaders maintained that exclusive and patriarchal hegemony extended from the Church councils, even to the particulars of missing persons and missing love. Still, the Inquisitors raised no alarms about magical practices in the early colonial era, perhaps because they were relatively rare or merely the work of women. While Inquisitors repeatedly quizzed confessants and denunciants about pacts with the devil or demonic powers, they also asked if a practitioner seemed to be in her right mind or was given to drinking too much wine. An almost dismissive attitude is reflected in the admonitions of the Portuguese Inquisitor to Guiomar d'Oliveira noted above: after she insisted that she made no pact with the devil, she was censured for her gullibility. Similarly, Maria Villela's confession concerning love magic appears only in a marginal comment that "she was reprimanded and ordered to confess and warned not to use these superstitions again."[98] Yet in these and similar exchanges we may see the continuing significance of magic in women's lives as an extension of religion. Women accepted God's powers, appealed to God as part of their love magic and divination, and considered their glimpses of the future or revelations of a thief to be, in Maria de Penhosa's words, "a work of God and not of the Devil."

*Women's Magic in the Later Colonial Period, 1763–1769*

Magical practices and practitioners flourished during the eighteenth century, as may be seen in the records provided by the third and final Visitation of the Inquisition to Brazil. The first and second Visitations had taken place between 1591 and 1620 in the coastal colonial centers of Salvador, Olinda, and nearby parishes, but the third began in Grão-Pará in 1763—nearly two centuries later, in the heart of the Amazon region. And it might as well be a different world, for the magic, witchcraft, and sorcery reported in the 1700s were essentially different from that of the earlier era: the practices and practitioners had changed, and the assessment of the place of magic had also shifted dramatically. By this later period, colonial Brazilian magical practices had been irrevocably reformulated through centuries of interchanges with native Brazilian and imported African religions. At the same time, magic was more readily linked to demonic powers from the perspectives of all concerned—practitioners, denunciants, and ecclesiastical and Inquisitorial officials.

Several factors may be responsible for the changes that can be observed. The first, and probably most important, is the sweeping impact of the Roman Catholic Council of Trent. Held in 1545–1563—a generation before the first Inquisition visit—the council created decrees and canons that slowly and inexorably changed the face of Roman Catholicism in Europe over the 1600s and finally in the colonial worlds through the 1700s. Although traces of the Tridentine doctrines concerning biblical and papal authority may be read in texts guiding the establishment of the missions to Brazil in the late 1500s and early 1600s, the absolutist and centralizing sentiments at the heart of the Trent Council were felt decades later. Second, at about the same time, the European Christian views on magic had changed as well. Influenced by the writings of demonologists like Jean Bodin of France, Catholic elites accepted the demonization of witchcraft and magic, and the scourge of witch trials had raced across Western Europe during the seventeenth century.[99] No longer just part of popular practices to ameliorate difficult lives and relationships, witchcraft and sorcery were associated by ecclesiastical and juridical authorities with heresy and apostasy—and with the devil's real powers to damage and pervert God's law and creation.

The third factor is the changed condition of Brazil. By the late 1700s, Brazil had been transformed from an outpost for a few Portuguese immigrants stranded along the coast to a complex and self-sustaining colonial enterprise. It had already undergone several cycles of expansion, financial change, and political reorganization, and had shifted the center of its economic productions. Its culture was a thorough intermixture of Portuguese culture with the separate but surviving indigenous and African languages, cosmologies, and customs. Most importantly, its religious life had changed.

The late eighteenth century was witness to two nearly contradictory developments, the centralization of the Catholic Church and the blossoming of
alternative religious groups. The Brazilian Catholic Church was no longer
a mission field dominated by Jesuits with plantation family chapels as the
spiritual centers; by the late 1700s the Jesuits had been expelled, and the
new archbishoprics in the colony were overseeing a thoroughgoing expansion of the hierarchical demands of conformity to the ecclesiastical institution. At the same time, nonconformist and even dissident religious leaders
and communities were emerging where folk Catholicism persisted. These
included, for example, independent religious communities led by female
visionaries and the first small Afro-Brazilian religious centers. The clash
of these two trends resulted in the sudden intrusion of diocesan reviews,
admonitions from the Portuguese ecclesiastical elite, and, of course, the
Visitation of the Portuguese Inquisition.

The *Constituiçōens Primeyras do Arcebispado da Bahia* (First Constitutions of the Archbishopric of Bahia), promulgated in 1707 by Bishop D.
Sebastião Monteiro da Vide, testified to the serious challenge still presented in the early eighteenth century by "witchcrafts, superstitions, fortunes, and auguries" in the colonial capital of Bahia.[100] The Fifth Book of
the *Constitutions*, on the grave sin of heresy, mandated excommunication
for "any person who does any work known to proceed from the Magical
Art, such as forming fantastical apparitions, transmutations of bodies, and
voices, that are heard, without seeing anyone speak, and other works that
exceed the efficacy [powers] of natural things." Pacts with the devils to
accomplish "witchcrafts for evil or for good, principally if they do it with
*pedras de ara* [pieces of altar stone], bodies, or sacred or blessed objects, so
as to devise or undo, conceive, move, or bring forth, or for whatever other
effects good, or bad" were condemned as "grave malice" and an affront to
God. So, too, were consultations with *feiticeiros* for cures, divination or
love magic, especially using "words, touch-cards, and things, that incline or
alienate husbands to their wives, and wives to their husbands, and medica-
tions, that mar the senses or consume the body," even if the prayers or rituals were only tricks done for monetary gain. Finally, the bishop attributed
all occult predictions—whether for personal travel or crop planning—that
relied on "the movements of the Sun, Moon, and Stars" or transgressive
ceremonies that called on the saints and interpreted natural events and
dreams—to "weakness of Religion." Even if perpetuated by ignorance or
superstition, all such heathen traditions supported "commerce, familiarity,
and pacts with the Devil," and their practitioners were to be severely castigated. D. Sebastião Monteiro da Vide made no separate condemnation

of women for magic, but the comprehensiveness of these articles includes all of the prayers and ceremonies that Brazilian women had introduced in the 1500s and perpetuated through the end of the 1700s.

Such magical practices in Brazil were renewed regularly by *feiticeiras* who immigrated to the colony voluntarily or involuntarily—the latter exiled as punishment for their heretical defiance of the Church. Brazilian historian Laura de Mello e Souza uncovered the names of twenty-two women banished to Brazil for sorcery, most of them during the 1600s. Others were notorious for their powers and spells in both Portugal and Brazil and crossed the Atlantic independently. One such, Antonia Maria, was tried in Lisbon, continued her practices in Pernambuco in 1715, and returned to Portugal later for another trial. Mello e Souza also tracked the persistence of harmful magic and curses, love magic, divination, and magical healing practices to the mid-1700s, unearthing trial records from Pernambuco, Minas Gerais, and Maranhão.[101] In those individual cases, European and Christian magical formulae continued to dominate most women's magic, except for healing rituals whose creative performers incorporated both African and Brazilian-Indian symbols and gestures by the 1750s. It is not surprising, given the common practices reported during the second Visitation of the Portuguese Inquisition in the early 1600s, that women continued and revitalized their core traditions in the healing arts and cherished their powers over life, love, and the future through the following century.

From 1763 to 1769, during the Visitation of the Portuguese Inquisition to Grão-Pará, forty-six statements of confession and denunciation were recorded, and of them twenty-seven—more than half—center on magical practices.[102] Of those, eleven specifically involved women—as the confessants to magical practices or as the principal witch, healer, or diviner denounced in the statement. The changes in the magical practices during this era in Brazil can already be seen: magic constituted the principal crime brought to the Inquisitors, but not even half of the statements centered on women. By contrast, in the earlier visitations discussed above, magical statements were infrequent—from 2.5 to 14 percent of the statements made overall—but women were 75 to 85 percent of those confessing or denounced in them. Moreover, in the 1760s, men's magic edged out women's, in all categories that women dominated in earlier years. The nature of the presentations was different as well: they are longer with more details, not as far in the past, and none of them offer mere rumor or "public opinion" as their source for information.

The reports of women's magic in the confessions and denunciations revealed another, sharper dimension of difference. Women's magical practices in the late 1700s fell into only four categories: there was only one statement of harms threatened by curses or caused by magical powers, one confession of love magic, three statements of divination, and six statements about magical healing. No statements described magical transformations into animals or magical transport. Here, the contrast is remarkable, for women's confessions of the late sixteenth and early seventeenth centuries had emphasized their powers over relationships, while denunciations had embellished the accounts of curses and resultant suffering, secrets revealed, witches' familiars or transformed appearances, and the powerful spells and powders they created. The details of the few statements made and their interpretations by the speakers and listeners provide even more contrasts, as the following cases using the previous four categories demonstrate.

First, the single denunciation in the late 1700s concerning harm involved the poisoning of one slave by another identified as Joana, "a *feiticeira*" who was "fond of saying and doing evil." On November 28, 1763, Nicolao Jozé da Costa, a Portuguese immigrant, related the particulars of the lengthy and puzzling illness of "an Indian woman named Phelypa" who had fallen "suddenly and gravely ill" the previous May on his sugar plantation Nossa Senhora da Guadalupe. Since remedies from the apothecary helped little, Costa suspected that she had been harmed by unknown *maleficios* or evil objects that she had handled or eaten. Phelypa recalled eating fish stew flavored with suspicious roots and cooked by Joana, a black slave jealous of her privileged position. Only with the local curate's blessings and Phelypa's own prayers did the illness finally abate. Joana had already been punished and imprisoned for threatening her mistress with a knife, and when accused of witchcraft, she first confessed to gesturing and chanting over the victim and then to using roots to help Phelypa.[103] Joana's recourse to domestic magic, through poisoned food and whispered words, recalls the curses and threats from witches of previous centuries, although her chosen root was locally grown.

Love magic, seemingly the province of women in the earlier era, was only admitted by one female confessant in 1763, Maria Joanna de Azevedo. Where a wider range of spells, powders, and practices were available to those who sought to control their relationships or "improve" their husbands in the late 1500s, Azevedo knew only European Christian prayers to sway young men's love.[104] The "natural" daughter of a single mother who lived by her own means, Azevedo had cultivated a "dishonest" relationship, when her neighbor Rosa Maria dos Santos taught her the popular *oração* or "prayer of São Marcos":

> May São Marcos of Venice mark you, may Jesus Christ soothe you, may the Consecrated Host incarnate you, [and] the Holy Spirit confirm you [under] my will: your pious eyes will look at the ground, other women seem as mud and earth to you, and only I will be like pearls [and] gold. My glorious São Marcos, you overcame high mountains, you faced brave bulls with your holy words, thus as I ask soften the heart of [this] man, that he not be able to eat, drink, sleep, . . . without seeking me to speak with me.[105]

After repeating this at midday or midnight, crossing herself as she spoke, and spitting on the ground at her feet, Azevedo expected that the small "ceremony" would bring her young lover to marry her. She also performed a second oration or prayer calling on "the Blood of Christ" and "the milk of the Virgin Mary" as spiritual potions to bring her lover, afflicted like "the most holy Virgin . . . when she saw her beloved Son dead," to her side. Her friends Maria Josepha, the wife of a tailor, and Lucia, the widow of a sentry officer, taught her other variations "that never worked," including the Brazilian "oration to São Cypriano" calling on the "Bishop, and Archbishop, Preacher and Confessor of my Lord Jesus Christ, By Thy Sanctity and Thy Virginity" to "drag so-and-so to me."[106]

Admitting that "nothing worked" on her lover, Azevedo had tried other orations, all calling on Jesus, São Marcos, and the Virgin Mary while the speaker walked, spit, and crossed herself or her fingers at midnight at a crossroads. When her "certain man" came to her one morning after her late-night ceremonies, Azevedo believed "firmly that she had made him come by virtue of the said orations"—though he stayed only three hours. Still, as her results and resolve failed her, she was overcome by the death of her daughter and four subsequent dreams of the afterlife, glimpsing glory and angels on the *escada* or stairway to heaven. She finally repented of her magic and "declar[ed] all of it to her Confessor," realizing that "she lived in danger of Eternal Damnation." Azevedo divulged the widest range of prayers and list of instructors in the published records of that era—and the Inquisitor concurred in her concern for the "discharging of her conscience and the salvation of her soul."[107]

Like the love magic "orations" that incorporated Christian phrases and gestures, women's divination in the late 1700s still relied on traditional

European folk practices to uncover secrets about the past and present. Three such denunciations and confessions clung tightly to such traditions, while a fourth case — the confession by the slave Marçal — revealed that even an Indian woman might teach a medieval European spell. Two of the three presentations by women focused on Dona Izabel Maria da Silva, who was first denounced in a secondhand account from Josepha Coelho. Coelho reported that her friend Anna Basilia, a young white woman serving in the captain's household, had seen "the said Dona Izabel call with chants and that then in the middle in the house . . . appeared three little black men or devils." Dona Izabel addressed the little dancing creatures in a language unknown to Basilia, and they responded and then disappeared, leaving the unperceived spy "stunned at what she had seen." Borrowing the indigenous Tupí term *xeri'mawa* for "wild pets," Coelho concluded that it was widely known in the neighborhood that Dona Izabel "had commerce and communication with some *xirimbabos* or demons and by this means she knew all she wished to know."[108] Coelho conceded that she herself had never witnessed anything of the ten-year-old event and ventured that Dona Izabel drank too much wine at times and had other bad habits.

Dona Izabel herself offered a brief confession of her "crimes" from the distant past before the Inquisitional officials only three days later. With no mention of dancing demons, Dona Izabel described only a divination ritual that she had been taught as a young maiden to foretell what might happen in the coming year. As part of the *"sorte de São João"* or "magic spell of Saint John," she learned to "fill a glass cup with water on the Night of the said Saint" and drop both the white and yolk of a broken egg into it "forming a cross," while praying an "Our Father" and "Hail Mary." She tried it for three successive years, discovering first that a student was destined for the priesthood when "the form of a Church appeared" in the egg-and-water mix, and then that an orphaned girl would marry a Portuguese man when the image of a ship emerged. These predictions proved true, as did the third divination that a young *mulata* woman would marry a Brazilian-born man, but she ended her "observations" abruptly when her new husband "reprimanded her sharply" for her spells.[109]

Finally, the young slave Marcelina Thereza denounced what she had seen only eight days before while doing laundry for the "Reverend Master of the bishopric School." Knowing that two other slaves were missing money, she asked Maria Fernandez "that she might look into who had the said money." Fernandez requested a basket and a pair of scissors for divination: she "thrust the points of the scissors into the hoop of the basket," and held it up by the scissors' hoops with the help of one of the complainants.

She spoke words that only one observer—a student named João Joze de Lira Barros—understood and then pronounced the names of the suspects. When the chaplain's servant Calisto was named, "the said Basket gave a turn and Fell on the floor" to indicate that he was the thief. After the ritual, Barros insisted that she tell the visiting Inquisitor, since this was "not a good thing but a superstition." Marcelina Thereza defended the diviner, however, explaining that she was sensible, sober, and religiously observant.[110]

The same basket-and-scissors technique appeared in the presentation identifying Quiteria as the Indian woman who taught the sole male diviner, Marçal. Twelve years earlier, Quiteria had recited to him the rhyming chant used in the divination: "By Saint Peter and Saint Paul he passed by the Door of Saint James, Saint Peter and Saint Paul." It cannot be ascertained if the diviner Fernandez used the same words as Quiteria, but Marçal noted that he had carefully kept the powerful words to be chanted "in his heart."[111] His statement, part confession and part denunciation, adds that much more detail to these cases of divination and love magic, performed by women of varying ethnicities and social ranks in Brazil but still relying on a European heritage of occult lore and demonology. Only a brief denunciation of divination by Domingos Rodrigues—included below for his statements against the healer Sabina—revealed the use of a smoky, darkened room that might suggest non-European rituals.

During this Visitation of the Portuguese Inquisition, most statements concerned magical healing and curing, the fourth and last category of women's magic in the late 1700s. The women who confessed or were denounced to the visiting Tribunal were mostly of Portuguese descent, but native Brazilians, a slave born in Africa, and a woman of mixed ethnic heritage also appeared. The origin of the cures was, however, quite different from those of the love magic and divination practices: all but one used recognizable Brazilian Indian practices, elements, and chants or prayers. Representative of this trend was the denunciation of Luduvina Ferreira cited at the beginning of this chapter. Ferreira (who was denounced twice) healed a sick woman with instruments, symbols, and chants from indigenous shamans. Other healers similarly used songs, gestures, and words that only a few onlookers—presumably native Brazilians—could decipher as they diagnosed and treated illnesses. Only Domingas Gomes da Resurreição, a young slave of mixed African and Indian parentage, was the exception in her confessed use of European Christian magical prayers.

Luduvina Ferreira first came to the attention of the visiting Inquisitor on October 14, 1763, when the seamstress and lace-maker Ignes Maria denounced her for her magical cures. Twenty years earlier, Ignes Maria had been servant to Dona Maria Barreto when the lady suddenly fell ill "from a flux of blood." A family friend, Constança Maciel, sent for Ferreira, who first examined the patient, then commenced "to play a Maraca or rattle made from a small calabash bound to an arrow that served as its handle" and "sing in an unknown language" used only by Indian healers, "*pajés* or masters of *feitiçarias*." Announcing that Dona Maria suffered due to "*feitiços*," Ferreira arranged a small ceremony to uncover the source of the ailment and heal its victim. Singing and balancing her rattle on an up-ended drinking gourd, Ferreira circled the house and then left "all of her equipment" under Dona Maria's bed. Several later sessions of "superstitions or devilish things" brought Ferreira and two young male Indians into a "little storeroom with no light" in which "those Indians or some demons commenced to create a racket" with their hands and feet, and to whistle shrilly. Ignes Maria concluded that her mistress was finally "disillusioned" and died of the very illness Ferreira failed to cure; for herself, she added that she had "no good opinion" of Ferreira, but had not seen her since the incident.[112]

Constança Maciel, the longtime friend of Dona Maria, followed with her own denunciation of Ferreira and her daughter Ignacia, describing much the same events—although she set them "thirty years ago, more or less." Ferreira, she noted, was a white widow, who made use not only of her Brazilian *maracá* but also of a pipe or cigar from which "she drank the smoke" of burning tobacco. After chanting and shouting with her *pajés* in the darkened storeroom, Ferreira had discovered "the head of a cobra with a pepper in its mouth" buried "at the street entrance" and identified it as the *feitiço* that had brought illness on the house. Maciel explained that as part of Ferreira's "deviltries," she had caused the apparent death of one of her *pajés* and then revived him with smoke. When asked, Maciel informed the Inquisition officials that while the healer was not intoxicated, she was "certain that the said Luduvina as well as her above-mentioned daughter . . . were familiar with and dealt with the devil."[113]

Another healer, the Indian woman Sabina, brought three different denunciations to the Inquisitor in 1763; her practices similarly utilized native Brazilian prayers and objects within a framework of demonic magic. Domingos Rodrigues offered a lengthy account of Sabina's many powers and practices in Pará. Fifteen years earlier, his wife, Caetana Thereza, had fallen ill and, with no sure remedies, her father had sent for Sabina, who was then known for her power to "uncover and remedy hidden evils." Sabina immediately recognized bewitchment, charged a Tapuia woman with witchcraft, and had the accused dig into the dirt floor of the house to extract "a bundle that consisted of various bones, feathers, thorns, pierced lizards and yet other things" made as a *feitiço* to harm the young Caetana Thereza. After the abrupt confession of the witch, Sabina threw leaves onto a brazier to create healing smoke in the room, blessed Caetana Thereza with holy water, and from "the mouth of the sick woman extracted a lizard," but only a later exorcism healed her. Rodrigues had also witnessed Sabina's discovery of *feitiços* in the governor's house and her use of smoke to draw "three live animals the size of a chick-pea" from the afflicted man. Despite the dramatic cures, Sabina was "suspected of evil," and considered only a "*bruxa* and *feiticeira* inasmuch as she did not have the powers to discern what was hidden and she had not been well behaved."[114]

Sabina performed her rituals for two other men, Manoel de Souza Novaiz and Raymundo Joze de Betancurt, men of property and position in Grão-Pará who both denounced her. Sabina had attempted to cure the slaves on Novaiz's farmlands, following a wave of deaths that he attributed to "curses and *feiticerias*." Although Sabina quickly discovered the *feitiço* that threatened his well-being, a buried bundle containing the bones of a *jaracara* or venomous snake, Novaiz suspected that "she had discovered the said bundle by diabolic means," since "she had no powers so great that God might work that wonder through her." Still, Novaiz admitted that his uncertainty about its having been "the work of the Devil" had delayed his confession some seven years.[115] Betancurt had no scruples about denouncing Sabina's rituals to cure his own eye disease only two months before his late statement in 1767. After smoking her pipe, blessing him with her thumb, and mumbling something about "Father, Son, and Holy Spirit, and [the] Virgin Mary," Sabina licked his eyes and spit out the malevolent beasts she found there—including a wasp and a chimeric creature resembling a fish whose belly "was full of already dead offspring." His eyes healed quickly after the subsequent anointing with holy water and recommended exorcisms, but Betancurt determined that—despite her "innumerable" successful cures—her work was all sorcery.[116]

Luduvina Ferreira and Sabina interwove European Christian and native Brazilian Indian healing practices, invoking the Trinity before using tobacco smoke in darkened rooms, inducing trances, sucking out the *bichos* or little beasts that caused pain or illness, and then—after a holy water blessing—sending their patients for an ecclesiastical exorcism. The third woman whose healing rituals are represented in these texts, however, offered no such New World creations despite her own maternal Indian heritage. Domingas Gomes da Resurreição confessed to using a set of prayers to heal the eye and skin disease and the affliction known as *quebranto*, weakness and indeterminate ill health caused by the personal curses of the "evil eye." To cure *quebranto*, for example, she blessed the sufferer, recited the "Our Father" and "Hail Mary to the Passion and Death of Our Lord Jesus Christ by the souls needing more in the fire of Purgatory," and added the spell: "Two Bad Eyes they gave you, With three you take them away Who are the Three Persons of the Most Holy Trinity, Father, Son, and Holy Spirit." For skin rash, she stroked the injured skin with a knife while invoking the mercy of God and the Virgin Mary, while eye pain might be removed with prayers to "my Lord Jesus Christ with Your precious wounds."[117]

Gomes da Resurreição had known the Christian prayers and ritual blessings for nearly thirty years, having learned them from her mistress, who — after taking third order vows — had been ordered to stop her magical healings by her Catholic confessors. She added that at least one variation for curing "bad air," or general malaise, came originally from a local friar, but that only recently had she realized "there might be something of superstition" in her cures. Insisting that she had never intended harm, she begged mercy from the Inquisitor. The words and gestures she employed had clear antecedents in European folk cures, though Gomes da Resurreição may have interjected a few colonial innovations.[118] Her cures, together with those of other female and male healers of the era, complete the pattern for magic in the late 1700s: traditional Christian rituals used against the evil eye or traditionally defined ailments gradually gave way to or intermixed with native Brazilian cures.

In their confessions, Domingas Gomes da Resurreição, Dona Izabel Maria da Silva, and Maria Joanna de Azevedo protested their innocent use of "orations" and "spells," but acknowledged the necessity of their appearance before the visiting Tribunal. All of the statements to this last Visitation of the Inquisition were mandated, as with previous cases, by the obedience due this powerful religious and political institution. Women who confessed or denounced women's magic in the late 1700s echoed the formulas prescribed by the officials: at the beginning of each record they petitioned to appear before the Holy Office and vowed their sincerity before the Holy Evangelists, and at the end agreed to abide by canon law for the salvation of their souls. The few women who indicated their motives for appearing before the Inquisition stated that confessors, husbands, and other male authorities had sent them, or that they had realized — having recently heard the Tribunal's announcements — that they had witnessed or practiced forbidden prayers or rituals. With only thirteen women named and another three unnamed in this set of records, fewer patterns emerge concerning social standing, ethnic background, or birthplace, but overall the women healers, diviners, and witches of this era—and their denouncers—are quite different from those of the early colony. The most important characteristic of the women who confessed, denounced, or were denounced for their magical practices was their diversity, for they seemed to have little in common beyond their magic. The three women who confessed to magical cures, love prayers, and divination ranged in ages from thirty-seven to "more than 60 years old" and represented the diverse ethnic heritage of Grão-Pará: Domingas Gomes da Resurreição, a former slave, was the daughter of a white father and Indian mother, Maria Joanna de Azevedo's mother was descended from Indian and African forebears, and Dona Izabel Maria da Silva stated that she was white and "Old Christian."[119] Similarly, the women who denounced magical practices were mostly mixed-race or of unknown fathers and ranged in age from the twenty-year-old single slave Marcelina Thereza to the fifty-nine-year-old Luso-Brazilian widow Constança Maciel; some were slaves, some cited their husbands' occupations in trade or the military, and some were slave owners and landowners. Two women denounced for "demonic" magic were identified as "white," but three women were from the lower social ranks, as black or Indian slaves.

The diversity of ethnic heritage and social ranks of the women was appropriate for the magic they practiced, for in this late colonial report, the magical practices have themselves become "creolized," that is, diversified with the creative interconnections of Portuguese and Catholic folk traditions, native Brazilian Indian rituals and objects, and a few African elements. Further, women availed themselves of traditional magic crossing the three cultures: women of European descent learned indigenous healing rituals, while African-descended slaves recited Portuguese chants during divinations. The spells and gestures for love magic retained most of the medieval and early modern European forms, with the invocations of Jesus and the saints accompanied by signs of the cross and midnight vigils to secure a marriage. Divination similarly perpetuated old European practices such as the basket-and-scissors ritual successfully used to identify thieves, while afflictions known in Portugal—such as the evil eye or demonic ailments—were healed with European magical prayers and blessings.

Women who were accused of divination or denounced for harm and healing had, however, developed a wider repertoire of magic for the novel colonial ailments. Luduvina Ferreira and the Indian woman Sabina diagnosed and healed diseases that did not respond to the apothecary's tonics, using the imported techniques of blessings with holy water, exorcisms, and incenses alongside indigenous gourds, tobaccos, drums, and trances. Both women identified the sources of evil and illness as *feitiços*, or works of magic inspired by the devil, but opened the bundles to find indigenous snake bones and leaves. Sabina, who resided in a house owned by Padre Jose Carneyro, merged European and indigenous medicine in her use of smoke and sucking to draw the illnesses out of the sufferers.[120] The denunciation of Dona Izabel Maria da Silva brought the three colonial cultures together in the identification of her little spirits: Josepha Coelho identified them as *diabretes*, *pretinhos*, and *xerimbabos*, giving Portuguese, African, and Tupí references for the imps that provided her with "all she wished to know."

The smaller number of confessions and denunciations of women's magic recorded by the visiting Inquisitor to Grão-Para need not be understood as an indication that magic in eighteenth-century Brazil was waning or less powerful than it had been in the early colony. Women's power to heal and influence the world was, in fact, widely known and magic and witchcraft employed by every rank and class of person in the colony. Magical practices had been incorporated into daily life, and one need only ask other women in the neighborhood—as did Maria Joanna de Azevedo— to learn more magical "prayers" and rituals. Healers such as Sabina and Luduvina Ferreira had "innumerable" cures, and they and other *feiticeiras* passed words, techniques, potions, and gestures to their daughters and other younger women. As powerful and commonplace as it might have been, magic still invoked otherworldly forces—nearly always viewed as demonic in these later reports. The disquieting presence of magic compelled practitioners, patients, and witnesses to divulge their experiences to the Inquisitor, and to admit that the powers that cursed, healed, and rearranged their lives were not divine but demonic.

As these later confessions and denunciations were heard, then, they were seldom characterized by the Inquisitors as folklore or superstitions. By the eighteenth century, the European literature of demonology had so infiltrated the Portuguese Inquisitional viewpoint that the visiting officials expected demonic presence and power in the denounced or confessed magical practices and more often judged them heretical rather than foolish. In most cases, the officials inquired about the circumstances of the magical event and the mood, state, and demeanor of the practitioner. Denunciants were asked whether the diviner or healer seemed drunk or crazy, under the influence of some passionate emotion, or even trying to trick or fool the observers. The officials pressed further with questions that might lead to more serious conclusions: What were the practitioner's usual behaviors, habits, and beliefs? Under such pressure, women might reveal more damaging details and expose demonic magic and devilish pacts.[121] So too the men denouncing the healer Sabina and the poisoner Joanna added further details toward the end of their statements and castigated the women variously as *bruxas* and dangerous women doing the "work of demons."

Many of the denunciants and confessants were thus compelled to adopt the Inquisitors' demonization of unorthodox practices, a transposition rarely found in the earlier era. Love magic began with the devil, divination called on demonic sprites, and the indigenous cures of course were demonic by nature, originating as they had with the devil-worshipping native cults. The denunciations of the healer Luduvina Ferreira illustrate this last point: her chant to the spirits in a darkened room was recast as an appeal to demonic forces. Ignes Maria explained that she knew little of Ferreira beyond her "superstitions or devilish acts" with her companion "masters of *feitiçarias*," but insisted that the sounds she heard were either the Indians "or some devils" causing a great noise. Constança Maciel maintained that the fatal illness originated with *feitiços* created by Indians "or demons" and that the strange sounds heard during the "devilish acts" could not have come from Ferreira or her assistant, since their voices were well known. When Maciel was questioned, she added that Ferreira's daughter had a demonic familiar and "dealt with the devil."[122]

Even when the confessants insisted on the usefulness of their cures and prayers and on their own ignorance concerning proper adherence to canon law, the Inquisitor and representatives insisted on the distinctions between the divine domain and the devil's work. As had been the case in the 1590s, the only source for unusual power outside of the realm controlled by the Catholic Church was the devil. Natural powers for healing with herbs were disallowed, no miracles might be obtained by old European prayers, and the evil eye—that ancient threat—was the devil's own orb. Confessants then followed the demonic discourse, moving their own practices out of their control and into the devil's world. The statements by Domingas Gomes da Resurreição followed that pattern: she first characterized her healing practices as cures taught to her by her pious mistress when she was a slave. Subsequently, although she had used them "without intending to do wrong," she began to think of them as superstitions. Finally, with the inquisitorial intervention challenging her motives and acts, she admitted that they were nothing but the devil's lies.[123]

Magic persisted in the late colonial period, however, because it remained a powerful and independent spiritual force for women, useful in domestic religious life alongside and enhanced by the domestic religion allowed by the Catholic Church. Prayers to Jesus and the saints were accepted private family devotions before a painted statue or image of the sacred presence, and the powers present during Catholic prayers—by extension—certainly might also heal a broken heart or drive off the spiritual infections of a buried *feitiço*. Women's responses to their marginalized and enclosed lives, to the problems rarely addressed or even incurred by the formal rituals of the Catholic Church, incorporated European and Brazilian-Indian folk rituals in new syntheses for their new colonial experiences. The appeal of power glimpsed in the darkened chapels with their gilded statues was brought home, and the domestic religious life for colonial Brazilian women—and men—encompassed magical *orações, ceremônias, rituais*, and even *curas* in the names of Jesus and the women who remembered them.

CONCLUSION

In their magical practices for divination, love relationships, curses, and cures, women in the early colonial period had preserved fragments of folk Catholicism in their prayers and spells drawn from the remarkably widespread magic of medieval Europe. Fragmented lives and fragmented religion were reconstructed in the colony with small ceremonies of love magic and divination and limited claims of supernal power, while the centrifugal forces that created their dissonance reappeared in rumors of witches, sorceresses, curses, and even demonic forces. But in the 1500s, the colonial community and the visiting Tribunal of the Inquisition had only begun the struggle against the New World's threats. There were, certainly, trials and executions of witches and magical healers in the sixteenth and seventeenth centuries sent from Brazil to Portugal, but European conceptions of the demonic pact and witches' perversions simply did not control the discourse to the extent that they would in later centuries.

By the late 1700s, much had changed: the colonial enterprise had produced a complex network of intermingled cultures so that European traditions were not the only model for alternative spirituality and the miraculous amelioration of colonial life. At the same time, the scope and content of women's practices and the characterization of their magic were thoroughly transformed. Among women's practices and prayers, one finds the near-complete eclipse of European magic by that later date and a clear indication of a revolution in religious thought in the few survivals of longstanding and popular practices. The primary change involved the incorporation of indigenous practices into healing and other religious rituals, and the comprehensive descriptions emergent from the Inquisition records suggest a new understanding of the development of religious lives in the colonial context. Among women healers, there was surprisingly little reliance on African religious elements, especially in healing rituals. Even the women descended from African slaves perpetuated European and Brazilian Indian symbols, words, and gestures. African ceremonies may have been more carefully shielded from the scrutiny of Church officials in Brazil, for several singular reports of African-style ceremonies in the early 1700s and the later emergence of Afro-Brazilian religions indicate that the knowledge of herbs, prayers, rituals, and roles was indeed preserved through the colonial era.[124]

The demonization of magic during the eighteenth century resulted from the efforts of the Portuguese Catholic Church to recapture its power over women's religious lives and to reassert a single dominant interpretive perspective. While no "witches' Sabbath" was constructed for the colony and no witch craze drove the Inquisitors to scour the countryside for malfeasants as happened in Europe, the otherness of magic could only derive from the devil himself, and in the Brazilian context, one can observe the application of demonology not only to dramatic curing rituals and but also to relatively insignificant remedies using herbs, inscribed notes, and unorthodox prayers. This demonization within the Church was short lived, however, and only a few decades later, the attribution of demonic reality to magic would meet with the skeptics' derision.

While few women stepped into the realm of magic to secure the devil's own powers, participants nonetheless endangered their own status and honor in their attempts to control their own lives and material conditions or those of others. The privilege and prestige that an upper-class or propertied woman might savor would have been jeopardized by her public patronage of a seer or witch, but she had as much to lose in the failure of her marriage or theft of household goods. In such cases, a surreptitious lesson in love magic or consultation with a diviner might have supported the dignity and honor prized by the wives of plantation owners and city officials. But the practitioners of magic, when discovered or denounced, had little honor left before the Inquisition; their public reputation as decent or Christian women was damaged, and further accusations accrued. Powerful women who defied the Christian ideal were suspected not only of witchcraft, but also of sexual misconduct, including prostitution, as can be seen in the details provided about their personal lives by their accusers: they were single, "lived as if married" with one or more men, or were *solteiras*, a term for older unmarried women that suggested loose morals.[125] The marginalization of witches and unmarried women according to the transmitted standards of the Catholic Church may have left them with little recourse but the heterodox traditions of magic.

Outside of the ecclesial institution, the designation of non-Catholic religious life as "magical" and demonic persists in Brazil to the present day in two forms. First, the folk culture of northeastern Brazil has preserved "mystical" and magical prayers for love and protection — including a prayer to São Marcos using almost the same formulation as that recited by Maria Joanna de Azevedo in 1763.[126] Second, Afro-Brazilian religious rituals, especially private herbal cures and blessings, are often designated "magic" by the popular press, an ascription that may be found in dictionaries of folklore beginning in the 1950s. With those two divergent remnants, women's magical lives continue as part of the fabric of Brazilian culture, interwoven with other preserved alternatives and creative innovations challenging the now-receding dominant culture that long kept them suppressed.

# Closing the Colonial Era

O ver the course of Brazil's colonial history, women faced numerous and sometimes insuperable barriers to their full expression as religious persons. In the earliest conception of the colonial enterprise, women's presence was portrayed in otherness, representing the otherness of America itself. The alien continents nurtured alien women who signified the others, the Amazons, cannibals, and—finally— witches of the Old World transposed to the New. These restrictive images reduced women to a status outside of their own self-understanding, and, with so few written accounts of their responses to the invasion, I have had to rely primarily on men's documents, letters, books, and reports to reconstruct women's religious lives, perspectives, and activities during the long years from 1500 to 1822.

The challenges for women in the colony began long before its shores were breached by the Portuguese imperial power, for the Catholic Church and Portuguese elite classes had already constructed the fundamental expectations for women's lives, including religious and social norms. When Pero de Caminha wondered at the nudity of Brazilian Indian women in 1500, he articulated the first demands for women in the Land of the Holy Cross; women were to be bound by the imported codes for morality and honor in all of their characteristics and behaviors, from their clothing and comportment to their occupations and daily activities. Few native Brazilians and few witches reflected the characteristics of honorable women, for few were modest and submissive, with an impeccable reputation for chastity—and none were elite white women of respectable ancestry. The ideals perpetuated by the Portuguese empire and religious officials granted prestige and precedence to married women of illustrious families, and those estimable rewards might have been available to women of lower classes if only they, too, paid with their lives the rather steep costs of honor. The historical records, however, leave little indication that enslaved or mixed-race women could meet those costs, overcome the social and religious limits, and be deemed honorable. Family wealth or personal virtue gained some respect for a handful of devout and chaste women, but the social distinctions required for the attributes of honor lay primarily in generations of nobility and in demonstrable family accomplishments or religious purity, so that the male writers of the seventeenth through the nineteenth centuries had little to add to the historical record but the failures and shortcomings of women.

In the first chapter, I examined the stereotypes of compliant and resistant women composed during the early colonial encounters with indigenous Brazilian women. From innocent and vulnerable maidens to vicious anthropophagous hags, the images utilized to portray women were not new sketches but drew on centuries of iconography about the "other" positioned to oppose and define the civilized Western Christian man. Explorers, conquerors, state officials, and Catholic missionaries could scarcely believe, let alone record, what they saw in the New World. As their astonishment left them wordless, motifs of sylph-like maidens, innocent virgins, wily Amazons, and frightening cannibals filled in the gaps. Yet the choice of symbols to present and represent the Brazilian women was not haphazard; instead, the symbols served distinctive purposes for establishing the imperial state and holy mother church in the colony. Docile and compliant women were more likely, I would suggest, to be assimilated into the Portuguese cultural empire, just as the accessible coastal regions of Brazil seemed to permit easy entry for the invaders. And as the outsiders struggled through the impassable interior forests and encountered genuine resistance, so their reports emphasized the otherness of women—as inhuman, degenerate, violent creatures whose eventual submission would fulfill the divine promise.

Brazilian Indian women had few opportunities to express their own responses to the encounters with the European colonists, and the sources permit us few authentic moments from their lives. Missionaries or colonial officials did not evangelize indigenous women merely for their own sake but for the service and submission to their husbands, church, and state, and did not consistently describe their responses. Women themselves left no direct records of their experiences as "others" in the early colony, and attempts to discover some trace of their reactions are thwarted by the bias of the sources. To whose voices should we attend? The Tupinambá women who gloated over Hans Staden's imminent demise? His contempt for the indigenous women along with his expectations of their evil intent could not possibly permit a reliable report on women's sentiments as he and other colonists demolished their traditions. The eager women who flocked to Jesuit catechists after their day's work? Padres Anchieta and Nóbrega rarely regarded indigenous women as separate, autonomous beings worthy of direct catechism and could not be considered trustworthy sources when their reports counted hundreds of willing converts after a few hours of limited indoctrination in Portuguese or Latin. Even a contravening case might prove suspect: a sympathetic cannibal might represent the certain downfall of her violent culture, and the treachery of a formerly compliant woman might symbolize the duplicity of her "race."

Just as indigenous Brazilian women found themselves ensnared and marginalized by the colonial images of Amazons and cannibals, so too women of all ethnic groups confronted the narrow expectations for feminine virtue crafted in Western Europe and transplanted to colonial Brazil. The ideal for Christian women, explored in Chapter 2, articulated the desire for control over women through political and religious laws, social norms, and personal and familial expectations. Women embodied physical imperfection and moral insufficiency, falling well short of religious and secular authors' expectations for the personal virtue and accomplishments that might accord with recognition of feminine honor. The Roman Catholic Church and Portuguese medieval and early modern society set standards for European women of the upper classes and nobility that few of them might ever reach. Parents, tutors, writers, and preachers regarded silence, modesty, self-restraint, chastity, and even ignorance as worthy traits that honorable girls and women might practice in the embrace of a secluded household. Outside of that restricted world, girls and women who worked in households, kitchens, shops, markets, and fields faced exploitation because of their ventures into the public sphere and accusations of sin because of their inescapable shortcomings.

In Brazil, members of the small governing class re-created that European ideal for Christian girls and women as they established traditional social norms, but even there few exemplars reached the ideal. White women barely satisfied the norms of meritorious behavior when, by most accounts, the highest honor devolved to those who were so compliant as to be (nearly) invisible in colonial society. Women of mixed ethnic heritage or of Brazilian Indian or African descent could hardly be so self-effacing as to disappear from view, for they too performed essential roles in the colonial world. Thus working women, including immigrant women of the mercantile and artisan classes, servants, and slaves, were expected to express the innate feminine virtues of submission and chastity, but they—at the same time—violated the virtuous norm because they were still considered un-controllable women. Since the implicit norms for feminine behavior appeared in the literature that only men among the colonial elite might read, colonial women of all classes were barred from knowing let alone shaping the communal discourse.

The images of Brazilian women and the ideal for virtuous women thus cannot be seen as representative of the lives and responses of women in the colony. Indigenous and immigrant women were not consulted about their models for virtuous behavior or their reactions to the criticism or praise concerning their achievement of those paradigms—of virtue or of vice. The concepts of honor were primarily bound to the Portuguese ruling classes and perpetuated the success of those worthies who had inherited or secured such rank by appointment. Whether by birth or marital fortune, most women simply could not achieve that rank and would not be considered "honorable." Most, too, could not attain the ideal for Christian virtue articulated during the colonial period by the Catholic Church. That ideal was not a set of aspirations created by women to convey their own highest values, but a doctrinally fixed list of beliefs and deeds modeled on religious concepts of perfection—almost by definition unachievable.

Still, that ideal served as the foundation for educational plans for girls and women in colonial households and schools, as I explained in Chapter 3. Rhetorical assertions about feminine virtue might not suffice to instruct women about their failings and guide them to appropriate accomplishments, so secular and religious writers provided explicit guidance about the moral duties and daily behaviors befitting honorable girls and women in Europe and in the Brazilian colony. Pedagogical distinctions separated the expectations for young Brazilian Indian women from those for the white, upper-class girls of colonial ruling families, but most men admitted that women of any rank profited from religious formation and training in the domestic arts. In early colonial efforts, the indoctrination of indigenous women completed the mission of the Roman Catholic Church to convert the heathen population. Jesuit and Franciscan clergy understood that religious instruction benefited women directly, but also envisioned that such transformed women would serve as models for all and as wives for male converts.

Beyond the basics of religious instruction, a few girls and women learned feminine skills in private and domestic schools, and their training in sewing, cooking, and cleaning earned them suitable positions in service and marriage to skilled laborers. For impoverished, enslaved, and working-class girls and women, even that education was transformative if rare; women of African and mixed ethnic backgrounds found few opportunities for instruction and advancement. For girls and women in the middle and upper ranks of colonial society, family wealth and position might permit education in reading, writing, arithmetic, and the decorative arts, but only so that they might be better wives, mothers, and managers of a household. In the guidelines for the school at the Recolhimento de Nossa Senhora da Glória as in the informal plans formulated by Jesuit missionary Manuel da Nóbrega earlier, education provided girls with the means to improve their moral and spiritual condition but not to consider or question their own lives and choices. Even the founding statutes for the Collegio de Educação de Meninas barely advanced the concepts of women's education toward the models offered during the European Renaissance, so that Brazilian women in the 1800s might fall short of humanistic accomplishments of educated women in Italy or France of the 1500s.

Married women might have come close to the Christian ideal, and reclusive religious women closer still, as seen in Chapters 4 and 5. The honorable estate of marriage opened the door for women to enact feminine virtues and behaviors and to fulfill their worldly purpose according to most secular and religious moralists of the sixteenth and seventeenth centuries. By the sixteenth century in Europe, church and state had cooperated in specifying the requirements for marriage for men and women, even while economic and personal situations continued to limit access to sacramental marriage for those outside of the elite families. Women were nonetheless expected to devote themselves faithfully to their husbands and to obey their commands because of the moral and social superiority of their mates. Guidebooks on appropriate marital behavior from both religious and secular authors echoed the ideal for virtuous girls, differing only in their emphases: the religious extolled chastity while the secular insisted on social subordination.

In early colonial Brazil, the governing families were particularly careful about women's conveyance to an appropriate married state, and so kept girls in isolation before marriage and under control afterward. Married women needed little education to succeed in that career, though Juan Luís Vives and Francisco Manuel de Melo similarly insisted that women attend to their humble appearance, modest demeanor, and personal restraint as much as to the household skills in sewing, cooking, and management of accounts. Religious authors emphasized the cultivation of spiritual virtues such as obedience and fidelity for married women, leaving domestic activities beyond their purview, perhaps relegated to servants and slaves. In this heedless dismissal of household needs, religious and secular authors alike neglected the lives of women in the lower classes, who might never marry but who might arrange temporary, consensual relationships. Marriages among slaves were not forbidden, but native Brazilian and African slave women found the sacrament of marriage elusive and expensive, and abusive relationships more likely. Domestic workers thus completed a full range of menial tasks while they lived as the sexual partners for the single or married men, or even priests, whom they served.

As wives, concubines, common-law partners, and temporary mistresses, women recorded their responses to marital demands through the most unlikely of recorders: the secretary to the Visitor for the Portuguese Inquisition. Under the Roman Catholic mandates to confess their own sins and denounce those of others, Brazilian women in the sixteenth through the late eighteenth centuries divulged more to the Inquisitors about their intimate lives than we might garner from other sources of those eras. Finally released from the ideals of silence and ignorance, women revealed that their marriages were sometimes successful, but oftentimes led them to arguments with husbands, disputes with neighbors and landlords, and violations of canon law. While confessing to blasphemous oaths or practices attributed to hidden Judaism, women spoke of living "as if married" and of their children borne to the men who had deserted them, and they denounced other women and men who broke with religious teachings and social norms in their irregular relationships. These records, despite their problems as third-party recordings of social and religious offenses, still permit the first glimpses of women's lives as they themselves might have understood them — complicated, disrupted by colonial reorganization, and distorted by unreachable ideals. The impact of failed social demands and the injustice of the colonial slave system reached all women who confessed to the Inquisition, and only a few moments of amelioration emerged from the life stories of free and working women who worried more about food and rents than about honor and virtue.

With married life perpetually fraught with personal challenges, many women desired the cloistered life as a religious nun or *recolhida* even though there were few religious houses in the first two colonial centuries. As detailed in Chapter 5, diverse religious, social, and personal motives inspired women to live as recluses, novices, or sisters in an informal or formal convent. Before the institution of formal convents in Brazil, priests, friars, and women themselves established informal retreat houses or *recolhimentos* where devout women, and those who sought refuge from the temporal world for other reasons, might reside under a semblance of conventual rules. Women such as Clara da Paixão de Jesus petitioned the Portuguese king directly for royal sanction for a house where she and her few companions might live a simple, pure, and dedicated life of prayer, offering their vows to support the royal family as well. Other women from the elite families similarly petitioned for royal permission and more formal religious recognition of the residence in which they and their female relatives already lived in austere seclusion, promising to educate younger women for marriage or cloistered life as well. Visionaries inspired several such informal retreat houses, especially when their irregular religious behavior or lower social status barred them from the *recolhimentos* funded by city charters.

The earliest *recolhimentos* date to the 1500s, with increasing numbers established through the 1780s. For most, the initial charters were approved by local religious and civil authorities and their stated purposes included the housing of unmarried girls and women from the upper ranks of the local society. Such shelters protected the virtue of devout women and the honor and fortunes of their families, which might seclude marriageable women until a groom of suitable rank and property emerged. Important and respected *recolhimentos* in Bahia, Pernambuco, and São Paulo drew women to their shelter for centuries, and women chose the rigors of a prayerful and obedient life that offered a few advantages to married life: independence, education, and personal responsibility. Successful directors and instructors guided other women through their accomplishments, although even the most astute bookkeepers and teachers could not overcome the repeated hardships that limited finances brought. Early financial support was supplemented with the dowries that accompanied women to their religious refuge, tuition payments from live-in students, and boarding fees paid by widows and older women who stayed only briefly at the retreat houses. Some still faced closure and so appealed to the civil and religious authorities for loans and grants to allow them to fulfill their missions as religious and social housing for the anomalous women of the colony.

Until the end of the seventeenth century, Brazilian women seeking the vows of the formal convents of the Carmelite and Conceptionist Orders traveled to Portugal with the financial and family support necessary to sustain them there. While some elite families preferred religious seclusion to marital disasters for their daughters, the imperial government planned to expand the population of white immigrants in colonial Brazil, and so forbade first the establishment of formal convents and then the transport of unmarried girls to convents in Portugal. In 1677, the city of Salvador, Bahia, opened the first Brazilian convent, Convento de Santa Clara do Desterro, and three more in the early 1700s. Only two more convents were permitted in Rio de Janeiro during the colonial era, but none in smaller cities and towns. At the Convento do Desterro, the original fifty places for professed nuns were quickly filled, as were the twenty-five for lower-ranking sisters, and when no further places were permitted, women simply moved in with family members or took up temporary residence as pupils and boarders there.

Because convents and *recolhimentos* required statutes to commence and financial and residence accounts to continue, their records preserved many aspects of affluent women's lives within their walls. Women themselves wrote petitions, entry requests, and letters about their own activities there, offering rare but distinctive glimpses of their own understanding of the demands and purposes of religious life in the colonial era. Pious but poor women composed and signed dramatic letters begging for support for their reclusive lives, and cloistered noblewomen pleaded to be freed of their forced stays at convents. Records of room and board payments reveal the longer-term stays of widows and abandoned wives and the shorter stays of their daughters, as each used the shelter for her own purposes. One particular source has provided the most poignant accounts: convent documents from the 1700s included affirmations from young girls that they entered voluntarily, as was required by civil and religious laws of the era. Most were rote statements about their dedication to the convent and deeply felt devotion to the church, but some added personal details that suggest both real vocations on the part of religious women and social seclusion at the behest of their families. Many more women worked as servants and slaves in these same convents and *recolhimentos*, but little can be known of *their* responses to the cloistered life.

In the last chapter, I recalled the women who dissented from the dominant culture and flouted the religious and social norms of colonial Brazil—the healers, diviners, and practitioners of magic. Women's magic opened new realms of power, autonomy, and creativity for women in that era, realms that few devout Catholic women might inhabit. Whatever gains women might have perceived through magical means, however, did not result in consistently improved circumstances and position: women lost virtue and honor through their contact with magical practices, and found little recompense in the wider society. Their confessions and denunciation statements before the visiting Portuguese Inquisition, however, indicated that some women consistently used magical chants and rituals to determine their own lives, loves, and fortunes in the more turbulent times of colonial Brazil, to continue traditional practices from Portugal, and to adapt new symbols and powers from the indigenous religions.

As tempting as it might be to follow the scholarly conclusion that marginalized women used magic to obtain some small improvements in their lives or the judgment of Catholic Church officials that females trafficked with Satan to introduce discord into their community, I have chosen instead to follow the methods of Portuguese scholar José Pedro Paiva. I have attempted to determine in the language of the recorded statements how and why colonial women used magic and to understand the patterns in the early and later colonial era from their perspectives. As I have noted, the confessions and denunciations came from working women or wives of relatively successful immigrant artisans and functionaries, and suggested a widespread acceptance and use of magic to harm and curse others, discover the whereabouts of missing persons and property, bind lovers in marriage, and change the course of ordinary lives. Many women borrowed the language of the Inquisitors—or the recording secretary recast their admissions in those terms—to admit that magic might be dangerous or interdicted, but some still affirmed its efficacy in gaining hidden knowledge or power over others. In addition, most statements from the first Visitations of the Inquisition focused on the manipulation of interpersonal relationships: women sought to control neighbors and husbands, or influence the future for their family and friends.

Women's magic underwent several changes by the time of the later Visitation of the Portuguese Inquisition to Grão-Pará in 1763–1769, if those limited records provide an accurate portrait of their beliefs and practices. Following the extraordinarily detailed condemnations of magic and sorcery in the *Constituições Primeyros do Arcebispado da Bahia* promulgated in 1707 by D. Sebastião Monteiro da Vide, magic itself seemed to proliferate in the colony. Evidence in the Inquisition records suggests that women's powers and claims extended beyond their own homes, and, more importantly, their magic drew on a wider range of religious rituals and symbols. Even the proportion of statements changed: over half of the denunciations and confessions described personal encounters with magic of some sort. While the older European tradition still shaped the chants and rituals for love magic and divination, the magical cures incorporated ritual structure, elements, and terminology taken from native Brazilian healing ceremonies. This expanding magical tradition enticed women of diverse ages and ethnic backgrounds to learn and practice rituals and to convey their successes, but they also—not surprisingly—came under the scrutiny of the Inquisitors.

Despite the diversification of traditions, the later records suggest that magic was less exclusively a feminine realm: unnamed or nicknamed women were no longer denounced for their reputation as witches according to "public report," and over half of the statements detailed men's involvement in magical curses, healings, and divinations. This did not, however, reduce the condemnation of women's magic by male denouncers and the Inquisitor himself. In fact, the Catholic Church officials replaced their dismissive responses to "superstitions" and "foolishness" with harsher rebukes of women's evil deeds. The Inquisitor pressed confessants and denunciants to detail pacts with the devil, demonic powers, and evil forces in women's activities, and routinely assigned the dissident spiritual tradition to the realm of heresy and apostasy, that is, to the devil's world. Following suit, male denouncers repeated that women who harmed or healed were dangerous and demonic. Confessants such as Domingas Gomes da Resurreição might have previously considered their practices mere superstitions, but could no longer avoid the condemnation from the Church: Gomes da Resurreição herself admitted their demonic origins. In spite of those condemnations, however, women's magic persisted and provided a realm for creative spiritual practitioners beyond the reach of the stereotypes for ideal Christian behavior.

These six chapters on the images, ideals, roles, and realities created about and by women offer only a hint at how women might have responded to the first Portuguese missionaries and conquerors and to the later authors, Church officials, and governors who had, at best, little time or sympathy for women's individual and independent existence. Brazilian Indian women's presence and power in the colonial theater was probably the most fleeting, for so many tribal communities were either "descended" by the Jesuits or decimated by the colonists. Still, indigenous women faced and fought off the earliest violation of their identities and bodies, and their legacy as the warriors, farmers, concubines, and healers of colonial Brazil can be tracked through the discourse that marginalized them, in Brazilian legends, Inquisition records, and contemporary Brazilian folklore. Women who emigrated from Portugal with their families or at the behest of Church or government courts had more opportunities to communicate their expectations and accomplishments in Brazil, but their literary production was slender—too few were literate and with sufficient wealth and leisure to record their ideas and experiences. Luso-Brazilian women remained in the shadows of male colonists through the first two centuries, and produced a small number of letters, reports, poems, and songs to represent their own observations on their land and lives. African women brought to the colony as slaves emerge in Brazilian history only toward the end of the colonial era, and then only as they served or confronted the dominant classes, still defined in relationship to them.

The limits forced on women's lives remain in the contemporary scarcity of sources, and the six studies completed for this book depended primarily on the writings of colonial men. I uncovered some documentary evidence of women's views and, in a few cases, just the echoes of women's own words, but with all of these I could only suggest how women might have understood their places and roles in colonial Brazil. Much more could be done to bring women's religious lives into the center of Brazilian history, of course, and the full range of perspectives from native Brazilian women and women of African descent has yet to be heard. Further research in the local public or religious archives in Salvador, Olinda, and Diamantina or in the Torre do Tombo in Lisbon will surely shed more light on these topics and open the discussion of still more perspectives from women themselves. Still, I hope that my studies might provide the foundation for recovering women's religious lives in the colonial era, and that my work might contribute to writing women back into their own history.

In colonial Brazil, then, women were simultaneously marginalized and misrepresented, idealized and demonized—all as a counterpoint to the dominant discourse of the Luso-Brazilian elites in the Roman Catholic Church and colonial government. Even the most accomplished and privileged woman—an educated white plantation owner, for example—might find her life forcibly restricted, while enslaved women of African descent might find a moment of freedom in healing rituals or devotional prayers. Women of diverse ethnic heritage, whose numbers increased through women's sexual exploitation, lived alongside the privileged classes and created a diverse cultural heritage within and alongside the very perspective that marginalized them. Placed at the center, however, a new understanding of women's religious lives might reorder the colonial universe and upend the subaltern mentality, transform the littoral coast and translate the literal past from its shackling confines to its most expansive possibilities.

# Notes

INTRODUCTION

1. [Brás Lourenço], "Por commissão do P. Brás Lourenço ao P. Miguel de Torres, Lisboa, Espírito Santo, 10 de Junho de 1562," in *Cartas dos primeiros jesuítas do Brasil*, ed. Serafim Leite, vol. 3: 462.

2. Mesa do Desembargo do Paço, 1808–1828, Caixa 778 [antiga 129], Divisão de documentação escrita, Arquivo Nacional; "Carta de doação que faz D. Ana de Sousa de Queirós e Silva para a construção de um seminário, Bahia, 10 de maio de 1728" [II 33, 27, 3], and "Petição da Madre Regente do Recolhimento de Santa Teresa de São Paulo, ao Príncipe D. João VI [1809]" [II 35, 25, 15], Seção dos Manuscritos, Biblioteca Nacional, Rio de Janeiro.

3. "Livro de Receitas e Despesas do Patrimônio da Igreja de N. S. do Parto, 1786–1797," Arquivo da Cúria Metropolitana, Catedral de São Sebastião do Rio de Janeiro, folios 1–2.

4. "Processos das Noviças do Convento Nossa Senhora da Conceição da Ajuda," Noviças para Conventos, 2a. Caixa, Arquivo da Cúria Metropolitana.

5. Sergio Buarque de Holanda, *Raizes do Brasil*, Coleção Documentos Brasileiros; Pedro Calmon, *História da civilização brasileira*, 14; Caio Prado Júnior, *The Colonial Background of Modern Brazil*, trans. Suzette Macedo (Berkeley: University of California Press, 1971); Gilberto Freyre, *Casa-grande e senzala: Formação da família brasileira sob o regime de economia patriarchal* (Rio de Janeiro: Maia & Schmidt, 1933); C. R. Boxer, *Mary and Misogyny: Women in Iberian Expansion Overseas, 1415–1815, Some Facts, Fancies, and Personalities* (London: Duckworth, 1975).

6. Asunción Lavrin, ed., *Latin American Women: Historical Perspectives*; Susan Migden Socolow, *The Women of Colonial Latin America*.

7. Maria Luiza Marcílio, ed., *Família, mulher, sexualidade e Igreja na história do Brasil*; Mary del Priore, *História das mulheres no Brasil* and *Mulheres no Brasil colonial*, Coleção repensando a história; Anna Amélia Vieira Nascimento, *Patriarcado e religião:*

*As enclausuradas clarissas do Convento do Desterro da Bahia 1677–1890*; Leila Mezan Algranti, *Honradas e devotas: Mulheres da colônia*; Muriel Nazzari, *Disappearance of the Dowry: Women, Families, and Social Change in São Paulo, 1600–1900*; Laura de Mello e Souza, *O Diabo e a Terra de Santa Cruz: Feitiçaria e religiosidade popular no Brasil colonial* and *Inferno Atlântico: Demonologia e colonização, séculos xvi–xvii*; Ronaldo Vainfas, *Trópico dos pecados: Moral, sexualidade e Inquisição no Brasil.*

8. The history and impact of European codes of honor have been explored in David D. Gilmore, ed., *Honor and Shame and the Unity of the Mediterranean*; John G. Peristiany, ed., *Honour and Shame: The Values of Mediterranean Society*; and Frank Henderson Stewart, ed., *Honor.* Interpretations of honor for colonial Latin America have been addressed in Lyman L. Johnson and Sonya Lipsett-Rivera, eds., *The Faces of Honor: Sex, Shame, and Violence in Colonial Latin America*; Ann Twinam, *Public Lives, Private Secrets: Gender, Honor, Sexuality, and Illegitimacy in Colonial Spanish America*; and, most important for this work, Algranti's *Honradas.*

9. Raphael Bluteau, *Vocabulario portuguez & latino: Aulico, anatomico, architectonico* . . . , vol. 4: 51, s.v. "honra."

10. David D. Gilmore, "Introduction: The Shame of Dishonor," in Gilmore, *Honor and Shame*, 9.

11. Ibid.

12. Ann Twinam, "The Negotiation of Honor: Elites, Sexuality, and Illegitimacy in Eighteenth-Century Spanish America," in *The Faces of Honor*, ed. Johnson and Lipsett-Rivera, 74–75, 85.

13. Rae Flory and David Grant Smith, "Bahian Merchants and Planters in the Seventeenth and Early Eighteenth Centuries," 583–585.

14. Muriel Nazzari, "An Urgent Need to Conceal," in *The Faces of Honor*, ed. Johnson and Lipsett-Rivera, 105.

15. Bluteau, *Vocabulario*, 51, s.v. "honra"; emphasis in the original.

16. Alzira Campos, *Casamento e família em São Paulo colonial: Caminhos e descaminhos*, 155.

17. Algranti, *Honradas*, 113.

CHAPTER ONE

1. Manuel da Nóbrega, "Informacion de las partes del Brasil," in *Cartas dos Jesuítas do Oriente e do Brasil, 1549–1551*, ed. José Manuel Garcia, 1v (page references are to the apparent original pagination).

2. Maria Cândida Ferreira de Almeida, *Tornar-se outro: O topos canibal na literatura brasileira*, 112.

3. See, for example, Fred Chiappelli, ed., *First Images of America: The Impact of the New World on the Old*; Tzvetan Todorov, *The Conquest of America: The Question of the Other*; Bernadette Bucher, *Icon and Conquest: A Structural Analysis of the Illustrations of de Bry's Great Voyages*, trans. Basia Miller Gulati; Peter Mason, *Deconstructing*

*America: Representations of the Other*; Ronald Raminelli, *Imagens da colonização: A representação do índio de Caminha a Vieira*; and Roger Bartra, *Wild Men in the Looking Glass: The Mythic Origins of European Otherness*, trans. Carl T. Berrisford.

4. Hayden White, "The Forms of Wildness," in *The Wild Man Within: An Image in Western Thought from the Renaissance to Romanticism*, ed. Edward Dudley and Maximilian E. Novak.

5. Ibid., 19–21.

6. Bartra, *Wild Men in the Looking Glass*, 43–62.

7. Annette Kolodny, *The Lay of the Land: Metaphor as Experience and History in American Life and Letters*, 10–25. Kolodny argues that "harmony between man and nature based on an experience of the land as essentially feminine" may be North America's "oldest and most cherished fantasy" (4); that characterization—with significantly less peaceful or maternal overtones—recurs in South American literature as well.

8. Carol Douglas Sparks, "The Land Incarnate: Navajo Women and the Dialogue of Colonialism, 1821–1870," in *Negotiators of Change: Historical Perspectives on Native American Women*, ed. Nancy Shoemaker, 139.

9. Ibid., 142, 140.

10. Pero Vaz de Caminha, *Carta a El Rei d. Manuel*, ed. Leonardo Arroyo.

11. A. de Silva Rego, *Portuguese Colonization in the Sixteenth Century*, 32–33.

12. Caminha, *Carta a El Rei d. Manuel*, 38. An alternate reading of the last difficult phrase, offered by the editor, is "we were not ashamed to look closely at them." In either case, Caminha was surely playing on the words "vergonhas"—his euphemism for genitals—and "envergonhar," to be ashamed.

13. Ibid., 40.

14. Ibid., 47–48. Here again Caminha plays on the Portuguese euphemism, referring to her "shameful parts" as innocent and free of shame.

15. Ibid., 66.

16. The presence of Jesuits in early colonial Brazil is explored by Serafim Leite in *Artes e ofícios dos Jesuítas no Brasil, 1549-1760*; *História da Companhia de Jesus no Brasil*, vol. 1, *Século XVI, O estabelecimento*, and vol. 2, *Século XVI—A obra*; *Páginas de história do Brasil*; and *Novas páginas de história do Brasil*.

17. Manuel da Nóbrega, "Carta 7, do P. Manuel da Nóbrega ao P. Simão Rodrigues, Bahia 9 de agosto de 1549," in *Cartas dos primeiros jesuítas do Brasil*, ed. Serafim Leite, vol. 1: 127.

18. Luís da Grã, "Carta 46, do P. Luís da Grã ao P. Inácio de Loyola, Piratininga 8 de junho de 1556," in *Cartas dos primeiros jesuítas do Brasil*, ed. Leite, vol. 2: 293–294.

19. Manuel da Nóbrega, "Apontamento de coisas do Brasil, Bahia, May 8, 1558," in *Novas cartas jesuíticas*, ed. Serafim Leite, 79.

20. Manuel da Nóbrega, "Carta 11, aos Padres e Irmãos de Coimbra, Pernambuco, 13 de setembro de 1551," in *Cartas do Brasil e mais escritos*, ed. Serafim Leite, 93.

21. José de Anchieta, "Carta trimensal, de maio a agosto de 1556," in *Cartas do Pe. José de Anchieta: Correspondência ativa e passiva*, ed. Hélio Abranches Viotti, 109.

22. José de Anchieta, "Carta 56, do Irmão José de Anchieta [aos Padres e Irmãos de Portugal], São Paulo de Piratininga, fim de abril de 1557," in *Cartas dos primeiros jesuítas do Brasil*, ed. Leite, vol. 2: 365–366.

23. Pero Correia, "Carta 23, do Irmão Pero Correia ao P. Belchior Nunes Barreto, Coimbra, S. Vicente 8 de junho de 1551," in *Cartas dos primeiros jesuítas do Brasil*, ed. Leite, vol. 1: 222n.

24. Luís da Grã, "Carta 46," 294.

25. António Pires, "Carta 44, do P. António Pires aos Padres e Irmãos de Coimbra, Pernambuco 4 de Junho de 1552," in *Cartas dos primeiros jesuítas do Brasil*, ed. Leite, vol. 1: 326. The interpreter is elsewhere identified as Maria da Rosa, founder of the first independent *recolhimento* in Olinda, Brazil.

26. Fernão Cardim, "Narrativa epistolar de uma viagem e missão jesuítica pelo Bahia, Ilheos, Porto Seguro, Pernambuco, Espirito Santo, Rio de Janeiro, São Vicente, etc. [1583–1590]," 26.

27. Ibid., 50.

28. Jean de Léry, *Histoire d'un Voyage fait en la terre du Brésil* [1556–1558].

29. Jean de Léry, *History of a Voyage to the Land of Brazil, Otherwise Called America*, trans. Jane Whatley, 26; Léry, *Histoire*, 47.

30. Léry, *History*, 57; *Histoire*, 110.

31. Léry, *History*, 65–66; *Histoire*, 126–128.

32. Léry, *History*, 67; *Histoire*, 130.

33. Léry, *History*, 66; *Histoire*, 128.

34. Laura Fishman, "Crossing Gender Boundaries: Tupí and European Women in the Eyes of Claude D'Abbeville," 81–98.

35. Claude d'Abbeville, *História da missão dos padres capuchinos na ilha do Maranhão e terras circumvizinhas* (n.p., 1614; reprint, São Paulo: Editora da Universidade de São Paulo, 1975), 216.

36. Ibid.

37. Ibid., 217.

38. Raminelli, *Imagens da colonização*, 13–15.

39. Bartra, *Wild Men in the Looking Glass*, 19.

40. Ibid., 83.

41. Christine de Pizan, *The Book of the City of Ladies*, trans. Earl Jeffrey Richards, 18, 40–41.

42. Ibid., 42, 47, 51.

43. Ibid., 51, 36.

44. Candace Slater, *Entangled Edens: Visions of the Amazon*, 83.

45. Christopher Columbus, *Four Voyages to the New World: Letters and Selected Documents*, trans. John Major, 15.

46. Christopher Columbus, *The Journal of Christopher Columbus*, trans. Cecil Jane, 147, under the entry for January 13, 1493.

47. Chivalric romances such as Garci Rodrígues de Montalvo's *Las Sergas de Explandián* (1510) and Feliciano de Silva's *Amadis de Grecia* portrayed some of the

Amazon women as vicious and dangerous, but their queens were typically valorous but ignorant—and readily converted to the Christian faith. Alison Taufer, "The Only Good Amazon Is a Converted Amazon: The Woman Warrior and Christianity in the Amadís Cycle," in *Playing with Gender: A Renaissance Pursuit*, ed. Jean R. Brink, Maryanne C. Horowitz, and Allison P. Coudert, 35–44.

48. Slater, *Entangled Edens*, 86; Batya Weinbaum, *Islands of Women and Amazons: Representations and Realities*, 131.

49. Raminelli, *Imagens da colonização*, 27; Simão de Vasconcelos, *Crônica da Companhia de Jesus*, 3rd ed. (Petrópolis: Editora Vozes, Ltda., 1977), vol. 1: 97.

50. Slater, *Entangled Edens*, 86.

51. Gaspar de Carvajal, "Discovery of the Orellana River," in *The Discovery of the Amazon*, ed. José Toribio Medina and H. C. Heaton, trans. Bertram T. Lee, 204.

52. Ibid., 214.

53. Ibid., 214.

54. Ibid., 220.

55. Ibid., 220–221.

56. Ibid., 222.

57. Leite, ed., *Cartas dos primeiros jesuítas do Brasil*, vol. 1: 167–168.

58. Gabriel Soares de Sousa, *Tratado descriptivo do Brasil em 1587*, Brasiliana, vol. 117 (São Paulo: Editora Nacional, 1987), 337.

59. Ibid.

60. Simão de Vasconcelos, "Notícias antecedentes, curiosas e necessárias dos cousas do Brasil," *Crônica da Companhia de Jesus* (Petrópolis: Editora Vozes Ltda., 1977), 1: 49–166.

61. Ibid., 64–65.

62. Leite, *Páginas de história do Brasil*, 128, 130, 131, 134. Rodrigues had just entered the Jesuit order in 1553 and may have been the source for Nóbrega's claim about Amazons in the interior.

63. Schuma Schumaher and Érico Vital Brazil, eds., *Dicionário Mulheres do Brasil de 1500 até a atualidade: Biográfico e ilustrado*, 43.

64. Luiz Mott, "As amazonas: Um mito e algumas hipóteses," in *América en tempo de conquista*, ed. Ronaldo Vainfas, 43.

65. Pero Magalhães Gandavo, *História da província de Santa Cruz e tratado da terra do Brasil* (São Paulo: Obelisco, 1964), 56, quoted in Mott, "As amazonas," 47.

66. Mott, "As amazonas," 45.

67. Ibid., 46–48.

68. Columbus, *Journal*, 52 [entry for November 4, 1492].

69. Ibid., 69 [November 23, 1492], 74 [November 26, 1492].

70. Stephen Greenblatt, *Marvelous Possessions: The Wonder of the New World*, 71–72.

71. Ernest Brehaut, *An Encyclopedist of the Dark Ages: Isidore of Seville*, 219; see also Jonathan Z. Smith, "What a Difference a Difference Makes," in *Relating Religion: Essays in the Study of Religion*, 265, 292n107.

72. Kirkpatrick Sale, *The Conquest of Paradise: Christopher Columbus and the Columbian Legacy,* 133–134.

73. Peter Martyr D'Anghera, *De Orbe Novo,* trans. Francis Augustus MacNutt, 163. It is worth noting that the preservation and cooking methods reported were certainly European and not used by Taino or island Caribs for meat and fish preparation.

74. Ibid., 63, 72–73. Martyr also entangles two legends, recounting the Spanish report that the cannibal men occasionally cohabited with Amazon women and fathered their children.

75. Mason, *Deconstructing America,* 54.

76. Bartra, *Wild Men in the Looking Glass,* 25.

77. Richard Bernheimer, *Wild Men in the Middle Ages: A Study in Art, Sentiment, and Demonology,* 33–40.

78. Hans Staden, *Warhaftig Historia und Beschreibung eyner Landschafft.*

79. These issues are explored in the introductions of translations ranging from Malcolm H. Letts, ed., *Hans Staden: The True History of His Captivity* (London: G. Routledge & Sons, Ltd., 1928) to Neil L. Whitehead and Michael Harbsmeier, ed. and trans., *Hans Staden's True History: An Account of Cannibal Captivity in Brazil* (Durham: Duke University Press, 2008).

80. Hans Staden, *Duas viagens ao Brasil,* trans. Giomar de Carvalho Franco, 81, 82.

81. Staden, *Duas viagens ao Brasil,* 89, 91, 95.

82. Ibid., 90, 91.

83. Ibid., 97–118.

84. Ibid., 175, 177–188.

85. Ibid., 183–184.

86. Almeida, *Tornar-se outro,* 135–137.

87. Raminelli, *Imagens da colonização,* 93–98. A similar discussion is found in Whitehead and Harbsmeier, *Hans Staden's True History,* lxxvii–lxxviii.

88. Manuel da Nóbrega, *Cartas do Brasil e mais escritos,* 48.

89. Ibid., 73.

90. Leite, *Páginas de história do Brasil,* 125, 127.

91. Ibid., 127, 129.

92. Vasconcelos, *Crônica,* vol. 1: 96–97.

93. Ibid., 102.

94. Ibid., 199–200.

95. Léry, *Histoire,* 126.

96. Léry, *Histoire,* 127.

97. Raminelli, *Imagens da colonização,* 85.

98. Almeida, *Tornar-se outro,* 18, 19. The identification of Brazilians as cannibals came full circle in the twentieth century, when Oswaldo Andrade embraced the epithet and its essential "Otherness" for modern Brazilians in his prose-poem, "Anthropofagia."

99. Claude Rawson, "Unspeakable Rites: Cultural Reticence and the Cannibal Question," 168.

100. Neil L. Whitehead, "Hans Staden and the Cultural Politics of Cannibalism," 739.

101. Neil L. Whitehead, "Carib Cannibalism: The Historical Evidence," 72.

102. Raminelli, *Imagens da colonização*, fig. 8, opposite page 65. Rebecca Parker Brienen analyzed the cultural and historical significance of this painting, also called *Tapuya Woman*, in *Visions of Savage Paradise: Albert Eckhout, Court Painter in Colonial Dutch Brazil*, 95–129. It should be noted that the most important Eckhout paintings are widely available electronically and in scholarly image collections.

103. Raminelli, *Imagens da colonização*, 86. For further analysis of the *Tapuya or Tupí Woman and Child*, also called *Tupinamba/Brasilian Woman and Child*, see Brienen, *Visions of Savage Paradise*, 113–117.

104. Albert Eckhout, *Mameluca*, in *Albert Eckhout: Pintor de Maurício de Nassau no Brasil, 1637–1644*, ed. Clarival do Prado Vallardes and Luiz Emygdio de Mello Filho, 75, with commentaries on 119 and 134. For further analysis of the *Mameluca*, see Brienen, *Visions of Savage Paradise*, 162–168.

CHAPTER TWO

1. Antônio Vieira, "Sermão Sétimo do Rosário," in *Sermões*, ed. Gonçalo Alves, vol. 4, tomo 11: 50–51. Here the noun "deshonestidade" bears the unavoidable connotation of sexual licentiousness.

2. Mary Douglas, *Natural Symbols: Explorations in Cosmology*, 93.

3. Ibid., 97, 99, 100, 101.

4. Suely Creusa Cordeiro de Almeida, *O sexo devoto: Normatização e resitência feminina no império português XVI–XVIII*, 89; emphasis in the original. The "moralist" was the seventeenth-century collector of proverbs, Antonio Delicado.

5. Douglas, *Natural Symbols*, 100.

6. Pierre Bourdieu, *Outline of a Theory of Practice*, 78, 80, 81.

7. Aristotle, *Politics*, bk. 1, chaps. 5–6.

8. Ibid., bk. 1, chaps. 12–13.

9. The first creation story ends with humans in "the image" of God in Gen. 1:27; Eve's tale is in Gen. 2:21–3:23.

10. Prov. 9:13; Prov. 31:11–29, 31:30.

11. Luke 8:3, 10:38–42; John 4:1–42; Matt. 27:55–56, 61, 28:1–10.

12. Rom. 16; Col. 3:18; 1 Cor. 11:2–15, 14:33–35.

13. 1 Pet. 3:1–6; 1 Tim. 2:11–15.

14. Merry E. Wiesner-Hanks, *Christianity and Sexuality in the Early Modern World: Regulating Desire, Reforming Practice*, 31.

15. Thomas Aquinas, *Summa Theologica*, I, q. 92, arts. 1–4; q. 93, art. 4.

16. Carla Casagrande, "The Protected Woman," trans. Arthur Goldhammer, in *A History of Women in the West*, vol. 2, *Silences of the Middle Ages*, ed. Christiane Klapisch-Zuber, 99.

17. Wiesner-Hanks, *Christianity and Sexuality*, 43–44; Jacques Dalarun, "The Clerical Gaze," trans. Arthur Goldhammer, in *Silences of the Middle Ages*, ed. Klapisch-Zuber, 15–42.

18. Christine de Pizan, *The Treasure of the City of Ladies*, trans. Sarah Lawrence, 5.

19. Ibid., 7, 10, 11, 14, 15, 19–27.

20. Ibid., 31, 58–63, 87, 120–129.

21. See Joan Kelly, "Did Women Have a Renaissance?," in *Women, History, and Theory*, 19–50.

22. Gonçalo Fernandes Trancoso, *Histórias de Proveito e Exemplo* [1575], ed. Agostinho de Campos, 4–5, 6–7.

23. Ibid., 74, 75–76.

24. Ibid., 101, 106, 107–108, 118–121.

25. Ibid., 183, 193, 189.

26. Ibid., 199–223.

27. Ibid., 91–92.

28. "O qual é que o A [quer] dizer que seja amiga da casa; o B, ben-quista da vizinhança; o C, caridosa para com os pobres; o D, devota da Virgem; o E, entendida em seu ofício; o F, firme na fé; o G, guardadeira da sua fazenda; o H, humilde a seu marido; o I, inimiga de mexericos; o L, lial; o M, mansa; o N, nobre; o O, [h]onesta; o P, prudente; o Q, quieta; o R, regrada; o S, sisuda; o T, trabalhadeira; o V, virtuosa; o X, xã; Z, zelosa da honra." Ibid., 92–93. The editor noted that in the 1624 edition, the "X" was for "*XPãa*" or *Christian woman*, with reference to the Greek letter abbreviation *Χραα*.

29. Diogo de Paiva de Andrada, *Casamento perfeito* [1630], 376, 387, 389, 396. The author's name is occasionally spelled "Andrade."

30. Juan Luís Vives, "Instruction of a Christian Woman" [1532], 34.

31. Elisa Maria Lopes da Costa, introduction to Rui Gonçalves, *Dos privilegios & praerogativas que ho genero feminino ttem por dereito comun & ordenações do Reyno mais que ho genero masculino*, 11.

32. Gonçalves, *Dos privilegios & praerogativas*, 6, 9, 14, 17, 20.

33. Ibid., 18, 22, 23, 30, 31.

34. Alice R. Clemente, "Rui Gonçalves: An Early Portuguese Jurist and the Status of Women," 352.

35. Luís dos Anjos, *Jardim de Portugal*, 190.

36. Ibid., 216.

37. Ibid.

38. Ibid., 230–231, 292, 304, 310.

39. Antonio Delicado, *Adagios portuguêses reduzidos a lugares communs*, ed. Luís Chaves, 74, 255, 260–269. Prior of the diocesan church in Évora, Padre Delicado published the first known collection of Portuguese proverbs in 1651, though private copies following the models of Spanish or French collections may have circulated earlier.

40. Ibid., 211, 212.

41. Ibid., 212, 219, 213.

42. Ibid., 218, 217, 215, 217.

43. Ibid., 213, 214, 216.

44. Pero Vaz de Caminha, *Carta a El Rei D. Manuel*, ed. Leonardo Arroyo, 38.

45. "The Mission to the Carajós, 1605–1607," related by P. Jerónimo Rodrigues, in *Novas cartas jesuíticas*, ed. Serafim Leite, 229–230.

46. Frei Vicente do Salvador, *História do Brasil, 1500–1627*, 278.

47. Ibid., 116; Charles R. Boxer, *Women in Iberian Expansion Overseas, 1415–1815: Some Facts, Fancies and Personalities*, 55.

48. Madre Maria Angela [Leda Maria Pereira Rodrigues], *A instrução feminina em São Paulo: Subsídios para sua história até a proclamação da Republica*, 32; Stuart B. Schwartz, "Plantations and Peripheries, c. 1580–c. 1750" in *Colonial Brazil*, ed. Leslie Bethell, 141.

49. A. J. R. Russell-Wood, "Female and Family in the Economy and Society of Colonial Brazil," in *Latin American Women: Historical Perspectives*, ed. Asunción Lavrin, 60, 61.

50. Kátia da Costa Bezerra, "'Pernambuco illustrado pelo sexo feminino': A condição feminina no relato de Dom Domingos Loreto Couto," 60.

51. Antônio Vieira, "Sermão Décimo Sétimo do Rosário," in *Sermões*, vol. 4: 414, 415, 417, 419. Vieira apparently completed this sermon in 1686 with others in a small group of writings dedicated to the rosary, in reverent thanks for surviving a fever.

52. Vieira, "Sermão do Demónio Mudo, pregado no Convento de Odivelas, Religiosas do Patriarca S. Bernardo, no ano de 1661," in *Sermões*, vol. 1, tomo 3: 329, 330, 333–334.

53. Nuno Marques Pereira, *Compendio narrativo do peregrino da America*, vol. 1: 164. See also Feliciano Joaquim de Sousa Nunes, *Discursos políticos-morais*, 133–134.

54. Domingos Loreto Couto, *Desagravos do Brazil e glórias de Pernambuco* [1759], ed. José Antônio Gonsalves de Mello, 463, 464.

55. Ibid., 465, 466.

56. Ibid., 480, 475, 482.

57. Ibid., 485–492, 495, 501, 500.

58. André João Antonil [João Antônio Andreoni], *Cultura e opulência do Brasil* [1711], 94; L. F. de Tollenare, *Notas dominicaes tomadas durante uma residencia em Portugal e no Brasil nos annos de 1816, 1817 e 1818, Parte relativa a Pernambuco* (Recife: Empreza do Jornal do Recife, 1905), 78–87, quoted in *Children of God's Fire: A Documentary History of Black Slavery in Brazil*, ed. Robert Edgar Conrad, 65.

59. Tollenare, *Notas dominicaes*, 67; Mrs. Nathaniel Kindersley [1764], British Museum, Sloane ms. 1572, fls. 61–2, quoted in Boxer, *Women in Iberian Expansion Overseas*, 60.

60. Manuel da Nóbrega, "Informação das terras do Brasil [aos Padres e Irmãos de Coimbra, Bahia agosto de 1549]," in *Cartas do Brasil e mais escritos*, ed. Leite, 61.

61. Eduardo Hoornaert, "Terceiro período: A Cristandade durante a primeira época colonial," 375.

62. Bluteau, *Vocabulario portuguez*, vol. 4: 52; vol. 8: 820.

63. Antônio de Morais Silva, *Diccionario da lingua portugueza composto pelo*

*padre D. Rafael Bluteau, reformado, e accrescentado por Antonio de Moraes Silva natural do Rio de Janeiro*, vol. 1: 684, s. v. "Honra."

64. José de Anchieta, "Carta 4, do José de Anchieta ao Ignacio de Loyola (Quadrimestre Maio-setembro, 10. de setembro de 1554)," in *Cartas do Padre José de Anchieta: Correspondência ativa e passiva*, ed. Hélio Abranches Viotti, 63.

65. Jorge Benci, *Economia christã dos senhores no governo dos escravos*, 98, quoted in Hoornaert, "Terceiro período," 374.

66. D. Sebastião Monteiro da Vide, *Constituiçoens Primeyras do Arcebispado da Bahia feytos & ordenadas pelo illustrissismo, e reverendissimo senhor D. Sebastião Monteyro da Vide, 50. Arcebispo do dito Arcebispado, e do conselho da Sua Magestade: Propostas, e Aceitas em o Synodo Diocesano, que o dito Senhor Celebrou em 12 de junho do anno de 1707*, 359. The sin of *molicie* was probably any sort of sexual contact between members of the same sex or of the opposite sexes, without penetration.

67. Ibid., 361, 363.

68. Emanuel Araújo, "A arte da sedução: Sexualidade feminina na colônia," in *História das mulheres no Brasil*, ed. Mary Del Priore and Carla Bassanezi, especially 65–68; Lígia Bellini, *A coisa obscura: Mulher, sodomia e Inquisição no Brasil colonial*, 39, 67–69.

69. Alzira Campos, *Casamento e família em São Paulo colonial: Caminhos e descaminhos*, 154.

70. Tollenare, *Notas dominicaes*, 93–96, quoted in *Children of God's Fire*, 69–70.

71. Andrada, *Casamento perfeito*, 356–357; Francisco Manuel de Melo, *Carta de guia de casados, ou um livro só para homens* [1651], ed. João Gaspar Simões, 72.

72. João de Nossa Senhora da Porta Siqueira, *Escola de politica, ou tratado pratico da civilidade portugueza* [1791], 169.

73. Raymond Cantel, "La place de la femme dans la pensée de Vieira," *Caravelle-Cahiers du Monde Hispanique et Luso-Brésilien* 1965, no. 4, 6, cited by Mary Lucy M. Del Priore, "O corpo feminino e o amor: Um olhar," in *Amor e família no Brasil*, ed. Maria Angela d'Incao, 35; Vieira, "Sermão da Quinta Quarta-Feira da Quaresma, pregado na Misericórdia de Lisboa, no ano de 1669," *Sermões* vol. 2, tomo 4: 119.

74. A. J. R. Russell-Wood, "Women and Society in Colonial Brazil," 3.

CHAPTER THREE

1. Gabriel Soares de Sousa, *Tratado descriptivo do Brasil em 1587*, 313–314.

2. Feliciano Joaquim de Souza Nunes, *Discursos políticos-morais*, 134, 88–101, 115; emphasis in the original.

3. Mary Douglas, *Natural Symbols: Explorations in Cosmology*, 97–101.

4. Susan R. Bordo, "The Body and the Reproduction of Femininity: A Feminist Appropriation of Foucault," in *Gender/Body/Knowledge: Feminist Reconstructions of Being and Knowing*, ed. Alison M. Jaggar and Susan R. Bordo, 13, 14.

5. Pierre Bourdieu, *Outline of a Theory of Practice*, 94.

6. Bordo, "The Body and the Reproduction of Femininity," 14.

7. Bourdieu, *Outline of a Theory of Practice*, 80, 95.

8. Plato, *Republic*, bk. 5, 455–458.

9. Aristotle, *Politics*, bk. 1, xiii, 1260a.

10. Silvana Vecchio, "The Good Wife," trans. Clarissa Botsford, in *A History of Women in the West*, vol. 2, *Silences of the Middle Ages*, ed. Christiane Klapisch-Zuber, 119.

11. Ibid., 119, 118–120.

12. Merry E. Wiesner, *Women and Gender in Early Modern Europe*, 144–150; A. H. de Oliveira Marques, *Daily Life in Portugal in the Late Middle Ages*, trans. S. S. Wyatt, 229, 234–237; Ann Pescatello, *Power and Pawn: The Female in Iberian Families, Societies, and Cultures*, 23–25.

13. Martine Sonnet, "A Daughter to Educate," trans. Arthur Goldhammer, in *A History of Women in the West*, vol. 3, *Renaissance and Enlightenment Paradoxes*, ed. Natalie Zemon Davis and Arlette Farge, 102; Wiesner, *Women and Gender in Early Modern Europe*, 146–159.

14. Wiesner, *Women and Gender in Early Modern Europe*, 159.

15. Ibid., 163, 159.

16. Marques, *Daily Life in Portugal in the Late Middle Ages*, 235, 230–236; Pescatello, *Power and Pawn*, 28.

17. Foster Watson, "Introduction," in Juan Luís Vives, *Vives and the Renascence Education of Women*, ed. Foster Watson, 5–7.

18. Ibid., 21.

19. Juan Luís Vives, "Instruction of a Christian Woman," in ibid., 34.

20. Ibid., 41, 43, 46–47, 55.

21. Ibid., 54, 56.

22. Ibid., 65, 71–80, 81, 88.

23. Ibid., 96, 97–98, 101.

24. Roberto López-Inglésias Samartim, *A dona do tempo antigo: Mulher e campo literário no Renascimento português, 1495-1557*, 227.

25. Maria de Lurdes Correia Fernandes, "Francisco de Monzón e a 'princesa cristã,'" 116.

26. Madre Maria Angela [Leda Maria Pereira Rodrigues], *A instrução feminina em São Paulo: Subsídios para sua história até a proclamação da Republica*, 33, 35.

27. Ibid., 34.

28. Francisco Manuel de Melo, *Carta de guia de casados, ou um livro só para homens*, ed. João Gaspar Simões, 93.

29. Ibid., 85, 87.

30. Ibid., 87, 70; 69–70; 90.

31. Schuma Schumaher and Érico Vital Brazil, eds., *Dicionário mulheres do Brasil de 1500 até a atualidade*, 350.

32. Luís da Grã, "Carta 46. Do P. Luís da Grã ao P. Inácio de Loyola, Piratininga 8 de junho de 1556," in *Cartas dos primeiros jesuítas do Brasil*, ed. Serafim Leite, vol. 2: 294.

33. José de Anchieta, "Carta trimensal, de maio a agosto de 1556," in *Cartas do Pe. José de Anchieta: Correspondência ativa e passiva*, ed. Hélio Abranches Viotti, 109.

34. Pero Correia, "Carta 23, do Irmão Pero Correia ao P. Belchior Nunes Barreto, Coimbra, do S. Vicente 8 de junho de 1551," in *Cartas dos primeiros jesuítas do Brasil*, ed. Leite, vol 1: 222.

35. António Pires, "Carta 44, do P. António Pires aos Padres e Irmãos de Coimbra, Pernambuco, 4 de junho de 1552," in ibid., vol. 1: 326.

36. António Blázquez, "Carta 21, do P. António Blázquez ao P. Diego Laynes, Bahia, September 10, 1559," in ibid., vol. 3: 37.

37. Brás Lourenço, "Carta 65, do P. Brás Lourenço ao P. Miguel de Torres, Espírito Santo, June 10, 1562," in ibid., vol. 3: 466.

38. Angela, *A instrução feminina em São Paulo*, 18.

39. João Adolfo Hansen, "A Civilização pela palavra," in *500 anos de educação no Brasil*, ed. Eliane Marta Teixeira Lopes, Luciano Mendes Faria Filho, and Cynthia Greive Veiga, 19–41; José Maria de Paiva, "Educação jesuítica no Brasil colonial," in ibid., 43.

40. José de Costa Pôrto, *Nos tempos do visitador: Subsídio ao estudo da vida colonial pernambucana, nos fins do século XVI*, 202; Schumaher and Brazil, *Dicionário mulheres do Brasil*, 63–64, 121–123; José Joaquim Machado de Oliveira, "Notas, apontamentos e noticias para a história da provincia do Espirito Santo," 164.

41. João Capistrano de Abreu, ed., *Primeira visitação do Santo Officio às partes do Brasil: Confissões da Bahia, 1591–92*, especially 80, 154; José Antônio Gonsalves de Mello, ed., *Primeira visitação do Santo Officio às partes do Brasil: Confissões de Pernambuco, 1594–1595*.

42. A brief account of Branca Dias may be found in Schumaher and Brazil, *Dicionário mulheres do Brasil*, 115–116, and an overview of her life and school in Pôrto, *Nos tempos do visitador*, 200–201.

43. The full denunciation statements concerning Branca Dias's school are in Leonardo Dantas Silva, ed., *Primeira visitação do Santo Ofício às partes do Brasil: Denunciações e confissões de Pernambuco, 1593–1595*, 30–32, 44–47, 181–183.

44. Ibid., 44–45, 182, 32; 45.

45. Ibid., 65.

46. Ibid., 47, 30, 181, 46, 44.

47. Ibid., 65, 150, 361.

48. Angela, *A instrução feminina em São Paulo*, 17–19.

49. Ibid., 17.

50. Arilda Ines Miranda Ribeiro, "Mulheres educadas na colônia," in *500 anos de educação no Brasil*, ed. Lopes et al., 79–81.

51. António Vieira, "Carta LXVI, ao Provincial do Brasil, 1654," in *Cartas do Padre António Vieira*, ed. João Lúcio de Azevedo, vol. 1: 391.

52. Schumaher and Brazil, *Dicionário mulheres do Brasil*, 49.

53. Fernão Cardim, "Narrativa epistolar de uma viagem e missão jesuítica pelo Bahia, Ilheos, Porto Seguro, Pernambuco, Espirito Santo, Rio de Janeiro, São Vicente, etc. [1583–1590]," 46.

54. Angela, *A instrução feminina em São Paulo*, 43.

55. Nuno Marques Pereira, *Compêndio narrativo do peregrino da America*, vol. 1: 169, 177.

56. Ribeiro Sanches, "Educação de uma menina até a idade de tomar estado . . . 1754," in *Plano para a educação de uma menina portuguesa no século XVIII*, ed. Luís de Pina (Porto: II Centenário da publicação do Método de Ribeiro Sanches, 1968), quoted in Maria Beatriz Nizza da Silva, *Sistema de casamento no Brasil colonial*, 185.

57. Archbishop of Bahia, Pastoral of 20 July 1751, *Anais do IV Congresso da História Nacional* 11 (1951): 85, quoted in C. R. Boxer, *The Golden Age of Brazil: 1695–1750*, 137–138.

58. José Joaquim da Cunha de Azeredo Coutinho, *Estatutos do Recolhimento de Nossa Senhora da Glória do lugar da Boa Vista de Pernambuco*, 1, 2. Maria Beatriz Nizza da Silva has pointed out that Coutinho's preamble and pedagogical claims seem to be near copies of the French text *Traité de l'éducation des filles*, written by François de Salignac de La Mothe Fénelon in 1687. In "Educação feminina e educação masculina no Brasil colonial," 151–156.

59. Coutinho, *Estatutos do Recolhimento de Nossa Senhora da Glória*, 96, 105, 76, 109, 80.

60. Maria Beatriz Nizza da Silva, *Cultura no Brasil colônia*, 99.

61. Ms., Departamento do Arquivo do Estado de São Paulo, Ofício Diversos da Capital, 871–c76–P01–d58, quoted in Maria Odila Leite da Silva Dias, *Quotidiano e poder em São Paulo no século XIX*, 26.

62. "Estatutos do Collegio de Educação de Meninas, denominado de 'Nossa Senhora dos Humildes' fundado pela beneficencia de seus Devotos o Padre Ignacio dos Santos e Araujo, em honra do Desaggravo do Santissimo Sacramento na Villa de Santo Amaro da Purificação na Capitania da Cidade da Bahia no anno de 1813," folios 1r–1v.

63. Ibid., folios 2r, 23v, 24r.

64. Ibid., folios 2r, 3v, 24.

65. Ibid., folios 2r, 10v.

66. Ibid., folio 2r.

67. Ibid., folios 14–15; 17r, 17v, 11.

68. Ibid., folios 9v, 22–23.

69. Ibid., folios 16, 29–30; 16v; 15v.


CHAPTER FOUR

1. João Capistrano de Abreu, ed., *Primeira visitação do Santo Officio às partes do Brasil: Confissões da Bahia, 1591–92*, 66, 67.

2. José Antônio Gonsalves de Mello, ed., *Primeira visitação do Santo Officio às partes do Brasil: Confissões de Pernambuco*, 1594–1595, 43. In other texts, the Inquisitor's family name is spelled "Mendonça."

3. Feliciano Joaquim de Souza Nunes, *Discursos políticos-morais*, 115, 124.

4. Ibid., 124–125.

5. Nuno Marques Pereira, *Compêndio narrativo do peregrino da America*, vol. 1: 296.

6. Because the documents of the colonial era distinguished different household relationships, I have chosen to use the somewhat archaic terms that might best reflect historical roles. *Esposas*, sometimes simply called *mulheres*, held religiously and legally recognized roles as "wives," while "common-law" wives were recognized as long-term partners and kept house or lived with men "as if married." The Portuguese term *concubinato*, here translated "concubinage," typically referred to short-term relationships and more casual sexual encounters but also designated longer-term relationships between unmarried women and married men or priests, or, less commonly, adulterous relations of any kind.

7. Jutta Sperling, "Marriage at the Time of the Council of Trent (1560–70): Clandestine Marriages, Kinship Prohibitions, and Dowry Exchange in European Comparison," 97.

8. António Henrique de Oliveira Marques, *Daily Life in Portugal in the Late Middle Ages*, trans. S. S. Wyatt, 166.

9. Ibid., 165.

10. Ibid., 176.

11. Duarte [King of Portugal], *Leal Conselheiro, o qual fez Dom Duarte, Rey de Portugal e do Algarve e Senhor de Ceuta*, 1. The treatise was probably composed in 1435.

12. Marques, *Daily Life in Portugal*, 164.

13. Duarte, *Leal Conselheiro*, 257.

14. Ibid., 257, 261.

15. J. Waterworth, ed. and trans., *The Canons and Decrees of the Sacred and Oecumenical Council of Trent, Celebrated under the Sovereign Pontiffs, Paul III, Julius III and Pius IV*, 202.

16. Much has been written about the "types" of marriages in medieval and early modern Portugal. In dealing with colonial Brazil, I have chosen to follow Ronaldo Vainfas's thoughtful conclusion that while judicial decisions recognized verbal promises in certain legal suits (against prospective bridegrooms who breached such promises) and "irregular" unions continued after the Council of Trent, religious sanctions applied to all but those blessed by a priest. Vainfas, *Trópico dos pecados: Moral, sexualidade e Inquisição no Brasil*, 70–75.

17. In Portugal, especially in the early modern period, two ranks were distinguished: the "nobles and people of property" and the "commoners." Brazilian elites added the stipulation of white skin to the former, and the two gender roles followed their lead. Colonists who were not of the elite, propertied white group, however, tended to blur the

distinctions not only by modeling idealized appearance and behaviors but also, more importantly, by raising lower groups to higher status. Thus, for example, *lavradores de cana* who were owners or even renters of substantial cane farms considered themselves among the local elite, claiming respectable titles of *Don* or *Dona*, and the children of even minor government employees reported themselves to be from "among the governors of the land." Stuart B. Schwartz, *Sugar Plantations in the Formation of Brazilian Society: Bahia, 1550–1835*, 295–296. In colonial Brazil, the daughter of *lavradores* might marry into the governing families, and the daughter of "nobles" might marry a *lavrador*. Leonardo Dantas Silva, ed., *Primeira visitação do Santo Ofício às partes do Brasil: Denunciações e confissões de Pernambuco, 1593–1595*, 130, 142.

18. The sources consulted for this overview include Asunción Lavrin, "Introduction: The Scenario, the Actors, and the Issues," in *Sexuality and Marriage in Colonial Latin America*, ed. Lavrin, 1–43; Maria Beatriz Nizza da Silva, *Sistema de casamento no Brasil colonial*; A. J. R. Russell-Wood, "Women and Society in Colonial Brazil," 1–34; Anna Maria Moog Rodrigues, ed., *Moralistas do século XVIII*; and Madre Maria Angela [Leda Maria Pereira Rodrigues], *A instrução feminina em São Paulo: Subsídios para sua história até a proclamação da Republica*.

19. Angela Mendes de Almeida, *O gosto do pecado: Casamento e sexualidade nos manuais de confessores dos séculos XVI e XVIII*, 96–97.

20. "Carta 7, do P. Manuel da Nóbrega ao P. Simão Rodrigues, Lisbon, Bahia, 9 August 1549," in *Cartas dos primeiros jesuítas do Brasil*, ed. Serafim Leite, vol. 1: 120.

21. Afonso Costa, "As Órfãs da Rainha," 105–111.

22. Vainfas, *Trópico dos pecados*, 49, 52. For his complete discussion of Brazilian historiography and its moral discourse, see 49–122.

23. Juan Luís Vives, "Instruction of a Christian Woman"; and Juan Luís Vives, *Instrucción de la mujer Cristiana*.

24. Foster Watson, Introduction to *Vives and the Renascence Education of Women*, 21.

25. Ibid., 34.

26. Vives, *Instrucción*, 44.

27. Francisco Manuel de Melo, *Carta de guia de casados, ou um livro só para homens* [1651], ed. João Gaspar Simões, 34.

28. Ibid., 88, 72.

29. Ibid., 99–100, 85–86, 69–70.

30. Ibid., 69–70, 85, 90.

31. Nóbrega received his baccalaureate from Navarro and corresponded with him from Brazil; the opinions of the senior Azpilcueta influenced Jesuit policies on catechizing Brazilindians. Leite, *Cartas dos primeiros jesuítas do Brasil*, vol. 1: 134n1, 132–145, 361.

32. Martín de Azpilcueta Navarro, *Manual de confessores y penitentes: Que contiene quase todas las dudas que en las confessiones suelen occurrir de los peccados, absoluciones, restituciones, censuras, & irregularidades*. First printed in Latin in 1554, it

was subsequently printed in Portuguese in Coimbra by J. de Berreyra in 1560. It is supposed to have been based on Rodrigo do Porto's 1549 *Manual de confessores*, which was—according to its extended title—"approved . . . by Dr. Navarro."

33. Ibid., 137.

34. Ibid., 138.

35. Ibid., 137, 138, 173.

36. Ibid., 158–173. Navarro's view on sexual relations offers an interesting contrast to modern judicial thought: he follows Iberian and Catholic tradition in deeming marital sex a "debt" owed to the spouse, but states that a woman is not "obligated" to struggle or even scream to prevent rape—"it is sufficient that she does not consent" (159).

37. Eduardo Hoornaert, ed., *História da Igreja no Brasil*, vol. 1: 331.

38. Serafim Leite, *História da Companhia de Jesus no Brasil*, vol. 4: 121.

39. Antônio Vieira, to the Father General Gosvínio Nickel, Amazon River, March 21, 1661, quoted in Bertha Leite, *A mulher na história de Portugal*, 295.

40. Antônio Vieira, *Sermões*, ed. Gonçalo Alves, vol. 4: 43–50.

41. Vieira, "Sermão da Quinta Quarta-Feira da Quaresma," 414.

42. Ibid., 153.

43. Ilana Novinsky argued that the economic success of the colony also engaged the interest of the Portuguese Inquisition in establishing religious conformity and detecting hidden Jews. Novinsky, "Heresia, mulher e sexualidade: Algumas notas sobre o Nordeste Brasileiro nos séculos XVI e XVII," in Maria Cristina A. Bruschini and Fúlvia Rosemberg, eds., *Vivência: História, sexualidade e imagens femininas*, 229.

44. José de Anchieta, "Do José de Anchieta ao Ignacio de Loyola, September 1, 1544," in *Cartas do Pe. José de Anchieta: Correspondência ativa e passiva*, ed. Hélio Abranches Viotti, 63.

45. This heretical statement about "simple fornication" appears regularly among men's confessions and denunciations in the Inquisition records of the 1590s and 1610s. See João Capistrano de Abreu, ed., *Primeira visitação do Santo Officio às partes do Brasil: denunciações da Bahia, 1591–93*, 376, 498; Mello, *Confissões de Pernambuco, 1594–1595*, 48–49, 76–77; Silva, *Denunciações de Pernambuco, 1593–1595*, 73–74, 107–108, 114–115, 118; and Eduardo D'Oliveira França and Sonia A. Siqueira, eds., "Segunda Visitação do Santo Ofício às partes do Brasil: Livro das confissões e ratificações da Bahia, 1618–1620," 407.

46. Leite, *Cartas dos primeiros jesuítas do Brasil*, vol. 3: 37, 365, 514, 466.

47. Silva, *Denunciações de Pernambuco, 1593–1595*, 30–32, 46–47, 54–55, 181–183, 200–203. Then deceased, Dias was denounced for working on Sundays and treating Saturdays as holy days, that is, for covert Judaism. She also taught her own step-granddaughter and a girl whose later husband was "of the government" (44–47, 149–151).

48. Hoornaert, *História da Igreja no Brasil*, 312–315; Donald Ramos, "Marriage and the Family in Colonial Vila Rica," 209–221; and Stuart B. Schwartz, "A população escrava na Bahia," in *Brasil: História econômica e demográfica*, ed. Iraci del Nero da Costa, 52–55.

49. Alida C. Metcalf, *Family and Frontier in Colonial Brazil: Santana de Paraíba, 1580–1822*, 163, 165.

50. Charles R. Boxer, *The Golden Age of Brazil: 1695–1750*, 17–21; Hoornaert, *História da Igreja no Brasil*, 316–317; Maria Beatriz Nizza da Silva, *Cultura no Brasil colônia*, 16; and Leite, *Cartas dos primeiros jesuítas do Brasil*, vol. 1: 270, 438–439. Ecclesiastical and colonial powers forbade concubinage and cohabitation, usually blaming immoral women, but the repetition of condemnations suggests that few heeded them.

51. A. J. R. Russell-Wood, *Fidalgos and Philanthropists: The Santa Casa da Misericórdia of Bahia, 1550–1755*, 192–193.

52. Susan A. Soeiro, "The Feminine Orders in Colonial Bahia, Brazil: Economic, Social and Demographic Implications, 1677–1800," 187.

53. Mary Lucy M. Del Priore, "O corpo feminino e o amor: Um olhar (Século XVIII, São Paulo)," 33–34.

54. Silva, *Denunciações de Pernambuco*, 24, 108–110, 39.

55. A. J. R. Russell-Wood, "Black and Mulatto Brotherhoods in Colonial Brazil: A Study in Collective Behavior," 580, 584.

56. Following Kathleen Higgins, I employ the contemporary term "concubine" here to underscore the "evident inequalities of both race and class in the majority" of the relationships between men and unmarried women. Higgins, *"Licentious Liberty" in a Brazilian Gold-Mining Region: Slavery, Gender, and Social Control in Eighteenth-Century Sabará, Minas Gerais*, 109.

57. Silva, *Sistema de casamento*, 37.

58. Eliana Maria Rea Goldschmidt, *Convivendo com o pecado na sociedade colonial paulista, 1719–1822*, 133–135; Silva, *Sistema de casamento*, 112, 44; Donald Ramos, "Gossip, Scandal, and Popular Culture in Golden Age Brazil," 890–892.

59. D. Sebastião Monteiro da Vide, *Constituiçoens Primeyras do Arcebispado da Bahia feytos & ordenadas pelo illustrissimo, e reverendissimo senhor D. Sebastião Monteyro da Vide, 5o. Arcebispo do dito Arcebispado, e do conselho da Sua Magestade: Propostas, e Aceitas em o Synodo Diocesano, que o dito Senhor Celebrou em 12 de junho do anno de 1707*, 364.

60. Ibid., 365.

61. Boxer, *The Golden Age of Brazil*, 17–21.

62. Vide, *Constituiçoens*, 197–198, 369.

63. Fernando Torres-Londoño, *A outra família: Concubinato, igreja e escândalo na colônia*, 175–176.

64. Higgins, *"Licentious Liberty,"* 110, 111.

65. Muriel Nazzari, "Concubinage in Colonial Brazil: The Inequalities of Race, Class, and Gender," 108.

66. Goldschmidt, *Convivendo com o pecado*, 133.

67. Alessandra da Silva Silveira, "O Amor possível: Um estudo sobre o concubinato no Bispado do Rio de Janeiro em fins do século XVIII e no XIX," 60–61.

68. Higgins, *"Licentious Liberty,"* 112.

69. Torres-Londoño, A outra família, 14.

70. Ibid., 59, 62, 111–113, 194; Goldschmidt, Convivendo com o pecado, 129–130.

71. Higgins, "Licentious Liberty," 113–114.

72. "Carta 7, Do P. Manuel da Nóbrega ao P. Simão Rodrigues, Lisbon, Bahia, 9 August 1549," in Cartas dos primeiros jesuítas do Brasil, ed. Leite, vol. 1: 119.

73. "Carta 33, Do P. Manuel da Nóbrega ao P. Simão Rodrigues, Pernambuco, August 11, 1551," in ibid., 270.

74. "Carta 60, Do Irmão Pero Correia ao Padre Simão Rodrigues, São Vicente, March 10, 1553," in ibid., 438–439.

75. "Carta 36, Do P. Manuel da Nóbrega aos Padres e Irmãos de Coimbra, Pernambuco, 13 setembro de 1551," in ibid., 287.

76. "Carta 22, Do Ir. José de Anchieta ao Ignacio de Loyola, São Paulo de Piratininga, 1 de setembro de 1554," in ibid., vol. 2: 103.

77. João Capistrano de Abreu, ed., Primeira visitação do Santo Officio às partes do Brasil: Confissões da Bahia, 1591–92, 160, 46.

78. Ibid., 46, 87, 95, 96, 97, 98, 104, 107, 117, 118, 121, 135, 146, 157, 160, 164, 167.

79. Mello, Confissões de Pernambuco, 77.

80. Leite, História da Companhia de Jesus no Brasil, vol. 4: 117.

81. França and Siqueira, "Livro das confissões e ratificações da Bahia, 1618–1620," 392, 459, 460.

82. Vide, Constituiçoens, 367.

83. Ibid., 132–133.

84. Jorge Benci, Economia cristã dos senhores no governo dos escravos: Livro brasileiro de 1700, 103.

85. Ibid., 111, 121.

86. André João Antonil [João Antônio Andreoni], Cultura e opulência do Brasil [1711], 90.

87. Schwartz, Sugar Plantations in the Formation of Brazilian Society, 351–352. Individual inventories and wills from eighteenth-century Minas Gerais revealed "extraordinarily unbalanced" sex ratios of 50 men to 6 women and even 22 men to 1 woman. Higgins, "Licentious Liberty," 60–61.

88. Mary C. Karasch, Slave Life in Rio, 1808–1850, 294; Linda Wimmer, "Ethnicity and Family Formation among Slaves on Tobacco Farms in the Bahian Recôncavo, 1698–1820," in Enslaving Connections: Changing Cultures of Africa and Brazil during the Era of Slavery, ed. José C. Curto and Paul E. Lovejoy, 149–162.

89. Laura de Mello e Souza, Desclassficados do ouro: A pobreza mineira no século XVIII, 160, 182.

90. Sheila de Castro Faria, A colônia em movimento: Fortuna e família no cotidiano colonial, 40–41, 60–61. Cf. Souza, Desclassificados do ouro.

91. Maria Beatriz Nizza da Silva, Donas e plebeias na sociedade colonial, 242.

92. Luciano Raposo de Almeida Figueiredo, O avesso da memória: Cotidiano e trabalho da mulher em Minas Gerais no século XVII, 76.

93. Ibid., 78.

94. Ibid., 133.

95. Goldschmidt, *Convivendo com o pecado*, 49–51.

96. Laura de Mello e Souza, *The Devil and the Land of the Holy Cross: Witchcraft, Slavery, and Popular Religion in Colonial Brazil*, trans. Diane Grosklaus Whitty, 219, 220–221.

97. Souza, *Desclassificados do ouro*, 181–182.

98. Pereira, *Compêndio narrativo*, vol. 1: 178, 180.

99. Benci, *Economia cristã*, 118.

100. Ibid., 119.

101. Antonil, *Cultura e opulência do Brasil*, 90. A few pages later, he advised that indulgent treatment of slave children would improve the likelihood that slaves would bear even more to increase their own ranks, while mistreatment would only drive female slaves to obtain some abortifacient, so that their children "would not come to suffer as they themselves had" (92).

102. Ambrósio Fernandes Brandão, *Diálogos das grandezas do Brasil*, 88; Pereira, *Compêndio narrativo*, vol. 1: 174, 296; vol. 2: 162–185; and Domingos do Loreto Couto, *Desagravos do Brasil e glorias de Pernambuco*, 485–521. Couto includes other "virtuous" women who "flourished in letters" (521–523) and those who defended their honor against Dutch invaders (524–526).

103. Luís dos Santos Vilhena, *A Bahia no século XVIII*, vol. 1: 54, 137–138, 136.

104. Antonil, *Cultura e opulência do Brasil*, 93, 94.

105. Pereira, *Compêndio narrativo*, vol. 1: 160.

106. Ibid., 238.

107. Ibid., 239.

108. Ibid., 287, 289, 290.

109. Ibid., 289–290, 290, 123.

110. Ibid., 291, 292.

111. Ibid., 292–293.

112. Ibid., 293.

113. Ibid., 296.

114. Mrs. [Nathaniel Edward] Kindersley, *Letters from the Island of Teneriffe, Brazil, the Cape of Good Hope, and the East Indies*, 39.

115. Ibid., 41, 41–42.

116. Ibid., 43. As I reported in Chapter 1, the subject of nudity and light clothing recurs with regularity in Brazilian historiography from its beginning: early French missionaries reported their struggles to cover indigenous women, as did contemporary Portuguese Jesuits.

117. John Mawe, *Travels in the Interior of Brazil, Particularly in the Gold and Diamond Districts of that Country*, 153, 154.

118. John Luccock, *Notes on Rio de Janeiro, and the Southern Parts of Brazil; Taken during a Residence of Ten Years in that Country, from 1808 to 1818*, 111, 112.

119. Ibid., 113, 114.

120. Jacques Arago, *Narrative of a Voyage round the World, in the Uranie and Phy-*

*sicienne Corvettes, Commanded by Captain Freycinet, during the Years 1817, 1818, 1819, and 1820,* 69–70, 79, 80.

121. From the letter written in December 1819. In Rose Marie Pinon de Freycinet, *A Woman of Courage: The Journal of Rose de Freycinet on her Voyage around the World, 1817–1820,* trans. and ed. Marc Serge Rivière, 18, 17.

122. Gilberto Freyre, *The Mansions and the Shanties,* trans. Harriet De Orís, 397, 322.

123. Katia de Queirós Mattoso, *Ser escravo no Brasil,* 125.

124. Ramos, "Marriage and the Family in Colonial Vila Rica," 207, 221.

CHAPTER FIVE

1. "Thereza Rosa e Mariana, 1756," "Processos das Noviças do Convento de N. S. da Conceição da Ajuda," ["Noviças para Conventos, Caixa 2"] "Portarias e ordens Episcopais."

2. Riolando Azzi and Maria Valéria V. Rezende, "A vida religiosa feminina no Brasil colonial," in *A vida religiosa no Brasil,* ed. Azzi, 25.

3. Anna Amélia Vieira Nascimento, *Patriarcado e religião: As enclausuradas clarissas do Convento do Desterro da Bahia 1677–1890,* especially 15–26.

4. Nuno Marques Pereira, *Compêndio narrativo do peregrino da America,* vol. 1: 220.

5. Leila Mezan Algranti, *Honradas e devotas: Mulheres da colônia, condição feminina nos conventos e recolhimentos do Sudeste do Brasil, 1750–1822,* 132.

6. Serafim Leite, *História da companhia de Jesus no Brasil,* vol. 1a: 21–22, 27. The first Jesuit chapel in Brazil was dedicated to Nossa Senhora da Ajuda, and that shrine, like many others, was established with an impressive reliquary housing a large image of Mary and small wooden figures of saints with their fragmentary relics. The "Eleven Thousand Virgins" were popular Western European icons, and the arrival of part of the three virginal relics was to be celebrated with the play composed by Jesuit missionary José de Anchieta, "Quando, no Espírito Santo, se recebeu uma relíquia das Onze Mil Virgens," *Documentação Lingüística* (bol. 3, 3), Museu Paulista, São Paulo, 1950.

7. "Clara da Paixão de Jesus pede licença para instituir hum pequeno Recolhimento no Termo de Caethé com o título de Nossa Senhora da Piedade," Ms., folio 2, doc. 50, "Documentos Eclesiasticos (Minas Gerais): Recolhimentos, Casas Pias, Irmandades, Compromissos," pt. 1, Mesa do Desembargo do Paço, Caixa 779 [Antiga 130], Arquivo Nacional, Rio de Janeiro.

8. Nascimento, *Patriarcado e religião,* 26.

9. "Recolhimentos, Casas Pias, Irmandades—Diversas Provincias," Mss., docs. 7, 3, 4, Pacote 2 [doc. 34], Mesa do Desembargo do Paço, Caixa 781 [Antiga 132], Arquivo Nacional, Rio de Janeiro.

10. Algranti, *Honradas,* 22.

11. Ibid., 17–21.
12. Luiz Mott, *Rosa Egipcíaca: Uma santa africana no Brasil*, 195–205, 257–258.
13. Ibid., 298–305; on her encounters with the Inquisition, see 625–721.
14. Algranti, *Honradas*, 90.
15. "Processos das Noviças do Convento de N. S. da Conceição da Ajuda."
16. Algranti, *Honradas*, 267–283.
17. Ibid., 298.
18. Ibid., 267.
19. Ibid., 307.
20. Ibid., 135.
21. Ibid., 264.
22. Ibid., 172–173.
23. "Processos das Noviças do Convento de N. S. da Conceição da Ajuda."
24. "Anna Acleta Felizarda de Menezes, Jozepha Thereza de Jesus, Isabel Maria da Conceição, 1756," "Processos das Noviças do Convento de N. S. da Conceição da Ajuda." The second page of the document offers income from their father's property, including several houses, to provide financial support for their lives within the convent.
25. Algranti, *Honradas*, 308.
26. "Recolhimentos, Casas Pias, Irmandades (Diversas Provincias)," Mss., Pacote 2, doc. 5, Mesa do Desembargo do Paço, Caixa 781 [Antiga 132], Arquivo Nacional, Rio de Janeiro.
27. "Livro de Receitas e Despesas do Patrimônio da Igreja de Nossa Senhora do Parto. 1786–1797," Mss., Arquivo da Cúria Metropolitana, Rio de Janeiro.
28. "Livro de Receitas e Despesas," folios 89, 107. Dona Caterina also supplies a fee for "the freedom of her old black slave Jozepha" that same year.
29. Ibid., folio 114.
30. Algranti, *Honradas*, 137. All girls had been enrolled when they were younger than seven.
31. Ibid., 155.
32. "Várias documentos referentes ao mesmo convento [da Lapa]. Lisboa/Bahia, 1733 a 1802," doc. 12, Ms., Seção de Manuscritos, Biblioteca Nacional, Rio de Janeiro [II 33, 29, 110].
33. Algranti, *Honradas*, 151n119.
34. Ibid., 154.
35. "Várias documentos referentes ao mesmo convento [da Lapa]," docs. 7–11, 13–14.
36. Maria Beatriz Nizza da Silva, *História da família no Brasil colonial*, 256. I am grateful for Silva's analysis and explanations of this confusing case (251–256) from her more extensive discoveries in the Lisbon archives, making sense of what she introduces as "a veritable soap opera."
37. Riolando Azzi, "Segundo período: A instituição eclesiástica durante a primeira época colonial," in *História da igreja no Brasil*, ed. Eduardo Hoornaert, 226–227, 288.

38. "Ofício de Antônio José da Silva Guimarães, Juiz Ordinario da Vila de Mara-gogipe, 1798," Ms., Seção dos Manuscritos, Biblioteca Nacional, Rio de Janeiro [II 33, 23, 32].

39. Algranti, *Honradas*, 174–177.

40. Raphael Bluteau, *Diccionario da lingua portugueza* (Lisbon, Officina de S. T. Ferreira, 1789), [vol. 2]: 157; quoted in Algranti, *Honradas*, 76.

41. "Costumes monásticos na Bahia: Freiras e recolhidas," *Revista do Instituto de Geografia e História da Bahia* 44 (1918); *Noticia historica da Ordem da Immaculada Conceição da Ajuda do Rio de Janeiro* (Rio de Janeiro: Typographia Leuzinger, 1913).

42. Azzi and Rezende, "A vida religiosa feminina no Brasil colonial," 24–60.

43. Laura de Mello e Souza presents a superlative interpretation of the dynamics of colonial religion in *The Devil and the Land of the Holy Cross: Witchcraft, Slavery, and Popular Religion in Colonial Brazil*, with a focus on the confrontations between ecclesiastical institutions and the residents of the New World.

44. Elisja Schulte van Kessel, "Virgins and Mothers between Heaven and Earth," in *A History of Women of Women in the West*, vol. 3, *Renaissance and Enlightenment Paradoxes*, ed. Natalie Zemon Davis and Arlette Farge, 137.

45. Azzi and Rezende, "A vida religiosa feminina no Brasil colonial," 30.

46. Ibid., 31.

47. Manuel da Nóbrega, "Carta 9, Do P. Manuel da Nóbrega aos Padres e Irmãos de Coimbra, Pernambuco, 13 setembro de 1551," in *Cartas dos primeiros jesuítas do Brasil*, ed. Serafim Leite, vol. 1: 149.

48. Nóbrega, "Carta 11, Aos Padres e Irmãos de Coimbra, Pernambuco, 13 de setembro de 1551," in *Cartas do Brasil e mais escritos*, ed. Serafim Leite, 93.

49. Nóbrega, "Carta 37, Do P. Manuel da Nóbrega a D. João III, Rei de Portugal, from Olinda [Pernambuco], 14 de setembro de 1551," in *Cartas dos primeiros jesuítas*, ed. Leite, vol. 1: 292.

50. "Document 1, 115, Documentos relativos ao Rio de Janeiro," Arquivo Histórico Ultramarino, Lisbon, Portugal, quoted in Azzi and Rezende, "A vida religiosa feminina no Brasil colonial," 28.

51. "Consulta do Conselho Ultramarino sobre a fundação de um recolhimento destinado às mulheres pobres e honestas da Capitânia do Rio de Janeiro, Lisboa, 16 outubro 1694," Ms., Consultas do Conselho Ultramarino, Governo do Rio de Janeiro e mais Capitânias do Sul, 1674–1731 [doc. 64], Seção dos Manuscritos, Biblioteca Nacional, Rio de Janeiro.

52. José de Costa Pôrto, *Nos tempos do visitador: Subsídio ao estudo da vida colonial pernambucana, nos fins do século XVI*, 204.

53. "Addendo para o Recolhimento de Olinda, Notícias sobre estabelecimento de ordens religiosas em Olinda e Recife, Pernambuco [1775]," Mss., Seção dos Manuscritos, Biblioteca Nacional, Rio de Janeiro [II 32, 33, 35].

54. "Capitulo 41, Noticias sôbre estabelecimento de ordens religiosas em Olinda e Recife, Pernambuco [1775]," Ms., Seção dos Manuscritos, Biblioteca Nacional, Rio de Janeiro; Azzi and Rezende, "A vida religiosa feminina no Brasil colonial," 38–39.

55. Azzi, "Segundo período," 227.

56. José Antônio Caldas, *Noticia geral de toda esta capitania da Bahia desde o seu Descobrimento até o presente ano de 1759*, 22.

57. Azzi, "Segundo período," 288.

58. Algranti, *Honradas*, 99.

59. "Estatutos do Collegio de Educação de Meninas, denominado de 'Nossa Senhora dos Humildes' fundado pela beneficiencia de seus Devotos o Padre Ignacio dos Santos e Araujo, em honra do Desaggravo do Santissimo Sacramento na villa de Santo Amaro da Purificação na Capitania da Cidade da Bahia no anno de 1813," Ms., folio 1v, Seção de Manuscritos, Biblioteca Nacional, Rio de Janeiro.

60. Ibid., folio 2.

61. Azzi and Rezende, "A vida religiosa feminina no Brasil colonial," 34.

62. Azzi, "Segundo período," 232.

63. Algranti, *Honradas*, 86.

64. "Petição da Madre Regente do Recolhimento de Santa Teresa de São Paulo, ao Principe D. João VI, solicitando isenção dos impostos, [1809]," Ms., Seção de Manuscritos, Biblioteca Nacional, Rio de Janeiro [II 35, 25, 15].

65. Ibid.

66. Algranti, *Honradas*, 97–98; Madre Maria Angela [Leda Maria Pereira Rodrigues], *A instrução feminina em São Paulo: Subsídios para sua história até a proclamação da Republica*, 53.

67. Azzi, "Segundo período," 231.

68. Luciano Figueiredo, *O avesso da memória: Cotidiano e trabalho da mulher em Minas Gerais no século XVIII*, 160.

69. Algranti, *Honradas*, 22–23, 93–94, 136.

70. Azzi, "Segundo período," 229, 232–233.

71. A. J. R. Russell-Wood, *Fidalgos and Philanthropists: The Santa Casa da Misericórdia of Bahia, 1550–1755*, 328.

72. Ibid., 331.

73. Algranti, *Honradas*, 197.

74. Michel Foucault, *History of Sexuality*, trans. Robert Hurley, vol. 1: 21–22; Algranti, *Honradas*, 203–204.

75. "Parecer sobre a petição da Regente do Recolhimento de Nossa Senhora da Glória que quer licença para transformar o referido Recolhimento em mosteiro, Recolhimento de Nossa Senhora da Glória, Olinda [18th Century]," Ms., Seção dos Manuscritos, Biblioteca Nacional, Rio de Janeiro.

76. Ibid.

77. Ibid.

78. José Joaquim da Cunha de Azeredo Coutinho, *Estatutos do Recolhimento de Nossa Senhora da Glória do lugar da Boa Vista de Pernambuco*, preface.

79. Ibid., 4.

80. Ibid., 46, 47.

81. Ibid., 29.

82. Ibid., 40–42.

83. Ibid., 113.

84. Ibid., 86.

85. Ibid., 89, 96.

86. Ibid., 100, 56.

87. Ibid., 67, 80.

88. "Estatutos do Collegio de Nossa Senhora dos Humildes," especially folios 15–28.

89. Ibid., folios 17, 17v.

90. Ibid., folio 16.

91. Ibid., folios 15v, 16.

92. José Justino Andrade e Silva, ed., *Collecção chronológica da legislação portugueza, 1603–1700* (Lisbon: Impresa de J. J. A. Silva, 1854–1859), vol. 1: 22 (September 2, 1603), quoted in Susan A. Soeiro, "The Feminine Orders in Colonial Bahia, Brazil: Economic, Social and Demographic Implications, 1677–1800," 175.

93. Soeiro, "The Feminine Orders," 190.

94. "Consulta do Conselho Ultramarino sobre a concessão de um convento de freiras ao Rio de Janeiro. Lisboa 15 março 1703" [#134], Ms., Consultas do Conselho Ultramarino, Governo do Rio de Janeiro e mais Capitânias do Sul, 1674–1731, Seção dos Manuscritos, Biblioteca Nacional, Rio de Janeiro.

95. Eduardo Hoornaert, "Terceiro período: A Cristandade durante a primeira época colonial," vol. 1: 372–373.

96. Soeiro, "The Feminine Orders," 179, 184.

97. Azzi and Rezende, "A vida religiosa feminina no Brasil colonial," 28–38.

98. Susan Soeiro calculated that only 14 percent of the wealthiest women married from 1677 to the end of the colonial period, and 77 percent entered convents in Brazil or other Portuguese territories. "The Feminine Orders," 180.

99. Ibid., 182.

100. Nascimento, *Patriarcado e religião*, 123.

101. Carta do Dom João de Lancastro Amaro, January 31, 1697, "Documentos relativos ao Convento de Nossa Senhora do Destêrro, 1696 a 1724," Ms., Seção de Manuscritos, Biblioteca Nacional, Rio de Janeiro [II 33, 29, 114n1].

102. Susan A. Soeiro, *The Social Composition of the Colonial Nunnery: A Case Study of the Convent of Santa Clara do Destêrro, Salvador, Bahia, 1677–1800*, 10; Nascimento, *Patriarcado e religião*, 115–128.

103. "Biografia de D. José Fialho, arcebispo da Bahia," *Revista eclesiástica brasileira*, 1956: 642; quoted in Azzi, "Segundo período," 225.

104. Universidade Católica do Salvador, "Um pouco de história: Convento da Lapa," http://www.ucsal.br/aucsal/hossa_historia.asp (2003), website, consulted online December 12, 2005.

105. "Provisão concedendo Licença para se Fundar o Convento da Lapa na Bahia: Várias documentos referentes ao mesmo convento, Lisboa/Bahia, 1733 a 1802," doc. 1, Ms., Seção de Manuscritos, Biblioteca Nacional, Rio de Janeiro [II 33, 29, 110].

106. Azzi, "Segundo período," 227.

107. Soeiro, "The Feminine Orders," 184; Azzi, "Segundo período," 227.

108. "Várias documentos referentes ao mesmo convento [da Lapa], Lisboa/Bahia, 1733 a 1802," doc. 4, Ms., Seção de Manuscritos, Biblioteca Nacional, Rio de Janeiro [II 33, 29, 110].

109. Ibid., doc. 5.

110. Carta da Dona Ursula Luisa de Monserrat, Ms., Seção de Manuscritos, Biblioteca Nacional, Rio de Janeiro [II 33, 26, 17], quoted in Soeiro, "The Feminine Orders," 190.

111. "Memorias da Fundação do Convento de Ursulinas da Cidade da Baia que fundou d. Ursula Luiza de Monserrate," Bahia, September 23, 1745, Ms., Seção de Manuscritos, Biblioteca Nacional, Rio de Janeiro [II 33, 26, 17].

112. Azzi, "Segundo período," 227.

113. Azzi and Rezende, "A vida religiosa feminina no Brasil colonial," 32; Soeiro, "The Feminine Orders," 183; "História do Colégio," http://www.colegiosoledade.com. br/historia.html, December 12, 2005. The Ursuline order continues to run a school near the original convent.

114. Soeiro, "The Feminine Orders," 184, 185.

115. "Consulta do Conselho Ultramarino sobre se fundar um mosteiro de freiras no Rio de Janeiro, Lisboa, 18 novembro 1678," doc. 16, Consultas do Conselho Ultramarino, Governo do Rio de Janeiro e mais Capitânias do Sul, 1674–1731, Ms., Seção dos Manuscritos, Biblioteca Nacional, Rio de Janeiro.

116. Algranti, Honradas, 84–85; Azzi and Rezende, "A vida religiosa feminina no Brasil colonial," 33–34.

117. Algranti, Honradas, 19.

118. Ibid., 17–22; Azzi and Rezende, "A vida religiosa feminina no Brasil colonial," 33–35.

119. Azzi and Rezende, "A vida religiosa feminina no Brasil colonial," 35–38.

120. Algranti, Honradas, 53–69; Jo Ann Kay McNamara, Sisters in Arms, 497–525.

121. Susan Soeiro, "The Social and Economic Role of the Convent: Women and Nuns in Colonial Bahia, 1677–1800," 210.

122. "Regra das Religiozas do Convento de Nossa Senhora da Conceição da Ajuda, 1750," Portarias e Ordens Episcopais, Livro 1, 1750–1761 (folio 11), Ms., Arquivo da Cúria, Catedral Metropolitana, Rio de Janeiro.

123. Ibid.

124. Ibid.

125. Ibid., folios 12v–14.

126. "Constituiçoins, e Leys, por que se haõ de governar as Religiozas da Conceição de Nossa Senhora da Ajuda . . . Rio de Janeiro, 1751," Portarias e Ordens Episcopais, Livro 1, 1750–1761, Ms., Arquivo da Cúria, Catedral Metropolitana, Rio de Janeiro.

127. Ibid., folio 16v.

128. Ibid., folio 19v.

129. Ibid., folios 22v–23.

130. Ibid., folios 24.

131. Ibid., folios 23, 25v, 26v.

132. Ibid., folios 27, 27v.

133. Ibid., folio 27v.

134. Letter from Dom Frei Antonio do Desterro, Bishop of Rio de Janeiro, 1761, "Portarias e Ordens Episcopais," Livro 2, 1761–1779, Ms., Arquivo da Cúria, Catedral Metropolitana, Rio de Janeiro, folio 5. David's "small fault" was adultery.

135. Ibid., folios 5, 7.

136. Algranti, *Honradas*, 212–215, 236–237.

137. Nascimento, *Patriarcado e religião*, 127–128, 156.

138. Frei Antônio de Sant'Anna Galvão, ed., *Escritos espirituais, 1766–1803*, 17.

139. Ibid., 21.

140. Algranti, *Honradas*, 231–233; Nascimento, *Patriarcado e religião*, 222–243.

141. Nascimento, *Patriarcado e religião*, 250–251.

142. Ibid., 272; Algranti, *Honradas*, 219–222.

143. Algranti, *Honradas*, 225–231.

144. Ibid., 236–237.

145. Ibid., 128.

CHAPTER SIX

1. João Capistrano de Abreu, ed., *Primeira visitação do Santo Officio às partes do Brasil: Confissões da Bahia, 1591–92*, 49. Like many confessants and denunciants at that time, Siqueira described events from her past: she had begun learning the different magico-religious practices twenty-three years earlier.

2. Leonardo Dantas Silva, ed., *Primeira visitação do Santo Ofício às partes do Brasil: Denunciações de Pernambuco, 1593–1595*, 25–26. This publication is a combined facsimile edition with the full title of *Primeira visitação do Santo Ofício às partes do Brasil: Confissões e denunciações de Pernambuco, 1593–1595*, reproducing the 1929 *Denunciações de Pernambuco, 1593–1595* with an unnamed editor (probably João Capistrano de Abreu) and the 1970 *Confissões de Pernambuco, 1593–1595* edited by José Antônio Gonsalves de Mello. In this chapter, all references to the Pernambuco denunciations will be taken from the Silva (1984) edition, and all references to the confessions will be taken from the Mello edition.

3. José Roberto do Amaral Lapa, ed., *Livro da visitação do Santo Ofício da Inquisição ao estado do Grão-Pará, 1763–1769*, 175–178.

4. Raphael Bluteau, *Vocabulario portuguez & latino: Aulico, anatomico, architectonico . . .* , vol. 4: 64.

5. Diogo de Paiva de Andrada, *Casamento perfeito*, 139; similar sentiments appear in Francisco Manuel de Melo, *Carta de guia de casados, ou um livro só para homens*, ed. João Gaspar Simões.

6. I explored these issues of theory and definition at length in "The Magic of Brazil: Practice and Prohibition in the Early Colonial Period, 1590–1620."

7. Edward B. Tylor, *Primitive Culture: Researches into the Development of Mythology, Philosophy, Religion, Language, Art and Custom.* See vol. 1: 112–144.

8. James George Frazer, *The Golden Bough*, vol. 1: 52–54.

9. Stanley Jeyaraja Tambiah, *Magic, Science, Religion, and the Scope of Rationality.*

10. Émile Durkheim, *The Elementary Forms of Religious Life*, trans. Joseph Ward Swain, 60. Italics in the original.

11. Bronislaw Malinowski, *Magic, Science, and Religion and Other Essays*, 17, 87–90.

12. E. E. Evans-Pritchard, "The Morphology and Function of Magic: A Comparative Study of Trobriand and Zande Ritual and Spells."

13. E. E. Evans-Pritchard, *Witchcraft, Oracles and Magic among the Azande*, 21–39, 387–422, 475–478.

14. Valerie I. J. Flint, *The Rise of Magic in Early Medieval Europe*, 3–9.

15. Richard Kieckhefer, "The Specific Rationality of Medieval Magic."

16. Keith Thomas, *Religion and the Decline of Magic*, 25–37.

17. Brian P. Levack, *The Witch-Hunt in Early Modern Europe*, 4–5.

18. Julio Caro Baroja, "Witchcraft and Catholic Theology," 28–29, 34–35. See also Baroja, *The World of Witches*, trans. O. N. V. Glendinning.

19. José Pedro de Matos Paiva, *Práticas e crenças mágicas: O medo e a necessidade dos mágicos na diocese de Coimbra, 1650–1740*, 27.

20. Laura de Mello e Souza, *Inferno Atlântico: Demonologia e colonização, séculos XVI–XVIII*, 22.

21. Malcolm Gaskill, *Crime and Mentalities in Early Modern England*, 3–6, 55.

22. Ibid., 119.

23. Gary K. Waite, *Heresy, Magic, and Witchcraft in Early Modern Europe*, 11.

24. Among the many valuable studies of the history of ancient and medieval European magic are Bengt Ankarloo and Stuart Clark, eds., *Witchcraft and Magic in Europe: Ancient Greece and Rome* (Philadelphia: University of Pennsylvania Press, 1999); Stephen Wilson, *The Magical Universe: Everyday Ritual and Magic in Pre-Modern Europe* (New York: Hambledon and London, 2000); Richard Kieckhefer, *Magic in the Middle Ages* (New York: Cambridge University Press, 1989); and Karen Jolly, Catharina Raudvere, and Edward Peters, *Witchcraft and Magic in Europe: The Middle Ages* (London: Athlone Press, 2002).

25. Karen Jolly, "Medieval Magic: Definitions, Beliefs, Practices," in *Witchcraft and Magic in Europe: The Middle Ages*, 3.

26. Ibid., 20–23.

27. Kieckhefer, *Magic in the Middle Ages*, 58–61.

28. Waite, *Heresy, Magic, and Witchcraft in Early Modern Europe*, 16–18.

29. Ibid., 12.

30. Jolly, "Medieval Magic," 24–25.

31. Waite, *Heresy, Magic, and Witchcraft in Early Modern Europe*, 134–135, 147, 190, 230–233.

32. Robert Rowland, "'Fantasticall and Devilishe Persons': European Witch-Beliefs in Comparative Perspective," in *Early Modern European Witchcraft: Centres and Peripheries*, ed. Bengt Ankarloo and Gustav Henningen, 180.

33. Robin Briggs, *Witches and Neighbors: The Social and Cultural Context of European Witchcraft*, 259.

34. Ibid., 261. See also Christina Larner, "Was Witch-Hunting Woman-Hunting?" in *The Witchcraft Reader*, ed. Darren Oldridge, 273–275.

35. Marianne Hester, "Patriarchal Reconstructions and Witch-Hunting," in *The Witchcraft Reader*, ed. Oldridge, 281–283; and James Sharpe, *Instruments of Darkness: Witchcraft in Early Modern England*, 180–183.

36. Lara Apps and Andrew Gow, *Male Witches in Early Modern Europe*, 136.

37. Levack, *The Witch-Hunt in Early Modern Europe*, 128.

38. José Pedro Paiva, "The Persecution of Popular Superstition in 17th and 18th Century Portugal."

39. Ibid.

40. Martín de Azpilcueta Navarro, *Manual de confessores y penitentes: Que contiene quasi todas las dudas que en las confessiones suelen occurrir de los peccados, absoluciones, restituciones, censuras, & irregularidades*.

41. Ibid., 73, 74.

42. Ibid., 76–77, 78.

43. Paiva, "Persecution of Popular Superstition."

44. Francisco Bethencourt, "Portugal: A Scrupulous Inquisition," in *Early Modern European Witchcraft: Centres and Peripheries*, ed. Ankarloo and Henningen, 403, 410–411.

45. Paiva, *Práticas e crenças mágicas*, 27–28.

46. Ibid., 184–189, 194.

47. Bethencourt, "Scrupulous Inquisition," 411–412.

48. Paiva, *Práticas e crenças mágicas*, 78–79, 128–132, 143–150; Bethencourt, "Scrupulous Inquisition," 414–415; Timothy D. Walker, "The Role and Practices of the *Curandeiro* and *Saludador* in Early Modern Portugal," 226–227.

49. Paiva, *Práticas e crenças mágicas*, 52.

50. Bethencourt, "Scrupulous Inquisition," 404–409; Waite, *Heresy, Magic, and Witchcraft in Early Modern Europe*.

51. Walker, "Role and Practices," 227.

52. Bethencourt, "Scrupulous Inquisition," 407; Paiva, *Práticas e crenças mágicas*, 29, 55.

53. Although some have suggested that there was another Visitation of the Portuguese Inquisition to Rio de Janeiro, there is as yet no historical evidence to support the suggestion. The edited publications of records were copied from the archived books of confessions and denunciations from each regional visit, and include some ratifications. The early records are published in Abreu, *Confissões da Bahia*, 1591–92; Abreu,

*Denunciações da Bahia*, 1591–593; Mello, *Confissões de Pernambuco*, 1594–1595; Silva, *Denunciações de Pernambuco*, 1593–1595; Eduardo D'Oliveira França and Sônia A. Siqueira, eds., "Segunda Visitação do Santo Ofício às partes do Brasil: Livro das confissões e ratificações da Bahia, 1618–1620"; and Rodolfo Garcia, ed., "Livro da Denunciações que se fizerão na Visitação do Santo Officio á Cidade do Salvador da Bahia de Todos os Santos do Estado do Brasil, no Anno de 1618."

54. James E. Wadsworth, "Children of the Inquisition: Minors as *Familiares* of the Inquisition in Pernambuco, Brazil, 1613–1821," 23.

55. Patricia Aufderheide, "True Confessions: The Inquisition and Social Attitudes in Brazil at the Turn of the XVII Century," 212; Abreu, *Confissões da Bahia, 1591–92*, iv–v.

56. Eduardo D'Oliveira França and Sonia A. Siqueira, "Introdução" and "Origem da Visitação de 1618," in "Livro das confissões e ratificações da Bahia, 1618–1620."

57. Lapa, *Livro da visitação do Santo Ofício da Inquisição ao Estado do Grão-Pará*, 26–32.

58. Abreu, *Confissões da Bahia, 1591–92*, xxx, xxxi–xxxiv. The Tribunal mandated that this first edict also be read from pulpits and posted at church doors in the later visitations in the sixteenth and seventeenth centuries.

59. Edited by Francisco Peña for reprint publication in Rome in 1578, the *Manual* defined heresy, in accord with Thomas Aquinas, as the free choice of renouncing the faith through personal opposition to an article of faith. Simple blasphemy, that is, blaspheming Mary or the saints, simple divination, or palm-reading, was not heresy and not typically under the purview of the Inquisition. Nicolás Eymerich, *Le manuel des inquisiteurs*, ed. and trans. Louis Sala-Molins, 49–50, 74.

60. The contemporary sources include Navarro, *Manual de confessores y penitentes*; and Bluteau, *Vocabulario portuguez*, especially vol. 5.

61. Abreu, ed., *Confissões da Bahia, 1591–92*, xxxiv.

62. Carole A. Myscofski, "Heterodoxy, Gender and the Brazilian Inquisition: Patterns in Religion in the 1590s."

63. The sixteenth- and seventeenth-century statements indicate little influence from indigenous Brazilian Indian or African religions; instead, the magical prayers and practices used Latin or Portuguese and resembled European magical practices, and the practitioners were mostly Portuguese immigrants. For this discussion, I use "European magic" for those occult practices and teachings common in Portugal or Western Europe, and "Christian magic" for those that included Christian prayers, structure, names, symbols, or objects.

64. In these texts, no apparent difference was marked between innate and learned magic, or between the powers of a *feiticeira* or sorceress and those of *bruxa* or witch. See, for comparison, Geoffrey Scarre, *Witchcraft and Magic in Sixteenth- and Seventeenth Century Europe*, 3–5.

65. In this first era, the numbers of statements are as follows: in the 1591–1593 Confessions of Bahia, 4 of the 121 statements described magic (3 by women); in the 1591–9153 Denunciations of Bahia, 26 of 212 mention magic (23 name women); in the

1593–1595 Confessions of Pernambuco, there is no mention of magic, but in the 1593–1595 Denunciations of Pernambuco, 7 out of 274 denounce magic (and 6 denounce women); in the 1618–1620 Confessions of Bahia, 5 of the 58 confess magic (1 woman only), but none in the Denunciation records include magic. Although the overall number of statements and the individuals involved cannot be calculated precisely due to the repeated appearances of some individuals and the confusion of similar names, there are at least 783 confessions and denunciations.

66. Abreu, *Confissões da Bahia, 1591–92*, 62. The Inquisitor's name is spelled "Mendonça" in other historical records.

67. See, for example, ibid., 48–51, 53–54, 59–62.

68. Ibid., 49, 54, 60–61.

69. For example, see Abreu, *Denunciações da Bahia, 1591–93*, 287–288, 303, 307, 319, 350, 385.

70. Ibid., 303.

71. Silva, *Denunciações de Pernambuco, 1593–1595*, 24–26; Abreu, *Denunciações da Bahia, 1591–93*, 349–350, 300, 318–319.

72. Abreu, *Denunciações da Bahia, 1591–93*, 385, 412.

73. Ibid., 288, 432, 395, 400, 424, 425–426.

74. Abreu, *Confissões da Bahia, 1591–92*, 49, 61; Abreu, *Denunciações da Bahia, 1591–93*, 311, 373.

75. Abreu, *Denunciações da Bahia, 1591–93*, 423–424; Abreu, *Confissões da Bahia, 1591–92*, 59–60.

76. Abreu, *Confissões da Bahia, 1591–92*, 50.

77. Ibid., 50, 59–62.

78. Silva, *Denunciações de Pernambuco, 1593–1595*, 396, 423, 109.

79. Abreu, *Denunciações da Bahia, 1591–93*, 396; Silva, *Denunciações de Pernambuco, 1593–1595*, 98, 121–122, 187.

80. França and Siqueira, "Livro das confissões e ratificações da Bahia, 1618–1620," 449–451. Her family name is also given as Despinhosa at the end of her statement.

81. Abreu, *Denunciações da Bahia, 1591–93*, 343, 349–350.

82. Ibid., 396; 478–479, 539–540.

83. Ibid., 319, 527, 299–300.

84. Ibid., 288, 424, 400–401.

85. Ibid., 385, 412; 395; 319, 396, 412; 342, 349.

86. Abreu, *Confissões da Bahia, 1591–92*, 47; Abreu, *Denunciações da Bahia, 1591–93*, 477; 424, 311, 373. There may be more overlapping testimonies, but the repetition of common colonial names creates some confusion.

87. Abreu, *Confissões da Bahia, 1591–92*, 533, 59; França and Siqueira, "Livro das confissões e ratificações da Bahia, 1618–1620," 449–451.

88. Abreu, *Denunciações da Bahia, 1591–93*, 307, 525; Silva, *Denunciações de Pernambuco, 1593–1595*, 121.

89. Abreu, *Denunciações da Bahia, 1591–93*, 548. The divining bowl was mentioned in two denunciations against African slaves in the same set of records.

90. Silva, *Denunciações de Pernambuco*, 1593–1595, 25–26; Abreu, *Denunciações da Bahia*, 1591–93, 432.

91. Silva, *Denunciações de Pernambuco*, 1593–1595, 321–322, 187. Other affirmations of successful divination are found in ibid., 98, 121; and França and Siqueira, "Livro das confissões e ratificações da Bahia, 1618–1620," 452.

92. Abreu, *Confissões da Bahia*, 1591–92, 50, 62.

93. Silva, *Denunciações de Pernambuco*, 1593–1595, 321–322, 108–109; Abreu, *Denunciações da Bahia*, 1591–93, 478.

94. Abreu, *Confissões da Bahia*, 1591–92, 53–54, 49–50.

95. Laura de Mello e Souza, *The Devil and the Land of the Holy Cross: Witchcraft, Slavery, and Popular Religion in Colonial Brazil*, trans. Diane Grosklaus Whitty, 193. For similar interpretations, see also Ronaldo Vainfas, *Trópico dos pecados: Moral, sexualidade e Inquisição no Brasil*, especially 32–38.

96. França and Siqueira, "Livro das confissões e ratificações da Bahia, 1618–1620," 450.

97. Comparative studies may be undertaken with reference to the following studies: Stephen Wilson, *The Magical Universe*; Guido Ruggiero, *Binding Passions: Tales of Magic, Marriage, and Power at the End of the Renaissance* (New York: Oxford University Press, 1993); Keith Thomas, *Religion and the Decline of Magic*; Timothy D. Walker, *Doctors, Folk Medicine and the Inquisition: The Repression of Magical Healing in Portugal during the Enlightenment*; and Paiva, *Práticas e crenças mágicas*.

98. Abreu, *Confissões da Bahia*, 1591–92, 62, 50.

99. William Monter, "Witch Trials in Continental Europe 1560–1660," in *Witchcraft and Magic in Europe: The Period of the Witch Trials* (Philadelphia: University of Pennsylvania Press, 2002), ed. Bengt Ankarloo and Gustav Henningen, 49–51.

100. D. Sebastião Monteiro da Vide, *Constituiçoens Primeyras do Arcebispado da Bahia feytos & ordenadas pelo illustrissimo, e reverendissimo senhor D. Sebastião Monteyro da Vide, 50. Arcebispo do dito Arcebispado, e do conselho da Sua Magestade: Propostas, e Aceitas em o Synodo Diocesano, que o dito Senhor Celebrou em 12 de junho do anno de 1707*, 335–340. That same section specifies that persons of lower rank be punished with public penances and exile for their magical crimes, while those of noble rank paid fines and the clergy faced suspension of their ranks, orders, and financial support.

101. Mello e Souza, *The Devil and the Land of the Holy Cross*, 94–95, 97, 101–102, 116–118, 125, 152.

102. In her discussion of healers in Grão-Pará, Laura de Mello e Souza provided details from documents that were apparently recorded by the Inquisition but not included among the 1978 texts of the *Livro da visitação do Santo Ofício da Inquisição ao Estado do Grão-Pará, 1763–1769*. In *The Devil and the Land of the Holy Cross*, 103, 290n58; 109, 291n84.

103. Lapa, *Livro da visitação do Grão-Pará*, 191–194. Mello e Souza provides additional details culled from an unpublished denunciation of Joana from the inquisitional manuscripts in the Arquivo Nacional da Torre do Tombo (*The Devil and the Land of the Holy Cross*, 128–129).

104. Lapa, *Livro da visitação do Grão-Pará*, 250–258. Interestingly, these records include seven confessions and denunciations of men practicing love magic, principally the oration of São Marcos to attract women. (Ibid., 129, 200, 207, 236, 239, 242, 245.)

105. Ibid., 251.

106. Ibid., 251–253, 255.

107. Ibid., 253, 255–258.

108. Ibid., 182–183. The contemporary Brazilian spelling may also be *xerimbabo*.

109. Ibid., 184–185. The spell was linked with "Sam João" in this report.

110. Ibid., 141–143.

111. Ibid., 156–158.

112. Ibid., 158–161.

113. Ibid., 175–178.

114. Ibid., 171–174.

115. Ibid., 165–167.

116. Ibid., 266–270. Betancurt had appeared before the visiting Inquisitors a month earlier to denounce Lazaro Vieyra for creating a protective *feitiço* holding bits of a Eucharist host and other Christian objects, and other men for providing the materials (Ibid., 203–205). His name is also spelled "Bitencurt" in the text.

117. Ibid., 180–181.

118. Ibid., 179–181.

119. Ibid., 179, 250, 184.

120. Ibid., 158–161, 175–178, 165–167, 171–174, 266–270.

121. Such questions were posed to Marcelina Thereza during her denunciation of Maria Francisca for divination (ibid., 142–143).

122. Ibid., 159–161, 176–178. The parallel phrasing in the two denunciations suggests some consultation or even collusion between the acquaintances before their appearances, or unrecorded promptings from the Inquisitor.

123. The published edition of the Visitation documents only includes Domingas's admission of superstitious practices (ibid., 179–181), but additional exchanges were discovered by Mello e Souza in the archival documents (*The Devil and the Land of the Holy Cross*, 199–200).

124. Luiz Mott also noted this absence, especially in comparison with the records from Minas Gerais of the same era, and suggested that the rituals must have been held clandestinely in Maranhão. In *A Inquisição no Maranhão*, 19.

125. Silva, *Denunciações de Pernambuco*, 24, 108–110; 39.

126. The new *"Oração a São Marcos e São Manso"* begins: "São Marcos, me marque! São Marcos, me amanse! Jesus Cristo, me abrande o coração e me aparte o sangue mal!" (Saint Mark, mark me! Saint Mark, tame me! Jesus Christ, soothe my heart and remove bad blood from me!) Regularly and devoutly repeated, that "prayer" will ostensibly confer divine protection and love. Joaquim V. Guimaraes, *O poderoso livro de São Cipriano* (Rio de Janeiro: Editora Eco, n.d.), 18. A similar version, for liberation from evil, was published online at http://www.oracoes.com.br/index.php?pg=osantos28.

# Bibliography

## MANUSCRIPT COLLECTIONS AND ARCHIVES

Arquivo da Cúria de São Paulo, Livros do Tombo. São Paulo, Brazil.
Arquivo Histórico, Manuscript Collection. Instituto Histórico e Geographico de São Paulo. São Paulo, Brazil.
Arquivo do Instituto de Estudos Brasileiros, Universidade de São Paulo. São Paulo, Brazil.
"Livro de Receitas e Despesas do Patrimônio da Igreja de N. S. do Parto, 1786–1797." Arquivo da Cúria Metropolitana, Catedral de São Sebastião do Rio de Janeiro. Rio de Janeiro, Brazil.
Mesa do Desembargo do Paço, 1808–1828. Divisão de Documentação Escrita. Arquivo Nacional. Rio de Janeiro, Brazil.
"Processos das Noviças do Convento de N. S. da Conceição da Ajuda." ["Noviças para Conventos, Caixa 2."] "Portarias e ordens Episcopais." Arquivo da Cúria Metropolitana, Catedral de São Sebastião do Rio de Janeiro. Rio de Janeiro, Brazil.
Seção dos Manuscritos, Biblioteca Nacional, Rio de Janeiro, Brazil.

## PRIMARY SOURCES: INQUISITION TEXTS

Abreu, João Capistrano de, ed. *Primeira visitação do Santo Officio às partes do Brasil: Confissões da Bahia, 1591–92.* Rio de Janeiro: F. Briguiet & Ca., 1935.
———. *Primeira visitação do Santo Officio às partes do Brasil: Denunciações da Bahia, 1591–593.* São Paulo: Homenagem de Paulo Prado, 1925.
França, Eduardo D'Oliveira, and Sonia A. Siqueira, eds. "Segunda Visitação do Santo Ofício às partes do Brasil: Livro das confissões e ratificações da Bahia, 1618–1620." *Anais do Museu Paulista* 17, 1963.
Garcia, Rodolfo, ed. "Livro da Denunciações que se fizerão na Visitação do Santo

Officio á Cidade do Salvador da Bahia de Todos os Santos do Estado do Brasil, no Anno de 1618." *Anais da Biblioteca Nacional do Rio de Janeiro* 49 (1927): 75–198.

Lapa, José Roberto do Amaral, ed. *Livro da visitação do Santo Ofício da Inquisição ao estado do Grão-Pará, 1763–1769.* Coleção História Brasileira 1. Petrópolis: Editora Vozes, 1978.

"Livro de depoimento de visitação do Santo Ofício, Salvador, 1591." Seção de Manuscritos, Biblioteca Nacional, Rio de Janeiro, Brazil. ["Copiado do Codice n°. 16 do Arquivo Nacional da Torre do Tombo — Livro 1°. de Denunciações — Brasil."]

Mello, José Antônio Gonsalves de, ed. *Primeira visitação do Santo Officio às partes do Brasil: Confissões de Pernambuco, 1594–1595.* Recife: Universidade Federal de Pernambuco, 1970.

Silva, Leonardo Dantas, ed. *Primeira visitação do Santo Ofício às partes do Brasil: Denunciações e confissões de Pernambuco, 1593–1595.* Combined facsimile ed. São Paulo: Homenagem de Paulo Prado, 1929; Recife: Universidade Federal de Pernambuco, 1970; Recife: FUNDARPE, 1984.

PRIMARY SOURCES: LETTERS, STATUTES, AND CHRONICLES

Abbeville, Claude d'. *História da missão dos padres capuchinos na ilha do Maranhão e terras circunvizinhas.* Translated by Sérgio Milliet. São Paulo: Editora da Universidade de São Paulo, 1975.

Almeida, Candido Mendes de, ed. *Codigo Philippino ou Ordenações e Leis do Reino do Portugal, Recopilados por mandado d'El-Rei D. Philippe I, 1603.* 14th ed. Vol. 2. Rio de Janeiro: Typographia do Instituto Philo-mathico, 1870.

Anchieta, José de. *Cartas do Pe. José de Anchieta: Correspondência ativa e passiva.* Edited by Hélio Abranches Viotti. 2nd ed. São Paulo: Edições Loyola, 1984.

———. "Na vila de Vitória e Na visitação de Santa Isabel." In *"Na vila de Vitória e Na visitação de Santa Isabel."* Edited by M. d. L. d. P. Martins. São Paulo: Museu Paulista, 1950.

———. "Sermão do Padre José d'Anchieta [sic]: In die convertionis S. Pauli, 1568, Piratininga." *Revista do Instituto Histórico e Geográfico Brasileiro* 54, no. 2 (1891): 109–130.

Andrada, Diogo de Paiva de. *Casamento perfeito* [1630]. 3rd ed. Rio de Janeiro: H. Garnier Editor, 1956.

Anjos, Luís dos. *Jardim de Portugal* [1626]. Edited by Maria de Lurdes Correia Fernandes. Porto: Campo das Letras, 1999.

Antonil, André João [João Antônio Andreoni]. *Cultura e opulência do Brasil* [1711]. 3rd ed. Reconquista do Brasil, vol. 70. São Paulo: Editora da Universidade de São Paulo, 1982.

Arago, Jacques. *Narrative of a Voyage round the World, in the Uranie and Physicienne Corvettes, Commanded by Captain Freycinet, during the Years 1817, 1818, 1819, and 1820.* London: Treuttel & Wurtz, Treuttel, Jr. & Richter, 1823.

Arraiz, D. Frei Amador. *Dialogos de Dom Frey Amador Arraiz*. Coimbra: Diogo Gomez Lourenzo, 1604.

Benci, Jorge. *Economia cristã dos senhores no governo dos escravos: Livro brasileiro de 1700*. São Paulo: Editorial Grijalbo, 1977.

Bluteau, Raphael. *Vocabulario portuguez & latino: Aulico, anatomico, architectonico . . .* 8 vols. Coimbra: Collegio das Artes da Companhia de Jesu, 1712–1728.

Brandão, Ambrósio Fernandes. *Diálogos das grandezas do Brasil* [1618]. Rio de Janeiro: Dois Mundos Editora, Ltda., n.d. [1943].

Bry, Theodor de. *Americae tertia pars memorabile[m] prouinciæ Brasiliæ historiam contine[n]s, germanico primum sermone scriptam à Ioa[n]nem Stadio Homburgensi Hesso, Omnia recens e vulgata, & eiconibus in æs incisis ac ad viuum expressis illustrata, ad normam exemplaris prædictorum autorum: studio & diligentia Theodori de Bry Leodiensis, atque ciuis Francofurtensis, anno M D XCII*. Frankfurt, Germany: Matthäus Becker, printer, 1605.

Calatayud, Pedro de. *Doutrinas Practicas, Que costuma explicar nas suas Missoens*. Coimbra: Companhia de Jesus, 1747.

Caldas, José Antônio. *Noticia geral de toda esta capitania da Bahia desde o seu Descobrimento até o presente ano de 1759*. Facsimile ed. [Salvador]: [Typografia Beneditina], 1951.

Caminha, Pero Vaz de. *Carta a El Rei d. Manuel*. Edited by Leonardo Arroyo. São Paulo: Dominus Editôra S. A., 1963.

Cardim, Fernão. "Narrativa epistolar de uma viagem e missão jesuítica pelo Bahia, Ilheos, Porto Seguro, Pernambuco, Espirito Santo, Rio de Janeiro, São Vicente, etc. [1583–1590]." *Revista (Trimensal) do Instituto Histórico e Geographico Brasileiro* 65 (1902–1903): 5–69.

———. *Tratados da terra e gente do Brasil* [1625]. 2nd ed. São Paulo: Companhia Editôra Nacional, 1939.

Columbus, Christopher. *Four Voyages to the New World: Letters and Selected Documents*. Translated by John Major. New York: Corinth Books, 1961.

———. *The Journal of Christopher Columbus*. Translated by Cecil Jane. New York: Clarkson N. Potter, Inc., 1960.

Coutinho, José Joaquim da Cunha de Azeredo. *Estatutos do Recolhimento de Nossa Senhora da Glória do lugar da Boa Vista de Pernambuco*. Lisbon: Typographia da Academia Real das Ciências, 1798.

Couto, Domingos do Loreto. *Desagravos do Brasil e glórias de Pernambuco* [1759]. Edited by José Antônio Gonsalves de Mello. Reprint ed. Recife: Fundação de Cultura Cidade do Recife, 1981.

D'Anghera, Peter Martyr. *De Orbe Novo*. Translated by Francis Augustus MacNutt. Reprint ed. New York: Burt Franklin, 1970.

Debret, Jean Baptiste. *Viagem pitoresca e histórica ao Brasil* [1816–1831]. 2 vols. Reconquista do Brasil, vols. 56 and 57. São Paulo: Editora da Universidade de São Paulo, 1978.

Delicado, Antonio. *Adagios portuguêses reduzidos a lugares communs* [1651]. Edited by Luís Chaves. Revised ed. Lisbon: Livraria Universal, 1923.

Dénis, Ferdinand. *Brésil.* Paris: Firmin Didot Frères, Ed., 1837.

Duarte. *Leal Conselheiro, o qual fez Dom Duarte, Rey de Portugal e do Algarve e Senhor de Ceuta, 1435.* Pariz: Em casa de J. P. Aillaud, 1842.

"Estatutos do Collegio de Educação de Meninas, denominado de 'Nossa Senhora dos Humildes' fundado pela beneficencia de seus Devotos o Padre Ignacio dos Santos e Araujo, em honra do Desaggravo do Santissimo Sacramento na Villa de Santo Amaro da Purificação na Capitania da Cidade da Bahia no anno de 1813." Seção de Manuscritos, Biblioteca Nacional, Rio de Janeiro, Brazil [I–32–13, 29].

Freycinet, Rose Marie Pinon de. *A Woman of Courage: The Journal of Rose de Freycinet on Her Voyage around the World, 1817–1820.* Translated and edited by Marc Serge Rivière. Canberra: National Library of Australia, 1996.

Galvão, Frei Antônio de Sant'Anna, ed. *Escritos espirituais, 1766–1803.* São Paulo: Centro Gráfico do Senado Federal, 1980.

Garcia, José Manuel, ed. *Cartas dos Jesuítas do Oriente e do Brasil, 1549–1551.* Facsimile reprint ed. Lisbon: Biblioteca Nacional, 1993.

Gonçalves, Rui. *Dos privilegios & praerogativas que ho genero feminino ttem por dereito comun & ordenações do Reyno mais que ho genero masculino.* Edited by Elisa Maria Lopes da Costa. Lisbon: Johannes Barreriun Regium, 1578; facsimile ed., Lisbon: Biblioteca Nacional, 1992.

Jorge, Marcos. *Doutrina Christã.* Lisbon: Geraldo da Vinha, 1624.

Kindersley, Mrs. [Nathaniel Edward]. *Letters from the Island of Teneriffe, Brazil, the Cape of Good Hope, and the East Indies.* London: J. Nourse, 1777.

Léry, Jean de. *Histoire d'un Voyage fait en la terre du Brésil [1556–1558].* La Rochelle: Antoine Chappin, 1578.

———. *History of a Voyage to the Land of Brazil, Otherwise Called America.* Translated by Jane Whatley. Berkeley: University of California Press, 1990.

Luccock, John. *Notes on Rio de Janeiro, and the Southern Parts of Brazil; Taken during a Residence of Ten Years in that Country, from 1808 to 1818.* London: Samuel Leigh, 1820.

Mawe, John. *Travels in the Interior of Brazil, Particularly in the Gold and Diamond Districts of that Country.* London: Longman, Hurst, Rees, Orme and Brown, 1812.

Melo, José Maria de. *Provisão de D. José Maria de Melo, Bispo titular do Algarve e Inquisidor Geral, prorrogando, pos mais dois anos, a redução dos encargos de missas dos conventos dos Carmelitas Descalças da Província da Bahia.* Lisbon, 1801; Ms., Arquivo do Instituto de Estudos Brasileiros, Universidade de São Paulo, Brazil.

Navarro, Martín de Azpilcueta. *Manual de confessores y penitentes: Que contiene quasi todas las dudas que en las confessiones suelen occurrir de los peccados, absoluciones, restituciones, censuras, & irregularidades.* Valladolid: Francisco Fernandez de Cordova, impressor de la Magestad Real, [1570].

Pereira, Nuno Marques. *Compêndio narrativo do peregrino da América.* 6th ed. 2 vols. Rio de Janeiro: Publicações da Academia Brasileira, 1939.

Pizan, Christine de. *The Book of the City of Ladies*. Translated by Earl Jeffrey Richards. New York: Persea Books, 1982.

———. *The Treasure of the City of Ladies*. Translated by Sarah Lawrence. Revised ed. New York: Penguin Books, 2003.

Silva, Antônio de Morais. *Diccionario da lingua portugueza composto pelo padre D. Rafael Bluteau, reformado, e accrescentado por Antonio de Moraes Silva natural do Rio de Janeiro*. 2 vols. Lisbon: Officina de Simão Thaddeo Ferreira, 1789.

Sousa, Gabriel Soares de. *Tratado descriptivo do Brasil em 1587*. Edited by Francisco Adolfo de Varnhagen. 5th ed. Brasiliana, vol. 117. São Paulo: Editora Nacional, 1987.

Staden, Hans. *Duas viagens ao Brasil*. Translated by Giomar de Carvalho Franco. Reconquista do Brasil, vol. 17. São Paulo: Editora da Universidade de São Paulo, 1974.

———. *Warhaftig Historia und Beschreibung eyner Landschafft.* . . . Marpurg: Andreas Kolbe, 1557.

Telles, Balthazar. *Chronica da Companhia de Jesu da Provincia de Portugal*. Lisbon: Paulo Craesbuck, 1645–1647.

Thevet, André. *La cosmographie universelle*. In *Les français en Amerique pendant la deuxième mortié du 16e Siècle*. Paris: Ed. S. Lussagnet, 1953.

Trancoso, Gonçalo Fernandes. *Histórias de Proveito e Exemplo* [1575]. Antologia Portuguesa. Edited by Agostinho de Campos. 2nd ed. Lisbon: Livrarias Aillaud e Bertrand, 1923.

Vasconcelos, Simão de. *Crônica da Companhia de Jesus*. 3rd ed. 2 vols. Petrópolis: Editora Vozes Ltda., 1977.

Vide, Dom Sebastião Monteiro da. *Constituiçoens Primeyras do Arcebispado da Bahia feytos & ordenadas pelo illustrissimo, e reverendissimo senhor D. Sebastião Monteyro da Vide, 50. Arcebispo do dito Arcebispado, e do conselho da Sua Magestade: Propostas, e Aceitas em o Synodo Diocesano, que o dito Senhor Celebrou em 12 de junho do anno de 1707*. Coimbra: Real Collegio das Artes da Companhia de Jesus, 1720.

Vieira, Antônio. *Cartas*. Lisbon: Seabra & Antunes, 1855.

———. *Cartas do Padre António Vieira*. Edited by João Lucio de Azevedo. 3 vols. Coimbra: Imprensa da Universidade de Coimbra, 1925.

———. *Obras escolhidas*. Edited by António Sérgio and Hernâni Cidade. 12 vols. Lisbon: Livraria Sá da Costa-Editora, 1951–1954.

———. *Por Brasil e Portugal*. Edited by Pedro Calmon. São Paulo: Companhia Editora Nacional, 1930.

———. *Sermões*. Edited by Gonçalo Alves. 5 vols. 15 tomes. Porto: Lello & Irmão Editories, 1959.

Vives, Juan Luís. *Instrucción de la mujer Cristiana*. 3rd ed. Buenos Aires: Espasa-Calpe Argentina, S. A., 1944.

Waterworth, James, ed. and trans. *The Canons and Decrees of the Sacred and Oecumenical Council of Trent, Celebrated under the Sovereign Pontiffs, Paul III, Julius III and Pius IV*. London: Dolman, 1848.

SECONDARY SOURCES

Abreu, João Capistrano de. *Chapters of Brazil's Colonial History 1500–1800.* Translated by Arthur Brakel. Introduction by Stuart Schwartz. New York: Oxford University Press, 1997.

Alden, Dauril, ed. *Colonial Roots of Modern Brazil.* Berkeley: University of California Press, 1973.

Algranti, Leila Mezan. *Honradas e devotas: Mulheres da colônia, condição feminina nos conventos e recolhimentos do Sudeste do Brasil, 1750–1822.* Rio de Janeiro: José Olympio, 1993.

Almeida, Angela Mendes de. *O gosto do pecado: Casamento e sexualidade nos manuais de confessores dos séculos XVI e XVII.* Rio de Janeiro: Rocco, 1992.

Almeida, Maria Cândida Ferreira de. *Tornar-se outro: O topos canibal na literatura brasileira.* São Paulo: Annablume, 2002.

Almeida, Suely Creusa Cordeiro de. *O sexo devoto: Normatização e resistência feminina no império português xvi–xvii.* Recife: Imprensa Universitária da Universidade Federal Rural de Pernambuco, 2005.

Ankarloo, Bengt, and Gustav Henningen, eds. *Early Modern European Witchcraft: Centres and Peripheries.* Oxford: Clarendon Press, 1990.

Apps, Lara, and Andrew Gow. *Male Witches in Early Modern Europe.* New York: Manchester University Press, 2003.

Arens, William. *The Man-Eating Myth: Anthropology and Anthropophagy.* New York: Oxford University Press, 1979.

Assumpção, Lino d'. *Os Jesuitas: O catolicismo no século XVI.* Lisbon: Guillard, Aillaud e Cia., 1888.

Aufderheide, Patricia. "True Confessions: The Inquisition and Social Attitudes in Brazil at the Turn of the XVII Century." *Luso-Brazilian Review* 10 (Winter 1973): 208–240.

Azevêdo, Carlos Alberto. "O heróico e o messiânico na literatura de cordel." *Coleção cadernos de sociologia da literatura* 1 (1972): 90–93.

Azevedo, João Lúcio de. *História de António Vieira.* 2nd ed. Lisbon: Livraria Clássica Editora de A. M. Tecxeira & Ca., 1931.

Azevedo, Thales de. *O catolicismo no Brasil.* Rio de Janeiro: Ministério da Educação e Cultura, 1955.

———. *Povoamento da cidade do Salvador.* 2nd revised ed. Brasiliana, vol. 281. São Paulo: Companhia Editora Nacional, 1955.

Azzi, Riolando. "Catolicismo popular e autoridade na evolução histórica do Brasil." *Religião e Sociedade* 1 (May 1977): 125–156.

———. *A cristandade colonial.* São Paulo: Edições Paulinas, 1987.

———. "Eremitas e irmãos: Uma forma da vida religiosa no Brasil antigo." *Convergência* 9, nos. 94–95 (1976): 1 parte, 370–383; 2 parte, 430–441.

———. "As romarias no Brasil." *Religiosidade popular na América Latina (Revista de Cultura Vozes)* 73, no. 4 (n.d.): 39–54 (279–294).

———. "Segundo período: A instituição eclesiástica durante a primeira época colonial." In *História da igreja no Brasil*, edited by Eduardo Hoornaert, 153–241. Petró-polis: Editora Vozes Ltda., 1977.

————, ed. *A vida religiosa no Brasil: Enfoques históricos*. São Paulo: Edições Pau-linas, 1983.

Baccarat, Maria Arruda. *Mulheres de outrora*. Rio de Janeiro: Linha Verde, 1993.

Baroja, Julio Caro. *Vidas mágicas e Inquisición*. 2 vols. Madrid: Taurus Ediciones, S. A., 1967.

————. "Witchcraft and Catholic Theology." In *Early Modern European Witchcraft*, edited by Bengt Ankarloo and Gustav Henningen, 19–43. Oxford: Clarendon Press, 1990.

————. *The World of Witches*. Translated by O. N. V. Glendinning. Chicago: University of Chicago Press, 1964.

Barros, João de. *Espelho de casados* [1540]. 2nd ed. Porto: Imprensa Portugueza, 1874.

Bartra, Roger. *Wild Men in the Looking Glass: The Mythic Origins of European Other-ness*. Translated by Carl T. Berrisford. Ann Arbor: University of Michigan Press, 1994.

Belchior, Elysio de Oliveira. *Conquistadores e povoadores do Rio de Janeiro*. Rio de Janeiro: Livraria Brasiliana, 1965.

Bellini, Lígia. *A coisa obscura: Mulher, sodomia e Inquisição no Brasil colonial*. São Paulo: Editora Brasiliense, 1987.

Beltrão, Luiz. *Comunicação e folclore*. São Paulo: Edições Melhoramentos, 1971.

Bernheimer, Richard. *Wild Men in the Middle Ages: A Study in Art, Sentiment, and Demonology*. New York: Octagon Books, 1970.

Bethell, Leslie, ed. *Colonial Brazil*. New York: Cambridge University Press, 1987.

Bezerra, Kátia da Costa. "'Pernambuco illustrado pelo sexo feminino': A condição femi-nina no relato de Dom Domingos Loreto Couto." *Colonial Latin American Review* 6, no. 1 (1997): 59–69.

Bodard, Lucien. *Green Hell: Massacre of the Brazilian Indians*. Translated by Jennifer Monaghan. New York: Outerbridge & Dienstfrey, 1972.

Bourdieu, Pierre. *Outline of a Theory of Practice*. Cambridge Studies in Social Anthro-pology. Translated by Richard Nice. New York: Cambridge University Press, 1977.

Boxer, Charles R. *The Dutch in Brazil: 1624–1654*. Hamden, CT: Archon Books, 1973.

————. *The Golden Age of Brazil: 1695–1750*. Berkeley: University of California Press, 1962.

————. *The Portuguese Seaborne Empire: 1415–1825*. New York: A. A. Knopf, 1969.

————. *Women in Iberian Expansion Overseas, 1415–1815: Some Facts, Fancies and Personalities*. New York: Oxford University Press, 1975.

Braga, Theophilo. *O povo portuguêz nos seus costumes, crenças e tradições*. Lisbon: Liv-raria Ferreira Editora, 1885.

Brehaut, Ernest. *An Encyclopedist of the Dark Ages: Isidore of Seville*. New York: Burt Franklin, 1912.

Brienen, Rebecca Parker. *Visions of Savage Paradise: Albert Eckhout, Court Painter in Colonial Dutch Brazil*. Amsterdam: Amsterdam University Press, 2006.

Briggs, Robin. *Witches and Neighbors: The Social and Cultural Context of European Witchcraft.* New York: Viking Penguin, 1996.

Brink, Jean R., Maryanne C. Horowitz, and Allison P. Coudert, eds. *Playing with Gender: A Renaissance Pursuit.* Urbana: University of Illinois Press, 1991.

Bruschini, Maria Cristina A., and Fúlvia Rosemberg, eds. *Vivência: História, sexualidade e imagens femininas.* São Paulo: Livraria Brasiliense Editora, S.A., 1980.

Bryant, William C., ed. *Colonial Travelers in Latin America.* Compiled and introduced by Irving A. Leonard. Newark, DE: Juan de la Cuesta, 1972.

Bucher, Bernadette. *Icon and Conquest: A Structural Analysis of the Illustrations of de Bry's Great Voyages.* Translated by Basia Miller Gulati. Chicago: University of Chicago Press, 1981.

Buescu, Mircea, and Vicente Tapajós. *História do desenvolvimento econômico do Brasil.* 2nd. ed. Rio de Janeiro: A Casa do Livro, Ltda., 1969.

Burkholder, Mark A., and Lyman L. Johnson. *Colonial Latin America.* 2nd ed. New York: Oxford University Press, 1994.

Burns, E. Bradford. *A History of Brazil.* New York: Columbia University Press, 1970.

Calmon, Pedro. *Historia da civilização brasileira.* Brasiliana, vol. 14. São Paulo: Companhia Editora Nacional, 1933.

———. *História social do Brasil.* 3 vols. Vol. 1, *Espírito da sociedade colonial.* Brasiliana, vol. 40. 3rd expanded ed. São Paulo: Companhia Editora Nacional, 1941.

Camargo, Paulo da Silveiro. *História ecclesiastica do Brasil.* Rio de Janeiro: Editora Vozes Ltda., 1955.

Campos, Alzira. *Casamento e família em São Paulo colonial: Caminhos e descaminhos.* São Paulo: Paz e Terra, 2003.

Cascudo, Luís da Câmara. *Coisas que o povo diz.* Rio de Janeiro: Block Editôres S.A., 1968.

———. *Folclore do Brasil.* 2 vols. Rio de Janeiro: Editôra Fundo de Cultura, 1967.

Castro, Luiz Christiano de. *A catechese dos indios: Inefficacia e perigo das missões leigas, necessidade da catechese religiosa.* Rio de Janeiro: Typographia da Patria Brasileira, 1910.

Chiappelli, Fred, ed. *First Images of America: The Impact of the New World on the Old.* 2 vols. Berkeley: University of California Press, 1976.

Christian, William A., Jr. *Local Religion in Sixteenth Century Spain.* Princeton, NJ: Princeton University Press, 1981.

Cidade, Hernâni. *A literatura autonomista sob os Filipes.* Lisbon: Editora Livraria Sá da Costa, n.d. [1948].

Clemente, Alice R. "Rui Gonçalves: An Early Portuguese Jurist and the Status of Women." *MLN [Modern Language Notes]* 108 (1993): 347–356.

Conrad, Robert Edgar, ed. *Children of God's Fire: A Documentary History of Black Slavery in Brazil.* Princeton, NJ: Princeton University Press, 1983.

Costa, Afonso. "As Órfãs da Rainha." *Revista do Instituto Histórico e Geográfico Brasileiro* 190 (1946): 105–111.

Costa, Francisco Augusto Pereira da. "Folk-lore pernambucano." *Revista do Instituto Histórico e Geográfico Brasileiro* 70, parte 1 (1907): 5–641.

Costa, Iraci del Nero da, ed. *Brasil: História econômica e demográfica*. São Paulo: Instituto de Pequisas Econômicas, 1986.

Costa, Luiz Edmundo. *Rio in the Time of the Viceroys*. Translated by Dorothea H. Momsen. Rio de Janeiro: J. R. de Oliveira & Cia., 1936.

Coutinho, José Lino. *Cartas sobre a educação de Cora*. Bahia: Typografia de Carlos Poggetti, 1849.

Couto, Manoel José Gonçalves. *Additamento á Missão Abreviada*. Porto: Sebastião José Pereira, 1882.

———. *Missão Abreviada para Despertar os Desciudados, Converter os Peccadores e Sustentar o Fructo das Missões*. 12th ed. Porto: Sebastão José Pereira, 1884.

Cunha, Manuela Carneiro da, ed. *História dos índios no Brasil*. São Paulo: Companhia das Letras, 1992.

Curto, José C., and Paul E. Lovejoy, eds. *Enslaving Connections: Changing Cultures of Africa and Brazil during the Era of Slavery*. Amherst, NY: Humanity Books, 2004.

Davis, Natalie Zemon. *Women on the Margins: Three Seventeenth Century Lives*. Cambridge, MA: Harvard University Press, 1995.

Davis, Natalie Zemon, and Arlette Farge, eds. *A History of Women in the West*. Vol. 3: *Renaissance and Enlightenment Paradoxes*. Cambridge, MA: Belknap Press of Harvard University Press, 1993.

Dias, Carlos Malheiro. *História da colonização portuguesa do Brasil*. Porto: Litografia Nacional, 1924.

Dias, José Sebastião da Silva. *Correntes de sentimento religioso em Portugal, séculos XVI a XVIII*. 2 vols. Coimbra: Universidade de Coimbra, 1960.

Dias, Maria Odila Leite da Silva. *Quotidiano e poder em São Paulo no século XIX*. São Paulo: Editora Brasiliense, 1984.

Diffie, Bailey W., and George D. Winius. *Foundations of the Portuguese Empire, 1415–1580*. Vol. 1, *Europe and the World in the Age of Expansion*. Minneapolis: University of Minnesota Press, 1977.

Douglas, Mary. *Natural Symbols: Explorations in Cosmology*. New York: Random House Vintage Books, 1973.

Dudley, Edward, and Maximilian E. Novak, eds. *The Wild Man Within: An Image in Western Thought from the Renaissance to Romanticism*. Pittsburgh: University of Pittsburgh Press, 1972.

Durkheim, Émile. *The Elementary Forms of Religious Life*. Translated by Joseph Ward Swain. New York: Free Press, 1965.

Estevão, Tomás. *Doutrina cristã em língua Concani* [1622]. Edited by M. Saldanha. Facsimile ed. Lisbon: Agência Geral das Colónias, 1945.

Estrada, José Possidonio. *Superstições Descubertas, Verdades Declaradas, & Desenganos A Toda A Gente*. Rio de Janeiro: Typographia de Torres, 1826.

Evans-Pritchard, E. E. "The Morphology and Function of Magic: A Comparative

Study of Trobriand and Zande Ritual and Spells." *American Anthropologist.* New Series, 31, no. 4 (October 1929): 619–641.

———. *Witchcraft, Oracles and Magic among the Azande.* New York: Oxford University Press, 1937.

Ewbank, Thomas. *Life in Brazil.* New York: Harper & Bros. Publishers, 1856.

Eymerich, Nicolás. *Le manuel des inquisiteurs.* Edited and translated by Louis Sala-Molins. Paris: Mouton Éditeur, 1973.

Falção, Edgard de Cerqueira. *Encantos tradicionais da Bahia.* São Paulo: Livraria Martins, 1943.

Faria, Sheila de Castro. *A colônia em movimento: Fortuna e família no cotidiano colonial.* Rio de Janeiro: Nova Fonteira, 1998.

Fausto, Carlos. *Os índios antes do Brasil.* Rio de Janeiro: Jorge Zahar Ed., 2000.

Fernandes, Gonçalves. *O folclore mágico do Nordeste.* Rio de Janeiro: Civilização Brasileira, 1938.

Fernandes, Maria de Lurdes Correia. "Francisco de Monzón e a 'princesa cristã.'" In *Espiritualidade e corte em Portugal, séculos XVI–XVIII,* 109–121. Porto: Instituto de Cultura Portuguesa, 1993.

Figueiredo, Luciano Raposa de Almeida. *O avesso da memória: Cotidiano e trabalho da mulher em Minas Gerais no século XVII.* Rio de Janeiro: José Olympio; Brasília, DF: Edunb, 1993.

———. "O avesso da memória: Estudo do papel, participação e condição da mulher no século XVIII mineira." In *Relatório final de pesquisa.* Rio de Janeiro: Fundação Carlos Chagas, 1984.

Filho, José de Figueirado. "Casa de Caridade de Crato fruto do apostolado multiforme do Pe. Ibiapina." *A Província* 3 (1955): 14–25.

Fishman, Laura. "Crossing Gender Boundaries: Tupí and European Women in the Eyes of Claude D'Abbeville." *French Colonial History* 4 (2003): 81–98.

Flint, Valerie I. J. *The Rise of Magic in Early Medieval Europe.* Princeton, NJ: Princeton University Press, 1991.

Flory, Rae, and David Grant Smith. "Bahian Merchants and Planters in the Seventeenth and Early Eighteenth Centuries." *Hispanic American Historical Review* 58, no. 4 (Nov. 1978): 571–594.

Foucault, Michel. *History of Sexuality.* Translated by Robert Hurley. 2 vols. New York: Random House, 1980.

França, Eduardo D'Oliveira, and Sonia A. Siqueira. "Introdução" and "Origem da Visitação de 1618." In "Segunda Visitação do Santo Ofício às partes do Brasil: Livro das confissões e ratificações da Bahia, 1618–1620." *Anais do Museu Paulista* 17 (1963).

Frazer, James George. *The Golden Bough.* Reprint ed. New York: St. Martin's Press, 1966.

Freyre, Gilberto. *The Mansions and the Shanties.* Translated by Harriet De Orís. New York: Alfred A. Knopf, 1963.

Gaskill, Malcolm. *Crime and Mentalities in Early Modern England.* New York: Cambridge University Press, 2000.

Gaspar, David Barry, and Darlene Clark Hine, eds. *More than Chattel: Black Women and Slavery in the Americas*. Bloomington: Indiana University Press, 1996.

Gilmore, David D., ed. *Honor and Shame and the Unity of the Mediterranean*. Washington, DC: American Anthropological Association, 1987.

Goldschmidt, Eliana Maria Rea. *Convivendo com o pecado na sociedade colonial paulista, 1719–1822*. São Paulo: Annablume, 1998.

Graham, Sandra Lauderdale. *House and Street: The Domestic World of Servants and Masters in Nineteenth-Century Rio de Janeiro*. Austin: University of Texas Press, 1988.

Graham, Thomas Richard. *The Jesuit Antônio Vieira and His Plans for the Economic Rehabilitation of Seventeenth-Century Portugal*. São Paulo: Secretaria da Cultura, Ciência & Tecnologia, Depto. de Arte e Ciências Humanos, Divisão de Arquivo do Estado, 1978.

Greenblatt, Stephen. *Marvelous Possessions: The Wonder of the New World*. Chicago: University of Chicago Press, 1991.

Greenleaf, Richard E. *The Roman Catholic Church in Colonial Latin America*. New York: Knopf, 1971.

Gross, Sue Anderson. "Religious Sectarianism in the Sertão of Northeast Brazil, 1815–1966." *Journal of Inter-American Studies* 10, no. 3 (1968): 369–383.

Harris, Marvin. *Town and Country in Brazil*. New York: Columbia University Press, 1956.

Hemming, John. *Red Gold: The Conquest of the Brazilian Indians*. Cambridge, MA: Harvard University Press, 1978.

Henningsen, Gustav. "'The Ladies from Outside': An Archaic Pattern of the Witches' Sabbath." In *Early Modern European Witchcraft*, edited by Bengt Ankarloo and Gustav Henningsen, 191–215. Oxford: Clarendon Press, 1990.

Hessel, Lothar, and Georges Raeders. *O teatro jesuítico no Brasil*. Porto Alegre: Editora da Universidade Federal do Rio Grande do Sul, 1972.

Higgins, Kathleen J. *"Licentious Liberty" in a Brazilian Gold-Mining Region: Slavery, Gender, and Social Control in Eighteenth-Century Sabará, Minas Gerais*. University Park, PA: Pennsylvania State University Press, 1999.

Holanda, Sergio Buarque de. *História geral da civilização brasileira*. São Paulo: Difusão Européia do Livro, 1960.

———. *Raizes do Brasil*. Coleção Documentos Brasileiros. Rio de Janeiro: José Olympio, 1936.

Hoornaert, Eduardo. *Formação do catolicismo brasileiro, 1550–1800*. 2nd ed. Petrópolis: Editora Vozes Ltda., 1978.

———. "Primeiro período: A evangelização do Brasil durante a primeira época colonial." In *História da igreja no Brasil*, edited by Eduardo Hoornaert, vol. 1: 9–15. Petrópolis: Editora Vozes Ltda., 1977.

———. "Terceiro período: A Cristandade durante a primeira época colonial." In *História da igreja no Brasil*, edited by Eduardo Hoornaert, vol. 1: 245–412. Petrópolis: Editora Vozes Ltda., 1977.

Incao, Maria Angela d', ed. *Amor e família no Brasil.* São Paulo: Contexto, 1989.

Ingraham, William. *Historical Scenes from the Old Jesuit Missions.* New York: A. D. F. Randolph & Co., 1875.

Jaggar, Alison M., and Susan R. Bordo, eds. *Gender/Body/Knowledge: Feminist Reconstructions of Being and Knowing.* New Brunswick, NJ: Rutgers University Press, 1989.

Jewel, Helen M. *Women in Late Medieval and Reformation Europe, 1200–1550.* New York: Palgrave Macmillan, 2007.

Johnson, Lyman L., and Sonya Lipsett-Rivera, eds. *The Faces of Honor: Sex, Shame, and Violence in Colonial Latin America.* Albuquerque: University of New Mexico Press, 1998.

Jolly, Karen. "Magic, Miracle, and Popular Practice in the Early Medieval West: Anglo-Saxon England." In *Religion, Science and Magic in Concert and in Conflict,* edited by Jacob Neusner, Ernest S. Frerichs, and Paul Virgil McCracken Flesher, 166–182. New York: Oxford University Press, 1989.

Jolly, Karen, Catharina Raudvere, and Edward Peters, eds. *Witchcraft and Magic in Europe: The Middle Ages.* London: Athlone Press, 2002.

Kanter, Rosabeth Moss. *Commitment and Community.* Cambridge, MA: Harvard University Press, 1972.

Karasch, Mary C. "Damiana da Cunha: Catechist and Sertaneja." In *Struggle and Survival in Colonial America,* edited by David G. Sweet and Gary B. Nash, 102–127. Berkeley: University of California Press, 1981.

———. *Slave Life in Rio, 1808–1850.* Princeton, NJ: Princeton University Press, 1987.

Kelly, Joan. "Did Women Have a Renaissance?" In *Women, History, and Theory,* edited by Joan Kelly, 19–50. Chicago: University of Chicago Press, 1984.

Kessler, Suzanne J., and Wendy McKenna. *Gender: An Ethnomethodological Approach.* New York: John Wiley & Sons, 1978.

Kieckhefer, Richard. *Magic in the Middle Ages.* New York: Cambridge University Press, 1989.

———. "The Specific Rationality of Medieval Magic." *American Historical Review* 99 (June 1994): 813–836.

Kittredge, George Lyman. *Witchcraft in Old and New England.* Cambridge, MA: Harvard University Press, 1929.

Klapisch-Zuber, Christiane, ed. *A History of Women in the West.* Vol. 2, *Silences of the Middle Ages.* Cambridge, MA: Belknap Press of Harvard University Press, 1992.

Kolodny, Annette. *The Lay of the Land: Metaphor as Experience and History in American Life and Letters.* Chapel Hill: University of North Carolina Press, 1975.

Koser, Frei Constantino. "Planos de sermões." *Revista eclesiástica brasileira.* Separata Selecta 8, 1956.

Kuznesof, Elizabeth. *Household Economy and Urban Development: São Paulo, 1765 to 1836.* Dellplain Latin American Studies, no. 18. Boulder, CO: Westview Press, 1986.

Lacerda, José Maria Corrêa de. *Diccionario Encyclopedico.* Lisbon: Francisco Arthur da Silva, 1874.

Larner, Christina. *Witchcraft and Religion: The Politics of Popular Belief.* New York: Basil Blackwell, 1984.

Lavrin, Asunción, ed. *Latin American Women: Historical Perspectives.* Contributions in Women's Studies 3. Westport, CT: Greenwood Press, 1978.

———. *Sexuality and Marriage in Colonial Latin America.* Lincoln: University of Nebraska Press, 1989.

Lea, Henry Charles. *Chapters from the Religious History of Spain connected with the Inquisition.* Philadelphia: Lea Brothers and Co., 1890; reprint, New York: Burt Franklin, 1967.

Leão, Duarte Nunez do. *Descripção do reino de Portugal.* Lisbon: Jorge Rodriguez, 1610.

Leite, Bertha. *A mulher na história de Portugal.* Lisbon: [Centro Tipográfica Colonial], 1940.

Leite, Serafim. *Artes e ofícios dos Jesuítas no Brasil, 1549–1760.* Lisbon: Edições Brotéria, 1953.

———. *História da companhia de Jesus no Brasil.* 10 vols. Rio de Janeiro: Civilização Brasileira, 1938–1950.

———. *Novas páginas de história do Brasil.* Brasiliana, vol. 324. São Paulo: Companhia Editora Nacional, 1965.

———. *Páginas de história do Brasil.* Biblioteca Pedagogica Brasileira, Brasiliana, vol. 93. São Paulo: Companhia Editora Nacional, 1937.

———, ed. *Cartas dos primeiros jesuítas do Brasil.* 3 vols. São Paulo: Commissão do IV Centenário da Cidade de São Paulo, 1956.

———, ed. *Novas cartas jesuíticas.* São Paulo: Companhia Editora Nacional, 1940.

Levack, Brian P. *The Witch-Hunt in Early Modern Europe.* New York: Longman, 1987.

Lopes, Eliane Marta Teixeira, Luciano Mendes Faria Filho, and Cynthia Greive Veiga, eds. *500 anos de educação no Brasil.* Belo Horizonte: Autêntica Editora, 2000.

Luther, Martin. "Treatise on Baptism" and "The Babylonian Captivity of the Church." *A Compend of Luther's Theology.* Edited by Hugh Thomson Kerr. Philadelphia: Westminster Press, 1943.

Malinowski, Bronislaw. *Magic, Science, and Religion and Other Essays.* Reprint ed. New York: Doubleday Anchor Books, 1954.

Marcílio, Maria Luiza, ed. *Família, mulher, sexualidade e Igreja na história do Brasil.* São Paulo: Edições Loyola, 1993.

Maria Angela, Madre [Leda Maria Pereira Rodrigues]. *A instrução feminina em São Paulo: Subsídios para sua história até a proclamação da Republica.* [São Paulo]: Faculdade de Filosofia "Sedes Sapientiae," 1962.

Marques, António Henrique de Oliveira. *Daily Life in Portugal in the Late Middle Ages.* Translated by S. S. Wyatt. Madison: University of Wisconsin Press, 1971.

Martins, Mário. "O penitencial de Martim Perez, em medievo-português." *Lusitania Sacra* 2 (1957): 57–110.

Martins, Padre Valdomiro Pires. *Catecismo romano: Versão fiel da edição autêntica de 1566.* Petrópolis: Editora Vozes Ltda, 1962.

Mason, Peter. *Deconstructing America: Representations of the Other.* New York: Routledge, 1990.

Massina, Nestor. *A igrega em Barbacena.* Rio de Janeiro: Serviço Gráfico do IBGE, 1952.

Mattoso, José. "Eremitas portugueses no século XII." *Lusitania Sacra* 9 (1970/1971): 7–40.

Mattoso, Kátia de Queirós. *Ser escravo no Brasil.* São Paulo: Editora Brasiliense, 1982.

McNamara, Jo Ann Kay. *Sisters in Arms.* Cambridge, MA: Harvard University Press, 1996.

Medina, José Toribio. *The Discovery of the Amazon.* Translated by Bertram T. Lee. Edited by H. C. Heaton. New York: Dover Publications, Inc., 1988.

Melo, Francisco Manuel de. *Carta de guia de casados, ou um livro só para homens* [1651]. Edited by João Gaspar Simões. Lisbon: Editorial Presença, Ltda., 1965.

Metcalf, Alida C. *Family and Frontier in Colonial Brazil: Santana de Paraíba, 1580–1822.* Berkeley: University of California Press, 1992.

Monteiro, John Manual. *Negros da terra: Índios e bandeirantes nas origens de São Paulo.* São Paulo: Campanhia das Letras, 1994.

Monter, William. *Ritual, Myth and Magic in Early Modern Europe.* Athens: Ohio University Press, 1984.

Moreira Neto, Carlos de Araujo. *Fontes documentais sobre índios dos séculos XVI–XIX.* Madrid: Fundación Histórica Tavera, 1996.

Mott, Luiz. *A Inquisição no Maranhão.* São Luis, Brazil: Edufma, 1995.

———. *Rosa Egipcíaca: Uma santa africana no Brasil.* Rio de Janeiro: Editora Bertrand, 1993.

Myscofski, Carole A. "Bounded Identities: Women and Religion in Colonial Brazil, 1550–1750." *Religion* 28 (1998): 329–337.

———. "Heterodoxy, Gender and the Brazilian Inquisition: Patterns in Religion in the 1590s." *Journal of Latin American Lore* 18 (1992): 79–94.

———. "The Magic of Brazil: Practice and Prohibition in the Early Colonial Period, 1590–1620." *History of Religions* 40, no. 2 (2000): 153–176.

Nascimento, Anna Amélia Vieira. *Patriarcado e religião: As enclausuradas clarissas do Convento do Desterro da Bahia 1677–1890.* Bahia, Brazil: Conselho Estadual de Cultura, 1994.

Nazzari, Muriel. "Concubinage in Colonial Brazil: The Inequalities of Race, Class, and Gender." *Journal of Family History* 21 (April 1996): 107–124.

———. *Disappearance of the Dowry: Women, Families, and Social Change in São Paulo (1600–1900).* Stanford, CA: Stanford University Press, 1991.

Nóbrega, Manuel da. *Cartas do Brasil e mais escritos.* Edited by Serafim Leite. Coimbra: Universidade de Coimbra, 1955.

———. *Diálogo da Conversão do Gentio do Pe. Manuel da Nóbrega.* Edited by Mecenas Dourado. Rio de Janeiro: Tecnoprint Gráfica S. A., 1968.

Novaes, R. P. Americo de. *Methodo de ensino e de catechese dos Indios usado pelos*

*Jesuitas e por Anchieta*. In *Terceiro centenário do venerável Joseph de Anchieta*. Lisboa: Aillaud & Cia., 1900.

Nunes, Feliciano Joaquim de Souza. *Discursos políticos-morais* [1758]. Rio de Janeiro, Officina Industrial Graphica, 1931.

Oldridge, Darren, ed. *The Witchcraft Reader*. New York: Routledge, 2002.

Oliveira, José Joaquim Machado de. "Notas, apontamentos e noticias para a história da provincia do Espirito Santo." *Revista do Instituto Histórico e Geográfico Brasileiro*, Terceira Serie 19, no. 22 (1856): 161–335.

Paiva, José Maria de. *Colonização e catequese, 1549-1600*. São Paulo: Autores Associados: Cortez, 1982.

Paiva, José Pedro. "The Persecution of Popular Superstition in 17th and 18th Century Portugal." Fourth Conference of the Sociedad Española de Ciencias de las Religiones: "Millennium: Fear and Religion." February 2000. http://www.ull.es/congresos/conmirel/PAIVA.htm.

———. "The Persecution of Popular Superstition in 17th and 18th Century Portugal." In *Miedo y religion*, edited by Francisco P. Díez de Velasco [Abellán] [and Raimundo Panikkar], 37–49. Madrid: Ediciones del Orto, 2002.

———. *Práticas e crenças mágicas: O medo e a necessidade dos mágicos na diocese de Coimbra, 1650-1740*. Coimbra, Portugal: Livraria Minerva, 1992.

Peristiany, John G., ed. *Honour and Shame: The Values of Mediterranean Society*. Chicago: University of Chicago Press, 1966.

Perrot, Michelle, and Georges Duby, gen. eds. *A History of Women in the West*. Vol. 2, *Silences of the Middle Ages*. Edited by Christiane Klapisch-Zuber. Cambridge, MA: Belknap Press of Harvard University Press, 1992.

Perry, Mary Elizabeth, and Anne J. Cruz, eds. *Cultural Encounters: The Impact of the Inquisition in Spain and the New World*. Berkeley: University of California Press, 1991.

Pescatello, Ann. "Ladies and Whores in Colonial Brazil." *Caribbean Review* 5 (1973): 26–30.

———. *Power and Pawn: The Female in Iberian Families, Societies, and Cultures*. Westport, CT: Greenwood Press, 1976.

Pimental, Antonio José de Mesquita. *Cartilha ou compendio da doutrina Christã*. Rio de Janeiro: Agostinho Gonçalves Guimarães e Cia., 1877.

Pinho, José Wanderley de A. "Costumes monasticos na Bahia—frades no seculo XVIII." *Revista do Instituto Histórico e Geográfico Brasileiro* 27, no. 46 (1920): 169–181.

———. "Costumes monasticos na Bahia—freiras e recolhidas" (parte 1a). *Revista do Instituto Geográfico e Histórico da Bahia* 25, no. 44 (1918): 123–138.

Pires, Antonio. "Carta que o pe. Antonio Pires escreveu do Brasil, da capitânia de Pernambuco, aos irmãos da companhia, de 2 de Agosto de 1551." *Revista do Instituto Histórico e Geográfico Brasileiro* 6, no. 21 (1844): 95–103.

Pires, P. Heliodoro. *Temas de história eclesiástica do Brasil*. São Paulo: São Paulo Editora, 1946.

Porro, Antônio. *O povo das águas: Ensaios de etno-história amazônica*. Rio de Janeiro: Vozes, 1995.

Pôrto, José de Costa. *Nos tempos do visitador: Subsídio ao estudo da vida colonial pernambucana, nos fins do século XVI*. Recife: Universidade Federal de Pernambuco, 1968.

Prado Júnior, Caio. *Formação do Brasil contemporâneo: Colônia*. 7th ed. São Paulo: Editôra Brasiliense, 1963.

Preto-Rodas, Richard A. "Anchieta and Vieira: Drama as Sermon, Sermon as Drama." *Luso-Brazilian Review* 7, no. 2 (1970): 96–103.

Prezia, Benedito, and Eduardo Hoonaert. *Esta terra tinha dono*. São Paulo: FTD, 1989.

Priore, Mary Lucy M. Del. "As atitudes da Igreja em face da mulher no Brasil colônia." In *Família, mulher, sexualidade e Igreja na história do Brasil*, edited by Maria Luiza Marcílio, 171–189. São Paulo: Edições Loyola, 1993.

———. "O corpo feminino e o amor: um olhar (Século XVIII, São Paulo)." In *Amor e família no Brasil*, edited by Maria Angela d'Incao, 31–56. São Paulo: Contexto, 1989.

———, ed. *História das mulheres no Brasil*. São Paulo: Contexto, 1997.

———. *A maternidade da mulher negra no período colonial brasileiro*. São Paulo: CEDHAL, 1989.

———. *Mulheres no Brasil colonial*. São Paulo: Contexto, 2000.

Querino, Manuel. *A Bahia de outr'ora*. 2nd ed. Bahia: Livraria Economica, 1922.

Raminelli, Ronald. *Imagens da colonização: A representação do índio de Caminha a Vieira*. Rio de Janeiro: Jorge Zahar Editora, 1996.

Ramos, Donald. "Gossip, Scandal, and Popular Culture in Golden Age Brazil." *Journal of Social History* 33, no. 4 (Summer 2000): 887–912.

———. "Marriage and the Family in Colonial Vila Rica." *Hispanic American Historical Review* 55, no. 4 (1975): 200–225.

———. "Single and Married Women in Vila Rica, Brazil, 1754–1838." *Journal of Family History* 16, no. 3 (1991): 261–282.

Rawson, Claude. "Unspeakable Rites: Cultural Reticence and the Cannibal Question." *Social Research* 66, no. 1 (Spring 1999): 167–193.

Rego, A. de Silva. *Portuguese Colonization in the Sixteenth Century*. Johannesburg: Witwatersrand University Press, 1959.

Reis, Padre Angelo dos. *Sermam da restauraçam da Bahia*. Lisboa: Miguel Manescal, Impressor do Santo Officio, 1706.

Rocha-Coutinho, Maria Lúcia. *Tecendo por trás do panos: A mulher brasileira nas relações familiaries*. Rio de Janeiro: Rocco, 1994.

Rocha Pita, Sebastião de. *História da América portuguesa* [1730]. São Paulo: Editora da Universidade de São Paulo, 1976.

Rodrigues, Anna Maria Moog, ed. *Moralistas do século XVIII*. Rio de Janeiro: Pontifícia Universidade Católica/Rio, 1979.

Russell-Wood, A. J. R. "Black and Mulatto Brotherhoods in Colonial Brazil: A Study in Collective Behavior." *Hispanic American Historical Review* 54, no. 4 (1974): 567–602.

———. *Fidalgos and Philanthropists: The Santa Casa da Misericórdia of Bahia, 1550–1755*. London: MacMillan, 1968.

———. "Women and Society in Colonial Brazil." *Journal of Latin American Studies* 9, no. 1 (1977): 1–34.

Sale, Kirkpatrick. *The Conquest of Paradise: Christopher Columbus and the Columbian Legacy*. Reprint ed. New York: Plume/Penguin Books, 1991.

Salvador, Frei Vicente do. *História do Brasil, 1500–1627*. 7th ed. São Paulo: Editora da Universidade de São Paulo, 1982.

Samartim, Roberto López-Inglésias. *A dona do tempo antigo: Mulher e campo literário no renascimento português, 1495–1557*. Santiago de Campostela [Galiza]: Edicións Laiovento, 2003.

Sampaio, Fernando G. *As Amazonas, a tribo das mulheres guerreiras: A derrota do matriarcado pelos Filhos do Sol*. São Paulo: Editora Aquarius, n.d. [1976].

Santos, Luci Rodrigues dos. *Bens reservados: roteção ao patrimônio da mulher casada*. São Paulo: Edição Saraiva, 1980.

Saraiva, António José. *História da cultura em Portugal*. 4 vols. Lisbon: Jornal do Fôro, 1950–1962.

Scarre, Geoffrey. *Witchcraft and Magic in Sixteenth- and Seventeenth-Century Europe*. Atlantic Highlands, NJ: Humanities Press International, Inc., 1987.

Schumaher, Schuma, and Érico Vital Brazil, eds. *Dicionário mulheres do Brasil de 1500 até a atualidade: Biográfico e ilustrado*. Rio de Janeiro: Jorge Zahar Editor, 2000.

Schwartz, Stuart B. "Magistracy and Society in Colonial Brazil." *Hispanic American Historical Review* 50, no. 4 (1970): 715–730.

———. *Sovereignty and Society in Colonial Brazil: The High Court and Its Judges, 1609–1751*. Berkeley: University of California Press, 1973.

———. *Sugar Plantations in the Formation of Brazilian Society: Bahia, 1550–1835*. New York: Cambridge University Press, 1985.

Sharpe, James. *Instruments of Darkness: Witchcraft in Early Modern England*. Philadelphia: University of Pennsylvania Press, 1997.

Shoemaker, Nancy, ed. *Negotiators of Change: Historical Perspectives on Native American Women*. New York: Routledge, 1995.

Silva, Innocencio Francisco da. *Diccionario bibliographico portuguez*. 23 vols. Lisbon: Imprensa Nacional, 1858.

Silva, Maria Beatriz Nizza da. *Cultura no Brasil colônia*. Petrópolis: Editora Vozes, 1981.

———. *Donas e plebeias na sociedade colonial*. Histórias de Portugal, 50. Lisbon: Editorial Estampa, 2002.

———. "Educação feminina e educação masculina no Brasil colonial." *Revista de História*, São Paulo, 109, no. 55 (January/March 1977): 149–164.

———. *História da família no Brasil colonial*. Rio de Janeiro: Nova Fronteira, 1998.

———. *Sistema de casamento no Brasil colonial*. Estudos brasileiros, vol. 6. São Paulo: Editora da Universidade de São Paulo, 1984.

Silveira, Alessandra da Silva. "O Amor possível: Um estudo sobre o concubinato no Bispado do Rio de Janeiro em fins do século XVIII e no XIX." Ph.D. diss., Departamento de História do Instituto de Filosofia e Ciências Humanas da Universidade Estadual de Campinas, 2005. http://libdigi.unicamp.br/document/?code=vtls000374338.

Siqueira, João de Nossa Senhora da Porta. *Escola de politica, ou tratado pratico da civilidade portugueza* [1791]. 9th ed. Pernambuco: Typ. de Santos e Cia., 1845.

Siqueira, Sônia. *A Inquisição portuguesa e a sociedade colonial*. São Paulo: Atica, 1978.

Slater, Candace. *Entangled Edens: Visions of the Amazon*. Berkeley: University of California Press, 2002.

Smith, Jonathan Z. *Relating Religion: Essays in the Study of Religion*. Chicago: University of Chicago Press, 2004.

Socolow, Susan Migden. *The Women of Colonial Latin America*. New York: Cambridge University Press, 2000.

Soeiro, Susan A. "The Feminine Orders in Colonial Bahia, Brazil: Economic, Social and Demographic Implications, 1677–1800." In *Latin American Women: Historical Perspectives*, edited by Asunción Lavrin, 173–197. Westport, CT: Greenwood Press, 1978.

———. *The Social Composition of the Colonial Nunnery: A Case Study of the Convent of Santa Clara do Destêrro, Salvador, Bahia, 1677–1800*. Occasional Papers, no. 6. New York: New York University Press, 1973.

———. "The Social and Economic Role of the Convent: Women and Nuns in Colonial Bahia, 1677–1800." *Hispanic American Historical Review* 54, no. 2 (1974): 209–232.

Sousa, Gabriel Soares de. *Tratado descriptivo do Brasil em 1587*. Rio de Janeiro: Companhia Editora Nacional, 1938.

Souza, Laura de Mello e. *Desclassificados do ouro: A pobreza mineira no século XVIII*. Rio de Janeiro: Edições Graal, 1982.

———. *The Devil and the Land of the Holy Cross: Witchcraft, Slavery, and Popular Religion in Colonial Brazil*. Translated by Diane Grosklaus Whitty. Austin: University of Texas Press, 2003.

———. *O Diabo e a Terra de Santa Cruz: Feitiçaria e religiosidade popular no Brasil colonial*. São Paulo: Companhia das Letras, 1986.

———. *Inferno Atlântico: Demonologia e colonização, séculos XVI–XVIII*. São Paulo: Companhia das Letras, 1993.

Sparks, Carol Douglas. "The Land Incarnate: Navajo Women and the Dialogue of Colonialism, 1821–1870." In *Negotiators of Change: Historical Perspectives on Native American Women*, edited by Nancy Shoemaker, 135–156. New York: Routledge, 1995.

Sperling, Jutta. "Marriage at the Time of the Council of Trent (1560–70): Clandestine

Marriages, Kinship Prohibitions, and Dowry Exchange in European Comparison." *Journal of Early Modern History* 8 (2004): 67–108.

Stewart, Frank Henderson. *Honor*. Chicago: University of Chicago Press, 1994.

Sweet, David G. "Francisca: Indian Slave." In *Struggle and Survival in Colonial America*, edited by David G. Sweet and Gary B. Nash, 274–291. Berkeley: University of California Press, 1981.

Tambiah, Stanley Jeyaraja. *Magic, Science, Religion, and the Scope of Rationality*. New York: Cambridge University Press, 1990.

Taufer, Alison. "The Only Good Amazon Is a Converted Amazon: The Woman Warrior and Christianity in the Amadís Cycle." In *Playing with Gender: A Renaissance Pursuit*, edited by Jean R. Brink, Maryanne C. Horowitz, and Allison P. Coudert, 35–51. Urbana: University of Illinois Press, 1991.

Thomas, Keith. *Religion and the Decline of Magic*. New York: Charles Scribner's Sons, 1971.

Tiffany, Sharon W., and Kathleen J. Adams. *Feminists Re-Reading the Amazon: Anthropological Adventures into the Realm of Sex and Violence*. Women in International Development Working Papers, no. 253. East Lansing, MI: Michigan State University, 1995.

Titiev, Mischa. "A Fresh Approach to the Problem of Magic and Religion." *Southwestern Journal of Anthropology* 16 (1960): 292–298.

Todorov, Tzvetan. *The Conquest of America: The Question of the Other*. Translated by Richard Howard. New York: Harper & Row, 1984.

Torres-Londoño, Fernando. *A outra família: Concubinato, igreja e escândalo na colônia*. São Paulo: Edições Loyola: 1999.

Twinam, Ann. *Public Lives, Private Secrets: Gender, Honor, Sexuality, and Illegitimacy in Colonial Spanish America*. Stanford, CA: Stanford University Press, 1999.

Tylor, Edward B. *Primitive Culture: Researches into the Development of Mythology, Philosophy, Religion, Language, Art and Custom*. 6th ed. 2 vols. New York: G. P. Putnam's Sons, 1920.

Vainfas, Ronaldo. *Trópico dos pecados: Moral, sexualidade e Inquisição no Brasil*. Rio de Janeiro: Editora Campus, 1989.

————, ed. *América en tempo de conquista*. Rio de Janeiro: Jorge Zahar Editor, 1992.

————, ed. *História e sexualidade no Brasil*. Rio de Janeiro: Edições Graal, 1986.

Vallardes, Clarival do Prado, and Luiz Emygdio de Mello Filho, eds. *Albert Eckhout: Pintor de Maurício de Naussau no Brasil, 1637–1644*. Rio de Janeiro: Livroarte Editora, 1981.

Varnhagen, F. A. de, ed. "Excerptos de varias listas de condemnados sela Inquisição de Lisbôa, desde o anno de 1711 ao de 1767." *Revista do Instituto Histórico e Geográfico Brasileiro* 7, no. 25 (1845): 54–86.

Vasconcelos, Simão de. *Vida do veneravel Padre José de Anchieta*. Rio de Janeiro: Imprensa Nacional, 1943.

Vilhena, Luís dos Santos. *A Bahia no século XVIII* [1802]. 2 vols. Bahia: Editôra Itapuã, 1969.

Vives, Juan Luís. "Instruction of a Christian Woman." In *Vives and the Renascence Education of Women*, edited by Foster Watson. New York: Longmans, Green & Co., 1912.

Wadsworth, James E. "Children of the Inquisition: Minors as *Familiares* of the Inquisition in Pernambuco, Brazil, 1613–1821." *Luso-Brazilian Review* 42, no. 1 (2005): 21–42.

Waite, Gary K. *Heresy, Magic, and Witchcraft in Early Modern Europe*. New York: Palgrave Macmillan, 2003.

Walker, Timothy D. *Doctors, Folk Medicine and the Inquisition: The Repression of Magical Healing in Portugal during the Enlightenment*. The Medieval and Early Modern Iberian World, vol. 23. Leiden: Brill, 2005.

———. "The Role and Practices of the *Curandeiro* and *Saludador* in Early Modern Portugal." *Manguinhos: História, Ciências, Saúde*. Fundação Oswaldo Cruz, Rio de Janeiro, Brazil, 11 (supplement 1, 2004): 223–237.

Watson, Foster, ed. *Vives and the Renascence Education of Women*. New York: Longmans, Green & Co., 1912.

Weinbaum, Batya. *Islands of Women and Amazons: Representations and Realities*. Austin: University of Texas Press, 1999.

White, Hayden. "The Forms of Wildness." In *The Wild Man Within: An Image in Western Thought from the Renaissance to Romanticism*, edited by Edward Dudley and Maximilian E. Novak, 3–38. Pittsburgh: University of Pittsburgh Press, 1972.

Whitehead, Neil L. "Carib Cannibalism: The Historical Evidence." *Journal de la Société des Américanistes* 70 (1984): 69–87.

———. "Hans Staden and the Cultural Politics of Cannibalism." *Hispanic American Historical Review* 80, no. 4 (2000): 721–751.

Wiesner, Merry E. *Women and Gender in Early Modern Europe*. 2nd ed. New York: Cambridge University Press, 2000.

Wiesner-Hanks, Merry E. *Christianity and Sexuality in the Early Modern World: Regulating Desire, Reforming Practice*. New York: Routledge, 2000.

Willeke, Frei Venâncio. *Franciscanos na história do Brasil*. Petrópolis: Editora Vozes Ltda., 1977.

Willems, Emilio. "The Structure of the Brazilian Family." *Social Forces* 31, no. 4 (1953): 339–345.

# Index

131; subordination decreases, 116; as
unnatural, 117; warnings against, 61,
63, 93; widows, 131
individual conscience, 116
inheritance: forfeited by cloistering, 153;
of husband's/father's position, 96, 113
Inquisition in Brazil, 7, 44, 80, 196–199;
1st Visitation (1591–1595), 97, 196–
197, 200, 209, 212, 236; 2nd Visitation
(1618–1620), 196, 200, 212, 214; attempts to retain orthodoxy, 157; confessions by gender and social standing, 206–208, 214–215; degree of
intimidation by, 210; lighter penalties
for women's sexual sins, 80; magic as
foolishness or heresy, 200, 223–224;
marital/sexual sins, 107–108, 120, 125,
128; regarding homosexuality, 44;
secret testimony, 206; signatures vs.
'X' on statements, 97; Visitation to
Grão-Pará (1763–1769), 197, 211–225,
236; Visitors to Maranhão, 7, 117,
125, 128; witchcraft/homosexuality
accusations against *solteiras* (unmarried women), 122; women accused
in Early Colonial Period, 200–211;
women accused in Later Colonial
Period, 211–225. *See also* demonic
powers/rituals
Inquisition in Portugal, 3, 10, 149;
changes in treatment of magic,
193–195; and Gabriel Malagrida, 160;
*Regimentos* (1640), 194
"Instruction of a Christian Woman"
(Vives), 91, 114–115
intellectual weakness of woman, 60
intertribal warfare, encouragement of,
49
invisibility of women, 66, 76–78, 112,
230
Isabella I of Aragon and Castile, 38, 90,
193

Isabel Maria, 160
Isadore of Seville, 44

Jacome, Ana, 183–184, 201
*Jardim de Portugal* (Anjos), 67–68
Jesuits: clothing Indians, 71–72; dominant in Brazilian Catholic Church,
157; establishing cloistered houses for
indigenous converts, 158; expulsion
of, 4, 94; as first missionaries in Brazil, 27; Gabriel Malagrida, 160, 163,
172; ignoring marital sins by/against
slaves, 107–108, 121; and Inquisitions, 196; less interested converting women, girls, 42, 95; struggles to
convert Indians, 38, 48, 95; teaching
feminine nature and virtue, 57, 80;
teaching indigenous women sewing
skills, 1; on virginity for nonwhites, 80
Jesus, Ana Maria de, 160
Jesus, Anna Maria de (Anna Corrêa de
Souza), 150
Jesus, Beatriz Maria de, 162
Jesus, Caetana Maria de, 152
Jesus, Catarina Maria do Coração de, 153
Jesus, Clara de Paixão de, 147–148,
233–234
Jesus, Jacinta de (Jacinta de São José),
173–174
Jesus, Margarida de, 162
Jesus, Mariana Maria de, 154
Jesus, Maria Pais de, 162
Jesus, Tereza Maria de, 152
Jews, 189, 193, 195, 197–198
Jezus, Josefa Clara de, 171
"Joana," 215
Joana of Aveiro, 68
Joanna Bernardina (Joanna Maria da
Conceiçam), 149–150
João III, 158, 193
João V, 171
João VI, 6, 162

Milton Keynes UK
Ingram Content Group UK Ltd.
UKHW040959120924
448236UK00001B/9